SIR JOHN DUNNE

Cumbria's First & Most Extraordinary Chief Constable

by Alan Bryant

Published in 2014

ISBN: 978-0-9927514-7-0

Cover and Book Design by Russell Holden
www.pixeltweakspublications.com

Photographs used by kind permission of the Chief Constable's Office and the current occupants of Dunne's former residencies.

Pixeltweaks
PUBLICATIONS
ULVERSTON • CUMBRIA

ACKNOWLEDGEMENTS

Clearly no book of such intensity could be completed without the assistance of a large number of people.

Primarily this includes those staff at the various Cumbrian archives who have literally been at my 'beck and call' when attempting to find that elusive piece of information.

I would especially like to thank

the Barrow-in-Furness archivists:

Michael Stephens

Glenn Lang

Susan Benson

Sonya Waplington

Selena Kendall

and the Carlisle archivists:

John Sinclair

Ann Gregg

Violet Chambers

Isaac Ray

To my wife Muriel, who has stood by me throughout a recent bad spell of illness, but more importantly has had to listen to me for more than six years speaking continuously of John Dunne and his various achievements whilst researching his story.

CONTENTS

FOREWORD

This is more than a biography, this is the professional life story of a truly remarkable and fascinating individual who as a 'boy' lied about his age to become a Police officer, dedicated his life to Policing the communities he served and subsequently achieved the role of Chief Constable in two counties as well as being honoured by Queen Victoria for his remarkable contribution.

It is fascinating to learn of the political and sociological context in which Sir John had to operate during his tenure as Chief Constable of Cumberland and Westmorland. Whilst the policing context differs substantially from that of today, what is striking are the many similarities contained in the principles and 'rules' which Sir John Dunne articulated over 150 years ago that are still pivotal to the effective delivery of modern day Policing.

Sir John Dunne's emphasis on the crucial importance of 'officers always giving their evidence in courts of justice in a fair and impartial manner' and stating candidly and readily "if they knew anything that may be favourable to the prisoner" is today enshrined in legislation. His ethos of delivering a 'faithful and fearless discharge of duty' has great similarities to the underpinning principles of the values and ethics of today's Constabulary in delivering with integrity the highest level of service possible to the public.

Policing today is complex and multi- faceted, dominated by fast changing environmental and technological factors such as the shift of criminality from traditional modes of offending to on line cyber crime where victim and offender may be thousands of miles apart. However, the challenges to policing presented by austerity, reduced budgets and diverse demographics pale into insignificance when compared to the difficulties and challenges that Sir John encountered in the mid nineteenth century.

The vivid descriptions, contained within this book, of the challenges caused by the increase in urbanity leading to acute overcrowding with living conditions described as 'receptacles of every kind of filth containing invariably pigsties, open privies, dunghills and stagnant pools' and eye witnesses describing routine and vicious fighting between men wearing nothing but their boots with iron spikes fixed around their toes, reminds one of the remarkable resilience and leadership required of Sir John Dunne and the officers he commanded over a protracted period of time.

As the current Chief Constable of Cumbria I have the privilege of leading a Constabulary of over 1150 officers and 650 police staff with a budget in excess of £105 million. My tenure of office is limited to five years and I am quite properly the subject of intense scrutiny for performance, public satisfaction, crime rates and data integrity to varying professional bodies including the Police and Crime Commissioner, Her Majesty's Inspectorate of Constabulary and most importantly transparency to the public. Compare this to the assets available to Sir John Dunne who commanded a total of 74 officers with a budget of less than £5500 for a marathon 45 years as Chief Constable.

At Cumbria Police HQ a display still exists in tribute to the contribution Sir John Dunne made to policing in the County. This includes his sword and a series of sepia photographs of a very serious minded and formidable looking individual. The stories contained within this book help to transport him from sepia and one dimensional to a colourful multi-dimensional individual whose legacy should be remembered and celebrated.

Jerry Graham

Chief Constable of Cumbria

WHY A BIOGRAPHY OF JOHN DUNNE?

For the simple reason that not only was John Dunne a highly complex and interesting individual, but more than anything else he made a solid contribution to policing in England and Wales throughout the Victoria era ... contributions which in a number of instances are still being used to this day.

His is an amazing story, for not only was he possibly one of the only police officers of this era to rise through the ranks from constable to Chief Constable of two county police forces simultaneously, but he was arguably the only Chief Constable during the Victorian era emanating from humble beginnings ... culminating in being honoured by Queen Victoria, and to be known thereafter as: Sir John Dunne, KB, DL,JP

Additionally he was amazing too in many other ways ... for example he was unquestionably the longest serving police officer ever from 1839 to 1902 an unbroken record of sixty-three years. He would have been one of the youngest police officers in history, possibly the youngest police officer when he joined the Manchester Police at just fourteen years of age (after falsifying his age a little) in 1839 ... and at the other end of the scale, the oldest serving police officer when he retired at age 77. He was in all probability the youngest police superintendent ever when he was appointed Superintendent of Bearsted Division of Kent County Police in 1850 aged just 25; yet even these achievement pale into insignificance when one compares his achievements in later years: Chief Constable of Norwich Police in (1852) at the age of 27, followed by a further similar appointment just two years later with the Newcastle Police, culminating in his appointment as the Chief Constable of two county forces simultaneously, namely the Cumberland and Westmorland Police in 1857 (now the Cumbria Police) where he served for an incredible 45 years.

During all this time ... 63 years in all, he introduced what was possibly the first training and instruction book for policc officers, introduced Merit Badges, recommended the title 'Officer' for all his men, (unheard of until now,) he also developed what were in its time novel counter measures for the slaughter, confinement and disinfection of cattle and which were methods which were later used to combat other contagious animal diseases and in fact proved so effective that they quickly became national policy, with many of his ideas still in use throughout the country to this day.

Another of his innovations was his procedures for police control of tramping vagrants which drastically cut the number of associated crimes and also became national law, as indeed did the rulings that he placed before a Commons Select Committee on the matter of Game Law Reforms, which more than anything else changed the laws on poaching ... a serious problem in rural counties.

In 1872 he was instrumental in the setting up of the Licensing Act, which came into law that year, and which went some way to reducing the number of drunkenness cases appearing before the Bench on a regular basis; as well as his considerable involvement in the Police Superannuation Act of 1875, and which was to prove so advantageous for the ordinary policeman in their later years.

There were to be many other acts of public interest in which Dunne would be involved over the years, amongst which would be the Reformatory and Industrial Schools Act of 1866 (otherwise known as Ragged Schools) which were the forerunner of the reform schools which we know today.

And of course throughout his career there is the story of a policeman ... whether that be pounding the beat as an ordinary copper as he did in both Manchester and Essex, or training and controlling the lives of the two hundred (plus) police under his overall command, in a rural area, where a policeman was more often than not expected to act on his own initiative.

Yet all this could not have been attained without a little subterfuge on Dunne's part, and possibly a little help from his wife, too ... But then, in part, that is what Dunne's story is all about.

THE OATH

I, do swear that I will well and truly serve our Sovereign Lady the Queen, in the office of Constable for the County of Cumberland , without favour or affection, malice or ill will; and that I will, to the best of my power, cause the peace to be kept and preserved and prevent all offences against the persons and properties of Her Majesty's subjects; and that while I continue to hold the said office, I will, to the best of my skill and knowledge, discharge all the duties thereof faithfully, according to the law, So help me God.

PROLOGUE

Born, 12th February, 1825,

fourth son of William Dunne, Boley, Queen's County,

Direct descendant of the ancient O'Dunne family,

High Reagain, Queen's County,

By Julia daughter of Denis O'Kelly, a direct descendant of the ancient O'Kelly's of Aodh, Slain, Magh Druichtain, Gailin, Lugucurran, and Rathascul, Leinster;

Educated at Montabaun and Dublin.

Well ... that is what his entry in Dod's Peerage states for 1898

... but then Dunne was, at times, a little economical with the truth!

CHAPTER ONE

JOHN DUNNE

His story begins on the 12th February 1852, when John Dunne was born in the little town of Boley, Southern Ireland ... to Catholic parents, William and Julia Dunne ... or as near to the 12th February 1825 as we can be. A quirk in Irish tradition was that birthdays were never celebrated in the 19th century, and no special heed was given to precisely how old someone was. This of course has created problems for genealogists today, as it did for bureaucrats some one hundred years ago, when they were endeavouring to institute a system of old age pensions – still as we will see, the lack of such evidence was to prove something of an advantage to Dunne in future years.

Boley, today is still a small pleasant little village just west of Abbeyleix. Located in Queens County (since 1922 Co. Laois) and offers very little of importance other than a small population, a number of shops (built since Dunne left) and of course the Catholic Church. Nearby in Maryborough there was the county gaol, plus bridewells (houses of correction) at Burros-in-Ossory, Stradbally and Abbeyleix. The local government at this time would have been vested in a Lieutenant, 18 deputy lieutenants, and 82 other magistrates besides whom there were the usual county officers including 4 coroners. There were in addition some 42 police stations in total offering a force of a sub-inspector, 9 Chief officers, 45 sub-constables, 291 men not overlooking the fifteen horses, and besides that there were three stations of what was known in those days as the *'peace preservation police'.*

Industry in the main for this area was coal production, indeed there were a total of sixty-four coal mines which together employed some 700 men. All were poor and there were regular fights and broils which to some degree explains the high number of constabulary. Somewhat surprisingly everyone (bar the elderly) spoke English fluently.

According to Dod's Peerage of 1898, following his investiture as KB by Queen Victoria in 1897, Dunne declared that he was descended via his father from the renowned and ancient O'Dunne family of High Reagain, Queen's County, (now Co.Laois) and his mother was a direct descendant of the similarly renowned and ancient O'Kelly's of Aodh, Slain, Magh Druichtain, Gailin, Lugucurran, and Rathascul, Leinster, however, such information has proven to be false in the main ... declared by Dunne, probably as early as 1839 when joining the Manchester Police in order that he would forever be recognised as someone of hereditary importance and hopefully accepted by his superiors as someone a little different from the normal 'run of the mill' policeman (labourer, agricultural worker etc) and perhaps could be directed towards higher things in the then fledgling police forces.

Dunne's father William had been married before, on the previous occasion to a certain Rose Grace, who was the grand aunt of William Russel Grace, the first Roman Catholic Mayor of New York, (1881-1882 and 1885-1886). It was he that accepted the Statue of Liberty as a gift from France.

Though our John Dunne would have us believe that he was descended from the famous 'Brittas' Dunnes, in reality his family background was a little more inferior, for records show that he was actually descended from the 'Darby' Dunne side of the family who had nothing of note to report in their background. I can however establish his roots back to the Thomas Fitzgerald family in 1700 when their daughter Mary married Nicholas Warron of Killeen,Queens Co in 1725 and who in turn produced just the one child Honoria. and who in 1747 married Darby Dunne of Raheenahown,Co.Wexford.

They had two children – Patrick Dunne and John William Dunne, the latter being our John Dunne's grandfather, and he in turn married Marion Stafford of Dunmain with whom he had three children, namely: John Stafford Dunne,Gerald Dunne and William Dunne (John Dunne's father.)

This union, of course, produced John Dunne, along with three brothers, only one of which is there any current knowledge of, William, for he too emigrated to England in later years, and after attending religious college entered the ministry and was pastor of St Patrick's Catholic Church, Walsall, in Staffordshire until his death on the 9th February 1872.

It is possible that the Darby Dunne side of the Dunne name could have achieved more but for the 1798 Rebellion, for records of 6th April 1799 following this rebellion show Darby Dunne declaring a loss of land in Boley to the value of £76.16s 6d (£76.57p) or at today's value around £152,000 ... a not inconsequential sum. This of course could have been the beginning of the end for the fortunes of the Darby Dunne side of the family. The value of £76 would have been an enormous amount of money then, roughly equivalent to around six years wages and could well have been the turning point in their fortunes.

And this was only some twenty-seven years before Dunne's birth.

The 1798 rebellion certainly was a turning point in Ireland's history as it was recorded as being possibly the most concentrated outbreak of violence in Irish history which resulted in many thousands of deaths over the course of the three months. Contemporary estimates put the death toll from 20,000 to as many as 50,000, of which 2,000 were military and 1,000 were loyalist civilians. Atrocities were committed on both sides, the majority being committed by the government forces, but rebel killings of Protestants in Wexford were given greater emphasis by the victors in the following years as the loyalist version of events reduced the rebellion to a sectarian Catholic plot to massacre Protestants – which was in fact a repeat of the Irish Rebellion of 1641. However the rebellion did at least result in the 1801 Act of Union, though not necessarily the way the Irish intended as it brought Ireland tighter still under British control.

As a comparison to the Darby Dunne background however, John Dunne declared to anyone who would listen, and hopefully further his career, that he originated from the 'Brittas' side of the family which had been mostly far more successful and influential over the years, and one can quite see why Dunne would have chosen this side of the family to have been developed stemming as it did from a strong military and religious background, not overlooking the fact their was a castle in the family (Brittas, at Ballybrittas)

Some evidence of this is indicated in his choice of names for his children in later years.

For example his second born child in 1871was named Francis Plunkett Neville Dunne no doubt after the Major-General Francis Plunkett Dunne who was born in 1801,or even more likely William Plunkett 4th Baron Plunkett, who ended up being the Archbishop of Dublin (1828- 1897). In fact the same could be said for the third (and last) born child of Dunne's; namely Gerald Fitzgerald Dunne, (born 1875) with the 'Fitzgerald' name cropping up regularly in the 'Brittas' background. Obviously as far as his daughter was concerned (born 1870) the historical names were not so important as she was named after Dunne's mother ... Henrietta (though she preferred the name Julia).

According to the Landed Estates database we learn that the ancient family of O'Doinn or Dunne were confirmed in their possession of the manor of Brittas in Clonaslee, County Laois, Republic of Ireland, as early as the 17th Century. By the time of Griffiths Valuation (published between 1847-1848) the same Brittas Dunnes owned land in the Parish of Fuerty, Barony of Athlone, County Roscommon and by the 1870's are recorded as owning 1,544 acres in the county as well as 9,215 acres in Queens County.

In 1771 Francis Dunne, then head of the Brittas Dunne's built a thatched parish chapel in the village of Ballybrittas and continued to finance the construction of other landmark buildings. The parish church itself was erected in 1814 under the direction and finances of General Edward Dunne ... this is the general who had made a name for himself at the time of the 1815 Battle of Waterloo, for all the wrong reasons. General Edward Dunne was known locally as *'shun-battle Ned'* because of his failure to appear when summoned at the battle. For this he was court-martialled, but in his defence stated that he had never got the order for battle as he later discovered it had been intercepted by his wife, Amadeus.

In later years these allegations have been denied by the Dunne family, and in fact Michael Corey in his book *A History of the Queens County* actually states that he was *'one of the best cavalry officers of his day'.*

Besides his nick-name he was also unpopular with the locals because he sold a large portion of his estate in order to relieve his financial difficulties as well as charging rack-rent (the word at this time indicated an excessive or extortionate rent) which in turncaused misery and poverty among the people of Hy-Regain in the early 1800's.

However he was not all bad for following the 1798 Irish Rebellion he treated leniently the men of Hy-Reagain, but not so the Wicklow rebels some 350 strong, who had actually laid down their arms, for they, under General Dunne's orders, were butchered in cold blood on the Curragh of Kildare.

This same Edward Dunne besides being a general, was also Deputy Governor and High Sheriff of Queen's County, as well as being MP for Marlborough (Portaloise). In 1803, the Viceroy, the Earl of Hardwicke appointed him Commander of the Dublin garrison from where later that year he was be involved in quelling the rebellion against British rule led by Robert Emmett. Emmett was later captured, tried and executed on the 20th September of that year, for high treason. As a result of General Dunne's involvement the Corporation of Dublin presented him with the Freedom of the City, and an address (which is held in Brittas) states that *'under his leadership they feared no enemy'.* He contested the election for Queen's County again in July 1818 and later in 1820, but failed on both occasions. He died at Brittas Castle on 3rd November 1844.

It was interesting to learn that this same General Edward Dunne was the eldest son of Francis Dunne who had married his cousin Margaret in the late 1760s who just happened to be the third daughter (and co-heiress) of a certain Nicholas Plunkett of Dunsoghly Castle, County Dublin who himself eventually succeeded to the Plunkett estate. Some hundred years later our John Dunne was to name his second child 'Plunkett'

Edward's Dunne's son Francis (born 1731) (who in later years was also to marry a Plunkett) also followed his father in the same military tradition joining the army at age 18 and after many promotions eventually too attained the rank of Major-General. He also took an active part in politics ... though for some years he was unsuccessful in gaining a seat in many elections. Between 1858 and 1859 he was private secretary to the Earl of Eglinton, who was then Lord Lieutenant of Ireland. At the general election in 1859 and again in 1865 Francis was more successful in his attempt to enter politics when he was returned for the Queen's County. For the latter election he actually topped the poll. Unfortunately it was all downhill after that for he failed to get elected in any subsequent elections. He did however contest the election as a Home Ruler in 1874 but was again defeated. He died at Brittas Castle in 1878 at the age of 73.

The Brittas-Dunne family home and estate, was Brittas Castle and built to a neo-Gothic design by Francis Dunne in 1869. It is believed that Francis obtained loans from Germany to build the castle with rental income from his tenants being used to repay the lenders. His son inherited the castle when Francis died. When he died in 1925 the castle became the property of a grand-nephew, who was the last male Dunne to own the estate. The castle was later destroyed by fire on the 25th June 1942 though before that had been sold to the Irish Government around 1924.

From the above it is quite clear why John Dunne would have decided at an early age that his hereditary family were the 'Brittas' Dunnes, rather than the 'Darby' Dunnes ... such an aristocratic background which offered Major-Generals, Politicians, Deputy-Governors and High Sheriffs (not overlooking the castle) would clearly look a lot better on his curriculum vitae especially at a time when such backgrounds were vitally important if one wanted to reach high office in whatever career he pursued.

As far as his mother's background is concerned, she, as has been declared by Dunne was a member of the 'famous' O'Kelly's of Aodh, Slain, Magh Druichtain, and Rathascul, Leinster.

To demonstrate this, Dunne stated (in Dod's Peerage) that the information had been obtained from The Annals of the Four Masters and Page 733 in particular. BUT the reliability and usefulness of the Annals as a historical source has regularly been questioned over the years on the grounds that they were limited to accounts of births, deaths and activities of the Gaelic nobility of Ireland and written (in Gaelic) between1632-1636.

It would be relatively easy for anyone to declare that they were members of such 'nobility' after a gap of some two hundred years, especially when that person had also declared some untruths about another side of the family. Usefully for him, the records only go up to 1616! It was first translated into English in 1846 by Owen Connellan (a useful year for Dunne, as he was on the promotion ladder in Essex at this time) Additionally there is no known copy of another reference book to which he refers namely: *Irish Histories of O'Herin and Rawson.*

His report of being educated at Montabuam and Dublin is yet another anomaly which requires clarification. I think it is safe to assume that he never attended Trinity College, Dublin, or indeed any other college/university in his youth. Trinity was set up in part to consolidate the rule of the Tudor monarchy in Ireland and it was seen as the Protestant Ascendancy for much of its history, although Catholics had been permitted to enter as early as 1753 certain restrictions on their membership of the college remained until 1873 and in any case the Catholic Church in Ireland forbade its adherents from attending until the late 20th century.

The alternative for Dunne could well have been Castleknock College, also in Dublin which opened in 1833. This was a college which at the time was in the forefront of Irish Catholic education, and certainly if Dunne would have been unacceptable at Trinity, then a place could certainly have been offered to him there. Still as we know neither happened for by the age of fourteen he was a police constable in Manchester thus there is little doubt that Dunne never did have a university education.

His declared 'education' at Montabuam would also be a further mystery. Admittedly it looks good on a CV namely a primary education in a French public school, but it is arguable whether that did in fact happen, especially when one considers the distance involved, the cost of such education for a lower-middle class family, not overlooking the lack of ability to speak French – at no time in his long career does the ability to speak French arise or indeed is even mentioned. However there was a school close by to his home in Boley which would have given him a sound educational background even if he did leave by the age of fourteen, and in truth would have been a better education than most of his contemporaries would have been getting at this time.

In all probability life for the young Dunne would have been comparatively good, his father owned and ran a business known as the Fruitlawn Woollen Mill in Boley, (though it is likely this was not established until around 1837) and he would certainly have had the opportunity of an education ... even if it was only until the age of fourteen and of course it was still some years before the onset of the Potato Famine which affected so many of the population (1845).

Thus following the end of John's limited schooling, we see him in 1839 setting off for England via the Dublin-Liverpool Ferry no doubt alongside vast numbers of passengers whose only reason to travel to England, and Liverpool in particular, was to obtain a passage on a ship to America and start a new life with their families. It is highly probable that Dunne actually travelled to England with some family members doing exactly that, even staying with them in Liverpool until the date of their sailing.

In order to cross the Irish Sea from Dublin to Liverpool, there were at this time at least three boats daily and the journey took 12 to 14 hours. In fact from the 1820s onwards Liverpool was connected with all the main Irish ports by a fleet of relatively fast cheap steam vessels, mainly paddle driven, though some were screw-driven.The leading company of the Dublin-Liverpool trade was the Dublin and Liverpool Steam Packet Company. The crossing would have been a traumatic experience for passengers and not just for the journey time either. There was little cabin accommodation and moreover most ships were carrying animals below decks and these were usually taken better care of.

Few of these early ships had steerage accommodation so most passengers had no shelter, they were therefore exposed to the elements and often arrived exhausted and scarcely able to walk. The alternative route would have been to take a ferry to Holyhead and then travel by stagecoach to Liverpool (a distance of about 85 miles). From Liverpool Dunne would have almost certainly have taken the short railway journey to Manchester utilising the relatively new Liverpool and Manchester Railway (L & MR) ... the world's first steam passenger railway which had started operations some nine years earlier. After the extremes of the boat crossing, this would have had to have been the highlight of his long journey.

Though it is clear that Dunne has attempted to hide his true background, a quick search of the name Dunne in Ireland will make clear that around the time Dunne was leaving Ireland there were recorded in excess of 3,300 households with the name Dunne, living in 36 different locations, with the largest number 803, in Queens County alone. It would be a safe bet that no one would be checking his credentials.

There is no clear indication as to why a fourteen year old boy suddenly chose to 'up sticks' and move to Manchester any more than I can offer an explanation for his joining the police at such a young age. Though there are records of a Dunne joining London's Metropolitan Police in 1829 and indeed reaching the dizzy height of Chief Inspector, there is no proof that this was any relation of

Dunne, but it could have been one reason for John doing the same. Perhaps it was the ongoing poverty in the country which precipitated his move, as history tells us the Potato Famine during the period of 1845-1852 was the most disastrous period in Ireland's history when some one million died and a further million emigrated, (though of course was after Dunne left) but, in fact the potato failure had already been around for some years by 1839, since 1830 in fact when the potato crop failure that year was to cause food riots in Limerick and Leitrim and cause widespread famine. The coldest summer in fifty years (in 1836) didn't help matters either for this too brought about widespread failure once again of the potato crop, as indeed it did the following year and again led to widespread famine.

This is not to say that such a period of uncertainty actually affected the Dunne household, but at least it would have been a clear indication to him that perhaps Ireland was not the best place to consider his career options...and would certainly have had some bearing on his decision to leave the country.

Perhaps it was the Great Storm of January 6th 1839 that finally helped him to make up his mind – it was certainly the same year that he chose to leave his homeland. The newspaper reports of the time state that more than 300 people were killed with reports of houses collapsing on people as well as houses burning to the ground. For most of the night until just before dawn, the winds caused total chaos throughout the countryside, uprooting large trees, tearing the thatched roofs off houses, as well as toppling barns and church spires. As the worst part of the storm occurred after midnight, residents were especially terrified as they couldn't see what was happening as the relentless winds extinguished candles and lanterns. In many instances homes were burned down because the bizarre winds blasting down the chimneys threw hot embers from hearths across the floors of houses thus igniting the entire structure. Certainly many thousands were made homeless with the economic devastation inflicted on the population (that was already severely impoverished) would have been massive and of course this was happening at a time before their was any government disaster response programme, so the people affected had to fend for themselves.

It was perhaps the sight (to him) of an efficient police force in his own area coupled with the introduction of the Police Act of 1839 ... which could quite easily have been his reason to see the police as a sensible career move ... we shall probably never know.

Personally I'm inclined to think that because many of the population were leaving Ireland in their droves around the 1830-40s, it is quite likely that many of Dunne's family were doing the same and emigrating to USA or Canada;.

Today there is a Dunne website listing many thousands of families with that name, a clear indication that many did choose that route around the mid 1800s.

The likelihood is that he did not want to go with the others and (in all probability following a family argument) instead hopped on a ferry to Liverpool and thence to Manchester, where, possibly through a newspaper advertisement, he was aware that the Manchester Police were setting up their new force, and thus were recruiting constables. The likelihood is too that he was not alone ... whose to say that friends too were not joining him for the self same adventure.

Whatever it was, there is no doubt that the young John Dunne had decided some time in the early part of 1839 that the police force was to be his chosen career, and with the newly formed Manchester Force beckoning ... then that was the place to be.

CHAPTER TWO

JOHN DUNNE

Manchester 1839-1842

'If you say in any other part of England that you are from Manchester you are at once supposed to be a thief' (W.B Neale, 1840)

Picture the scene as a young Dunne arrives at Manchester railway station off the Liverpool-Manchester train on that day in mid 1839, a picture which is best described by a local reporter Angus Reach of *The Morning Chronicle* at that time and which could perhaps portray more eloquently than I at just what a fourteen years old Irish lad would have seen upon arriving in Manchester for the first time.

'The traveller by railway is made aware of his approach to the great northern seats of industry by the dull leaden-coloured sky, tainted by thousands of ever smoking chimneys, which broods over the distance. The stations along the line are more closely planted, showing that the country is more and more thickly people. Then, small manufacturing villages begin to appear, each consisting of two or three irregular streets clustered round the mill, as in former days cottages were clustered round the castle.

You shoot by town after town-the outlying satellites of the great cotton metropolis. They have all similar features-they are all little Manchester's. Huge, shapeless, unsightly mills with their countless rows of windows; their towering shafts, their jets of waste steam continually puffing in panting gushes from the brown grimy wall. Some dozen or so of miles so characterized, you enter the Queen of the cotton cities- and then amid smoke and noise, and the hum of never ceasing toil, you are borne over the roofs to the terminus platform. You stand in Manchester.

There is a smoky brown sky over head-smoky brown streets all round long piles of warehouses, many of them with pillared and stately fronts-great grimy mills, the leviathans of ugly architecture, with their smoke-pouring shafts. There are streets of all kinds-some with glittering shops and vast hotels, others grim and little frequented-formed of rows and stacks of warehouses, many mean and distressing monotonous visas of uniform brick houses.

There are swarms of mechanics and artisans in their distinguishing fustian-of factory operatives, in general undersized, sallow-looking men-and of factory girls somewhat stunted and paled, but smart and active-looking with dingy dresses and ark shawls speckled with flakes of cotton wool, wreathed round their heads.'

It would be good to know just what image the young Dunne had in his mind prior to his arrival in Manchester that cold and miserable day, but whatever it was it almost certainly would have been nothing like that facing him, and certainly one quite different to the rolling green fields of a rural Ireland, coupled with its laid-back life. It would certainly have been one hell of a culture shock This was totally different ... probably far more so than he could have ever imagined, and it is likely that their were moments during those first few weeks and months on English soil that he wished he was back in his homeland.

One supposes that if you were a fourteen year old lad keen on making the police your chosen career then arriving in Manchester city centre in mid 1839 just at the time the town's magistrates had decided to formulate its first police force, and with recruitment of said police force under way, would have indeed proved a fortuitous time for Dunne.

When the well-built, six foot tall John Dunne was accepted into the Manchester Borough Police in 1839, initially as an 'Expectant' Constable, but later as a fully-fledged (though untrained) police constable and having almost certainly adjusted his age by a year or so, it was still a very disorganised force, though in all fairness it was only a few weeks old, as this new force had only been approved by the Watch Committee as recently as the 23rd January. This had happened almost immediately following the merging of the township of Manchester with five other townships thus creating the Borough of Manchester in late 1838, though it wasn't to see its first policeman on the streets until the July of 1839. Indeed until the Watch Committee meeting in early 1839 policing for the borough had been handled by each individual township – of a sorts.

It was by learning of the introduction of the new County Police Act of this year (also known as the Rural Police Act or the Rural Constabularies Act) which actually initiated the setting up of Manchester's first police force. This Act actually received the Royal Assent on the 27th August of this year, though by this time the Borough's Watch Committee were already well advanced with their plans for a police force. The County Police Act was the Act which enabled Justices of the Peace in England and Wales to establish police forces in their counties if they so wished, though the Act was not compulsory and in fact constabularies were only established in 25 out of the 55 counties, Manchester

Borough Police Force being one of them. Policing was of course a relatively new concept, as prior to this Act the town had relied for its limited policing solely on the provisions of the Lighting and Watching Act (of 1833) which was the first statute to deal with the establishment of a paid police force in the country generally. It was this earlier Act which enabled a quorum of ratepayers to adopt its provisions for their parish, and which meant in effect appointing several of their number to be 'inspectors' and levy a rate for the employment of watchmen, 'sergeants of the night', patrols, street keepers and 'others' to be sworn in as constables.

The 1839 Act however was different as this was set up with the intention of preventing crime, rather than as in the past, reacting to what had already occurred, and to a major degree was occasioned by the threat of Chartism unrest which was rearing its head throughout the country. Richard Beswick, then aged just 27, was appointed as Manchester's first Head Constable (at a salary of £400.0.0 p.a.) (around £80,000 in today's pay) though unlike just about every other head constable in those days he did at least bring with him extensive policing experience, having originally joined the Manchester police some sixteen years earlier as a police constable. Beswick was regretfully to die in 1855 at the early age of just 43. (Incidentally this would have been the first, and only instance where the young Dunne would have met a relatively young officer who had reached the highest position in the police force, through his own achievements, and almost certainly would have been instrumental in determining Dunne's own career.)

Towards the latter end of 1838 the borough's Justices of the Peace would have already decided that Manchester would benefit from having a full time paid police force for, as stated, it was on that cold January morning in 1839 that the Manchester Borough Watch Committee was first formed with a membership of twenty two members of the Council – their job being of overseeing the inception and the initial running of the local police force.

From the minutes of that first meeting we learn that funding of this new police force was to be an ongoing source of dispute and which was to take some considerable time to determine. In fact by mid 1839, around the time the new fledgling force was just starting to step foot on the streets of Manchester, a Special Bill was introduced by Government which empowered the Crown to appoint a Chief Commissioner of Police specifically for the Borough of Manchester and to establish a new police force, this new Chief Commissioner to replace Beswick, who when his replacement took up office in the September had had a short lived career of just three months. This commissioner (as he would be titled) was to hold office for two years during which time it was hoped the litigation with regards to the Manchester municipal charter would be settled, and indeed was the reason for the appointment of a commissioner in the first place.

At the Watch Committee's further meeting on the 25th March a number of momentous decisions were made, when it was agreed that a total of 310 constables would be appointed, both for day and night duty at a wage of seventeen shillings per week, (around £160.00 today) along with 20 inspectors with their wage fixed at twenty-seven shillings a week.(£250.00 today) The initial salary of the Head Constable would be £400 per year. One month later these numbers were increased to allow for 5 superintendents (one indoor at £250 per annum, and four outdoor at £150 per annum), plus 7 lock-up keepers and 7 clerks. However it was to be another four months before the first police constables were actually to be seen on the streets of Manchester (July 1st) ... most of whom had been previously employed as Manchester Watchmen, under the old Act, and would have at least been knowledgeable about the people and streets of the metropolis.

Before that date however their was clearly a need to appoint a Chief (or head) constable to oversee the appointment and setting up of the new force. A total of five men were interviewed and from these Richard Beswick was appointed as the first Head Constable of Manchester Borough Constabulary – his appointment based solely on the fact that he was known to the Watch Committee and had served as a police officer in Manchester for some years. It was soon discovered that the 310 constables initially recruited would not be enough to cover Manchester and deal with its many on going problems, for between the 4th and 8th June a further 73 constables were recruited ... amongst whom was a certain John Dunne.

On the 8th June another momentous decision was made by the Watch Committee when it was decided that the uniform of the police constables would consist of a top coat, body coat, trousers and hat, all to be the same colour and style as that worn by constables of London's Metropolitan Police. In addition it was agreed that each man would receive a bell (for night duty) along with staves and rattles. By the 26th August the night duty constables were additionally provided with a lantern. Dunne would certainly have met the criteria for admission – ***not to be above forty years of age*** (no mention of minimum age fortunately!) ***over five feet seven inches in height, to be able to read and write perfectly*** ... well we certainly know he had an education, though perhaps not as much as he would have his superiors believe; ***be free of 'bodily complaint'*** so clearly he must have passed the medical ... ***have been of strong constitution,***

and generally intelligent. For Dunne this would have been a pass on all counts.

However Dunne did not immediately find himself pounding the streets of Manchester, for he was initially employed as what Beswick termed an *'Expectant Constable'*, which meant that he was amongst a number of constables who were temporarily employed on stand-by (on a lower salary of course) solely for the purpose of going out on the Beats of the permanently employed who could be absent through sickness, and whose pay was stopped, thus allowing for the paying of the temporary constable. Apparently such sickness was a serious problem of the Chief officer during those first few months.

However this appointment was only of short duration as the minutes of the Watch Committee for 12th September 1839 show Dunne being accepted as a full time constable following his period as an *'expectant constable'*.

It is interesting to learn from the minutes of the Watch Committee meeting of the 4th July meeting, that this new police got off to an auspicious start, when just four days after the first policeman was seen on the streets of Manchester a certain PC William Fletcher had to be summoned before the Borough Council for being drunk when going off duty as well as absenting himself from duty for the past four days ... or indeed from day one of the new force! This would unquestionably have been the first discipline case recorded for the fledgling police force and it was to be another whole seven days before a certain PC James Groom also found himself before the Borough Court, and who had also absented himself from duty.

And it wasn't just the lowly poorly paid constable who found himself in trouble either, for the minutes of the Watch Committee meeting of the 22nd July show a certain Inspector Love being reported for neglecting his duty. For that misdemeanour he was immediately dismissed probably the first Inspector to be so disciplined just three weeks after the formation of the force., or indeed any force. In the September we learn that two inspectors, Chadwick and Bennett have been reduced from the office of inspector to that of constable – indicating that it certainly wasn't just the ex-agricultural workers who were being disciplined so early in their new career.

As will have been gathered by now Manchester's new police force was formed along pretty much the same lines as the earlier formed Metropolitan Police in London, some ten years earlier. The first Chief Officer of Manchester Richard Beswick, though only in the post for three months would too have incorporated the same *'Nine Points of Law'* as introduced by Robert Peel.

These were:

1. The basic mission for which the police exist is to prevent crime and disorder

2. The ability of the police to perform their duties is dependent upon public approval of police actions.

3. Police must secure the willing co-operation of the public in voluntary observance of the law to be able to secure and maintain the respect of the public.

4. The degree of co-operation of the public that can be secured diminishes proportionately to the necessity of the use of physical force.

5. Police seek and preserve public favour not by catering to public opinion but by constantly demonstrating absolute impartial service to the law.

6. Police use physical force to the extent necessary to secure observance of the law or to restore order only when the exercise of persuasion, advice and warning is found to be insufficient.

7. Police, at all times,should maintain a relationship with the public that gives reality to the historic tradition that the police are the public and the public are the police; the police only being members of the public who are paid to give full time attention to duties which are incumbent on every citizen in the interests of community welfare and existence.

8. Police should always direct their attention strictly towards their functions and never appear to usurp the powers of the judiciary.

9. The test of police efficiency is the absence of crime and disorder, not the visible evidence of police action in dealing with it.

Such instructions would have formed the basis of every constable's terms and conditions.

Dunne being just fourteen years of age when he presented himself as a possible candidate for the newly formed Manchester Police Force at the police office located in the Town Hall on King Street, Manchester makes one wonder whether, as is supposed, that he falsified his age to gain acceptance, or did in fact admit to his age. There is certainly evidence to support the fact that some police forces did accept candidates at this age. Surrey Constabulary being one such example, for they had no minimum age and it is recorded that they recruited constables at age fourteen and fifteen.

Still, be that as it may, that first year for Dunne must have been quite an experience ... and not just for the fact that he was some hundreds of miles away from home, but due in part to the force's almost immediate change of leadership of the newly formed police force under its Head Constable Richard Beswick but it would also have been clear to him that Beswick's first choice of constables, being all the forces original watchmen, were certainly not for the good of the force, which in all probability explains partly why he only held this office for three months, thus making him the only individual holding the record for the shortest term of office for a Chief Constable. He did however continue in employment with the force – though at the lower rank of Chief superintendent.

Within a few months (December 1840,) he was to find himself the subject of a complaint directed to his successor Charles Shaw in respect of his past conduct, something which Shaw apparently felt best left alone, as certainly no further action was taken.

When Brigadier-General Sir Charles Shaw was appointed Commissioner in the October of 1839, the first thing he did was to replace a large number of the then existing police force... partly due to the funds that were available to him for his force, but also to some degree to 'sort the wheat from the chaff'. Initially he retained 157 of the force (including a certain PC 155 Dunne) but dispensed with the services of a further 111 of whom 23 were considered unfit and another 11 had refused to attend for a medical examination. This action upset at least 9 inspectors who were amongst those to be dismissed for they wrote directly to the Watch Committee declaring their surprise at actually being on the list and stating the difficulty they would have at finding any other form of employment. As it happened Shaw did consider their request but only retained 4 of the inspectors.

By the 6th January 1840, Shaw's financial problems appeared to have resolved for in his report to the Watch Committee of that date he was able to report that the strength of the force was now 383 in total made up of 64 officers and 319 constables. We also learn from this same report that beside the main police office in the Town Hall, further station houses were now in operation, namely at Ridgefield, Oldham Road, Great Jackson Street, Hulme and a station and division house on Allum Street, Ancoats, though in truth his report goes on to say that this was by no means sufficient number of stations for the numbers of populace, or indeed to deal with the expected number of felonies.

When the new Commissioner was appointed at then enormous salary of £700 per annum (roughly equivalent to £140,000 today) as stated, he immediately began to make serious adjustments to the strength of the police force. Only 157 men of the old force were sworn in on 17th October (out of an original total of 343) though a further 73 men were placed upon a supplementary list headed: *'where they may be chosen to fill the vacancies which may from time to time occur in the police force'.* A further 23 were deemed unfit by the surgeon and an additional 15 were advised that they were inadmissible to the police as they had not turned up for a medical examination by the surgeon.

By the 6th January 1840, Sir Charles Shaw was reporting to the Watch Committee that he now had in total 383 policemen, made up of 64 officers and 319 constables ... and declares this as being one Chief commissioner, one Chief superintendent, one Chief clerk, one receiver (or treasurer) 4 superintendents, 9 inspectors, 16 superior sergeants, plus 31 sergeants, along with the aforementioned 319 constables and that 7 police stations/lock ups were in place.

It is also from this same report of Shaws that we learn something of a policeman's duties and thus Dunne's in particular at this early stage of his new career for we now know something of the police beats themselves. Shaw is advising that he now has 80 police constables on beats employed on permanent day duty ... these commenced at 6am and terminated at 9pm with 40 of them going on duty at 6am and remaining until 9am, when they were relieved by the remaining 40, who would continue on duty till 2pm the first relief of 40 then returned on duty at 2pm and remained until 9pm.

The second relief of 40 also returned at 5pm and remained until 9pm so that during the last four hours. viz from 5pm until 9pm there were 80 police constables performing duty throughout the borough and this was of course for seven days a week with just four days off a year ... clearly indicating that anybody willing to accept such hours on pay equivalent today of around £160.00 per week had to be very keen indeed if the police was to be his chosen career ... though on the other hand it also explains why so many stayed little more than a few weeks – or turned to drink.

Naturally the police were to be on duty both day and night for Shaw advised further that there were then during the night time from 9pm until 6am a total of 130 police constables on beats throughout the borough, the largest of which beats may be *'paced on the first round, when the doors and windows are or ought to be examined, in 45 minutes'* and the shortest of such beats in 16 minutes or thereabouts, the average time for going around the beats being about 28 minutes.

By the 10th December we are aware of a letter from Shaw addressed to the Mayor of Manchester which clarifies the position of the police since the time he had taken responsibility for the force, as well as the problems he had encountered within the first few months. The letter read:

My Dear Sir.

With reference to our conversation on the 6th December last (1839) upon the subject of police matters I have the pleasure of enclosing to you the answers attached to the queries which you left with one upon that occasion. I can only say that I trust they may be considered at least sufficiently explanatory if not satisfactory.

Having thus acquainted you with the general detail of the arrangements which I have after mature reflection in every case found it necessary to adopt I have thought that it would not be inexpedient to take this opportunity of bringing likewise to your knowledge, the various and vexatious difficulties which have been thrown in my face since my arrival in Manchester.

The results of the opposition (to this new force) have been to circulate reports of every possible nature, calculated to cause either a misapprehension of the measures I have from time to time adopted, or to uphold them to public disapproval. Had I therefore in any degree permitted my mind to have been influenced by the conflicting advice and criticisms, even of those who were, I verily believe, purely activated by a feeling on general interest for the welfare of Manchester, I should have been in all probability now, where I had commenced, and perhaps by this time have really merited some portion of that misunderstanding which has so industriously been spread abroad.

I therefore, my dear sir, request your attention to the following sketch of the organisation of the police force, and of its working from the commencement to the present period.

Upon my arrival in Manchester, I found three distinct police establishments, but my mind had been fully made up (as it is now) carefully to avoid entertaining personal feelings either in favour or otherwise of any party, but to be guided by a fine sense of duty in every instance.

The numerical strength of these forces I found to amount to somewhere about six hundred constables under no general control, and possessing no intercommunity of information, or any unity of action. Their numbers under the circumstances appeared to me to have been more than sufficient; I am however convinced that two thirds of their numbers would, if not immediately dispensed with, eventually be necessary for the formation of an efficient police force. The sums however expended upon these establishments I found to be about £40,000, while to the contrary the means at my disposal were £16,500, a sum which it must be confessed, is obviously inadequate, and which necessarily prevented my competing in a numerical point of view with these united establishments.

Under the circumstances I was constrained to proceed with extreme caution, and my operations were commenced by selecting from the various forces as merely as circumstances would admit, a proportionate number from each, and in making this selection I was thrown entirely upon the candour and good faith of their respective officers, as to their previous conduct and merits, the officers themselves likewise, who had served in these forces, were selected by me with a due regard to their qualifications and with reference to the information I obtained respecting them from their superiors, but in some instances it is true contrary to my opinion and misgivings as to their fidelity or zeal and these appointed purely with the view of yielding (to the utmost limits consistent with my duty) to the declared wishes of their former employers.

Upon the 17th October last, therefore, the day fixed upon by me for entering upon my duties as Chief Commissioner, I swore in and embodied the comparatively small number of two hundred constables, thus at once, making an unfavourable impression in the eyes of the public at the first outset, an unavoidable circumstance, which however every man of the world will allow is a disadvantage difficult to overcome.

But this force having been placed in active operation, in the course of ten days, I found that it would be necessary to increase its numbers and accordingly fifty additional constables were appointed. In a few days after, fifty more were added, and these together formed a force (as it is at present constituted) of three hundred constables exclusive of officers.

Pending these arrangements the working of the police force for the first month, i.e. from the 17th October to the 17th November even under all these manifold and striking disadvantages, has not been unsatisfactory, but on the contrary, its daily increasing efficiency has inspired me with every confidence and I take the liberty of directing your attention to the grounds upon which I have formed so favourably an opinion.

I find then, by a reference to the public records of the three former police establishments in Manchester, the number of prisoners taken by them conjunctively, during the four months viz, from 16th June to 16th October of this year was 4936 averaging per a month 1234 of which number 4963 there were discharged by the magistrates 3184 cases, and committed for trial 1752, being an average of committals per month of 438. The present police force (which I have before stated consisted only for the last ten days of 300 constables) has during one month i.e. from 17th October to 17th November apprehended 928 criminals of whom 492 were discharged and the remainder committed for trial viz 436 this leaving a balance of two in favour of the above three united establishments. And may I be permitted here to draw your attention to the great number of prisoners taken by the old forces, as compared with the number committed for trial, viz less than ¼, whereas those taken by the new police nearly ½ were committed for trial. And surely this services some little discernment and discretion on the part of the new force.

I was however further gratified by an enquiry of another nature, to which I had been prompted, by vague rumours that had come to my knowledge, of the 'alarming increase' of information's lodged at the various stations of the present force, regarding robberies, which had been committed since its commencement.

Upon a reference to the records however I find that the district information of this nature lodged at the three former police establishments in four months i.e. from 10th June to 16th October this year amounted to 542, averaging per month over 182. The number of information's lodged at the various stations of the present force from 17th October to 17th November was 143 and may I here take the opportunity of stating that during that month, I have directed to be sent sixty-eight letters to proprietors of houses who had left their property exposed to plunder by leaving their warehouse doors and windows open.

In conclusion I deem it a duty which I owe to myself to draw your special attention to the very responsible situation I have placed myself in, by appointing a force so much more numerous than the means at my disposal (£16,500) will warrant. I have however been led to take this step by the universal opinions expressed by the inhabitants, that the force which I at first embodied, and which was adapted for the protection of the borough. With this opinion I entirely agreed and I rely with confidence on the cordial support of the public when it becomes needful to appeal to them for a supply to meet the deficiency which must necessarily occur by continuing the present establishment

Signed Charles Shaw.

What Shaw has left out from his letter is the problems then, and later associated with the Chartists, for it was during these early days that the rumblings of unease were starting to affect the residents of Manchester. Additionally Shaw was endeavouring to create a neutral force which was both independent of the many hundreds of mill owners who until then had been dominating the municipal authorities ... and of the unionists and Chartists. Though he was only to subsequently be in this post for the next two years his was not an uneventful time for in 1841 he is recorded as having led the hunt for the 'Ashton Murderers', and then during the Anti-Corn Law Riots and Plug Plot Riots in the summer of 1842 Shaw was forced to call on military assistance (the second time this had been necessary in Manchester.) At one point he actually led a charge by a troop of dragoons against a mob of rioters.

Shaw had considerable sympathy for the Chartists as well as the poor of Manchester. However he did last a little longer than his predecessor until 1st October 1842 to be precise, which was when the Manchester municipal authorities took over responsibility for the Borough Police. Coincidentally, as we shall learn it was also the time that Dunne decided to move to another force. This was to prove Shaw's only police career move for shortly after leaving he returned to the army for a short period though it was only to give him the opportunity of selling his commission and retire.

The fact that the Borough were now taking over the operation of the police force, and Shaw's appointment had been Government authorised meant yet another change of Chief officer as well as the need for all the current force to re-apply which for some of them meant a third time of applying for the exact same job. Perhaps this was proving just too much for Dunne in fact the earlier Chief officer Richard Beswick actually found himself temporarily Chief officer once again until a new man was appointed ... who was to be yet another one-time military man, namely Captain Edward Willis who was appointed on the 24th October of that year (1842) the advertisement requested that the selected man should have *'a practical knowledge of police affairs'*, and as Willis had previously been assistant Chief Constable of Lancaster police, then at least he met that criteria, unlike his immediate predecessor. Their were in total seventeen applications for the position, including Richard Beswick, who was even short-listed for the job of which eight actually had previous police experience and at high rank too. Unfortunately the newly appointed Willis did not fare so well as Shaw in the salary stakes receiving £450.00 per annum compared to his predecessors £700. Beswick ended up back in his old job as Chief Superintendent at a salary of £350 per annum.

Chartism did indeed prove a problem for the new force during its early days, and we know that Dunne himself was involved regularly in the many riots and skirmishes, as he himself declared in 1853 when giving evidence to the Select Committee on Policing.

Chartist meetings were actually banned by proclamation of the government in 1839. Mass arrests followed with Chartists being imprisoned and transported. In a movement that nurtured personality cults and where Chartist leaders vied for the hero worship of their followers, rancour and rivalry was inevitable.

The background to this movement was that a certain William Lovett, a member of the London Workingmen's Association, published his People's Charter in May 1838. Among its provisions the Charter made a number of political demands which became known as the 'six points', these were:

1. universal manhood suffrage
2. payment of Members of Parliament
3. equal electoral districts
4. abolition of property qualification
5. annual parliaments
6. the ballot

It was these people who subscribed to the aims of the Peoples Charter who were to become known as Chartists. Many of these (predominantly) working-class Chartists who were involved in the movement during the late 1830's and early 1840's often lived in abject poverty. In fact according to one historian (Mark Hovel, writing The Chartist Movement) *'intolerable conditions of existence'* were the driving force behind Chartism, and in addition to the many hardships they had to endure, they also risked the blacklist and imprisonment for their involvement in the movement.

By May of 1840, there were more than 200 Chartists in prison, 18 had by then been transported ... which included 11 who had been transported for life. Six months later by the November, the number of prisoners being held had risen to 480. In October of 1840, Chester Castle alone held 15 Chartist prisoners *'twelve of them for collecting arms'*, with many of them coming from Ashton-under-Lyne and Stockport.

In a year or two to come, the Chartist Movement would be giving the young Dunne some serious problems, however that very first meeting of the National

Charter Association was held at Kersal Moor in September 1838 (obviously overlooking the fact that this venue had been the scene of the Peterloo Massacre in Manchester some nineteen years earlier) with a second meeting at the same site in the May of 1839. Another was held on the 20th July 1840 at the Griffin Tavern, Great Ancoats Street, Manchester which fortunately went without incident – no record exists today as to whether their was a police presence at this meeting, however amongst the items agreed was that the organisation would only employ peaceful and constitutional means for gaining approval of the People's Charter. Six other meetings were held in Lancashire in 1841.Thus it was that the Chartist Movement came to dominate British politics in the 1840s with Manchester being the flashpoint for the nationwide chain reaction which it caused, and for the eventual political reforms which were brought about through the constant efforts of its supporters, as Dunne would later find out, that agreement from the 20th July meeting would be sorely pushed.

Many of the later skirmishes were to cause injury and death to some of Dunne's colleagues. As we know Dunne himself was involved in many of these riots for in 1853 when giving evidence to the Select Committee on Police to Parliament he declares *'that he was detached with a party of police and special constables on three occasions and when called into action the special constables ran away. Three active policemen were beaten so severely, that they died in hospital some two days afterwards'* And, the Watch Committee minutes of July 1839 also report that a PC John Pullien would *'continue to receive his wages following receiving severe injuries received in the discharge of his duties'*... which could indicate injuries received during one of the above meetings or perhaps dealing with a group of drunken Irish or navvies (or both) all of which were to be a continuous problem for the police. This was not the only case of injury reported to the Watch Committee for there is a further report dated 1st August regarding two police constables namely PC William Taylor and PC T. P. Rouse suffering injuries in the discharge of their duties.

There is a clear indication of disturbances at the mills during Beswicks' short term too, which was once again linked to the Chartists, as in the July of 1840 the Chief officer received a letter from one of the mill owners stating that:

> *'in consequence of a turn out of some of my work people my mill is regularly beset at the time when workers are proceeding to and from their work. To prevent disturbance,I consider it absolutely necessary a strong force of police should be in the neighbourhood. If you could put a policeman near my mill until this disturbance is settled I shall willingly pay for this extra service'. (Signed Chas Pooley)*

The same minutes indicate that the head constable was authorised to station a police constable *'out of uniform'* at Mr Pooley's mill for the purpose of watching the proceedings of the turnouts on the condition that Mr Pooley pay 3/- (15p) per day for such services AND the Minutes of 25th July tell us that this was not the only instance of 'trouble at the mill' for some 17 inspectors along with 208 police constables were on extra duty for four hours on the night of Saturday 13th July in readiness of an expected case of riot or disturbance. They all received an extra 1/- (5p) for their trouble ... and a few cuts and bruises too.

Naturally it was not only the Chartists that were causing the new force many headaches. Manchester was renowned at this time for its poverty, from which many crimes would stem, in most cases purely out of a necessity to stay alive.

Although the Industrial Revolution stemmed from the latter end of the 18th century and brought great wealth to a small portion of the population of Manchester, it also brought with it poverty and squalor to a much larger part. After all the population figures at this time were reported as 235,507. It was the historian Simon Schama writing in *'A History of Britain'* who noted that *'Manchester was the very best and the very worst taken to terrifying extremes, a new kind of city in the world, the chimneys of industrial suburbs greeting you with columns of smoke'. He also stated that an American visitor taken to Manchester's black-spots saw 'wretched,defrauded, oppressed human nature, lying and bleeding fragments".* Which pretty much sums up precisely what Dunne faced in the 1840s.

Records from this era clearly show that Manchester actually began expanding at a fast rate around the turn of the 19th century, which thanks to the Industrial Revolution brought about an unplanned urbanisation of the town so that by 1835 Manchester would have been the first as well as the greatest industrial 'city' in the world. (Manchester did not actually receive 'city' status until 1853).

In the beginning it would have been the engineering firms that initially made machines for the burgeoning cotton trade, though many diversified into general manufacture. At the same time the chemical industry started to make a name for itself by producing bleaches and dyes, though later many expanded into others areas too. Naturally commerce was supported by the financial services industries such as banking and insurance. It was around this time too that Manchester was being dubbed *'Cottonopolis'* and *'Warehouse City'* due to the fact that it was, for a time, the most productive centre of cotton processing as well as later being the world's largest marketplace for cotton goods.

However, regardless of the wealth for the limited few, the majority of the streets were still unpaved at this time, and on most of them rubbish such as rotting vegetables would be piled in heaps, invariably for months at a time. It was only removed when it was considered ready to be sold as fertiliser. People were still using cesspits, and these were only cleaned infrequently. The worst slums however were the cellar dwellings, and invariably whole families would be living in just one room .More often than not they had little or no furniture and most slept on piles of filthy straw. The rooms were damp andunventilated, and because of these conditions disease was rife... in fact as recently as1832 there had been a cholera epidemic in Manchester which had killed 674 people.

It was not until 1845 that the council took responsibility for removing refuse, and sewage, though initially only to a limited degree. Generally speaking throughout Dunne's time here, the poverty and sanitation would have got increasingly worse, simply because the population was increasing all the time. It was reported that in some parts of Manchester the number of toilets averaged only two for 250 people. Further reports tell us that only 40% of the children living in this area actually reached their fifth birthday. (according to Edwin Chadwick writing *The Sanitary Conditions of the Labouring Population* in 1842.) At the same time Dr Robertson, a Manchester surgeon, was penning a letter to the Parliamentary Committee on the Health of Towns in 1840, stated *'Manchester is a huge overgrown village, built according to no definite plan. The factories have sprung up along the rivers Irk, Irwell, and Medlock, as well as the Rochdale Canal. The homes of the work-people have been built in the factory districts. The interests and convenience ofthe manufacturers have determined the growth of the town and the manner of that growth, while the comfort, health and happiness have not been considered. Manchester has no public park or other ground where the population can walk and breathe the fresh air. Every advantage has been sacrificed to the getting of money'.*

The situation of the poor was not made any better because the then current Victorian attitudes was that they were regarded by the middle classes as largely being in a situation of their own making frequently stating that *'God wished them to be poor'.*

Overall the poor were considered a semi-class with almost certainly criminal tendencies. In fact one could go so far as to say that the more affluent Victorians actually distinguished between the 'deserving' and the 'undeserving' poor.

Widows, orphans, old people and those whose sickness rendered them incapable of work were regarded as deserving and thus could receive help through the system of Poor Houses, degrading though these were. The remaining poor (or unemployed) were regarded as undeserving and without any social support system in place, and were left entirely to their own devices, which invariably meant that just to survive they were forced to lead a life of crime with all its attendant penalties. As far as the Victorians were concerned acquired wealth on the other hand was commonly seen as a visible sign of virtue; the poor were bad, the rich were good – it was a natural order.

Another popular concept was that if one worked hard, this would be rewarded by an increase in wealth. Strong evidence of the plight of the poor was made clear when John Kay published *'The Moral and Physical Conditions of the Working Classes'* in 1832. However other than publicise the fact to a limited few, little action was taken upon its publication. Engels too wrote his well known *'The Condition of the Working Class in England'* in 1844, which was actually based on the Manchester under-class. In fact the area around Withy Grove and Shude Hill is described at some length by Engels as being insanitary and 'down at heel', but markedly more ordered than the area around St Ann's Square, which is also described. Nevertheless the houses are *'dirty, old and tumbledown, and the constructionof the side-streets utterly horrible'.* He also writes of *'pigs walking about in the alleyways, rooting in offal heaps'.* In addition in 1842 Edwin Chadwick was to publish his *'Report on the Sanitary Conditions of the Labouring Population'*, which amongst other disturbing facts clearly indicated that the official paupership figures for the 'Township of Manchester' were the highest in Britain – higher even than in London's east end.

As we know immigrants, especially from Ireland, also formed a large proportion of these poor. Indeed Dunne was of Irish descent himself of course, and probably recognised how fortunate he was not to be one of these under privileged. By 1851 these Irish immigrants comprised some 15% of the city's poor. Half of the population registered in the New Bridge Street Workhouse at this time were Irish Catholics. Most lived in Ancoats, probably the poorest and most deprived area of the city. By 1851 the total population of Ancoats was 53,737 making it larger than towns such as Bury and Blackburn and according to that years census, with half the population being born in Ireland. In addition to the Irish immigrants a small area of Chorlton-on-Medlock came to be known as 'Little Italy' on account of the large numbers of immigrant Italians who lived there in a sort of ghetto situation. They actually formed the largest section of the vast casual labour force which put in long hard hours when the trade was good but were the first to be laid off in leaner times. They formed the largest part of the Smithfield labour force, comprised the majority of the city's street sellers and hawkers and dominated the building trade and figured largely in domestic service (females in particular).

Coming from a rural background Dunne would, above anything else, have found Manchester to be a very unhealthy place to live in the early 1840's. For starters coal burning domestic fires and innumerable factory chimneys (with cotton still at its peak there were for example some 180 cotton mills each with a chimney spewing out vast amounts of polluted smoke) meant that Manchester was permanently overhung with the pall of smoke, drenched with acid rain thus ensuring the area continuously suffered plagues of various respiratory diseases ... bronchitis, influenza, pneumonia, asthma, along with many other dust related diseases. Clearly that newspaper reporter knew what he was writing about. And where did this vast horde work? Well two of the biggest mills hereabouts was Redhills Street Mills which employed 1500 workers all of whom would have laboured some 69 hours a week for an average wage of 11/- (60p). Three quarters of their workforce were women and children. Close by was the Cambridge Street Mill which employed 2000 people, and in the early 1840s was the largest mill in Manchester. However, in truth this was only the tip of the iceberg where mills were concerned as it has been estimated that in 1830 alone there were some 560 cotton mills in Lancashire employing around 110,000 workers, and of which 35,000 were children, some as young as six years of age, and working for as little as 2/3d per week (11.5p).

Life expectancy for the working man at this time was also a problem, for we now know it was just seventeen years. None of the areas health problems were helped by the lack of proper sanitation,though Manchester was not alone with that problem, it certainly exasperated the overall situation. In sewage disposal the city, until the middle of the nineteenth century, had little or no policy; ash-pits and communal cesspits were common and these were regularly overflowing especially in rainy periods which meant they had to be emptied and carried away ... though in truth this was rarely done. There were frequent accounts of 'middens' overflowing into cellars in which a large number of workers lived, with no attempt by the authorities to relieve the problem.

From 1840 onwards, Manchester's reputation was to get worse. This was almost entirely due to the living conditions of the many thousands of workers ... factory workers, miners, and railway workers predominantly which could well be attributed to the area's continual descent into squalor and subsequent crime. Both men and women on the low incomes sought relief from the filthiness of not just their homes, but their workplaces too, and 'pickled' their brains with large amounts of the cheap and easily available beer and gin from any one of the 502 public houses and/or the 812 beer houses. Troublesome children would in all probability have been treated with a large dose of laudanum ... though in truth they would have been the lucky ones, for according to

W B Neale, the author of Juvenile Delinquency in Manchester. Its causes and history and some suggestions concerning its cure, (Manchester 1840) who undertook a personal survey into the problems of juvenile delinquency in Manchester for 1840, he estimated that there were some 3650 homeless children on the streets at this time, many, if not all, being involved in some crime or other. Is it any wonder that Shaw was anxious to increase policing numbers as well as lock-ups?

The juvenile crime rates for this time are clear enough too – criminal statistics for Manchester in the early 1840s indicated that there were 3571 convictions of which 475 were boys and 26 girls, both of which were under the age of fifteen. As Dunne quickly came to learn drink was a contributory factor in the many cases of wife-beating and assault cases that regularly came his way and for which he would regularly testify before the magistrates. It would certainly have been a common sight for him to see heavily-bandaged women testifying against drunk brutish husbands. No doubt those that did get caught would have been just the tip of the iceberg, with many wives simply deciding to suffer in silence.

Life too would have been particularly harsh for women. They were paid a much lower salary than the men – even though they were doing exactly the same work, though being barred from many trades and professions they were invariably dependant on their men-folk, whether in or out of work, with many of the men preferring to hand their money over to the hundreds of publicans than to their wife and children.

Given the choice between the long hours as well as the hard graft of domestic service or factory work, it is quite understandable why so many women turned to prostitution to make ends meet. It is difficult to imagine a young immature naïve police constable from Ireland being faced with the harsh realities of this form of life… it would certainly have been a swift 'learning curve'. An indication of exactly what another outsider would have seen following their arrival in Manchester at this time, would be the words of General Sir Charles James Napier who when taking command of troops in the North of England in 1839, following the expectation of Chartist riots, he wrote that: '*Manchester is the chimney of the world. Rich rascals, poor rogues, drunken ragamuffins and prostitutes form the moral, soot made into paste by rain the physique, and the only view long chimney, what a place! The entrance to hell realised!*'

Besides the shock of such a place at least Dunne soon learnt that he was amongst his own kind ... sort of! – for as we have learnt there were at this time some many thousands of Irish patriots living in and around Manchester, with a high proportion of them living in an area commonly known as Little Ireland.

It is difficult to imagine how Dunne would have coped with his fellow compatriots during periods of unrest, especially so when he was personally involved in the removal of over 2600 of them between 1841-1842, when they were moved away from Little Ireland. At that time there were as many as 2,647 Irish immigrants living there, and their removal had been authorised as many were on poor relief ... and thus a strain on the limited council reserves.

By 1841 there were 33,490 Irish living in Manchester ... and this was before the major emigration brought about by the Potato Famine still to come some four years later. So to some degree our young John Dunne may well have felt at home, though in truth more because many of his police colleagues who would also have hailed from Ireland, as compared to those living in Little Ireland.

Earlier, in 1840 there had already been a riot in Little Ireland which had been sparked off when the police entered the area to halt the regular practice of Sunday morning gambling, which the law saw as a desecration of the Sabbath. At the time the police only managed to arrest just two young boys, namely William Donnelly and Patrick Connelly who were simply playing pitch and toss, though there would have been a small amount of money changing hands. The arrests set off what the local newspaper called *'a most despicable battle'* between nine policemen and scores of Irish'. Two of the officers were seriously injured.

Unquestionably times were hard for the Irish, as indeed they were wherever they settled London, Liverpool, Glasgow, and parts of Cumberland being the most popular (the latter Dunne would discover for himself in the years to come) they were pressed into the ghettos and *'whenever they did emerge from their quarters they were subjected to considerable prejudice'* ... even though in many instances those who were doing the complaining at their presence were little better accommodated then them.

There were in fact two Irish areas in Manchester from 1832. Little Ireland was where the smallest contingent was, and their location was just south of the city in a depression situated at a bend of the River Medlock. Altogether some four thousand lived there. The other Irish area was known as Irish Town and was located north-east of the city centre, between the River Irk and St George's Road (now Rochdale Road). It was much larger than Little Ireland, this time with over twenty thousand people huddled into similar cramped houses and cellar dwellings. Engels, in his book *The Conditions of the Working Class in England*, explains it well: *'But the most horrible spot (in Manchester) lies immediately south-west of Oxford Road, and is known as Little Ireland. In a rather deep hole, in a curve of the Medlock and surrounded on all four sides by tall factories and high embankments covered with buildings, stand two groups of about two hundred cottages, built Chiefly back to back, in which about four thousand human beings live,most of them Irish'* He continued *'The cottages are old, dirty, and of the smallest sort,the streets uneven fallen into ruts and in part without drains or pavement, masses of refuse, offal and sickening filth lie in the puddles. In short the whole rookery furnishes such a hateful and repulsive spectacle as can hardly be equalled in the worst part of the irk. The race that lives in these ruinous cottages, behind broken windows mended with oilskin, sprung doors and rotten doorposts, or in dark, wet cellars, in measureless filth and stench, in this atmosphere penned in as if with a purpose, this race must really have reached the lowest stage of humanity'. And 'this is the impression and the line of thought which the exterior of this district forces upon the beholder. But what must one think when he hears that in each of these pens, containing at most two rooms, a garret, perhaps a cellar, on the average twenty human beings live in the whole region, for each one hundred and twenty persons, one usually inaccessible privy is provided, and in spite of all the preaching of the physicians, in spite of the excitement into which the cholera epidemic plunged the sanitary police by reason of the condition of Little Ireland, in spite of everything, in the year of grace 1844, it is almost in the same state as it was in 1831'* In fairness it should be noted that Engels wasn't putting down the Irish rather he was highlighting their plight along with the failure of British capitalism, and it wasn't just the Irish either as pretty much all working people in Manchester at this time were living in a similar situation of deprivation though the Irish did face significantly worse conditions as well as encountering discrimination; as Father Daniel Hearne, the parish priest in IrishTown, pointed out in the Report on the State of the Irish Poor in Great Britain. He said that the Irish *'were prevented from advancing from feelings of jealousy. A manufacturer would prefer employing English to Irish simply on the ground of they being Irish and not being worse workmen'.* Furthermore as Fr Hearne told the newly set up commission to investigate the conditions *'the Irish were attacked for working for lower wages than other workers and for placing too much of a burden on poor relief.* This same official report (of 1836) also quoted a Constable Sadler who said that applying the law in Little Ireland was *'a most daunting task, my officers are often maltreated by brickbat and other missiles'*, with the result that they were often driven off when they came to arrest an Irishman for reasons of rent arrears or debt.

Chartism, poverty, and the Irish contingent were not the only problems that Dunne and his colleagues had to contend with at this time, for this was also the time of the Anti-Corn Law Riots and Plug Plot Riots.

The 1842 General Strike which came to be known as the Plug Plot Riots. (so named because the mills were stopped from working by the removal or drawing of a few bolts or plugs in the boilers thus preventing steam from being raised).

The strike was influenced by the same Chartist movement which I have mentioned, and came about because on the 4th May Thomas Duncombe (an MP who believed it was his responsibility to represent the views of the working people as well as those who had actually voted for him) presented to Parliament a Chartist petition signed by more than 3,250,000 people. The Chartists were furious when the House of Commons rejected the petition by 287 votes to 47. This decision was followed by a series of strikes which started amongst the miners in Staffordshire but was soon to spread throughout Britain eventually affecting not just the mines, but factories and mills too. The strike in turn brought about a movement of resistance to the planned imposition of wage cuts in the mills, a movement which came to be known as the Plug Riots. This spread rapidly and eventually involved nearly half a million workers throughout Britain and at its time represented the biggest single exercise of working class strength in Britain.

On the 13th August there was a strike at Bayley's cotton mill in Stalybridge, (understandable when one considers that this area alone contributed in excess of 10,000 signatures to the petition.) and it was from there that roving cohorts of operatives carried this stoppage not only to the whole area of Stalybridge and Ashton, but onwards to Manchester and all towns adjacent, using as much force as was necessary to bring the mills to a standstill ... Which, of course included the removal or drawing of a few bolts or 'plugs' in the factories boilers. It was Wednesday the 10th August that the strike reached Manchester when thousands of angry men from Stalybridge arrived in the town calling out mill workers as they went.The following morning a mass meeting of workers was held on Granby Row Fields in Manchester, after which they marched through the city, ignoring magistrates who read the Riot Act at the Town Hall and from there moving on to Blackfriars Bridge over the Irwell, where they forced the gate and moved on to Salford. Generally speaking the strikers were peaceful though where the factory owners tried to impede their actions there were the expected clashes with the police and the recently arrived troops led by General Napier. By the evening virtually all of Manchester was at a standstill and by two days later the strike had spread to many neighbouring towns. In dealing with the rapidly growing situation, the Prime Minister Sir Robert Peel apparently favoured a non-intervention approach to the problem, but Arthur Wellesley, the 1st Duke of Wellington (backed by Sir James Graham) argued for troops to be sent into deal with the strikers and who was going to argue with the man who defeated Napoleon at Waterloo? Thus Peel eventually agreed with them and the Home Secretary along with the army were dispatched to assist such police as there were at that time in bringing the problem to a speedy conclusion.

Leaders of the strikes, which included members of the Manchester Conference who had voted for linking the dispute with the Chartist demands, were soon arrested. Several Chartist leaders namely: Feargus O'Connor, George Julian Harney and Thomas Cooper were detained. In total 1500 people were arrested, 79 were found guilty and sentenced to between seven and twenty-one years transportation ... still a popular form of punishment at this time. By the end of August rioting had come to an end with most strikers returning to work though the cotton operatives of Lancashire and the Staffordshire miners who had started it all, did manage to hold out for another month.

The strike spread to involve nearly half a million workers throughout Britain and represented the biggest single exercise of working class strength in nineteenth century Britain. The movement remained, to outward appearances, largely non-political. Although the Peoples Charter was praised at public meetings, the resolutions that were passed at these were in almost all cases merely for a restoration of the wages of 1820, a ten hour working day, or reduced rents.

Though the Government deployed soldiers to swiftly suppress violence, it was the practical problems in sustaining an indefinite stoppage that ultimately defeated the strikers. The drift back to work began on 19th August. Only Lancashire and Cheshire (which included Manchester) were still strike-bound by September, with the Manchester power loom weavers being the last to return to work on the 26th September. Several Chartist leaders, including Feargus O'Connor, George Julian Harney and Thomas Cooper were arrested along with nearly fifteen hundred others. Around 250 were sentenced to prison for major offences, ranging from sixteen months and from two to twenty-one years; 50 more were sentenced to transportation to Australia. However the government's most ambitious prosecution, personally led by the Attorney General, of O'Connor and 57 others (including almost all Chartism's national executive) failed, none were convicted of the serious charges, and those found guilty of minor offences were never actually sentenced. Cooper alone of the National Chartist leadership was convicted (at a different trial) having been involved in events leading up to the strikes in North Staffordshire, where violence was especially serious.

Clearly the young Dunne was experiencing a somewhat exciting time during his formulative time in the police force but dealing with the Chartist problem was clearly only part of his experiences ... another problem at this time in

Manchester would have been the vast numbers of navvies, most of whom were involved in building the Summit Tunnel beneath the Pennines for the planned Manchester and Leeds Railway.

Today the tunnel is one of the *oldest* railway tunnels in the world – then it would have been the *longest* railway tunnel in the world. Before Dunne joined the Manchester Police there had been numerous problems associated with its construction not least of which would have been the large numbers of fatal accidents especially during the period February to September 1838 when sixteen were killed.

It was not just accidents however that beset the progress of the tunnel, it was labour troubles too. In February of 1841, 16 of the labourers were brought before the magistrates charged with having intimidated a number of workmen and in so doing prevented them from following their employment. The men threatened were 32 from North Shields engaged on a six month contract, by the renowned engineer John Stephenson, at a wage of 5/- per day (25p) which in fact was 1/- (5p) above the rate paid to the existing workforce. All the accused were found guilty of the offence, 7 of them were sentenced to hard labour for three months. Others for one month, whilst others, for reasons not recorded, were allowed to return to work. (Hard labour would have meant breaking stones, walking the treadmill, or turning the crank in the cell for many hours a day ... not something many would have relished.) This clearly indicates that there would have been plenty of fights between the men.

It would be certain that the North Shields men hired by Stephenson at the higher rate of pay were not, and never would be, welcomed by the workmen already contracted at the lower rate, and there were ongoing disputes between the men with most of the confrontation sending up before the magistrates. These navvies usually earned between 3/- (15p) and 4/- (20p) per day, though the stonemasons faired a little better earning 4/- and joiners at 22/- (£1.20) per week.

The majority of these navvies lived in shanty huts built of sods or stone roofed with sticks and clay. This at the time, would have been the normal practice, the navvies and their families forming their own community, buying their food locally but at the same time keeping well apart from the village.

By the August of 1842 for reasons which still remain unknown, Dunne clearly decided that his career in the Manchester Police was not proceeding as he would have liked. Perhaps it was the change of leadership that convinced him to move, after all their had been three changes in three years, or it could simply have been the fact that the municipal authorities had taken over responsibility for the police, perhaps it was because Shaw left. We shall never know. What we do know however is that Dunne's short career with the Manchester Police came to an end on the 20th August of 1842, immediately after the last set of riots, when he decided to move across to Chelmsford, in Essex, to join yet another newly formed police force, this time the Essex Police under the leadership of Admiral McHardy. By then he was just seventeen years of age, but even at that young age, he would be taking with him a vast amount of experience.

CHAPTER THREE

JOHN DUNNE

Essex 1842-1848

'If one were to ask what in my opinion was the dullest and most stupid spot on the face of the earth, I should decidedly say Chelmsford'.
(Charles Dickens in a letter to Thomas Beard, January 11th 1835)

Based on the fact that Dunne was to spend a total of six rewarding and busy years in this fair town, I have my doubts whether Dunne would have agreed with Dickens sentiments!

Thus it was that in September 1842 we see the seventeen year old John making another excursion into the unknown – though unlike his previous journey three years earlier I think it would be safe to assume that this is a stronger more confident John than the one who stood on those Liverpool Docks backs in 1839. Unquestionably much had happened to him over the past three years which would have broadened his outlook on life ... and no doubt taught him a few lessons too, thus the need to make a lengthy train journey would have been unlikely to have phrased him. Anyway it was clearly his decision to move from an urban to a rural force, and in all probability he would have been expecting perhaps as lightly more comfortable life plodding the streets of a country town and perhaps even the early possibility of a promotion.

His train journey this time would of necessity take in London, utilising the Manchester to London train, though he would have had to initially travel on the Manchester to Birmingham train before joining the Birmingham-London Railway train. Unfortunately for him it was to be another four years before the London and North Western train was introduced giving direct access from Manchester to London. No doubt that all added to the excitement.

Almost certainly this too would have been John's first, though not his last, visit to the metropolis that was London, and one can safely assume that he took full advantage of the opportunity to visit the many sights. From London he would have been able to catch a train on the newly opened Eastern Counties Railway (ECR) running then from Mile End in London to Chelmsford town centre, his ultimate destination.

Chelmsford these days is better known as the *'birthplace of radio'* for this is the town where Guglielmo Marconi opened the world's first wireless factory and employed many staff ... though that was to be a further 57 years hence, but when John first set foot in Essex's county town (since 1215) it was totally different. Located just 32 miles from London, and with a population of just over 9,300, it was like so many other towns at this time, dirty and unsanitary, and again just like Manchester, sewers had at this time still not been installed. Indeed the town had suffered an outbreak of cholera as recently as 1832. The atmosphere of poverty would not have been helped at this time by the streets being lit by gas. In some respects Chelmsford was a little like Manchester, the streets in the main parts of the town were well paved and there were many large inns and taverns as well as plenty of well stocked shops with *'handsome glass windows'*. There was a market twice a week at the junction of Conduit Square and the High Street.

I suppose what would have been especially noticeable to Dunne immediately upon his arrival would have been the lack of Irish voices, (or Italian for that matter) which he would have been used to. Whether that would have been a cause for celebration it would be difficult to know – for on the one hand he could expect far fewer fights and skirmishes, but on the other hand his Irish accent would be one of a few, instead of one of many. Mind you if he arrived in Chelmsford just a year or two earlier the situation would havebeen entirely different as the Eastern Counties Railway was then still under construction and which would have certainly entailed the employment of many hundreds of Irish navvies since 1836.

The County Police Office, and the residence of the Chief Constable Capt McHardy (as he was in Dunne's time) occupied a large building in Springfield which was formerly a military depot. The rural police, or county constabulary force comprised then of 15 superintendents, 20 inspectors and 156 constables for the fourteen divisions of the county. There were lock-ups in each division and for prisoners taken in Chelmsford, the police had use of the prison under the Shire Hall. Messrs W.Oakley and J May were the two superintendents stationed at the Chelmsford Division, and as such would have been Dunne's immediate superiors. The latter were also the Inspector's of Weights and Measures for Essex. The Chief Constable of the Essex Constabulary, who like Dunne had been a police officer for just 2/3 years, was the aforementioned Captain (later Admiral) McHardy, and as it was he that was to strongly influence Dunne for the rest of his career it would perhaps be useful to give some background to the Chief Constable.

At the time of Dunne's appointment in 1842, Captain John Bunch Bonnemaison McHardy had been the forces' Chief Constable for just over two years ... indeed the force, like Manchester had only been set up in 1839 and was too on a strict learning curve, though on this occasion it was to be the first time that Dunne had been under the supervision of a strict ex-military man, rather than as with Richard Beswick in Manchester who at least had had a lengthy background in policing. Still as he soon discovered a senior officer with a military background was not going to do him any harm whatsoever. On the contrary there is strong evidence of the time to suggest that McHardy was a particularly moral commander, for faced with the task of gathering a disparate group of men into a team and moulding them as he wanted them, would come as no surprise that he favoured strict disciplinary action.

Considering that many of his men had been soldiers and labourers, McHardy, no doubt given half a chance would almost certainly had favoured the enforcement of the 'cat o'nine tails' which the majority of his new force would certainly have been used to ... indeed such discipline was still being enforced in the military services at this time. However that was not to be the case in McHardys new police force fortunately – simply because it was totally illegal outside the military services.

The background to this force dated back to November 1839 when the Essex Justices ofthe Peace met at the Shire Hall in Chelmsford on the 25th November. They had already earlier decided that the county would benefit from having a full time paid police force and so when the Home Secretary's approval was received they immediately advertised for a Chief Constable. There were 31 applicants who applied in total, and of the nineteen who were short-listed for interview the majority were military or naval officers.The application form stated that applicants had to be under 45 years of age, free of debts, and certified by a doctor to be in good health with their approval being subject tothe final agreement of the Home Secretary. Following lengthy discussion and numerous interviews the JP's finally decided on appointing McHardy who started work on the 11th February 1840. Although only 38 years of age, (he was born in 1802) John McHardy already had a long career in the Royal Navy as well as the Coastguard service, and it was this background that clearly satisfied the justices.

McHardy's working life had actually begun at age eleven when he joined the Royal Navy from his home in the British-owned Bahamas. Researching Essex Police History website we learn that McHardy was the son of a Scottish migrant who had left his home country at the latter end of the 18th century to settle in

New Providence, capital of the island of Nassau. John McHardy's mother had died when he was very young so he went to live with his mother's sister and her wealthy husband, who just happened, and very fortunately for the young McHardy to be, the Chief Justice of the Bahamas. It seems quite likely that his uncle and aunt were already acquainted with a Royal Naval captain named John Pasco for when Essex's future Chief Constable decided to join the Royal Navy in 1813 he was taken on as a boy third class on Captain Pasco's ship – the Tartarus.

Captain John Pasco himself was already something of a Naval celebrity, for he had been signal lieutenant to Nelson at the Battle of Trafalgar, and in fact was responsible for sending the famous signal which began *'England expects that every man would do his duty'.* It is a well-documented fact that Nelson's original choice of words for the now famous signal had been *'England confides ... that every man would do his duty'.* Pasco had suggested the alteration, because he knew that confides was not in the naval signal vocabulary (still isn't).

It is clear that Captain (later Admiral) Pasco did a lot to shape John McHardy's early naval career, (and by default Dunne's also one could say) as the future Chief Constable remained under his command until August 1815. However their relationship continued for much longer, for in December 1830 McHardy was to marry one of Pasco's daughters, Horatia Elizabeth Atchison Pasco, then aged 22 (he was 28). Also in the early 1800s in order to progress through the naval ranks up to lieutenant at least, an applicant had to produce certificates showing that he had been on a ship's books for at least six years, and of which at least two years had been spent as a midshipman. Midshipman without ability or more importantly patronage, could sometimes remain as 'middies' until they were well into their thirties. McHardy served as a midshipmanal together on seven different ships where he was able to acquire a wide variety of practical nautical experience, before being promoted to lieutenant on 19th August 1824, when he was 22 years of age.

Influence and patronage were important elements in those early Navy days, even Nelson himself is said to have owed his rapid promotions to a well placed uncle. Of course it is impossible now to say if anyone, other than Pasco, received promotions through their own efforts, a fact of which he was rightly very proud and to which he made reference on several occasions whilst Chief Constable of Essex. I have been able to obtain some additional background to McHardy's navel career from Clowes printed: *History of the British Navy* which refers to McHardy as being *'the terror equally of pirates and of slavers in the West Indies'.* An example of this is shown too for while acting as captain on the Icarus prior to his promotion he was involved in the capture off Havana of the pirate schooner Diableto.

On 1st January 1828 McHardy was given command of his own ship, the schooner HMS Pickle, which was manned by 30 men and 6 boys. On the 6th June 1829 the Pickle captured a famous slave ship called Boladora, which had 60 men as well as armed black's on board. After a severe action lasting more than an hour, and the loss of eleven of her own sailors, Pickle succeeded in capturing the Boladora. Thanks to the success of his men in that action, McHardy received a special promotion to commander in December 1830.

Having been married only two weeks before this latest promotion, it would be fair to say that McHardy might have welcomed the chance to live at home, especially as the Navy was operating a 'run-down' in the number of its sea-going ships, an action which just happened to coincide with his marriage. But no, that was not for him for he began his new career with the coastguard in March 1831. As an inspecting commander of the Burnham (Norfolk) district of the Coastguard, many of his new duties were concerned with the control of smuggling; though co-operation with other law enforcement agencies such as the police (limited though they were at this time) was also encouraged.

His senior officer, a certain Captain Bowles who went under the title of the First Controller General of the Coastguard, set high standards and issued frequent instructional memoranda to his officers – indeed it has now been established that McHardy actually adapted many of these coastguard rules, instructions and methods of working when he became Chief Constable . Later McHardy also supported the Home Secretary's belief that police in maritime counties such as Essex should co-operate with the Coastguard and in fact one of the earliest places outside Chelmsford to be policed by county constables was the remote Foulness Island... then well known as a smugglers paradise.

At least Dunne could expect some alternative forms of policing than he had until now been used to. Such then was McHardy's background, clearly a man not to be argued with.

As an inspecting commander with Customs and Excise for the past two years, as well as his background in the Navy there was no question that McHardy had been used to commanding men, and who would additionally *'be occasionally assembled in armed bodies for the protection of the Public Peace, and in co-operation with the Civil Power'.*

His personal and professional qualifications for the post of Chief Constable were therefore considered to be *'so perfect that you may obtain your wish'.* Having been appointed on the 11th February 1840 he began work almost immediately by purchasing a copy of *'Standing Rules and Regulations for the Constabulary Force of Ireland'*, and acquiring copies of coastguard forms which he then adapted for police use. One example of this was 'Form 50' for travelling and subsistence expenses that was still being used in the Essex Constabulary in the early years of the 20th century. In later years comparison with these 'standing rules' and those issued by Dunne for the Cumberland and Westmoreland Police show a clear similarity indicating that he had kept his copy from1842 for possible future use.

McHardy held his first batch of selection interviews on 26th February 1840 initially to appoint the first fifteen superintendents for Essex and which he stated:, *'on whose zeal and activity the efficiency of the service depends'.* Their salary was agreed at £80 per annum.

Two of the first superintendents to be appointed were Henry Riom and Charles Greaves, both of whom had been amongst those who had applied for the post of Chief Constable; it seems hardly surprising that neither stayed long in Essex, although Riom was later dismissed for 'misappropriating county funds'.

The second batch of his initial interviews i.e the selection of 100 police constables, on a starting wage of 19/- per week (95p) were equally as important, though as we have already learnt possibly harder to select than the superintendents due tothe fact that the majority would have had a background of being farmers, soldiers and sailors, the latter two generally having only recently returned from service overseas; and of course illiteracy would have deleted large numbers of those first applicants.

From the evidence so far it certainly looks unlikely that Dunne moved across to Essex for any monetary gain. It fact it is far more likely it was because he didn't like Manchester or did not think he stood any chance of promotion, OR, as I would prefer to think, he knew something about McHardy he felt would give him a better chance of promotion – and I guess on that score he was proved right.

Like Manchester, the criteria for recruits was much the same: under forty years of age, to stand 5'7" without shoes, to read and write and to keep accounts, to be *'free from bodily complaint'*, of strong constitution and generally intelligent. Unlike Manchester however their was one additional requirement, namely that an applicant was required to provide a certificate of character from one or more respectable persons who had personal knowledge of him during the last five years and confirm that he was *'sober, honest and of good temper, and that his connections and associates were respectable'.* One would assume that Dunne's testimonials from the Chief Constable of Manchester Police would have done the job admirably. Subject then to the applicant being passed fit by the police surgeon he would then be sworn in as a constable before the magistrates at Shire Hall, Chelmsford.

It is clear from later records however that the definition of *'a respectable person'* had never been made clear to the referees, for their were many instances of police constables reporting drunk for duty, or even getting drunk whilst on duty – not something one is inclined to do on the spur of the moment. In fact the records from 1840 alone, show that some forty constables were dismissed the service for drunkenness within the first few weeks of their recruitment. One supposes that the excuses of those caught would always have been that their refreshment breaks were at their discretion and of course this meant the nearest beer or public house. Thus, not their fault!

On the basis of the constables local knowledge, the county was split up into fifteen divisions which was based on the old Hundreds system and then into detachments, and finally into guards (later to be called beats). Initially this meant their was about one constable to 1,750 head of population, though by 1842 the force had been increased by a further fifty men allowing one constable to 1,325 of the population.

Uniform once again was much the same as Manchester with a basic uniform consisting of a blue dress coat with embroidered collar, dress trousers, 'undress' trousers, waterproofed greatcoat, cape, pair of boots, pair of shoes and a black stove pipe. Constables at this time, and at their own expense were expected to supply themselveswith a pair of white drill trousers which were to be worn *'whenever the superintendent may direct'.*Besides strict discipline McHardy also insisted that Divine Worship was encouraged, in fact *'duties would be so arranged as to allow the attendance of the Constabulary at the Divine Service, and constables are expected to show an example of due respect for the observance of the Sabbath Day'* was his clear instructions to all his men.

Research tells me that from the very outset McHardy had to contend with widespread distrust, mostly from the public, and especially the taxpayers, though gradually he won the support of the magistracy and the majority of the local communities.

In many respects his contribution to the establishment of county police forces (and in later years of Dunne's too) throughout the country, was equally comparable one could say to that of Rowan and Mayne in the establishment and development of the Metropolitan Police. Frankly the establishment of any police forces in the country was founded on a number of deep rooted fears, (as the Metropolitan Police had earlier discovered) the traditional fear of a standing army coupled with the political uses which might be made of such a force, along with the effects of police intrusion upon daily neighbourhood life as well as the fear that they would be used to enforce the new Poor Law. Middle classes invariably objected solely out of a fear of an increase in rates, whilst those living in rural areas did at least see a need for policing in cities but at the same time felt that having them in the countryside far outweighed their potential usefulness. It was clearly McHardy's job to prove them all wrong.

Under his guidance the Essex County Constabulary quickly became a 'sort of nursery for policemen' as many men were appointed and trained in Essex before being 'head-hunted' by newer police forces in other parts of the country. I suppose this would be a bit like what we now know as 'fast track promotion'… though in the Victorian era one's social background and education would have played a much bigger part in their selection.

Clearly as we have learnt something that was always very much in the back of Dunne's mind. Still, regardless of his aspirations it was still be to another five years before he was to be offered promotion, which given his attitude must have been extremely frustrating for him. Why this took so long, knowing what we now know is unclear – was he perhaps a slow learner, or was it as one supposes his age, perhaps reaching the age of 22 before promotion to inspector was McHardy's guideline. There is however a precedent for this as a colleague of his namely one Andrew Rome was also promoted to Inspector at the age of 22, though in his case he found himself spending the rest of his career policing the oyster beds at Burnham on Crouch with four police constables under his command until his retirement in 1897. One supposes it is a little argumentative in Rome's case whether that was indeed promotion or not... 57 years policing oyster beds ? In fairness to Rome however it would be true to say that the oyster industry was important to Essex and in 1844 (as an example) the Colne Fishery Company actually employed no less than 200 smacks along with 2,000 men, whilst equally as many worked in the Blackwater for the Tollesbury and Mersea Company. Amazingly some 144 million oysters a year were being sold on the streets of London alone at this time so perhaps Rome had an important promotion after all

Right from the outset stress was laid upon securing the goodwill and co-operation of those living in areas where the police had to operate. An early instruction stated *'Constables are always to take the outside of the footpath, and when walking along thestreets should not shoulder past respectable people but give way in a mild manner, for the more respectful and civil the Constabulary are, the more they will be supported and respected by the public'.* The constable worked long hours often under difficult conditions. The average working day was between ten and twelve hours split into two shifts. A day shift of three or four hours was followed by a night shift between 10pm and dawn. This was performed seven days a week, a rest day not being granted until 1914. A week's annual leave was granted each year however unpaid! All patrols were on foot and it was not uncommon for a constable on a rural beat to walk over twenty miles each day. Horse and cart (an early form of Black Maria) was however provided in every division for the conveyance of prisoners and the use of constables who were being posted.

Under McHardy's instructions even getting married was a hardship and if a constable wished to get married (but not before serving for seven years in order that he had accumulated a sufficient amount of 'wealth' to allow them to live comfortably, and support a family) he firstly had to request permission from the Chief Constable ... even the background of his future wife was examined to see if she was of good character.

Many trades were forbidden to McHardy's policemen (and his spouse) and they were forbidden from selling goods or keeping lodgers.

A superannuating scheme was introduced from the outset, but a pension was not granted as an automatic right; only men recommended by the Chief Constable and approved by the justices received one. After 15-20 years service a police officer (of what ever rank) was entitled to a half-pay pension, a two-thirds pension being received after twenty or more years service. The superannuating fund was established from deductions from wages, selling off cast clothing and fines imposed for disciplinary offences...which for the latter were many.

Clearly as we have seen McHardy was totally dedicated to the formation of an efficient and disciplined force and as a result a strict discipline code was maintained with many constables falling foul of even the slightest misdemeanour. Such dedication being soaked up by Dunne throughout his career with the Essex Police, and as we shall see, all inherited by him in later years.

This was of course the situation of the still relatively new police when John Dunne joined them in the September of 1842. From the records we know that PC 150 John Dunne joined at this time and that by 1846 he had been appointed an Inspector, a rank he continued to hold until he left in 1849.

Interestingly his records also show that when he joined he gave his trade as clerk for the Manchester Police, rather than PC. Quite why, we shall never know, for certainly he himself regularly referred to himself as a serving police office with the Manchester Police in the early part of his career. Perhaps he had done both, for there is evidence to show that it was not uncommon for an educated lad of around fourteen years of age to be employed as a clerk in a Chief Constables office, indeed, McHardy had one himself.

His application form from 1842 details him as 6'0"tall, and hailing from Queen's County, Ireland. Under general character at the time of his departure it states: *'Conduct strictly correct and discharge of duty satisfactorily'*.

It is clear that in those early policing days McHardy was if nothing else enthusiastic in his work and that of his men for he had volunteered the services of his officers in far more ways than they could have imagined. Almost right from the beginning he decided that they would not just be pounding the streets of Essex, his men were far more valuable than that, they too would also be responsible for acting as Inspectors of Weights and Measures, Inspectors of Nuisances, Inspectors of Common Lodging Houses, Assistants to H.M Revenue Officers (a requirement somewhat peculiar to Essex), along with acting as Relieving Officers for Casuals under the Poor Law, and Inspectors under the Explosives Acts, just to name a few. One wonders if Dunne realised just what he had let himself in for!

Clearly too for the next few years it wasn't entirely policing duties that McHardy was interested in for obviously family life was important to him too, as John and Horatia McHardy between them managed to produce at least fifteen children, although six are known to have died in infancy . Interestingly two of his sons in later life were also to become Chief Constables in their own right.

Hardy McHardy was to become Chief Constable of Ayr, and Wallace McHardy the Chief Constable of Lanarkshire (in 1890 however, suffering from stress he committed suicide by jumping into the harbour in Glasgow). McHardy went on to serve a total of 41 years as Chief Constable and retired at the age of 79. He must have been doing something right!

This then was the man who was to influence John Dunne for the next seven years and mould his future. Strangely enough when John joined the Essex County Constabulary on that day in 1842, he had precisely the same amount of police experience as did his Chief ... though perhaps in John's case it was perhaps a little more 'down to earth'. Now would come the theory to add to that practical experience.

An early test of the resolve and determination of the new Essex Constabulary and one in which PC 150 John Dunne was almost certainly to have been embroiled was that which came just a few years after the force's formation.

Coggeshall was the place, a town which was in the Witham Division coming under the command of a Superintendent Charles Cooke, who had just two constables at Witham along with two constables stationed at Coggeshall. Between 1844 and 1848 there had been a series of violent crimes taking place in Coggeshall and the surrounding villages which had the local inhabitants in fear for their safety, amongst whom was a Mr Dell who appeared to have suffered far more than many other victims. A group of up to fourteen men known locally as the Coggeshall Gang had been carrying out many of the crimes, until now without interruption. They had made their headquarters at the Black Horse Inn, in Stonegate Street, the landlord of which was a William French, the half brother of the leader of the gang, namely Samuel Crow. French himself benefited from the proceeds of these crimes by receiving the stolen property from the gang. Crow himself was legally employed in driving post-chaises for innkeepers and gentry and was well known throughout the neighbourhood. Armed with pistols and cudgels and wearing masks, the gang operated mainly at night terrorising the local inhabitants. Quite how they remained free until 1847 and with such a record, is something the writer would dearly love to ask McHardy (or Dunne) about. However they were eventually caught with a little subterfuge by the police themselves and the trial of the gang eventually took place at the Essex Lent Assizes at Chelmsford on the first Monday in March 1849 with the Right Honourable Sir James Parke, KTpresiding. By the end of the trial those of the gang who had been found guilty were sentenced for their parts in the crimes. The main ring-leaders, namely: Samuel Crow, Tansley and Elliswere each sentenced to be transported for life. Indeed in sentencing Samuel Crow the judge said: *'For the part you have taken in this guilty transaction in robbing and injuring Mr Dell your life is forfeited to the laws of your country and if I did choose to interfere by recommending you to the merciful consideration of Her Majesty, the consequences would be that you would suffer an ignominious death. You have evidently not been concerned in this alone, but the circumstances of the injury to the prosecutor were not so great as to justify me in letting the sentence take its course, therefore your life will be spared, but the rest of it will be spent abroad'.* Two other gang members, Everett and French were sentenced to be transported for seven years and another John Crow received three months hard labour for assisting his brother to escape. Samuel Crow never served his sentence – he died in Chelmsford Prison in March 1850. Two other gang members were also transported for periods of seven years. Wade,who had been an active member of the gang, had his sentence reduced to transportation for seven years and thus ended the reign of terror that the Coggleshall Gang had brought to this quiet part of rural Essex and no doubt Dunne's continuous involvement too.

Another case Dunne would almost certainly have been involved in, as indeed all his colleagues were for a time, was the murder of a fellow officer, namely PC George Clark who was killed in Dagenham in the June of 1846. On the night of June 29th 1846 Police Constable George Clark, stationed at Dagenham, disappeared whilst on duty. It was to be a further four days before his mutilated body was found in a cornfield at Eastbrook End ... even after an extensive search.

The murder was shrouded in mystery and is still unsolved to this day. Partly due to the fact that they didn't have forensics experts in those days.There was, as now, plenty of speculation as to why this murder had happened, some reports from this period state that he may well have stumbled on some wrongdoing, whilst there were other stories which suggested he was perhaps getting too friendly with Maria, his sergeant's wife. Whatever the reason it is clear that at PC George Clark's inquest, this sergeant along with some fellow constables certainly did lie, which ultimately led to rumours that they too might be implicated in his murder. I have no evidence however to indicate that our John Dunne was in any way implicated in these rumours. George Clark was twenty years old at the time of his death. He hailed originally from Battlesden in Bedfordshire having previously been stationed in Stepney, East London. He had been in Dagenham for only six weeks and was patrolling the Wantz and Eastbrook End areas on his own, from 9pm to 6am each night. As stated the murder still remains a mystery to this day. Someone from the time, and almost certainly one of Clark's colleagues would have known who the murderer was, but they weren't telling. Was Dunne perhaps also in on the secret? (followers of true crime, especially unsolved crimes may be interested to learn that a book *The Dagenham Murder* was published in 2005).

One of the first superintendents to be appointed by McHardy was a certain Thomas Redin, then aged 25 who in later years Dunne was to become even more acquainted with when not only did he give evidence alongside him to the Select Committee on Policing in 1853 (McHardy was to give evidence too) but later still when he was appointed Governor of Carlisle Gaol. Clearly Redin did not continue with his Police career with the Essex Constabulary for he resigned in 1845, and after serving a term as Superintendent with Liverpool Police, as earlier stated he became the Governor of Carlisle Prison.

These next few years ... seven in total, would unquestionably have been Dunne's formulative years, certainly under the renowned Admiral McHardy, who, as he probably knew, had a reputation for training new officers for high office.

From the evidence submitted by McHardy to the Select Committee on Policing in 1853 we are able to learn much of what John Dunne experienced during these formulative years. The force was relatively large – 202 in total and which included both a Chief Constable and a deputy Chief Constable, and fourteen superintendents (in three distinct classes) (By 1853 it also included twenty inspectors). It is also clear that when Dunne joined in 1842 he would have been one of a small number who had any experience or indeed training for police work, for as McHardy himself states, there was simply no time to train the men under his command. He went on to say that though their had been an initial opposition to the new force, those who opposed it were now its strongest supporters *'and in some instances when I am under the necessity of removing a constable from their immediate locality, they write to say that they cannot leave home comfortably unless I replace the constable'.*

From this report we also learn something of Dunne's accommodation at this time, which like Manchester tended to be in barrack type accommodation, sharing with many of his colleagues. Also at the time there were still areas within Essex which had their own individual borough police forces, namely Maldon, Harwich, Saffron Walden and Colchester. However though they had their own police forces this did not mean that they were totally independent for we learn from McHardy that his men were regularly called upon to assist, especially during election periods when there was felt a need to ensure the preservation of the peace.

On one instance he refers to the supplying of 120 men to Colchester, and upon reflection felt that that was not enough. He admittedhowever that his men were always happy to go as they could always expect a little extra money in their weekly pay packet – usually 2/- (10p) a day and 1/- (5p) a night. Coincidentally they also received the same rate of extra pay for attending quarter sessions. McHardy's argument for this was simple: *'My object is to guard against the police officers profiting in any way by crime, one of the greatest evils which can exist in a system of constabulary is to permit any member of it to have an interest in crime; my object is to confine his interests solely to the prevention of crime'.* This extra pay for attending petty and quarter sessions was a very important and useful addition to their meagre wages. Still when we learn that the petty sessions were regular and many, and held in eighteen different locations across Essex, (Saffron Walden, Great Bardfield, Billericay, Orsett, Bocking, Brentwood, Castle Hedingham, Chelmsford,Chipping Ongar, Colchester Castle, Great Dunmow, Epping, Halstead, Maldon, Manningtree, Rochford, Waltham Abbey, and Witham) it becomes quite clear that such extra income was very much a regular part of their income.

Clearly too McHardy did not have much time for the 'Special Constables' who were sworn in at times of special needs, for he stated in his report to the Select Committee on Policing in later years: 'Generally I have sworn in special constables; they have written to me since we have had the county police, the special constables are little more than useless, and that was my reason for giving the boroughs the assistance of the county constabulary, I think the special constables are useless on such occasions for many reasons and in answer to the question: *'Do you know any cases which they have been found so?'* he replied: *'I never swore them in but once, and that was to prevent their tending to disorder during the Chartist meetings. I thought it advisable to swear those men in, because then I had them under my immediate supervision'.* In due course Dunne was to make a similar observation, though in his case it was relating to his experiences with the Kent Police… clearly this was a nationwide problem.

It is also from this same report of McHardy's that we learn of Dunne's and his colleagues continual assistance with the coast guard in their ongoing prevention of smuggling, as and when required. For when asked he replied: *'I endeavoured to get them (the police)armed with the necessary powers, under the 33rd section of the Custom House Act. I did not succeed until I put in evidence that we fell in with wagons laden with contraband goods, subsequently two hundred policemen were armed with the power, and with the result I had anticipated. As I told the Board of Customs, on their having that power, we should never see a contraband article. One of my objects for urging it particularly was, that the Government was paying £9,000 for one hundred and twenty-seven men upon the coast of Essex, and if the county of Essex could give them a force of two hundred men without cost, they might ultimately have a claim for a part of the expenses of the constabulary'.*

In addition to these extra-curricular activities of his men McHardy was clearly satisfied with his force's involvement in acting as Inspectors of Weights and Measures, for we see him reporting that since taking over responsibility they had produced an annual saving to the county of £562.10.0d per year for a total of eight years. Such was the 1853 Selection Panels original disbelief that any police force could be actually saving money, McHardy was later re-called and asked the self same question about their collections under Weights and Measures, for when asked: *'Have you had anyexperience in the beneficial results of transferring local duties to the county constabulary?'*, he was able to reply: *The Essex Constabulary were the first that performed the duties of Inspectors of Weights and Measures; it effected a very great saving on the whole, it used to be the sum of £600. An expense was saved to the county by transferring the duty to the County Constabulary, and it is the opinion of the county generally that the superintendents have discharged that duty very satisfactorily; they have discharged it satisfactorily in this way, that a shopkeeper never knows when the superintendent is coming into his shop. The parish constable used to acquaint all his neighbours "The inspector of weights and measures is coming and you must look out". The superintendent of police can walk in any time and detect the fraudulent dealer. Also with reference to sanitary matters, all the duties in connection with the Board of Health are far better discharged by the police, than by the Inspector of Nuisances, as he is termed, the whole of those duties are performed by the police much better than the limited staff which they keep'.* Which for once seemed to satisfy the Select Panel.

We also learn that since the introduction of the police in Essex McHardy is clearly able to announce that their has been a great reduction in crime, for in reply to the question: *'Have you found that there is any great diminution in the cases of ordinary violence and petty assaults?'* He was able to reply: *'There has been a very great reduction in most ofthose cases. The establishment of a permanent and perfect police force in Essex has been a great check to sheep-stealing; in two divisions out of fourteen in the county of Essex one hundred sheep were stolen the year previously to the establishment of the police; that number has never been taken in the whole county subsequently'.* And in reply to the question: *'Do you think that any modifications of your system could be adapted to the wild districts of counties which are thinly inhabited where the distances are too large forthe men to travel over except on horseback, and the districts too thinly inhabited for much crime to go on in them, but in which there might be places for the concealment of stolen goods, and so on?'* His reply was: *'The principle upon which policemen are distributed over a county is, that the county is separated into divisions, the divisions into detachments, and these detachment are subdivided into guards or beats...in dividing them, it requires a local knowledge, a place thinly inhabited would not have anything like the number of men that there would be in a place thickly inhabited, those places would be inspected during the day, to guard against the practices which your Lordship refers to. A horse patrol is most inefficient in the detection of crime, (as) the very noise of a horse's feet upon the road will disturb a depredator, and he will conceal himself it is abeacon for him to avoid, and I would never recommend the introduction of a horse patrol, except for supervision'.*

Executions, and the attending thereof would too have been an integral part of a police constables duty throughout the Victorian era, and though Dunne had been fortunate not to have been involved in any during his time in Manchester, Essex was to prove his 'baptism of fire'. In fact since the formation of the Essex Constabulary in 1840 police officers had begun to attend executions for public order purposes, though their first real test was on 14th August 1848 when 38 year old Mary May was executed for the murder of her brother William Constable, alias Spratty Watts, at Wix. She was the first women to be executed at Springfield Prison, Chelmsford, and the event attracted over 3,000 spectators.

This in all probability would have been the first time that Dunne, now aged 23, would have attended ... it most certainly would not be his last! This particular execution was memorable, and almost certainly would have stayed in his memory for the very simple reason that it would have been one of only two occasions throughout his entire career that he was to be present at the execution of a woman, though as we shall later learn their were some women who passed his path who came very close to it. Mary's public execution was unexceptional, though about 3,000 people turned up and as stated, the police, including John Dunne were in attendance – though by this time he was in a more authoritative position as a newly appointed Inspector. To the end Mary maintained her innocence.

Mary May's execution, wasn't the only female execution in Chelmsford during this decade., though as this wasn't until 1851, two years after Dunne had left for pastures new, he would not have had the unpleasant job of controlling any crowds. Which we can feel sure he was not exactly unhappy about. Clearly Dunne's learning curve since leaving Manchester had over the years incorporated not just all aspects of crime, but as we have seen a vast amount of other areas which McHardy had introduced. Even so, if that wasn't enough arson too was another area which took up a great deal of his and his colleagues time, especially so during 1844 where their were many ongoing attacks on hay-stacks, barley-stacks, and farm buildings which were continually plaguing the farmers lives.

Unfortunately the detection of the arsonists was not one of Essex police finer points for only two actual arsonists were discovered and even then there appeared to be no links between them. Indeed there may have been an element of copy-cat of earlier fires set by others was the general consensus at the time.

As can be imagined, the economic costs for the farmers was high, though the local papers did report that the all the farmers involved were at least insured, which deadened the blow a little.

As we have earlier learnt, not only was McHardy clearly interested in involving his men in many activities earlier unheard of in policing work ... indeed there is little doubt that he was a forerunner in creating these activities for his newly formed police, but as we have also learnt, he didn't want to relinquish his earlier interests in his previous career move – namely the coastguard service and again he insisted that his police force should additionally be involved in a little 'smuggling arrests' also. Once again this would prove another area which Dunne would have known nothing about and as it happened would not have proved much use to him in the future. Still, like the rest of his colleagues a day chasing smugglers would probably have proven an enjoyable exercise from his usual work.

We already know that the area of Burnham-on-Crouch was famous for its oysters and indeed had a small force of police officers permanently based there, but for the smugglers of gin, brandy and silks, from abroad, they seemed to favour the area between the Crouch and the Blackwater. The narrow isthmus of land between The Crouch and Blackwateris isolated even to today but in the mid 19th century it was a favourite spot for smugglers. It is likely that Dunne and his fellow police officers in their guise as customs officers would have known the area well. There are many shallow inlets along with vast tracts of low marshland and saltings and the area would have made evasion a relatively simple matter and capture extremely difficult. The coastline too was desolate and isolated, and the ditches treacherous – especially at night, to all of course except the local folk who knew well the routes inland from the shore. The east-facing shore between Bradwell and Holliwell point remained a favourite landing place for many years. Most of the land hereabouts lies below the twenty metre contour and on a clear night a lantern on a high point could be seen many miles off which most certainly did not help the police in their endeavours.

Another area would have been Bradwell located at the mouth of the Blackwater Estuary. Though catching the smugglers here would have been equally as difficult, and it was not just for the tower of St Peter's Chapel which made a handy point for a warning beacon but possibly more so because of a certain Hezekiah Staines, a local constable who was reputed to have been a kind of smuggling double-agent ... special constable by day, smuggler by night. Foulness Island was also notorious for its ongoing smuggling activities, and was regularly the refuge of many a criminal or wanted man, especially so within the confines of The George and Dragon Pub due to its remote location. It was also an ideal spot for all kinds of other illegal pursuits too which appeared to continue unabated throughout a great deal of the 19th century – dog fighting, and bare fist fighting being but two of them.

Foulness Island, Bradwell, and Holliwell, were not to be the only areas along the Essex coastline which attracted the attention of the numerous smugglers, and their erstwhile custom agents. Mersea Island and its surrounding was another location in which Dunne and his colleagues would regularly have been visiting though with how much success is in doubt. Certainly the two pubs in this area were certainly more than happy to conceal the smugglers stock in trade.

The Dog and Pheasant Pub was one of them that was much used by the smugglers whilst another the Peldon Rose was also involved in this free-trade. Storage at the Rose was not the cellar as one would expect but the pond alongside! There was a large well hidden in the middle of the pond and the weighted tubs of spirits could be lowered down into this on ropes until the revenue men had completed their searches.

Close by at Fingringhoe en route from Mersea to Colchester there is still evidence to this day that their were instances when the revenue men were actually successful for it was here that a local smuggler was hanged just outside the churchyard and buried on the spot. An acorn placed in the mouth of the corpse grew into thespreading oak tree that now stands there. Close by the village of Salcott-cum-Virley would too have attracted the attentions of smugglers and revenue collectors/police alike. The churches this time, rather than pubs,were the haunts of the smugglers, no doubt believing they were in safe (or holy) ground in choosing them for their hiding places. There was always a good turn out for the Sunday church services at Virley due to the fact that the congregation was invariably swelled by local smugglers who were only there to keep an eye on their contraband which they had concealed in various parts of the church.

And quite why our intrepid customs officers rarely caught any smugglers at Tiptree is a mystery in itself. For this was the town where the smugglers would openly trade and store their goods ... possibly even resting their horses before moving on to the larger market of Colchester. Tiptree was a notorious spot for auctions of smugglers goods as these were invariably held here by gypsies and squatters, clearly rarely getting caught. Their storage areas was simplicity itself for they simply dug shallow holes in the sandy soil and covered them with turf and brushwood. And finally their was Goldhanger, which was sufficiently distant from Maldon to escape the attentions of all but the most diligent of the customs officers, including those who were permanently stationed there. A favourite trick apparently of these Goldhanger smugglers was to float rafts of tubs along the Blackwater and land them at Mill Beach opposite Northey Island.

Notwithstanding the exciting and unusual aspects of his career in Essex, a part-time customs officer being just part of those duties, nevertheless by 1849 Inspector John Dunne clearly thought it time that he moved to yet another area. Whether that was because he felt he had exhausted all possibilities for promotion in Essex and Bath City Police offered better opportunities we shall never know, perhaps it was the promise of the responsibility of the position of *'Relieving Officer for Vagrants'* which had been detailed as one of his more important duties which actually enticed him. What we do know is that vagrancy and vagrants were to be one of his prime areas of importance when in later years he took over responsibility for the Chief Constableship of Cumberland and Westmorland, so it is quite possible that the interest stemmed from these early days.

Thus it was that on that date in March 1849, Dunne left the Essex Constabulary, a far more experienced police officer than when he had arrived some seven years earlier. Certainly that naivety that had accompanied him back in 1839 when he first put foot on English soil was well past ... he was now 24 years of age, and had close on ten years active police service under his belt. He was clearly ready for new responsibilities,and hopefully the city of Bath offered just that.

CHAPTER FOUR

INSPECTOR JOHN DUNNE

Bath City Police 1849-1850

With the benefit of hindsight one wonders if John Dunne would have made this trip to the fair city of Bath that day in March 1849. No doubt the letter of introduction in his pocket from one Admiral to another (Admiral McHardy as he was now entitled to be called to Admiral Carroll, Chief Constable of Bath City Police) would have been sufficient to see him well on the promotion ladder. After all as Dunne well knew McHardy's reputation as the trainer of 'up and coming' police officers had preceded him, and it would have been difficult to improve on a letter of introduction and recommendation as one produced by McHardy. Mind you the extra salary of 28/- (£1.40) compared to his 25/- (£1.25) could have had something to do with it too.

In today's money this would have been equivalent to a rise of approximately £30.00 a week thus a not insignificant sum. All would have been well in his world that day he booked his train ticket to London, once again on the Eastern Counties Railway, before this time connecting with the GreatWestern Railway from London's Paddington Station which would wing him the ninety-seven miles on his way to Bath Spa Railway Station, the principal railway station in the city of Bath which had only been open since 1840.

Thus he was ready to start anew with a new area, new urban force, and a new Chief officer ... not overlooking the new job which had been offered as a carrot, that of Relieving Officer for Vagrants. Something somewhere went very wrong, for as we shall learn he was only to stay in Bath for a little over eighteen months, until October 1850 to be precise, still it was an interesting year, none the less.

The 'something' could well have been the fact that his new mentor Admiral Carroll, was only around for a few short weeks before he was replaced somewhat suddenly by a Mr W Oakley. The self same Oakley who had been his superintendent in Chelmsford for many years. Though Dunne didn't know it at the time, Oakley was only to be in position himself for just three years before accepting the post in1852 as Governor of Essex County Gaol at a higher remuneration.

The Bath City Police in 1849 had already been in existence for thirteen years when Dunne first set foot in the city, having been originally formed in 1836 following the Municipal Corporation's Act of 1835. It's first, and still current Chief Constable upon Dunne's arrival was Admiral F Carroll, though their association was short-lived as within weeks Carroll had retired (or been removed) to be replaced by Mr W Oakley who remained a little longer than Dunne ... till 1852 to be precise.

The strength of the force at this time was just 98. Dunne and Oakley quickly found out why Carroll had left, and it would be true to say that his and Oakley's arrival was none too soon, for according to the report that the new Chief Constable gave to the Select Committee in 1853, the active members of the Watch Committee were not satisfied that things under the previous Chief Constable, Admiral Carroll, were on the best footing, with many of the men being superannuated and who had been taken from the old constabulary force when the new force was formed (in 1836), and they were unfit for the job.

There were some other circumstances which the watch committee considered it would be necessary to reform but they had thought it best to leave those matters until the new Chief Constable was in place. Clearly the watch committee were delighted with their choice for they stated that they *'had a man thoroughly conversant with his business, a man who submitted to us such a statement in writing, that though we were a committee composed of the most heterogeneous materials, all his propositions were carried unanimously by the watch committee and also when submitted to the council.'* Whatever proposition it was necessary to submit to the council were equally approved by them. We soon learn what those 'other circumstances' were when in a report of Oakley's hestates: *'I found when I took the appointment at Bath, the force in an inefficient a state as I believe it possible for any force to be, there were two-thirds of the men locally connected, and before their appointment had been out of employment, or in low employment'* A large proportion of them were working at their various trades, there were instances of dishonesty which were substantiated before a Watch Committee, on the part of the members of the force, many were incapacitated, some unable to write, some at the previous sessions, the Recorder had noticed as giving false evidence. *'I found a system of supernumeraries existing there, and many of them were living on the prostitution of the women in the city of Bath'.* Then followed his analysis of a return which he had made for the Watch Committee shortly after his arrival.

Of the 98 officers he found that two were above the age of 70, one was between 60 and 70, fourteen were between 50 and 60, twenty between 40 and 50, thirty-one between 30 and 40, twenty-eight between 20 and 30, that six were keeping shops, six were unable to write and sixty-two were natives of Bath.

Oakley went on to report that after careful consideration he found only twenty-eight efficient out of the original ninety-eight; thirty-four entered as 'doubtful' were quickly 'disposed of', and twenty he had entered 'not efficient' and fourteen as 'worn out' also went the same route. He recommended that overall the numbers in his force should be reduced (by around ten) in order that others could be better paid, the old officers were then superannuated, and with the declared efficiency (as latter appeared in a resolution by the watch committee and town council) he actually effected a saving of £500 a year.

However, what was perhaps equally as important to the future of the police was his report that:

> *'a very great evil then existed in the mayor's officers, who had the management of cases of felony, without the control of my predecessor Admiral Carroll. Instances were reported to have occurred in which the mayors officers sat quietly in their rooms and obtained of thieves in their pay the information which was taken before amagistrate. The mayors officers were entirely abolished, but there still remained in the borough great evils from courts leet officers and the conflicting jurisdiction of the magistrates and the watch committee. In some instances the magistrates were given instructions to one effect, and the watch committee have given instructions to the contrary'.*

It is interesting to report that during Dunne's short time in Bath the Mayor of this fair city was a certain Edwyn Dowding, who besides being the mayor was also an alderman, and a partner in a local firm of solicitors. Though unmarried that apparently did not stop him having a twenty year affair with a local saddler's daughter by the name of Harriet Louisa Jones, and indeed having five children with her. Thanks both to the Victorian class system of the time, and his own reputation this relationship was continued in the greatest secrecy and it wasn't until many years later that the association was uncovered.

One of the first jobs Oakley undertook upon taking command was to confirm his appointment of Dunne as *'Relieving officer for vagrants'* (a job normally undertaken by a superintendent). This was but one of new responsibilities for the police following the passing of the 1834 Poor Law Amendment Act at which time Union workhouses were established (the Bath Poor Law Union was actually formed on the 28th March 1836). According to the same report this was a post which was seriously and urgently needed, and clearly he felt that Dunne was the right man for the job. As he was to later state *"Bath is very peculiarly situated as regards vagrants. There are an immense number of persons of very large property residing in Bath in a bad state of health, they are often imposed upon by the number of vagrants that flock to the city. In order to put a stop to vagrancy as far as possible, and at the same time to ensure that a really destitute person should be relieved, a Refuge for the Destitute was established under an influential committee".*

Initially there were two 'relieving officers' both of whom had been further approved by the Board of Guardians as well as the Poor Law Board, 41 persons in all. These 'relieving officers' were expected to examine travellers pleading destitution, and then if approved, send them to a house in Abbey Green, which had recently been opened as a night refuge. (Abbey Green Refuge for Destitute Travellers). In addition a further police officer was selected to act as resident or superintendent and housekeeper. In Oakley's *'Report to the Watch Committee of the City and Borough of Bath'* dated 4th October 1850, item number five shows a return of mendicants applying for and receiving relief at the central police station, since the appointment of the in-door inspectors as 'relieving officers for vagrants'. The advantage of their appointment is then clearly shown by Oakley's comparison with the only previous period of returns shown, namely:

> *'between the 18th March and 31st May 1849, and at that time some 991 persons received relief. From the appointment of the in-door inspectors, i.e.from 12th November 1849 to 1st October 1850, 998 had appliedfor relief with 961 actually receiving it, the remaining 37 for various good reasons, were refused, showing a diminution (the different lengths of time being taken into account) of more than three-fourths' ... 'at the same time, the number of persons apprehended for begging during this latter period had been only 139, showing, as compared with the year1847, when 247 had been apprehended, and the year 1848, when 232 were apprehended, a diminution of 30%'.*

Clearly the appointment of 'Relieving Officers' was working well, but as Oakley further pointed out the detection of crime was also improving thanks to their appointment, for he reports that:

> *'that I have known many instances where crime has been detected by a relieving officer due to the fact that vagrants have been recognised by them. In these cases he has invariably refused relief for good reason and then sent a person to watch that person and subsequently found that he was indeed a known offender as was, to use a police term 'wanted' for some offence which he had committed'.*

These 'relieving officers' had quite specific and important duties. All paupers, or vagrants as they were usually incorrectly called were supposed to approach these 'relieving officers' of the district in which they resided if they were in need of relief, though in most cases they would in all probability have approached the 'overseer of the poor' following which they would have been sent on to the relieving officer to obtain approval and the necessary documentation. No one could enter the workhouse without an order (or ticket).

There was a clear distinction between pauper and vagrants (they were often called one and the same). A pauper, as the name implies was clearly in need of assistance, whereas a vagrant was a person who was travelling and needed putting up for the night, though with the latter he/she would often be expected to perform some kind of work before leaving the following morning.

It would be true to say that the duties of a'relieving officer' didn't stop with paupers and/or vagrants. Many claimants would clearly be termed 'lunatics' whilst many pregnant women, invariably single, would too find themselves under the scrutiny of these officers. Clearly Dunne had an important job and was a very important person in the city. He was responsible for dispensing what limited amount of aid was available to the needy as well as needing a knowledge of the lunacy laws.

Clearly Oakley, no doubt assisted by Dunne would have been responsible for recruiting and training the replacement police constables within his first few weeks in Bath. Drilling the men would have been the first priority, along with the use of truncheon and cutlass. Oakley drew the line at entrusting his men with firearms for as he stated: *'I know of an instance where a police officer having a pistol with him at a time when he thought he was being interfered with in the execution of his duty, very serious evils arose from it, he fired at one of the men, but providentially the bullet merely grazed his temple. Later the magistrates took this action into action when considering the case and decided to discharge the prisoners'.*

Dunne may well have thought that his attendance at public hangings, especially where women were the culprits, was at an end when he left Essex, but within days of his arriving in Bath he found himself the officer in charge of a group of constables responsible for crowd control at the hanging of 17 year old Sarah Thomas, when she was hanged outside Bristol Prison on Friday the 20th April 1949. Sarah had found herself in this predicament after having been charged with the murder of her employer 61 year old Mrs Jefferies in March. She had apparently been beaten to death by her servant Sarah, who had additionally killed the women's dog and thrown it down the lavatory as well as ransacking the house, after which she had made off to her parent's house. Her last moments both for her and the witnesses (and probably too for Dunne and his colleagues) was certainly traumatic for six prison officers had to drag her screaming to the scaffold. Even the prison governor was reported to have fainted. Apparently, so the story goes, even William Calcraft, the longest serving executioner in England who performed the hanging was it is said *'moved by her youth and looks, and was deeply affected'*. Such a scene did not cause him to tender his resignation however for he continued in his chosen profession for a further 25 years! As it happened this scene was never repeated again as Sarah was the last person to be publicly hanged in the city.

The population of Bath had reached some 50,000 by 1850, (compared to Manchester which by the same date had reached 400,000) making it one of the largest cities in Britain.

Dunne would certainly have found Bath to have been an entirely different 'kettle of fish' than either Manchester or the rural community of Essex for the city had been a leading centre of fashionable life in England since the early 18th century, offered a wide range of theatres, and architectural developments, (including an Abbey and of course the famous Royal Crescent), various museums ... not overlooking the hot springs and spas of course, which even at this time attracted vast numbers of visitors. Not something that his previous postings could boast.

However be that as may, cleanliness was, like so many cities in Britain at this time, virtually non-existent, dirty and unsanitary. In fact shortly after Dunne's arrival in Bath the city had suffered a cholera outbreak ... which didn't bide well for his health. In fact so far in his travels he had been fortunate as he had just missed an epidemic ... this time however he was not so lucky.

The cholera was not just confined to Bath either, for over 33,000 people died this year throughout Britain, so Bath was certainly not alone. Cholera of course was caused not just by the dirty and unsanitary conditions of the time but also by poor sanitation, which explains why it was mostly the poor that suffered.

It was highly infectious and caused severe vomiting and diarrhoea which was enough to send the body into shock where upon dehydration rapidly followed, and in all likelihood death, all within a space of eighteen hours. Evidence of the disease, especially in the latter stages was clear by the fact that the patient would have a hollowed face and blue lips. The Victorians believed that it was caused by rancid or putrid food, by 'cold food' such as melon and cucumber, and by 'passionate fear and rage'. In fact the term cholera was often used to describe any acute attack of diarrhoea – a point worth remembering given that one quarter of all deaths in children under five was attributed to childhood diarrhoea ... which if considered would certainly alter the statistics issued for deaths somewhat for this time.

Bath, as stated, was too suffering from severe unsanitary conditions, regardless of the fact that it attracted many thousands of people to the city to take advantage of the 'waters'. Here like every other urban city rapid development had been unregulated and the ramshackle severely over-crowded housing left inhabitants more susceptible to infectious diseases.

Again, as Dunne had discovered before, access to fresh water was limited, with the water companies invariably only providing a supply just two or three times a week, and then for just a few hours at a time. Refuse was again a problem and was either stored in the home or left in piles for the scavengers carts to collect.

As well as being littered with rubbish the streets would also have been full of horse manure, and in fact the removal of horse manure was almost as big a problem as that of human waste.

The management of human sewage went hand in hand with the unsanitary conditions as to be expected, latrines and cesspits were common, and in the towns and cities a night soil collector made the rounds but only collected from those who used pails. Tons and tons of human waste was removed from the city and despatched to the countryside by road or train where it was spread on the fields …thus neatly extending the range of waterborne diseases. Though the first public water closets (WCs) were seen for the first time at the Great Exhibition in 1851, and their appearance heralded, it would be thought, the end of the sewage problems, they were of course initially only available for those who could afford them. Even so the disposal of flushed water was no more ethical; it was pumped into the sewer, and then directed straight into the nearest river… the source of drinking water for many. As a result of course drinking water was often spoiled by human waste, and as cholera and typhoid were waterborne diseases this then would be transmitted through contaminated faeces – a fact that was not recognised until the latter end of the 1850's.

As previously declared Dunne's stay in Bath was short-lived, for reasons of which we are unaware. The most likely possibility is that he spotted an advertisement in the July of 1850, in the Kent Messenger advertising the posts of Superintendents in some twelve districts in Kent. After a shortlist of four was drawn up he was clearly successful with his application, and in fact he was offered the choice of either Dartford Division or Bearsted Division. His letter of acknowledgment read:

> *I John Dunne hereby accept the office of Superintending Constable for the Bearsted Division of the County of Kent upon the Terms and Conditions now or hereafter to be agreed by the Justices in general sessions and I undertake to*

give in writing to the Magistrates Clerk of the said Division three months notice of my intention to resign the said office and in default thereof I will submit to such reduction in my pay and allowances as the Justices in General Sessions shall think fit.

Dated 14th Day of October 1850

Signed John Dunne.

The phraseology of his letter indicates that he was obviously very very keen to get this post even if it did appear that he was not entirely clear as to the conditions that may be imposed upon himself.

Thus, his duration in Bath was short-lived ... and once again, for the third time in his career he was to move to a totally new area. This time however he was promoted to superintendent, a responsible post, which would have been considered the equivalent of Chief officer of police. At just 25 years of age it looks highly likely that he would have been the youngest such individual in the country at such a post, though whether he himself was aware of that we shall of course never know.

CHAPTER FIVE

SUPERINTENDENT JOHN DUNNE

Kent County Police October 1850 - November 1851

Before the introduction of the County and Borough Police Act 1856, the county of Kent had relied almost exclusively on a system of policing utilising Parish Constables who had themselves been appointed following the introduction of the Parish Constables Act of 1842. This piece of legislation had been passed in response to the political unrest associated with the Chartist movement.

The appointed parish constables were part-time and poorly paid, sometimes unpaid, so the posts attracted a low calibre of person, certainly none who was prepared to risk life and limb to arrest anyone. In addition the constable's field of operation extended no further than the boundaries of his own parish and he was paid not out of the general county rate, but out of the poor rate, by the overseers. Also this same Act allowed for the provision to appoint and pay for a superintending constable, though this was something which in 1842 was not considered essential – at least not for another eight years.

However by the July of 1850 the justices for Kent clearly felt that something was amiss with this system and consequently following yet another piece of legislation, namely the Superintending Constables Act of 1850, as well as that same year the amended Parish Constables Act both of which pointed out to them that the way forward would be to appoint Superintending Constables for the twelve divisions across Kent, men who would then take overall responsibility and control of the parish constables in their respective divisions. Well that was the plan ...

Thus it was that in the July of 1850 the Kent Court of General Sessions appointed a Constabulary Committee to report on the need of appointing Superintending Constables for the twelve districts covered by them, and the salaries and fees which would be considered due . Their later report recommended that a Superintending Constable should be between the ages of 25 and 45 years of age and literate. Whilst so employed he was not to follow any other occupation and had to reside where instructed by the Court. He was not allowed to leave his district except in an emergency (unless it was with the written consent of a justice) and was to keep in contact with the other Superintending Constables informing them of any robberies, etc.

Evidence of this 'problem' is shown in a letter of October 1851 when Charles Neve of Shepway Court (Maidstone) wrote to the Town Clerk complaining that although he contributed to the borough rates the town's police did not patrol beyond the top of Upper Stone Street, He had applied to Mr Dunne, the superintending constable for the local county district who had told him that the Parish Constables under his command were not authorised to patrol within the borough. Poor Mr Neve was therefore excluded from both the borough police and the existing county system.

Dunne was further instructed to visit his constables at least once a month and visit all public houses in his district. He was to be notified of all serious offences and should attend the scene to investigate. Overall the superintending constable was put in charge of all parish constables and lock-ups. But in truth his powers extended no further than the division boundaries and even paying parish constables could not provide for a superintendent's control of them. His pay was to be £85 a year plus a £25 horse and £6 a year for a horse and cart (which he had to supply himself).

Vacancies were advertised in *The Times* as well as relevant local newspapers. Their responsibilities were extensive: record keeping, (journals, charges, accounts, reports to justices etc) plus the aforementioned monthly visits to each parish, superintending lockups and the parish constables; noting and reporting to Petty Sessions nuisances and highway obstructions; visiting pubs and beer-houses; communication with other superintendents; and execution of arrest and search warrants in criminal cases. Additionally they were to investigate and 'prevent' all crimes. All Superintendents would be mounted and be issued with pistols and short swords. Most of the men selected for Kent were veterans of the Metropolitan Police or of the Gloucestershire, Staffordshire and East Suffolk constabularies. Dunne, of course was the odd one out having been selected from Bath. Clearly these new superintendents could not do everything so it was proposed that the parish constables would be responsible for other warrants and summons, e.g for non payment of rates along with the responsibility of conveying wrong doers to gaol – Maidstone being the nearest.

Carolyn Steedman informs us in her book *Policing the Victorian Community* that these superintending constables occupied a particular position in what she saw as a reasonably well-understood hierarchy. She points out that the magistrates knew that with the money they offered these men (across the country they varied between £65-£125 per year) they were in the main buying expertise and experience. She informs us that by 1852 the thirteen counties that used this police system employed an aggregate of 118 superintending constables. Men who joined a county in this way had usually been inspectors in the forces they had left, and the most common experience among the total number was previous work in the Essex Constabulary. Correct on both those points as far as Dunne was concerned!

Interestingly Steedman advises us that these professional policemen, though universally condemnative of the system they had to work under, and as we shall later see, no one was more condemnative than Dunne, they were still willing to take jobs in counties like Buckinghamshire and Kent because the position of the superintending constable was recognised by many of them as a step towards the head constableship of a borough police force, and because the system offered faster promotion than a rural police force did. There was just one more little problem. Dunne was NOT the Chief Constable. Legally the watch committee was the Chief Constable, and the borough head constable was merely a Chief officer of a body of police ... in Dunne's case 35 men. Still he did get a nice staff bearing the number of his division, a pair of handcuffs, a sword and belt, cartouches and box ... double barrelled pistols and a holster were issued later.

So, as we have seen Dunne took up his new appointment as the Superintending Constable for the District of Bearsted in the October of 1850, presumably hopeful of a long career in this delightful part of England, and with a position of some authority. As we are aware he was still only 25 years of age, and assuming he was aware of the fact, proud that he had made such rank at a young age. This time too, he was visiting an area which for once was free of plague ... Just! Fortunately the great epidemics of the plague and smallpox were over by 1850, though Kentish society still suffered from an undercurrent of regular devastating outbreaks of contagious diseases such as measles and whooping cough, cholera and influenza. Some diseases, for example cholera, caused short-lived panics but it was diseases like tuberculosis, 'the white plague', that regularly killed thousands every year until well into the twentieth century.

The next cholera outbreak in Kent was in 1854, well after Dunne had left.

And at least his posting this time was not going to involve him in any public hangings for the most recent one had been that of John Millen at Maidstone on the 28th March 1849. After that their was a gap of eight years before the next. However that was something of an auspicious year for hangings at Maidstone for it held the record in the country for that year – namely five.

Before Dunne had been in position for more than five months the Court of General Sessions had sent a circular to the justices in the various divisions on 21st March 1851 setting out their new conditions for the employment of parish constables under the new 1850 Act. It stated:

'Constables to be appointed for one year only under the Parish Constables Act of 1842, by the justices who will select 'the most efficient men' in their Division from the lists sent in by the parishes of men who are liable to serve, as well as those who are willing to serve. When a parish has determined to have a paid constable the justices should take especial care to appoint the best man and to inform him that, in consideration of the salary paid, he will be required to perform all such business as appertains strictly to his own parish, such as serving summonses and warrants for non-payment of rates, apprehending vagrants, etc. All Parish Constables will come under the control of the Superintending Constable for their respective division'.

Although these appointments give the impression of an organised police force, it must be remembered that the constables and their supervisor were all appointed locally by the justices of the peace and most of the constables were unpaid. Nevertheless the supervisory posts were much sought after, by both experienced policemen and others. This then was the post that John Dunne had applied for ... little did he realise what he had let himself in for.

At first all seemed to be going well. Bearsted (or Beested) looked like an excellent posting. In the first place he must have been pleasantly surprised to find that he was to be based in a quiet Kent country village, especially after his hectic years in the large metropolis's of Bath, Chelmsford, and Manchester. Bearsted was listed as a parish two and a half miles from Maidstone and with a population for 1851 of just six hundred and twenty. In reality however his true responsibility was listed as the Bearsted Eastern Division of Aylesford which overall had a population of 20,515. That was his true responsibility, though with thirty -five men with each being responsible for just 506 people the future looked rather too easy, It was!

However, Bearsted was to be more than his home, it was actually a Division of the Kent Police (there were twelve altogether), the area was correctly named Bearsted Eastern Division of Aylesford. When the post was first declared Bearsted Eastern Division of Aylesford was but one section of Aylesford. Others were Malling Upper South, (George Hilton appointed Superintendent: population 24,216,) Rochester North (Thomas Everist appointed, population 44,226) and Tunbridge Lower South (Richard Gilbert, appointed population 27,683) four sections in all.

With Dunne having control of the smallest division in terms of population all bar Bearsted came under the jurisdiction of North Aylesford Petty Sessional Division. Bearsted had its own Petty Sessional Division for the period 1748-1974.

Dunne's time in Kent was relatively short-lived but at least he had the time to experience yet another English phenomenon. This time instead of smuggling it was hop pickers! And where better than the Garden of England.

Of course the hop pickers had been around for many years by the time Dunne had first sight of them. In fact by the middle of the nineteenth century hops were being grown in more than three hundred of the four hundred rural parishes of Kent with widespread building of hop kilns. Annual 'hopping' generally involved some 250,000 pickers with the East End of London generally supplying around one third of them. The balance were itinerants and travellers from as far afield as Ireland.

The hop picking season started in September and continued for some four-five weeks. This gave the hop-pickers the much needed opportunity of earning some money as well as giving them a 'holiday', and would have been a welcome break from the grime and smoke of London. It was mainly women and children in the family who did the work, with their men folk joining them at the weekend. Whole families would come down on special trains and live in 'hoppers huts' for most of the September, with even the smallest children helping in the fields. Hop-picking continued until the late 1950's when mechanical picking was introduced. However during the Victorian era accommodation was invariably in barns, stables, cattle sheds, pigsties, tents or in the roof space of buildings. This led to problems with hygiene and thus health. In fact an outbreak of cholera actually killed 43 hop-pickers at East Farleigh in the September of 1849 (just days before Dunne took up his new post) Effectively these visitors were living in near squalor whilst sleeping in straw-filled palliasses crawling with mice, earwigs and spiders, along with cooking their dinners on open fires ... even in the pouring rain. The very best that the hop-pickers could hope for were bell-tents that were invariably worn out and often not waterproof. These tents were shared by eight people and were extremely cramped. Hop-pickers had no drying facilities when it rained and the food available was of poor standard and insufficient. The water was often impure and difficult to obtain. It was not until the 1870's that conditions began to improve.

As earlier indicated things were not to go too well for Dunne, in fact just two years later when submitting evidence to The Select Committee on Police he clearly subjected the Kent system of the parish constable system to devastating criticism. The rationale for the scheme initially had been that the superintendents would rejuvenate a parish constabulary and was now meant to be of better quality than those men complained of so frequently in the past. But as Dunne quickly discovered these constables were no different than before, they were still disinclined to serve, and were refractory, hopeless, and overall expensive.

Naturally they were a charge on the Poor Rates especially so based on the scale of fees mandated by the Kent Quarter Sessions. He went on to say that when they were called out to watch, they were occasionally obstructive and most importantly were inclined to sabotage inspections of public houses by tipping off landlords about impending visits. (there were also suggestions that they frustrated superintendents by tipping off suspected felons too). It was pointed out that with no Chief Constable to supervise and co-ordinate the men and act as a counterweight to the whims of Petty Sessions magistrates, who themselves sometimes refused to allow their men to act within other divisions.

Above everything else, he stated the major deficiency was the lack of an embodied force of professional subordinates who would do what they were ordered to do, and when ordered to do it. An example of this would be the arrests of sheep-stealers which in a rural community was a serious and ongoing problem. No doubt, as we have learnt, this particular crime would have been a particular 'thorn' in Dunne's side following his many years in rural Essex. Dunne along with many of his superintendent colleagues complained of the torpor or lack of co-operation of parish constables and for that matter their victims.

Delays of five to fifteen days in initial complaints were regularly reported. Another of his gripes was the fact that, unlike the County Police Acts, the Parish Constables Act did not order the disbandment of the Lighting and Watching Act forces within the area where it was originally adopted, and the superintendents complained of lack of co-operation and assistance from those forces.

Clearly superintendents were overburdened by their numerous duties along with the demands on their time. Dunne considered that overall, efficient use could not really be made under these conditions. As he reported:

> *"I was very frequently obliged to go out with three horses a day in the performance of my duties; when I returned I would find waiting some communication from another part (of the division) to the effect that I was required; that there had been a serious robbery, or something requiring my attention, and the magistrates had sent me an order to go immediately".*

Dunne's report to the Select Committee didn't just stop with the above. A brief run though of some of the questions he was asked by the committee would perhaps be useful here ...

When asked: From your knowledge of the system, you would pronounce it to be a totally inefficient system for the purposes of the police ?

Dunne replied: Quite so. I think it is attended with great evils. There is a system in Kent – I am not aware of its being carried out in any other county under the 3rd and 4th William the 4th, Chapter 90, the vestry has the power of appointing paid watchmen, who act as police officers for the parish for which they are appointed. In twelve parishes in the division of Bearsted, the provisions of this Act were carried into effect, and for those twelve parishes, there were no parish constables appointed under 5th and 6th and 13th and 14th of Victoria, the men appointed under the Act were quite independent of my control; they were not under my jurisdiction in any way; the consequence was that if I wanted any assistance for the supervision of beer-houses or public-houses, or the performance of any other duty I had no person to assist me, for those men were generally acted against me instead of giving any cordial co-operation.

Then in a response to a question from the Chairman: Was the appointment of those persons made in consequence of a direct recommendation of the magistrates from the bench?

His reply: They were appointed upon the recommendation of a majority of the vestry in consequence of the feeling which prevails in that county among the middle classes in favour of an efficient police force, and finding the parish constables so inefficient, the vestry, under this Act, appointed those policemen.

And: How long did they continue?

He replied: They were there during the whole of my service. The Act provides that if it is once adopted it cannot be discontinued for a period of three years. The men were under no efficient control; the inspectors who supervised them were selected by the vestry, such as farmers and shopkeepers, who knew but little of the duties.

And then: Were not those duties more efficiently performed by those paid watchmen than by the parish constables who were not paid?

He replied: In some respects they were; still there was a want of supervision and a want of uniformity in the system which rendered them ineffective. They felt independent, they were under no control, and if applied to for assistance they would not generally render it. They were in no way subject to my control. I made an application to the magistrates at the Bearsted Petty Sessions on account of the want of assistance and co-operation on the part of those men.

Question: Were not those men under the control of a superintendent?

He replied: No.

Question: Had the superintending constables nothing to do with their appointment?

He again replied: Nothing, directly or indirectly.

Question: How many constables had you under you?

He stated: I had thirty-five.

And in response to the question: With how many rural policemen could you have effectually watched and guarded the district?

He replied: Judging from the extent of the division, and comparing its area with divisions of counties where police forces are established, if I had had twenty good active men, one inspector, and two sergeants, I could have carried out an efficient system in that division, providing the force was general.

Question: Are you of the opinion that it is impossible to make the superintending constable system act efficiently.

Reply: I am

Question: And you deem it to be quite inefficient.

Reply: Quite so.

And in response to a question from the Chairman: Do you know the whole extent of the divisions in Kent under the superintending constable?

Dunne replied: The largest division in the county of Kent is Wingham, which consists of fifty-six parishes

Question: Do you know how many superintending constables they have for that division?

Dunne replied: Only one.

Then in response to the question: Do you think it possible that one man can superintend such a district?

He firmly replied: It is not possible to do it efficiently; even in my division, which was composed of thirty-two parishes, I was very frequently obliged to go out with three horses a day, in the performance of my duties; when I returned home from one part of the division, I would find waiting for me some communication from another part of it, to the effect that I was required; that there had been a serious robbery, or something required my attention, and with effective co-operation or assistance from the local constables; they would not subject themselves to any control.

Followed by the question: Could you pursue criminals with the assistance of the local constables?

His reply was: Certainly not, with regard to the supervision of the beer-houses and public houses, I have frequently arranged to make a visit at an appointed time for the purpose of visiting some house, and the parish constable has gone and told the publican or the beer-house keeper that the superintendent was coming at such a time. They are so much mixed up with local connection in their general business that it is impossible for them to act independently; it is imposing upon them duties which they cannot perform consistently with their own interests, viewing it as a money question.

And then the question: Do you think that it is the fact that no police constable can get into a public-house unless he is called upon by the publican?

He replied: I know that it is a regulation of the police.

His next question was: Do you think that parish constables would generally consider it an invidious duty to have to enter upon public-houses for the purpose of control if they were called upon?

Dunne replied: I have known of many instances in which they have skulked out of the way to avoid it.

Then a question from Lord Lovaine: You have stated that under the method of appointing the police in the boroughs, it is hardly possible to make the force efficient?

Reply: Yes

And then the final the question for this session was: Is your opinion that it would be an advantage to those boroughs that they should be amalgamated, as far as regards the police with the counties?

His reply was: I do certainly think that it would tend to render them more efficient. I think consolidating the borough police with the county forces would be attended with the most beneficial results.

Dunne went on to say: I should refer to my experience during seven years in the Essex County Constabulary. I had an opportunity of making myself thoroughly acquainted with the working of that force, and the items of saving effected there, and comparing them with the expenses of the constabulary system in the county of Kent. I feel confident in saying that an effective police force could be carried out upon a similar principle to th atof Essex at a less real cost to the county than a superintending constable system, giving to the poor man the protection which he does not enjoy under the parish constable system. If a man applies to a local constable he may have to pay him for the duty performed.

Dunne's next question was: Was not the police force in Essex very effective for the suppression of vagrancy?

He replied: Yes, most effective.

But in reply to the question: Was the superintending constable system in the county of Kent efficient for the suppression of vagrants?

He made a firm reply: Certainly not.

Questioned why he responded: Because the constables were seldom on duty and the superintendent was unable to superintend the extent of ground placed under his supervision, therefore there was but little check upon vagrancy. Hordes of vagrants travelled from one part of the county to another, there was a regular migratory population which tramped from one county to another, previously to the establishment of the Surrey Constabulary that county was infested with gangs of gypsies, and those parties immediately on the establishment of that force came into Kent, and in Kent the number of vagrants increased to a great extent.

His next question was: When you were appointed superintending constable in the county of Kent was not one of your duties as far as you had the means, to suppress vagrancy?

He replied: It was my duty to suppress vagrancy, but in consequence of the want of efficient constables, I had not the means to do so.

Followed up by the question: Do you mean, having used your best endeavours during the period you were in Kent, that vagrancy was decreased?

He replied: I think the appointment of superintending constables, to a certain extent, did tend to decrease crime as regards the apprehension of offenders, but to suppress vagrancy was impossible, the man was utterly unable, both physically and morally to perform the duties which were expected of him. In Essex the performance of the duty and the strict supervision of all grades of the officers, arises from the superior uniformity of the system set down in that county. That was the final question for Dunne.

Dunne's stay in Kent thus lasted just 13 months. Though this short stay could have in all probability had a lot to do with his total disaffection with the posting, it was also brought about by a message he received from Admiral McHardy in Essex enquiring whether he would be interested in returning to Essex, but as a superintendent, rather than an inspector, as he had been when he left. It would appear that this offer came at an opportune time for Dunne jumped at the opportunity and before the end of the year found himself working with his mentor McHardy once again. This move did not however stop his insatiable need for a higher post clearly McHardy was not going to step down as Chief Constable of Essex Constabulary, so he needed to look elsewhere. Thus a little over one year later a further notice in *The Times* brought his attention to the fact that Norwich City Police were anxious to appoint a Chief officer of police. As it happened he found he had no need to apply ... the Justices of Norwich City Police contacted him.. and he was quick to accept their offer.

Though his move to Norwich to all intents and purposes could well have been based on his experiences over the past years, in truth his move came about due to a spot of head-hunting. Norwich City Police had been anxious to replace their existing Chief Constable for some months and Dunne had been approached during the summer of 1852. I am inclined to think that the offer of such a post coming after a time of much stress would have come as something of a godsend and he would have reached out with both hands to accept. Thus, once again after such a short period we see Dunne heading off to yet another new area Norwich, but this time as Chief Constable and at 25 years of age too.

Author's note: I am thankful to have been able to obtain much of my research on Dunne's short time in Kent by accessing the minutes of the 1853 Select Committee on Police. As regards police reports and transcripts of the police from this period in Kent, regretfully nothing now exists, as on the whim of a senior police officer earlier on in the twentieth century all the history of this period was destroyed.

CHAPTER SIX

JOHN DUNNE, CHIEF OFFICER

Norwich City Police late 1851- July 1853

At approximately the same time that Dunne was joining the Norwich City Police as Chief Officer (as opposed to the title Chief Constable) a certain Lt Col. Richard Oates, the then Chief Constable of Norfolk Rural Police, had decided to leave due, as he put it ... *to those meddling magistrates!'*. With the benefit of hindsight it is a pity Dunne had not had the opportunity of a meeting with Oates prior to taking up his new appointment as any such discussion could well have made him re-apply for the third time to the Kent Police – considering what he had to look forward to in Norwich. (Oakes went off into the twilight of permanent retirement and was superseded by Captain George Black, who was to remain in that post until 1880).

It is doubtful whether Dunne was happy with his new posting almost from day one. Yes, he had reached the dizzy heights of Chief Officer, (though the request to which he responded stated 'Superintendent') and he was now holding responsibility for 80 policemen together with 26 firemen, along with an area which housed some 70,000 people, but even so it was clear to him that his predecessor Mr Peter Master Yarington had left things in a bit of a mess ... and that was putting it mildly.

Not that he would have got any clues to this 'mess' from the Watch Committee who had selected him for as he soon learnt, Yarington, upon retirement, had been presented with a silver salver and a purse of 283 sovereigns *'in recognition of his efficient discharge of duty as superintendent of the Norwich Police'*. And this was despite the fact that disquiet over the efficiency of the force as late back as 1841 had led to sackings, warnings, along with various of his constables being called before the Watch Committee to explain themselves. Yarington went on to become governor of the city gaol shortly afterwards, though the post was to be short-lived, as he died just five months later, aged 41.

Norwich clearly needed to find a replacement superintendent for its force in 1851, when Peter Yarington was appointed governor of the city gaol on July 31st. Given the condition of policing in the City found by Dunne it is interesting to note the remarkable difference in treatment the two men received from the Watch Committee. Whereas Yarington had received an award for his service in the December of 1851, Dunne, just two years later was to be hounded for the return of a uniform coat in order that it could be re-issued to his successor.

John Dunne, then of course serving (briefly) in the Essex Constabulary, was actually one of thirty-seven who replied to an advertisement for a superintendent in Norwich at a salary of £150 a year. Then 26 years old, (coincidentally the same age as his predecessor when he had taken up the post in 1839), he defeated a Norwich inspector for the appointment when the applicants were narrowed to a final short list of two. Perhaps the fact that he came from outside the Borough would explain some of the resentment he almost immediately met.

Contrary to the apparent satisfaction with policing expressed in the presentation to Peter Yarington, John Dunne discovered practices which he described as *'disreputable and disgraceful, and which could not be tolerated in a well organised, well governed, and well conducted police force'.*

Apart from the separation of the Watch from the force and the abuse of an outmoded system of supervision, Dunne immediately discovered that no less than one third of the members of both organisations were aged between fifty and seventy years of age. And not only that, the whole of the watch and some of the force were in trade or business so that for those constables policing was only a part-time occupation. Constables were selected on political preference and many were *'violently political'*. John Dunne found that some were still serving after conviction for a criminal offence. And most had been subject to frequent punishments for breaches of discipline. It was only a few who carried out their duties with *'energy, zeal and efficiency'.*

Fees were demanded before any action would be taken and at Christmas these same constables would go from door to door *'begging Christmas boxes'*

John Dunne's attempts at reform quickly gained the respect of the press, though certainly not the Watch Committee. Within months of taking up his post a local paper was describing him as having a *'vigilant mind'* and being *'cautious, shrewd, fearless and determined'*. By the January of 1852 Dunne was already putting proposals before the Watch Committee calling for the amalgamation of the watch and force. He further insisted that all Christmas collections were to be forbidden and all fees from whatever source to be paid into the Borough Fund.

Not surprisingly opposition in local political circles to John Dunne intensified over the challenge he made to the authority of the Watch Committee and magistrates alike. I suppose one could call this an early example of concern over accountability which has been of prominence in recent years not overlooking the honesty of the Chief officer, would have made the situation worse.

In 1853, John Dunne was asked by theParliamentary Select Committee about the efficiency of Norwich Police and replied: *"It is not in such a satisfactory state of efficiency as I should like to see it".* (see below).

Part of the challenge he had to the then established authority came over the issue of prosecutions for offences by those keeping licensed premises. The Watch Committee continued to instruct their superintendent that no summons for such offences could be brought without their permission. This, as before, was rarely given and thus faced with many complaints from respectable citizens and members of the clergy John Dunne started a number of prosecutions of his own without reference to the Watch Committee. Yet, in two instances, despite those summoned pleading guilty, the cases were still dismissed. This only seems explicable given that some magistrates were members of the Watch Committee, together with three brewers. It was also apparently acceptable at this time for one Norwich magistrate, who was also a practising barrister, to allow his solicitor sons to appear on cases on which he adjudicated.

More generally, John Dunne took issue with the effects of a divided system of accountability where the force was subject to the orders of both Watch Committee and justices. There was an instance where a constable was suspended by magistrates who recommended his dismissal. The Watch Committee there upon immediately re-instated him. When the constable next appeared before the magistrates to give evidence, one justice who had been involved in the suspension said he would not believe the man on oath. A defiant Watch Committee again decided to retain the constable.

In his evidence to the same Parliamentary Select Committee in 1853 John Dunne had this to say:

> *"In many instances the Watch Committee lay down instructions and give orders which themagistrates countermanded. One of the magistrates in Norwich recently ordered a policeman to perform a certain duty, and while in the performance of that duty another magistrate came up and found fault with him, and spoke to him in the street in such a way that the man resigned".*

This confusion over the control of policing was unquestionably one reason why John Dunne proposed, over a hundred years before it was finally accomplished, the amalgamation of borough forces with those in the counties.

Speaking of borough forces nationally, but no doubt with Norwich firmly in mind, he told the same Parliamentary Select Committee: *"Every borough has some system or other peculiar to itself; there is no uniformity, no co-operation, no communication, no effectual action, thereby the ends of justice are frequently defeated; they are generally defective in numerical strength, unequal to any emergency, and rely too much upon military aid; local interests and influences are brought to bear'.*

It would be true to say that in this twenty-first century Chief Constables have become little more than political animals and are invariably too outspoken. In fact they are merely following the precedent which have been set by officers such as Dunne, who in two traumatic years at Norwich did more to develop and reform policing than his predecessor (Peter Yarington) had done in almost twelve. It was almost certainly because of the schemes which attempted to discredit him that Dunne resigned in 1853. A local newspaper reported that this action was on the grounds

> *'that he had been so much obstructed by those who ought to have assisted him in the discharge of his duties, that noalternative had been left him but to resign'.*

It was during this period (1853) that Dunne was called upon to give evidence to the House of Commons Select Committee on Policing. He was in good company for amongst others giving evidence at this time were his former employers Captain McHardy, along with Thomas Redin, who was by now the Governor of Carlisle Prison, and Mr W Oakley, Dunne's earlier Chief officer in Bath. Other senior police officers presenting evidence were Captain Harris, from Hampshire Constabulary, William Hamilton, Supt. Constable from Andover, Alfred Hughes the current Chief officer of Bath Police, Captain Woodford, the Chief Constable of Lancashire Police (Dunne would get to know him well in later years when he headed up the Police Inspectorate) Major George White, Chief Constable of Durham, Captain Henry Mackay, Chief Constable of East Sussex, Capt Edward Willis head of the police of the Borough of Manchester 1842-1857, Mr F M Mallalieu Metropolitan Police, Mr Robert Brown, Superintendent of Police in the Derwent division of the County of Cumberland. (someone, like Redin, and Woodford, Dunne would soon get to know well), Mr Richard Healy Chief Constable of the Hundred of Aveland, in the parts of Kesteven, Lincolnshire, Mr Henry Matthews, Detective from Lincolnshire, Mr David Smith, the Superintending Constable in Oxfordshire, Mr George Martin, Superintendent of the G Division of the Metropolitan Police in Clerkenwell, John List, Superintendent of the county police in Mid Lothian, Mr Smart Superintendent of the Glasgow Police, and finally Mr John Jones, Superintendent of the Dumfriesshire Constabulary.

The Committee itself was made up of twelve members amongst whom were some very notable names of the times, namely: Robert Handyside, the Lord

Advocate, Lord Walpole, the Home Secretary, Henry Fitzroy, Under Secretary of State, Lord Lovaine, 6th Duke of Northumberland, and Sir John Trollope. MP. The committee was chaired throughout by Mr E R Rice, MP for Dover.

This committee was set up following a motion raised by E R Rice ... *to consider the expediency of adopting a more Uniform System of Police in England and Wales and Scotland'*. Much of the discussion in committee focused on the value of a professional constabulary in suppressing vagrancy as it was convinced that the new constabularies had contributed to a decline in this as well as *'to the maintenance of order and the improved habits of the population'*. The Select Committee presented its report in 1853 which resolved:

> *'That the efficiency of all the existing police forces is materially impaired by the want of co-operation between the Rural Constabularies and the Police under the control of the authorities of the Boroughs or other local jurisdictions...your Committee are of the opinion that the smaller Boroughs should be consolidated with Districts or Counties for Police purposes and that the police in the larger Boroughs should be under a similar system of management and control to that of the adjoining District or County (where practical) under the same superintendence.'*

Palmerston, the then Home Secretary, appears to have had a personal interest in these questions considering he had been involved in a local attempt in Hampshire to pressure the Watch Committee of the Borough of Romsey to consolidate its force with that of the county. He responded favourably to letters from fellow aristocrats in non-adopting counties, complaining of the state of their police. Lord Fortescue even wrote from Devon complaining of the *'petty depredations'*, the sheep stealing, and the swarms of *'sturdy beggars'* who had to be repelled from his own house by a servant employed solely for that purpose. He went on to say that a proper police would be cost effective *'even were the whole to be charged to the Consolidated Fund' by the 'saving of private property now plundered and destroyed'*. Remarkably even Edwin Chadwick (the fellow noted for his work to reform the Poor Laws) found Palmerston sympathetic to his views on the police. It was Chadwick who advised him to create an unashamedly Benthamite 'General Police' which he recommended should be governed by a separate department within the Home Office which would be responsible for both London and the provinces.

Fortescue, Chadwick and Palmerston clearly all had a private fondness for the model of the Irish Constabulary which had already been around for a few years, for in his speech explaining his National Police Bill in June 1854,Palmerston praised it-which unfortunately proved to be the first of his many errors in that episode.

The Select Committee of 1853 overall, it has to be said, was well stacked with a bipartisan group of supporters of rationalisation of the provincial police. The Chairman, Dover MP, E R Rice, who had initially proposed the motion for the committee, was himself a long-standing supporter of the County Police Acts going back to 1839.

The committee produced a set of persuasive arguments for a universal national police system which proved very hard to rebut. Its witnesses and evidence were clearly chosen to extol the virtues of county policing and to highlight the deficiencies of the superintending constable systems and of the small borough forces, as became clear from the ongoing evidence.

Unlike the mid 1830's, proponents of reform would this time come armed with statistics along with other data purporting to show the good effects produced by functioning forces.

The Select Committee's Chief target was the superintending constable system (which as we know was still in force at this time). If the effectiveness of the only alternative was successfully impugned what was left would simply be an updated County Police Acts scheme.

The witnesses questioned by the committee included: the aforementioned Chadwick, along with a number of articulate county Chief Constables (or in Dunne's case Chief Officer) most of whom came laden with papers containing statistics of crimes, criminal committees, and costs along with further suggestions for police rationalisation; MPs, and various 'country gentlemen'; farmers living on the borders of counties, who stressed the contrast between a policed and an un-policed countryside; Quarter Sessions Chairmen, who spoke of the difference the county police had made in producing better order, control of vagrants and suppression of crimes against agricultural property; and a group of present and past superintending constables who made strong and well-informed attacks on the entire alternative policing system ... with possibly the biggest proponents as it happened being Dunne and McHardy.

At the end the Select Committee delivered a very short report, which though praising the efficiency of the existing county forces, at the same time condemned the permissive principle of the County Police Acts, which in their opinion had created irrational gaps in coverage. It lamented the lack of co-operation and co-ordination between borough and county police, and recommended that, at the least, the small boroughs be amalgamated with the counties. It also recommended immediate legislation 'rendering the adoption of an efficient

Police Force on a uniform principle imperative throughout Great Britain' and a central government subvention to assist with the cost of county forces. It praised the superintending constables, but severely criticized the system as *'too dependant on the aid of Parochial Constables'* who confirmed Dunne's evidence by agreeing that they were essentially useless 'for the protection of property ... the prompt detection and pursuit of offenders, and the maintenance of order'.

It is interesting to learn that there was at least one section of the evidence which proved quite startling. Three Chief Constables (which included Dunne) provided detailed comparative cost estimates showing expenditure for a county police, as compared to parish constables alone, and to a superintending constable scheme (with its attendant costs for the parochial constabulary). Captain McHardy of Essex (Dunne's one time mentor) by the simple formula of:

a) including sums formerly paid to parish constables,

b) claiming a large sum to represent money saved on the decrease of vagrancy

c) fines

d) conveyance of prisoners and

e) an estimate of the value of property recovered and protected by the county force

thus came up with a balance sheet purporting to show that the Essex Constabulary was in fact a 'self supporting force'.

Understandably the committee members found this difficult to believe. Another of Dunne's earlier colleagues was William Oakley of the Bath Police who estimated that for Somerset to use superintendents plus parish constables would cost much more than a police force. These balance sheets were noticed and reported elsewhere.

It took until 1854, following on from the Select Committee, until Palmerston introduced his National Police Bill. Unfortunately it was poorly conceived and badly handled and failed to get through ... the first time anyhow. And why not? well for one thing it had a somewhat 'Chadwickian' ring about it: counties would be compelled to form police forces (though MP's clearly changed their minds on this aspect just two years later) the five smallest counties would be amalgamated with surrounding counties; there would be government inspection (that too appeared to be overlooked later) county forces would be governed by new Police Boards elected by the magistrates ... from the magistrates.

For the boroughs, those with fewer than 20,000 inhabitants would have their forces taken over by the county (which would mean the un-elected county magistrates replacing the elected borough council as the authority in charge) and, even in those that retained their police, the power of Chief Constables would be increased in relation to their Watch Committees. But perhaps most importantly, the bill offered the counties and boroughs no financial aid from central government towards the cost of the force. Overall county members disliked the bill, though it provoked the greatest hostility from the boroughs which even sent representatives to London to protest en masse.

Consequently Palmerston had to bow to the strength of the objections and withdraw the bill. Though Palmerston attempted another bill shortly after, it was not until 1856 that the bill had been sufficiently tweaked' so that the *'objectionable compulsory principle'* was offered together with a central government subvention, namely their would be financial aid, that the entire matter proved to be negotiable after all. But that is still to come.

Their has to be little doubt that Dunne would have felt honoured to have been selected to give evidence to this committee ... he was after all, still just 28 years of age, and would be the youngest called to give evidence ... but then, as he states himself he did already have more than fourteen years policing experience under his belt – more than all the others. so why wouldn't his evidence have proved essential to the committee?

In Dunne's evidence to the Select Committee on Police in 1853, on the 3rd June 1853 he confirmed these fourteen years service when first giving evidence that day in June of 1853 firstly by stating that he was currently Chief Officer of Police at Norwich and had previously served as a superintending constable in Bearsted for thirteen months, and left in consequence of getting the appointment at Norwich, which was superior. (NB For unknown reasons Dunne has clearly not mentioned his brief return to Essex after Bearsted) ... and advised that he went with testimonials from the magistrates in Kent.

In answering whether he had served in a police force before Kent, he replied that he had joined the Manchester Police in 1840, and there served for one year under Sir Charles Shaw: he then served seven years as a constable and inspector in the Essex County Constabulary, under Captain McHardy. He then states he served as inspector in the Bath Police, under Mr Oakley, and served thirteen months as superintendent in Kent, from which he succeeded to his present position in Norwich (Again Dunne has overlooked mentioning his brief return to Essex) He advised the panel that he had been in a borough police twice before his present appointment, seven years in a rural constabulary and thirteen months as superintending constable.

Then the questions ...

Item 1938. Question: Will you state your opinion of those different systems of police in which you have served: take the borough police first: do you think the borough police is generally efficient?

Dunne: No I consider it inefficient; it is impracticable to establish an efficient police in any borough town, in accordance with the present divided system of organization and government, want of uniformity and cordial co-operation and communication in the pursuit, apprehension and conviction of offenders tend to render it most inefficient.

Item 1939. Question: Do you think the borough police in which you are serving is inefficient?

Dunne: It is not in such a satisfactory state of efficiency as I should like to see it.

Item 1840. Question. For what reasons?

Dunne: When I was appointed to the office of Chief of the police in the city of Norwich, I found existing there two distinct bodies of police: one was termed the day police, and the other the night watch: the day police consisted of twenty-seven men, six supernumeraries, six inspectors, and one Chief officer: the night watch consisted of an equal number: I found that in the day police the inspectors and constables received nearly the same pay: the inspector received 16/- and the constable 14/- they were permitted to receive fees and allowances for all special duties which they performed, which was considered sufficient to make up for any deficiency that existed as regarded their pay: the most ordinary duty which they were called upon to perform by any inhabitants they were paid for: and a similar system was connected with the night watch: those men were not at all supervised during the night; they checked themselves by a clock, an old system which I believe existed in connection with the constables in London previous to the establishment of the Metropolitan Police; in the course of inquiry I ascertained that it was possible for one man to attend to the clocks of three or four; the mode of ascertaining whether a man had attended to his clock was by the superintendent going round the city every morning and examining the face of the clock, which revolved; there was a peg which moved on the dial, which,on examination, showed whether the man had pulled at the time laid down in the regulations for him to do so. I found that nearly all the men were in trade and business in the city, and they generally used to attend it every day. It was the opinion of many of the respectable inhabitants that receiving fees by the watchmen and policemen was an indirect incentive to the commission of crime. If a policeman or watchmen apprehended any party he received a fee for it, and was allowed to retain that fee and appropriate it to his own uses. Viewing it then, as a whole, I considered it to be in a most inefficient and defective state: I stated so to the watch committee to whose authority I am subject, and also to the magistrates, and explained everything in connection with both forces, particularly alluding to the want of co- operation and communication existing between both bodies, especially as they were allowed to receive fees. If one of the night watchmen saw any suspected parties during the night, and observed anything which he ought to have communicated to the day policeman, so as to give the public the advantages of the services of an efficient police, he would attempt to do that duty himself, for the purpose of getting the fee, thereby frequently frustrating the end of justice so it was vice versa with the police force as regards the watchmen.

1941. Question: Has that system been altered?

Dunne: Yes I drew up a report in reference therein, which was adopted.

1942 Question: Does that report contain more in detail the objections which you have now stated?

Dunne: Yes

1943 Question: Was the system altered in consequence of that report?

Dunne: Yes, both the bodies were amalgamated and established, similar in detail to the Essex Constabulary and the Metropolitan Police Force.

1944. Question: Do you think the force is more efficient?

Dunne: I do. Serious crime has greatly decreased, pursuit, apprehension and conviction of offenders facilitated, life and property better protected, the system insures the performance of the duties, the respectable inhabitants have expressed themselves gratified with the duties, considerable savings are effected; my report however has not been fully carried out, particularly as regards the appointment and promotion of the men and other circumstances, which render the force still defective.

1945 Question (Mr Fitzroy): Have the numbers been increased?

Dunne: No the consolidated force is equal in numbers (eighty) to the two bodies previously existing.

1946 Question: What is the population of Norwich?

Dunne: Between 70,000 and 80,000

1947 Question (Chairman): Do you know what the cost of the old force was?

Dunne: About £3,687 16s.8d per annun the new about the same.

1948. Question (Lord Lovaine): What is the rating in the pound?

Dunne: About 2d police rate

1949 Question. (Mr Fitzroy): Will you point out in what respects the police forces in boroughs are deficient?

Dunne: I consider that the police force of a borough being placed under the divided control of the magistrates and the watch committee tends to render effectual action almost impossible. In many instance the watch committees lay down instruction and give orders which the magistrates countermand. One of the magistrates in Norwich recently ordered a policeman to perform a certain duty, and while in the performance of that duty another magistrate came up and found fault with him, and spoke to him in the street in such a way that the man resigned. Every borough has some system or other peculiar to itself, there's no uniform, no co-operation, no communication, no effectual action, thereby the ends of justice are frequently defeated, they are generally defective in numerical strength, unequal to any emergency, and rely too much upon military aid; local interests and influences brought to bear.

1950 Question (Chairman): Do you think the rural police in Essex is efficient?

Dunne: I do. I consider it the most efficient rural police force in England. The establishment of station-houses and police districts in connection with that force have been attended with most advantageous results, and to meet the gross expense, a variety of duties have been engrafted on the force, which, while adding materially to its efficiency, has considerably reduced the net expense, which example has been followed in Hampshire and other counties.

1951. Question: What is your opinion of the efficiency of the superintending constable system?

Dunne: I consider the system inefficient; it is quite impossible to ever become effective.

1952. Question: What difficulty did you find in carrying out your duties there?

Dunne: I found that the men from whom the rural constables were chosen under Act 5th and 6th of Victoria, were men generally disinclined to serve as constables, they never voluntarily or cheerfully accepted their office. In the general performance of the duties they are called upon to exercise there appears to be a reluctance on their part to do their duties, particularly in consideration of their being brought into collision with the parties from whom they obtain their livelihood. They are generally chosen from tailors, blacksmiths, agricultural labourers and men who keep little shops in the parish in which they may reside. I found that it was quite impossible to carry out any system so as to ensure the performance of the duties appertaining to a police force.

1953. Question: Did you find any difficulty in pursuing offenders?

Dunne: I did, I often found great obstruction in the pursuit and apprehension of offenders, which often entirely frustrated their detection, and defeated the ends of justice.

1954. Question: Have you any means of stating to the Committee what the expenses of the superintending constables were in the county of Kent?

Dunne: The expense of the superintending constable system I consider to be far greater than any person is able to show by statistics which can be obtained, insomuch as the performance of the duties by the constables is generally paid for, indirectly, by

individuals and by the overseers of the parishes, there are no accounts kept, and this makes it almost impossible to conceive the extreme expense incurred by the system; the superintending constables salaries amounted to £85 a year and £25 a year as an allowance for horse, cart and re-mount; then for the performance of special services there was a quarterly contingent account made, which was taken before the constabulary committee to be approved by them, in many instances charges were disallowed on examination by the constabulary committee; subsequently the salaries were increased to £150 per annum, with other allowances.

1955. Question: Were those charges independent of the fees paid by order of the magistrates to the local constables ?

Dunne: Entirely.

1956 Question: Have you the means of stating what those fees were in your division?

Dunne: The expense for the performance of any occasional duty required under a written order of a justice was at the rate of 2/6d per day, and 3/- a night, and all other fees and allowances were paid in accordance with a table laid down, and approved by court of quarter sessions.

1957. Question: Had the magistrates any power of ordering watch?

Dunne: Yes on the application of the superintending constables, or other person on his apprehension that any offence was likely to be committed, the magistrates had the power to order as many constables as they thought necessary to remain on duty, both day and night, as long as they deemed proper, at that rate of payment.

1958. Question: Do you know at all what the expense in your division was of a watch, under orders of magistrates?

Dunne: I tried what the effect might be of calling out the constables on one occasion, the neighbourhood was infested with a great number of vagrants and reputed thieves, and I considered that the calling out of the constables might have the effect of watching these parties, who were continually prowling about, and be thereby attended with the prevention and detection of crime; I made an application to a magistrate, and on his order I placed a great many constables on duty, but in the working out of the system I found it to be most defective, If I gave any orders to the constables to watch certain parties or to supervise beer-shops or public houses, I found that they deceived me and rarely performed the duties necessary to enable me to discharge my duty with any advantage to the county. The expense of ten constables on duty for one month under the system would be £77.

1959. Question (Mr Fitzroy): Under what Act was power given to magistrates to order parish constables to watch ?

Dunne: The 5th and 6th Victoria, c 109,and 13th and 14th Victoria c 20.

1960 Question: Does it give the magistrates power to call out constables to watch, in case of apprehended danger?

Dunne: Yes, it was exercised to a great extent. The indirect expense thereby incurred was very large. There was no return made of it, and it is impossible to conceive the excessive amount caused by this and other circumstances in connection with the superintending constable system.

1961. Question: Is that expense paid out of the county rate?

Dunne: Out of the poor rates, an order is made out by the magistrates clerk, signed by the magistrates, and paid by the overseer of the parish.

1962. Question: So far as your knowledge of that system goes, do you think that one great drawback to its well working is the want of a Chief Constable at the head of the whole of the superintending constables ?

Dunne: Certainly not. I consider that a Chief Constable at the head of the superintending constables would not at all improve the system. I cannot see how it can be improved by having a Chief superintending constable. He could not possibly establish an efficient system of supervision. The superintending constables are subject to no control, except to the court of quarter sessions. I have known instances of the superintending constable acting in such a manner as could not be allowed in a police force, where there was any system, so as to insure the legal and due discharge of his duty.

1963 Question: Would it not probably be the case that the appointment of a Chief constable would introduce more system into the working of that plan?

Dunne: I do not think it is practicable, particularly for the want of having a proper class of men as local constables, such as the superintending constables could derive assistance from.

1964. Question (Lord Lovaine): You mean that it is impossible to make a parish constable an efficient officer?

Dunne: It is impracticable to do so.

1965 Question (Chairman): Do you mean that in your opinion a superintending constable could not make the parish constables efficient police officers?

Dunne: I do, it is quite impossible.

1966. Question: If the superintending constable under whose immediate direction they were, could not improve them as police officers, do you think that one Chief Constable of the whole could make any difference in their efficiency as police officers.

Dunne: None whatsoever.

1989. Question: Would you give the appointment of the men to the head officer of the police, whoever he might be, or to any body or committee, either magistrates or town council?

Dunne: I think it is absolutely necessary that the Chief officer of the district should have the entire control of the force.

1990 Question: In the same manner as in the rural constabulary?

Dunne: Yes

1991 Question (Mr Fitzroy): By whom were you appointed at Norwich?

Dunne: By the Watch Committee

1992 Question: Does the watch committee appoint the whole of the other constables?

Dunne: Yes

1993 Question: Have the magistrates the power to dismiss or suspend the men?

Dunne: They have, the control is divided between the watch committee and the magistrates, the watch committee and the magistrates frequently differ as to the merits of cases in connection with the police which may be brought before them. I have known instances occur in which the magistrates have suspended a policeman, and recommended his dismissal, and when before the watch committee, the watch committee reinstated him. When that same officer again appeared before the magistrates to give evidence in court, one of the magistrates who suspended him stated on the bench that he would not believe the man upon his oath, and if he saw the man in a court of justice he should think it his duty to stand up and state that he thought the man was not worthy of belief on his oath. I reported that to the watch committee, but notwithstanding the man was retained in the service.

1994. Question: Is there a complaint on the part of the inhabitants of Norwich that a sufficient supervision is not exercised over the beer-houses?

Dunne: Yes

1995 Question: Is there a complaint that information is not laid by the police when the publicans are known to transgress the law?

Dunne: Yes

1996. Question: Is that attributable to the manner in which they are appointed?

Dunne: I believe so, in some measure

1997 Question (Lord Lovaine): How many brewers are members of the watch committee?

Dunne: Three; the late chairman of the watch committee was a brewer, there are in Norwich six hundred and seventy beer-houses and public-houses

1998 Question (Mr Fitzroy): When did you get that return?

Dunne: Last Monday. There is one fact in connection with these houses which is, I think, peculiar to Norwich, of this number three hundred and forty-four took a spirit license, one hundred and seven a wine license and two hundred and nineteen are little better than beer- houses, insomuch as they receive the magistrate's license to sell beer, but they have no spirit license, nor wine license; after receiving a beer license they save about £3 by not taking out a spirit license from the Excise.

1999 Question: Do you know that they do not take out a spirit license from the Excise?

Dunne: They pay £3. 6s 03/4d to the Excise for the spirit license, and £1.2s 0.½d for the magistrates beer license.

2000 Question (Lord Lovaine): Are the Committee to understand that those six hundred and seventy beer-houses, alehouses and wine shops are all under the control of one individual?

Dunne: No. there are eight owners of houses, exclusive of free houses

2001. Question: Under the control of the brewers there are six hundred and seventy houses, exclusive of free houses and those houses where spirituous liquors of one sort or another are sold, are all under the control of eight individuals ?

Dunne: Yes. Exclusive of free houses, which are about one hundred and twenty.

2002 Question (Mr Burroughes): When you speak of control, do you mean ownership?

Dunne: Yes. And with respect to the control exercised by the police, I have caused information to be laid against some of them for disorderly conduct; I have had the parties summoned, the offence has been proved by the police officers, and the party has been called upon to assign his answer to the charge, he has pleaded guilty and notwithstanding, the case has been dismissed. One was a case of a man keeping a disorderly house on Sunday morning during the hours of Divine Service.

2003 Question (Mr Fitzroy): Do you mean that he opened his house?

Dunne: Yes, and I felt it my duty to bring the case before the magistrates.

2004. Question: Do you mean than an information had been laid before a bench of magistrates?

Dunne: Yes, and the party summoned.

2005. Question: Had you received any instructions from the watch committee with respect to the public-houses?

Dunne: The watch committee told me not to summon any public-house keeper or beer-house keeper without first submitting the report for their approval, and to receive their orders and instructions thereon.

2006. Question: The information being laid, before whom was it laid?

Dunne: Before the magistrates.

2007. Question: You say that the information has been laid before the magistrates, the case has been heard, the man has pleaded guilty, and then the information has been dismissed?

Dunne: In two instances

2008. Question: Were any of those magistrates who heard the information members of the watch committee?

Dunne: They were.

2009 Question (Chairman): Of how many members does the watch committee consist altogether?

Dunne: Eighteen.

2010 Question (Mr Fitzroy): Were any of the magistrates who heard the information to which you have referred, brewers, connected with the public-houses in the town?

Dunne: I cannot say.

2011 Question: Had those information's which were laid before the magistrates been first submitted to the watch committee, and had you received their directions upon the subject?

Dunne: No, there were so many complaints from respectable inhabitants and the clergy, of the state of the public-houses, that to remove the responsibility from myself and to see what the magistrates would do, I laid those information's upon my own responsibility, and the result is what I have told you.

2012. Question: Are the committee to understand from the statement you have made, that the influence exercised by those members of the watch committee who are connected with the publicans, over the other members of the watch committee is sufficient to insure a decision such as will be convenient to the members of the watch committee who are connected with the public-houses?

Dunne: I am unable to say so.

2013. Question: Do you mean to say that these two cases in which information's were dismissed, although the parties pleaded guilty, are an example of the influence which the watch committee have over the conduct of the magistrates?

Dunne: I cannot say that those two cases were dismissed by the magistrates in consequence of the influence of the watch committee. I do not know the cause, these are only two of many cases I could refer to, to show the difficulties experienced by the police in the performance of their duties under the present system.

2014. Question: Do you mean to say that there is generally a total want of interference with the regulation of the public houses?

Dunne: It is very difficult to efficiently supervise them.

2015 Question: It is your impression that it is the wish of the magistrates that the public-houses and beer-shops should not be interfered with?

Dunne: Judging from the difficulty of carrying out strictly an information, it appears so.

2016 Question (Mr Burroughes): Has there been any application for a stipendiary magistrate at Norwich?

Dunne: I am not aware, I believe it is the feeling of the inhabitants generally that it would be a very great advantage to the city to have a stipendiary magistrate. I was told that some of the leading gentlemen in the city have got up a petition to the effect that a stipendiary magistrate is necessary for the advantage of the city, and the protection of the public.

2017 Question (Mr Fitzroy): But as a stipendiary magistrate would have nothing to do with the dismissal or the appointment of the police, would the evil to which you have referred, namely, the want of proper regulations of the public-houses and beer-shops, be remedied at all by the appointment of a stipendiary magistrate?

Dunne: No, I consider it would not, assuming the police to remain under the same control and jurisdiction, but if an information was brought, the party would be punished as he deserved, and injustice impartially administered.

2018 Question (Lord Lovaine): Which, in your opinion is not the case now?

Dunne: In my opinion it is not.

2019. Question (Mr Fitzroy): Are any directions issued to yourself to prevent the police interfering with these public-houses?

Dunne: None, excepting what I have stated.

2020 Question: It is your impression that such a course is understood on the part of the watch committee ?

Dunne: It is my impression, as Inspector Peck informed me that an order was put up in the station house, previous to my being in Norwich prohibiting interference unless in flagrant cases.

2021. Question (Lord Lovaine): You have said that no information is to be laid without having previously undergone the sanction of the watch committee?

Dunne: These instructions were given. I took the responsibility of laying information's against some houses.

2022 Question: And brought them direct before the magistrates of the city?

Dunne: Yes. In some cases the parties were fined.

2023 Question (Mr Fitzroy): Is Sunday trading carried on to a great extent at Norwich?

Dunne: Not so much as it used to be .

2024 Question: What are the principal offences which are committed by the public-house and beer-shop keepers in Norwich?

Dunne: It is said that in the city of Norwich there are two hundred houses that are used for the purposes of prostitution…it is difficult to supervise them.

2025 Question (Chairman): Do you mean that those houses are the resort of hired prostitutes?

Dunne: The resort of prostitutes, some of those houses are kept by returned convicts, or by men who have been convicted of felony, and in many of those low public-houses crime is fostered, many of them I suspect to be receivers of stolen property: I recently found a quantity of stolen goods in the house of a returned convict, and also an illicit still.

2026 Question: Did you take any measures in that instance to bring the offenders to justice?

Dunne: Yes. I had the man taken before the magistrates, but one of the magistrates who is a practising barrister, has two sons, solicitors and his sons appear before the bench; he adjudicates in cases where his sons appear as solicitors, he was there that day, and he suggested that the case was got up by the police, that it was a set-up robbery.

2027 Question: Was the case dismissed?

Dunne: Yes

2028 Question: Upon the representation of the magistrates that it was a got-up robbery by the police?

Dunne: I cannot say that it was dismissed upon that statement; that remark was made by that magistrate. The men vote at elections, there are generally from twenty-thirty men who vote at parliamentary and municipal elections, at the last election I submitted to the watch committee the impropriety of allowing the men to interfere in the election, directly or indirectly, only in the performance of their duties; that both parties were entitled to protection, one as much as the other. The committee met my proposition with a direct negative.

2029 Question (Lord Lovaine): Have you ever found it necessary to call in further assistance during elections?

Dunne: No, my experience only extends to one election at Norwich, and there was no occasion then to apply for further assistance, excepting posse-men; the military were ordered to remain in barracks, and they were in readiness to come out if called upon. I had been informed that they were obliged to avail themselves of military aid when a disturbance took place. During the riots in Manchester in 1841 the military were called out, large bodies of special constables were appointed. I was detached with a party of police and special constables on three occasions, when called into action the special constables ran away, three active policemen were beaten, in a day or two afterwards they died in hospital. It is my opinion that special constables are unequal to any emergency.

2030. Question (Mr Fitzroy): On the occasion to which you refer, regarding Norwich, did those members of the police vote?

Dunne: I am informed they always have done so.

This marked the end of his questions. Overall 33 persons were interviewed by the Select Committee of which ten were senior police officers.

However ... back to Dunne's day's in Norwich. One case that Dunne inherited was that of the attack on Superintendent Parker and Constable Greenacre of the Norwich City Police, which though happening three weeks before his arrival in Norwich, he would nevertheless have taken over the responsibility for the case. It was also one of those rare occasions when the city police assisted the county police with the permission and approval of the Norwich Watch Committee.

The offence, at this time, also coincided with numerous instances of poaching which were ongoing in Norfolk at this time. All participants in this crime were quickly apprehended and sent to Norwich Castle on the 9th December. At the Lent Assizes of 1852, William and John Hunter, Lincoln, Stagg, Lake, Buckle and Harwood were charged with having shot at Samuel Parker, a Superintendent of the rural police, with intent to murder him. There was also a second count which additionally charged them with having shot at Parker to prevent their apprehension along with a third count which charged them with having shot at him with intent to do grievous bodily harm. John Lakes was quickly discharged however due to insufficient evidence being found against him. Acting in his own defence Lincoln claimed he was persuaded to go by Stagg and the others, otherwise he would not have been there. The defence showed signs of disgust *'that six young men, who if the right love and feeling which the rich ought to show to the poor had been displayed towards them in their youth, would have grown up to be a comfort to their friends instead of being brought here for trial, and remarked that if a gentleman would preserve game they must take the proper means to preserve it, they had no right to employ the police for that purpose and further deplored that these young men should be allowed to grow up like so many weeds in the neighbourhood of the mansions of the rich; the care which ought to have been bestowed on them having been lavished on the game of their preserves'* The judge agreed that the landlord had no right to employ police 'who were in that sense like soldiers. They were to obey the orders of their Superintendent and acting under his orders they were justified in what they did. It appeared that they were there for a week and this thing should be guarded against because it was likely to lead to 'ill will'. Yet despite the plea of the defence and the general anti-police feeling the sentences were harsh; Lincoln, William Hunter and Harwood were to be transported for ten years, while Buckle, Stagg and John Hunter were to be imprisoned for two years with hard labour ... Postcript to this case would be that this trial, and the judges comments, would remain in Dunne's memory for some time to come, and in later years he was to instruct his constables NOT to be so employed, and indeed he was instrumental in changing the Poaching Act.

Shortly after Dunne's return from giving evidence to the Select Committee on Police (in June 1853) there was an announcement in the local paper of the resignation of Superintendent Dunne of the Norwich Police *'on the grounds that he had been so much obstructed by those who ought to have assisted him in the discharge of his duties, that no alternative had been left him but to resign'.* On 6th July Mr Stephen English of Pontefract was elected to the post. Throughout John Dunne's time with the Norwich Police he had not been sufficiently pretentious to style himself Chief Constable of Norwich Constabulary (he was happy with the title Chief Officer) but his successor Stephen English had no such pretensions for immediately on appointment. and with the approval of the Watch Committee he styled himself Chief Constable. A move which not only brought him into conflict with an officer who believed himself correctly titled Chief Constable for Norfolk but eventually brought about an unsavoury court case which eventually published a few items in English's background that he would have preferred to have kept in his 'closet' Stephen English, who having at one time served with the Essex Constabulary as Inspector would at first glance appear to have been yet another protégé of McHardy. In later years it was learnt that English had actually been 'required to resign'. However he still went on to serve as 'Chief Constable' of Norwich until 1859.

By now we are starting to get a picture of Dunne ... and indeed his honesty (up to a point) and his integrity. Twice now we have seen him leave previous postings on a point of principle – Bearsted (Kent) and now Norwich. However such principles do not appear to have been quite so important to both his predecessor in Norwich (Yarington) and indeed Stephen English who took over his post upon his resignation. We know that Yarington left a mess that Dunne tried to clear up...but with only a degree of success, whilst English went on to serve six years in the same post ... presumably without the same degree of concern that had bothered Dunne so.

Before he left Norwich the Chairman of the of Police Committee (amazingly) bore testimony to the able manner in which he had organised the police force *'to the advantage of the city and its several trading, manufacturing and other interests'* adding that he had proved himself *'an energetic and most efficient officer and a strict disciplinarian and had constantly discharged all his duties with firmness and attention'.* Mind you – that didn't stop them hounding him for the return of his dress coat!

And, a final word in recognition, this time by the: *The Norfolk Chronicle* in 1854 was reporting that poaching seemed to be declining in the neighbourhood so that which Dunne had inherited in the January of 1852 was, if the paper was to be believed, actually declining thanks in part no doubt to Dunne and the work of his men!

Now it was off to Newcastle. One wonders if his honesty and integrity would fare any better there?

CHAPTER SEVEN

CHIEF CONSTABLE JOHN DUNNE

Newcastle-upon-Tyne City Police July 1854 - December1856

It is at this point in Dunne's career, that we have something of an anomaly. We are aware that following various problems with the Norwich magistrates, Dunne had decided that 'enough is enough' and his career was not going anywhere, at least as far as Norfolk was concerned, and within a month of handing in his notice to the magistrates, in the June of 1853, he was to find himself 'footloose and fancy free' for the first time in his life, as did not take up his new position as Chief officer of Newcastle City Police until exactly one year later.

Clearly we have no way of knowing what he did with himself for a year, other than presumably write letters of application to other police forces ... and of course make at least two appearances before the Select Committee on Police during 1853 which in all probability would have taken up quite a bit of his time even if unpaid. Still considering that Newcastle in 1853 was suffering from its worst cholera epidemic in living memory, it was perhaps fortuitous that Dunne did not move across that year. In total 1,533 died, and he could so easily have been one of them.

Dunne must have thought upon his eventual arrival in Newcastle in that summer of 1854, that he was once again back to the worst of Manchester fourteen years earlier, especially so when he noticed the large numbers of Irish who too were living once again in filthy and unsanitary conditions in an area of the town known as Sandgate ... with the Corporation of Newcastle being the largest landlords for the area! In fact the Health Inspectors in their 1853 report referred to Sandgate specifically and confirmed that cholera had broken out in *'rooms in which as many as twenty or twenty-five occupiers were congregated, there being but fifty cubic feet of space or air for each individual'*

The worse of these epidemics was in 1853 just a few months prior to Dunne arriving to take up his post as Chief officer of police, when 1,533 people died from cholera. In fact on the 12th September of that year the Superintending Inspector of Health, Mr Grainger reported to the General Board of Health that *'there was no doubt that the general malaria, rising out of the neglected and miserable parts of Newcastle, overhangs the whole town and penetrates into every domicile,and acts in this epidemic period as an intensifying, predisposing and all-influential cause'.*

And, later in the same report, *'That there are districts in Newcastle which, in the totality of sanitary evil, or in respect of the many sanitary defects simultaneously exhibited are, according to three Superintending Inspectors of Health whom we have examined, more misconditioned probably than any other districts of anything like the same area in any other town in Great Britain; that a negative confirmation of this testimony may probably be gathered from the refusal of the present superintendent of police (John Stevens) in Newcastle (formerly a member of the Metropolitan Police in the Westminster District), to answer our questions in respect even of the very first point, in which we proposed to institute a comparison between the worst districts of Westminster and of Newcastle; and that, whatever be the comparative condition of these latter districts, their actual conditions is in the highest degree lamentable and prejudicial to health'.*

The aforementioned, John Stevens, who had not come out in too good a light from the above report, was of course Dunne's predecessor, who had been in the post since 1836.

Once again we learn that he too had been 29 years of age when he had taken up the post in 1836, exactly the same age as Dunne was in 1854. What was perhaps more interesting was the fact that this was the same John Stevens who had been Sir Robert Peel's one time personal valet who had become so inspired by his association with the great man that he joined the Metropolitan Police as a Police Constable in 1829 and eventually became the Chief Constable of Newcastle upon Tyne. He went on to become commander of his first love, the River Tyne Police until 1884. His would make an interesting story at some future date.

Dunne was nothing, if not a glutton for punishment for again, like Bearsted, and Norwich before he quickly found that he had yet another formidable task before him. The police of Newcastle like those of Norwich when he first went there, was in a deplorably disorganised condition, and the whole system was rotten to the core. Nevertheless by the application of the same principles which had operated with magical effect at Norwich he brought the force into such an efficient state that when he left in December 1856, he received a glowing ovation from the Chairman of the Police Committee.

Dunne, besides inheriting a population of 87,784 and a police strength of eighty-five (or one policeman per 1,000 head of population ... a very acceptable distribution) also inherited a town with history (Newcastle did not become a city until 1882 when the church of St Nicholas became a cathedral).

Unquestionably the biggest problem that Dunne had to contend with during his time in Newcastle, over and above his numerous arguments with the

Magistrates and Watch Committee would have been what became known as the Great Fire of Newcastle, which started on the 6th October 1854 ... just three months after Dunne had taken up the reins. I suppose one could call that a 'baptism of fire'. Considering that Dunne was of course Chief of Police, this would automatically have made him the head of the town's fire division too, thus he and his men would have been an integral part of the fire fighting team, along with the town's insurance companies own fire appliances, and firemen.

Indeed as we shall see one of his men was killed and many others were injured, with Dunne himself coming very close to being one of those injured or even killed. The fire was first noticed by a Newcastle policeman who spotted flames on the upper floors of a worsted mill in Hill Gate, and who then ran over the bridge to alert the Gateshead Police, who forced their way into the building. For those readers unfamiliar with the north east of England it should perhaps be pointed out that the towns of Newcastle upon Tyne and Gateshead actually sit opposite each other, on relatively steep slopes leading down to the River Tyne. On the north side is Newcastle, the quayside of which was one of the largest in the country, with much shipping and the concentration of town's business and commerce. Gateshead had similarly dense developments opposite the quayside with factories, mills, and warehouses built down to the water's edge, behind which and running up the hill were numberless densely occupied tenement dwellings. The two towns were linked by a short multi-arched stone bridge.

The Gateshead policemen's actions had the unfortunate effect of providing great gulps of fresh air on which the flames could feed. Within a short space of time two insurance companies' fire engines arrived, but due to their limited facilities within two hours the flames had spread to a six storey warehouse next door. It was said to be a *'double fireproof structure most strongly built'* but unfortunately it contained more than 4,000 tons of sulphur, as well as other goods including coal, tar, and rags, all exceptional nourishment for the flames. In one vault alone was 45 tons of highly explosive sodium nitrate.

About 3am, the whole building went up in a violent explosion which flung into the air lumps of masonry and burning beams that crashed through people's roofs killing them in their beds. Six people died on the opposite bank of the river. Burning debris set fire to ships in the river, and to offices and warehouses on the quay at Newcastle, and soon, in the words of *The Times*, *'houses and buildings on both sides of the river were one sheet of fire'*. Some people fled *'as if from an earthquake'*, others could not because they had fainted, overcome by the fumes from the burning sulphur. The explosion was heard in Sunderland eleven miles away, where miners even came rushing to the surface of the pit in alarm.

The fires that had been started on the Newcastle side now coalesced into one great conflagration that spread from Butchers Bank to Pilgrim Street.

With the fire now spreading to Newcastle, help was desperately needed and the message went out to as far afield as Berwick, Sunderland and even Carlisle – ninety miles distant. Horse drawn fire engines quickly came from all over the North East. However it appeared that nothing could stop the fire as it continued to spread in Gateshead, threatening the badly damaged St Mary's Church. In fact this church which for many years had been the only place of worship, marriage, baptism and funeral for the people of Gateshead, any further damage would have been giving enormous concern. It was an exciting sight to see all the vessels in the neighbourhood being hurried out of the region of the fire. After several warehouses had been involved in the conflagration this was when the terrific explosion took place and crowds of people who had assembled to see the fire were mown down as if by a discharge of artillery with many of them being killed. John Dunne himself had at this moment a narrow escape from death.

The river was all ablaze, and the Gateshead Police who were looking after the fire brigade which Dunne had additionally organised there, had crossed over the bridge to the Newcastle side of the river, just one hundred feet away. when the explosion took place. At that critical moment Dunne was making his way towards Ensign Cranbourne Hastings Paynter, (aged just 19) of the 26th Cameroonians, who was on duty, and was within a few yards of that officer when Paynter was killed by the force of the explosion. At the same time Alexander Ralph Dobson, a 25 year old architect who was by Mr Dunne's side was blown to smithereens and the only part of him ever found was a detached hand grasping a watch identified as his, which was picked up far away. He had evidently had his watch in his hand when the explosion took place, and its hands indicated the precise hour at which his death had occurred. It was a terribly trying time for Dunne and for the next three weeks he never slept in his bed, his only rest being obtained in a chair at the office of Mr Clayton, the Town Clerk. Still it wasn't all bad for Dunne for later that year he was awarded £5.5.0 (£5.25) for his devotion to duty during the Great Fire, and his force was increased by a further 22 men even getting its first sergeant. Whether his opposite number in Gateshead, W.H Schorey, who headed up the Gateshead Police Force, and with whom he was working alongside, was similarly awarded, is not recorded.

It was generally supposed that the explosion had been caused either by a cargo of gunpowder which was being prepared for exportation to Russia (it was during the time of the Crimean War) or by the fortuitous combination of sulphur and other chemicals, which made an explosive more powerful than gunpowder. As stated one policeman died in the fire Thomas Duke, and a Police Inspector was injured. In addition two firemen lost their lives, namely Martin Hall and James Todd, as well as their being numerous firemen injured. The fire was finally brought under control thanks to a group of army sappers and miners who blew up the buildings in its path.

Two inquests were later held into the events, one on the Gateshead side and the other on the Newcastle side. The main points of consideration for both were the causes of the fire and the cause of the explosion. The inquest juries found that no direct evidence as to the origin of the fire was presented. Mill hands responsible for various of the upper floor gave testimony that at the end of the day, all gas lights had been extinguished, and the gas supply isolated at a main tap; no cause was suggested and no progress made in this line of enquiry. The Gateshead jury however found that there must have been *'some want of caution displayed'* at the mill to occasion the fire.

Evidence in respect of the explosion was of more interest. A statement of the contents of the warehouse was given, the most interesting features of which were 2,800 tons of sulphur and one hundred and twenty eight tons of nitrate of soda. These goods lay on various floors, and in the vaults, arranged so that in the event of a destructive fire, they might mix. Evidence given suggests that there were no other obvious candidates as fuel for the explosion, no oils, no naphtha, nor oils of vitriol. Great lengths were taken, including the posting of a reward for information, to ascertain whether gunpowder was stored in the warehouse ... but all evidence pointed against it. A number of chemists, including a government chemist, tested residues found on the scene, as well as black dust which fell on the spectators, looking for the remains of combusted gunpowder, but none was found.

The Gateshead jury found that the explosion was caused by the interaction of sulphur and nitrate of sulphur, but were unable to determine a mechanism. They did make the recommendation that the two should not be stored together in future. They found a complete want of evidence for gunpowder.

Shortly after the fire spectators in their thousands came to look at the damage, with special trains running on the following Sunday bringing some 20,000 people into Newcastle and Gateshead. Some time later that year, Queen Victoria herself asked that her train be stopped on the High Level so that she and her family could look for themselves.

Nowhere in any of the newspaper reports of the time was there any mention about the lack of fire-fighting equipment, lack of firemen, or lack of equipment to save people from upper floors, nevertheless it would be true to say that those firemen and police that were in attendance certainly tried their hardest to control the many fires.

It would be quite understandable if there had been reports of increasing levels of crime around this time either from the conflagration and petty thieving, but more importantly perhaps from the increasing levels in the population but this was not to be the case in Dunne's time, for by the end of 1856 he was reporting to the Watch Committee that the detected crime rate was 87% compared with the 45% when he took office. When= considering those reported figures with today's, one wonders how many crimes weren't reported?

Youth crime was, as now, a substantial part of Dunne's problems ... though whether all were dealt with quite so severely as nine year old Francis Dixon who received six lashes for stealing oranges in 1856; and in the following year (1857) he was given a further ten lashes for stealing apples. Clearly this was not enough for just a few months later he got twelve lashes for stealing lead, followed by six weeks in prison with hard labour. The records don't state whether this final punishment was enough for him to mend his ways. It wasn't all bad for Dunne during his time in Newcastle.

There were those moments when as head of the police he would regularly have had the opportunity of meeting with visiting dignitaries, attending untold numbers of banquets, as well as officiating at other events. Prominent amongst the visitors to Newcastle at this time would unquestionably have been Guiseppe Garibaldi, not the biscuit manufacturer, but the hero of Italy's First War of Independence where he had led his legion to two minor victories (at Luino and Morazzone), and who later went on to take command of the defence of Rome where in April of 1849 he was able to defeat a far superior French army. Such defeat was short lived however for Napoleon sent vast numbers of reinforcements and Garibaldi found himself simply holding onto a sieged Rome ... until he was forced, along with his men to retreat Rome and continue his resistance from the Apennine mountains ... and thence into exile.

Garibaldi arrived in Newcastle on the 21st March 1854 on the ship Commonwealth. He was already a popular figure on Tyneside and was welcomed enthusiastically by local working men, although the Newcastle Courant reported that he refused an invitation to dine with dignitaries in the city. He stayed in South Shields on Tyneside for over a month, departing at the end of April 1854. During his stay he was presented with an inscribed sword which his grandson later carried as a volunteer in British Service in the Boer War.

He then sailed to Genoa where his five years of exile ended on 10th May 1854. Apparently all was forgiven for in 1859 at the time of Italy's Second War of Independence Garibaldi was appointed Major General and headed up a volunteer unit named The Hunters of the Alps with whom he was to win victories over the Austrians at Varese, Como and numerous other places ... and that was only the start of his success, for he was to eventually proclaim himself dictator of Sicily

Another famous visitor to Newcastle,this time in 1856, was the Hungarian patriot and statesman Louis Kossuth, and who was also the one time Governor-President of Hungary ... though such position was short lived as he was only in power for less than four months. There is still a plaque in Nelson Street to this day declaring that he called into a bookshop that stood on the site in 1856.

As we know Dunne was only Chief of police for Newcastle for two and a half years, having been originally appointed in the July of 1854. Nevertheless by the end of 1856 he was able to report to the Watch Committee that the detected crime rate in the borough was 87% compared with the 45% when he took office. This was clearly recognised by Mr Ridley, the Chairman of Newcastle's Police Committee, who wrote about his services:

> *'The police force, has under his able and judicious superintendence, been brought from a state of much disorganisation to one of perfection not to be surpassed by any in the kingdom, and the Judges and recorder from the Bench, as well as the Home Secretary in the House of Commons have adverted to its efficiency under the present management'.*

References don't come much better than that!

He was superseded by John Sabbage, coincidentally a superintendent from Carlisle where of course Dunne was destined. Later reports state that he was often to be seen on horseback in the streets of Newcastle *'a commanding figure the cynosure of all eyes'* where he commanded the force until 1867 satisfactorily until his death that year after catching a chill on *'Corporation Sunday'.*

Dunne's departure from Newcastle was not solely because '*he had done all he could*' as he later proclaimed, but more to do with the fact that the County Police Act (of 1856) had now come into being ... indeed Dunne could say that he had had a goodly part in its appearance following his lengthy interviews at the 1853 Select Committee on Police in London. This clearly put the idea in his head that this could well be the opportunity he had been looking for, and for some months prior to his departure he had been busily penning large numbers of letters to Watch Committees of counties across the country who were preparing the way for a new county police force, and thus advertising for a Chief Constable to head up their new force.

Amongst those that did reply was that of the joint police forces of Cumberland and Westmorland, who once reading his detailed CV, and learning of his successes in Norwich and Newcastle especially had no hesitation in offering him the post of Chief Constable of both forces, without even the necessity of an interview, with the request that he should present himself at Carlisle on the 1st January 1857.

Thus Dunne's time at Newcastle came to a swift close and he was off to start a whole new career, this time truly as head of a relatively large force (or two forces in his case) and ones with which he would stay for the next forty-five years ... but of course he didn't know that at the time.

CHAPTER EIGHT

POLICING IN CUMBERLAND & WESTMORLAND

Pre-John Dunne 1846 - 1856

January 1st,1857, clearly heralded the arrival of John Dunne to his new post as the Chief Constable of two counties in the north of England namely: Cumberland and Westmorland.

However, as before this was to be another area of England which was not new to policing of a sorts and it would perhaps be advantageous to the reader to know a little of the area, and its then background in policing in what is ostensibly the second largest county(s) in Britain, through the period 1846-1856 ie leading up to that momentous day when Dunne took control for the first time.

William Rollinson reminds us in his book *A History of Cumberland and Westmoreland* that:

> *'The decade between 1850 and 1860 marked a watershed in the history of man's contribution of the developing landscape of the Lake counties. Certainly in the early part of the century the economy was essentially rural and the steady pace of life was governed by the seasons... by seed-time and harvest, by lambing and clipping, as it had been for centuries. In the second half of the century the process of change clearly accelerated, the percentage of urban dwellers increased and entirely new towns came into being. In fact by the time of Dunne's arrival in the counties it was possible to travel by rail from Carlisle along the West Cumberland coast, through Furness and Cartmel to Carnforth and then return to Carlisle via the railway over Shap Fell.'*

In the second half of the 19th century the picture changed somewhat and in many cases a sharp increase in the number of urban dwellers gave rise to overcrowding and related health hazards. By 1850 Carlisle had long since outgrown the confines of the ancient city walls and linear suburbs extending finger like along Botchergate, Rickergate and Coldwater – the three main routes into the town, but within the city centre overcrowding became acute and hundreds of people lived in dark unsanitary courts, the worst of which were described by one observer as *'the receptacles of every kind of filth, containing almost invariably pigsties, open privies, dunghills and stagnant pools'.*

And of course it wasn't just Carlisle that saw such depredation. One observer, writing in 1858 stated *'There is only one street in England that we have seen beat Quay Street, Whitehaven for squalor and filth, and that was Lace Street, Liverpool before the Sanitary Act came into operation. Houses, shops, jerry-shops, courts, public houses, everything you come on speaks plainly of overcrowding. Sallow looking women covered with rags,thrust their heads and half their bodies through the windows to look after you, and as they do this they appear to gasp for fresh air'* And the problems were not overcome quite so easily either, for by 1871 we learn that the population of Millom, the southern most point of Cumberland along with the older nucleus of Holborn Hill had reached 3,000 and smallpox and typhus followed in the wake of the overcrowded and insanitary housing conditions and just three years later one of the most crowded and ill drained sections of the town was described by the local medical officer as: *'a reproach and antithesis to even a remotely sanitary state-the drainage in many places consisting of sweltering stagnant puddle-holes in which may be seen floating the carcasses of drowned cats and puppies, the backyard receptacles for house refuse, night soil and ash, unroofed and some filled to overflowing, pigs and goats roaming-horses going at large'.* So if that was the case many years hence, one can just imagine what it was like in 1857 ... and of course, with his background none of it would have come as any surprise to John Dunne.

The growth of such industries as textiles, brewing, biscuit-making and other manufacturing activities, together with the rise of Carlisle as a railway junction of national importance, further stimulated urban growth and the industrial suburbs of Denton Holme developed along the flat valley floor of the River Caldew. Mid nineteenth century Cumberland and Westmorland were of course overwhelmingly rural counties. They are both located in the extreme north-east of England, and bounded on the north by Dumfriesshire and Roxburghshire, on the east by Northumberland and Durham, and in the south-east by Lancashire and the estuary of the Duddon. On the west is the Irish Sea and the Solway Firth. By combining the two counties together the overall acreage is in excess of 1.5 million, making it the second largest county in the country.

The overall population at this time would have been 217,092, and the principal industries after agriculture would have been coal, iron ore mining and cotton. The principal towns are Carlisle, Whitehaven, Penrith and Kendal.

As I hope it has become clear by now it was the twin forces of industrialization and urbanisation which forced England to reform its antiquated police system in the first half of the nineteenth century. Parliament passed the Metropolitan Police Act in 1829 of course, which was followed by the Municipal Corporations Act in 1835 which effectively spread the 'new' police to the provinces, though in truth many were slow to take up this opportunity until actually forced to do so under the County and Borough Police Act, which in the case of Cumberland was confirmed at the Midsummer Quarter Sessions held at Carlisle on the 7th August 1856, and brought into being on the 6th January 1857.

As stated, by 1857 Cumberland and Westmorland was to form one police force but in 1846 the counties were both separated as far as policing was concerned and was unusual in that it was a hotch-potch or mosaic of policing across the whole of the two counties and was in desperate need of organisation. Also at this time the two counties were made up of a combination of various police forces, parish constables, and felons societies, none of which worked with the other to assist uniformity ... though in truth they did achieve a high degree of success. For many parts of Cumberland and Westmorland policing remained in the hands of the old style parish constables, often employing paid night watchmen as their police much the same as other regions which Dunne had experienced but there were also other areas where policing was taken more seriously.

At this time burglaries and other serious robberies were frequent and the state of terror for many was such that many people would have been in the habit of piling up cans, tea-trays, and anything else that would make a noise, behind the front doors of their homes before going to bed at night, in order that should their doors be forced open, than the subsequent noise of the collapsing tin-ware would be sufficient to waken them and hopefully frighten off the thieves.

Public houses at this time were kept open all night and gambling was openly carried on in them. Houses of ill-repute flourished, and were tolerated without hindrance. Men would run races on the streets naked (at least they did until the Amateur Athletic Association became the controlling force of athletics in 1880). Terrible fights were continuously witnessed, often by men with nothing on but their boots, and even these had iron spikes fixed around their toes, which could, and did, inflect terrible injuries though the latter were more inclined to be seen in the counties mining towns. Dog and cock-fighting were carried out to a great extent, with the authorities seldom interfering (even though dog and cock-fighting was banned outright under the Cruelty to Animals Act of 1835).

Gentlemen, as well as working men, would be in the habit of spending their evenings at the card table, playing for any amount of stakes, invariably not going home until daylight.

The populace, including women and children of tender age, were being kept at work in the factories for twelve or thirteen hours a day, six days a week. It would be these long hours along with little and poor food which these 'lower-classes' received that would have had a deteriorating effect on their constitution and appearance; scores of young men would invariably have been seen in the streets, bow-legged, knock-kneed, hunch-backed and of a stunted growth generally. And of course it was these same 'lower-classes' that were the ones living in the cellars and other ill-ventilated places regardless of age, sex or of sanitary arrangements.

Cumberland though given the opportunity of adopting the proposals put forward under the County Police Act of 1836, nevertheless felt that their county was sufficiently policed, especially after taking into account the financial implications, and decided that for the time being at least they would simply opt for just one area to be included under the new act, and agreed to set up a miniscule force for the Derwent Division of the county only (the area taking in Penrith and Keswick -with a population of 3,000) across to Maryport (with a population of 7,500) and Cockermouth) ... miniscule being the operative word with just four men spread across Keswick, Cockermouth and Maryport, under the control of one superintendent based at Cockermouth. The overall population at this time was 31,960 and the area to be patrolled two hundred and five square miles. By 1853 it had not grown any bigger.

Westmorland following the 1836 Police Act, totally chose to ignore the proposals outlined in the Act, though they later adopted the 1842 Parish Constable Act. Some areas within the extensive Cumberland and Westmorland counties did opt to have their own, paid for police forces well before the 1856 Act. For example on the west coast of Cumberland the Whitehaven Town and Harbour Trustees had a small police force to patrol the coastal area from Whitehaven to Millom, a distance of some thirty-five miles, with a superintendent, namely George Goodman, along with one sergeant and nine constables. In the years to come this would be the area which would give John Dunne the most problems in his early days as Chief Constable.

In the north, Carlisle in Cumberland, had had a city police force since 1827 with a strength of 22 constables paid for through public subscription. This police force had become unusual when it became the first in the country to accept a black man John Kent (the son of a slave) as a constable back in 1837. Regretfully like so many other policemen, whatever their colour, both before and after him, drunkenness was to prove his undoing, and the Watch Committee dismissed him in 1844. Under the Municipal Corporations Act of 1835 this force was to become the reformed Carlisle City Police.

From 1853 through to 1857 it came under the supervision of Superintendent Sabbage, though he preferred the title Chief Constable of Carlisle City Police.

Of course, as we now know, it was this same Sabbage who was to replace Dunne in Newcastle in 1857. Referring to the evidence given at the previously mentioned Select Committee on Police in 1853 we can learn something of the problems for the Carlisle area from the evidence given by the Derwent superintendent for this time. When asked about the rural police for this area he replied: *"The eastern parts of Cumberland and the border of Northumberland are infested with vagrants, robberies are rife, and the farmers frequently turn out in a gang and attempt to secure the depredators. But before they can be secured they have gone to the border of Scotland, and vanished from Cumberland".* And when asked about the population of Carlisle he replied: *"there are considerable numbers of Irish and Scottish, though he clarified that they had very few Scottish prisoners, with the prisoners in the gaol at this time being principally Irish, or at least persons born of Irish parents, resident in Cumberland".* He went on to tell the committee that over the last seven years (1846-1853) the committals for trial had been very light. In 1846 it was 144, and by 1853 it was down to 138 though he was quick to point out that that in itself was no criteria to work by, as he was sure there was far more crime though this had gone undetected. In asked to clarify that statement he replied: *"It remains undetected purely from the want of some channel to apply to."*

The subject of vagrants entering the city of Carlisle for this period was also discussed. In response to the question about these numbers he replied: *"The number of vagrants that slept in Carlisle in the year ended November 1852, which number was registered, and every information procured by the police, was 45,718, for the present quarter, ending the other night, the numbers amounted to 10,236, that is wholly independent of those who pass through Carlisle during the daytime, those are the parties that actually slept in Carlisle."* And when asked the class of the vagrants, he replied: *"Itinerant thieves principally"* ... and clarified that statement with: "*three fourths of my prisoners are that class.*"

We also learn from the same gentleman and the same committee something of the 'low lodging houses' for Carlisle at this time. For when asked if he felt these houses could be the receptacles for stolen goods, he replied: *"Unquestionably they are receptacles for stolen goods; according to the term made use of by the thieves as 'fence', if the thief does not know of any other method, he manages to dispose of 'his' property through the keepers of these houses."* And in reply to the question *"Were not some portion of this vast number of vagrants Irish, who were driven by the state of their own country into England or Scotland?"* He replied: *"I think so".* Clarifying this he stated: *"that in the opinion of the superintendent of police they have a great many in custody, with about 600 prisoners in the year committed to gaol."* From the same evidence we also get confirmation that the Derwent superintendent considers parochial constables inefficient, for when asked if they were capable of doing their work he replied: *"I think it is utterly impossible from their local connection, and their own interest, they are generally small tradesmen, such as tailors and shoemakers."*

In the south, Kendal in Westmorland had formed a Borough Police Force on the 6th January 1832 with one superintendent and three police constables, though this was later to be increased to four constables with the introduction of the Municipal Corporation's Act of 1835 and thus came under the auspices of the town's Watch Committee.

In addition to these small police forces, both Cumberland and Westmorland were policed by a small number of parish constables. These constables who would have been seen at this time scattered across some of the smaller towns of the two counties were in each and every case part-time constables, often unpaid and drawn from a body of ordinary ratepayers who were invariably small businessman or local traders. As a general rule they acted only when appealed to by a citizen, or instructed to do so by a magistrate.

And, not to be overlooked, was the increasing numbers of felon's societies which had been springing up all over the country, and Cumberland and Westmorland were no exception. Set up in the early 1800's as a hopeful means of deterring criminals, these societies were an asset to the already hard-pressed and limited police. An extract from the *Cumberland Pacquet* dated 11th January 1814, refers to the new society formed to cover the towns of Aspatria, Plumbland and Torpenhow. Such articles gave a clear indication of the scope and rewards offered, though research confirms that their policies were duplicated across the county, for example the Alston Moor Association for the Prosecution of Felons duplicates Aspatria almost exactly.

Each and every area of these two counties had their own story to tell in respect of policing. Whitehaven more than anywhere else had considerable anti-Irish violence, though it would be true to say that life there in the 1840's and 1850's should not be compared with the violence that was occurring in the far bigger towns and cities in the north of England, especially so in Liverpool and Manchester ... the latter being something that Dunne could certainly vouch for. Nevertheless there were towns and cities especially on the west coast, which were not exactly unaccustomed to violence in general, and the Irish presence was growing continuously at this time. For example in 1851 to 1852 during the turbulence of the 'Papal Aggression' an Irish mob prevented James Hughan, a Unitarian street preacher, from delivering an address in Whitehaven. Newspaper reports of the time show that the predominantly dock police were brought in to handle what could quite easily have turned into a riot and by all accounts managed to bring the problems to a speedy conclusion.

In 1841, the Whitehaven census showed a population total of 12,107, whereas by 1851 this had increased 50% to 18,916, of which the majority of the population were Irish. Whitehaven and its vast environs was controlled by the Whitehaven Town and Harbour Trustees having a board of 21 governors headed by William Lowther, the Second Earl of Lonsdale. Somewhat understandably the Trustees concentrated most of their efforts on the port, for not only had most of them a vested interest in its continued success (especially so with William Lowther) but there were at this time some 177 vessels belonging to the port which overall employed 1455 men. Interestingly most reports of the town of Whitehaven for this period concentrate on a modern well laid out town with plenty of gardens and monuments all coming under the auspices of an apparently efficient Town and Harbour Trustee Board. However scratch beneath the surface and you will find that the majority of the populace lived in filthy conditions with no water and no toilet or sewage facilities. With a population in 1850 of 18,000 people and a police force of just eleven men on low pay, then one can well understand why the port had first priority.

Whitehaven was certainly not alone with its outbursts of violence linked to the high Irish input, in fact the most notorious outburst of Irish-related violence in Cumberland also happened during this period, though on this occasion it did not involve religion, and instead of the west coast was centred in the north of the county; Carlisle and Penrith.

During the latter part of the 1840's the demands of 'Railway Mania' promoted a spiralling growth in the number of the Irish navvy communities throughout Britain, and Cumbria was no exception with both the opening of the Lancaster-Kendal line in 1846 and the arrival of the railway in Carlisle also that same year. In Penrith too there were serious riots involving Irish navvies, also in 1846, incorporating some 2,000 workers.

Vagrancy was also a problem over this period, though reports in Carlisle appear to far exceed those reported in other areas of the two counties. One particular police historian, DJV Jones noted this as a nationwide problem when he refers to the *'exceptional levels of vagrancy'* during the aftermath of the Napoleonic Wars and again in the twenty years from 1829-1849. In addition Chadwick's two commissions on the 'Poor Law and Constabulary' spelt out its physical, moral and financial dangers. It was becoming abundantly clear that in those early years of Victoria's reign the new poor-law policies together with the Irish famine problem were greatly increasing the numbers of 'travellers' on the road. Carlisle certainly was suffering greatly from vagrants, particularly so by 1852.

The city's superintendent Sabbage was so concerned that he undertook a three month survey of both tramps and vagrants at this time and came to a figure of 11,709 in the city, which in his opinion equated to some 46,836 annually. The newspaper report of his findings at the time state that from these figures he estimated that 31,688 were *'male, idle and of no fixed abode'* and *'who stayed in the city for just one night in lodging houses'*. According to Sabbage they made their living by begging and stealing, and he blamed them for most of the crime in the city. Nevertheless he felt that they were *'kept in check by an efficient and active police force'*. Though the article makes no mention of it, one has to assume that Sabbage was under extreme pressure to ensure such a high degree of vagrants were kept in check, particularly so when the workhouses regarded vagrancy as a matter for the police rather than any aspect of the Poor Law. The Poor Law Amendment Act of 1834 didn't actually make mention of 'vagrants' so they were wrong as technically the law to which the Board of Guardians of these workhouses referred was not in fact the responsibility of the police. However this appears to have been overlooked by Sabbage, as he saw vagrants as causing a high degree of the crimes anyway.

Rachel Vorspan in her work Vagrancy and the New Poor Law in late Victorian and Edwardian England actually clarifies these distinctions and outlines the assumptions of not just the Boards of Guardians of workhouses, but Victorian attitude in general. As she explains, the Poor Law Act made clear that the 'vagrant' or 'casual' was in fact a destitute person who lacked a permanent home and who sought temporary relief in a workhouse. There was no clarity as what was a 'vagrant' and to the Victorian this term could equally have applied to the returning soldier, a craftsman looking for work, or indeed a tramp.

Periods of unrest and concern associated with the rise of Chartism, especially in the principally industrial region of Carlisle, was to form yet another important area of policing under superintendent Sabbage's jurisdiction. The major period of unrest for Carlisle was in the 1840's when the predominantly textile workers were like most of their co-workers around the country, desirous of obtaining the vote. Carlisle though was to see very little riots, any militant action was normally linked to marches and the odd demonstration and such as there were, were handled by superintendent Sabbage who throughout the period saw no reason to call in the military to assist, relying totally on his own small force of men, and the aforementioned policy of careful observation and non- intervention. By 1850 however the militant Chartism was fading and the marches and demonstrations were going out of fashion.

The other area which warrants mention for this period is Kendal, which had had a small police force since 1832, though there were some changes to this force in 1836 with the introduction of the Municipal Corporations Act. Kendal, in the county of Westmorland, handled policing in a similar but smaller way to its Cumberland neighbour. Like Carlisle the railway was to come to Kendal in 1846, but there are no reported instances of wide-spread rioting associated with the Irish navvies, or for that matter instances of demonstrations and marches linked to Chartism. Kendal, in 1851, with a population of 14,800, was policed with just one superintendent (David Lipsett) one sergeant (Robert Hutchinson) and four constables. Their responsibilities took the form of somewhat normal policing activities with much of the reports of this period indicating crime associated with agriculture, with the occasional house-breaking, mugging and drunken assaults. Reports of the Assizes for this period confirm this. The Constable's Oath and Instructions to Constables and other peace officers, a forty page booklet printed in 1840, by Kendal's superintendent,clearly indicates that their Chief officer had firm ideas about policing long before many other areas.

For most of these early police forces the turnover of men was high, and there is no doubt that life was both gruelling and to some degree highly regimented. Even breaking a minor rule could mean a fine, suspension, or in serious case, dismissal. Drunkenness was the biggest problem and large numbers of men were dismissed, or 'asked to resign' solely for that reason, though absence from their beats regularly appeared on the charge sheet. This was not a problem solely encountered in Cumberland and Westmorland at this time, but seemed somewhat wide-spread, as we have already learnt from Dunne.

Due to lack of information and statistics for the period 1846 to 1856, it is difficult to determine the actual turnover of police in any of the areas, and one has to rely almost exclusively on newspaper reports for the period. Therefore comparisons with the newly formed Cumberland and Westmorland Police following the 1856 Act are difficult. Jennifer Hart in her article *'Reform of the Borough Police 1835-1856'* clearly identifies this problem, for she makes clear that it is not possible to make an estimate for the decade 1836/1845 and later, of the numbers of full-time police, *'for many, if not most, soon left for one reason or another'*. In addition we are advised that many of these police would only have been part-time, for example parish constables.

Current research for this period utilising fifty random cases published in the local newspapers and who had appeared before the magistrates and judges, indicate that not too surprisingly most crimes committed were primarily agricultural in nature (38%). Other cases in order of severity were assault at

22%, theft at 12%, and somewhat surprisingly, bigamy at 8%. There were also reports of wilful murder of new-born babies by their mothers, with at least two cases recorded in one year. There were just two reports of assaults which compare favourably with other regions of Britain at this time. However there were some instances of major crime, with at least five cases of murder and manslaughter. By and large however, most of the population of Cumberland and Westmorland continued to draw back altogether from any senseless taking of life, for as stated only five murders are reported over this entire ten year span: Jane Crosby in 1846, John Thompson in 1847, John and Nichol Hogg in 1849, Thomas Munroe in 1855 and William Graham in 1856. (the trial, and later transportation of this latter individual would be overseen by Dunne in 1857).

Many books on Victorian policing for this era dwell on the numbers of assaults on police during these early days, as well as extreme sufferings from crime and disorder. Charles Reith, in his book *The Blind Eye of History*, states *'that in every county throughout England crime has so rapidly and fearfully increased as to shake all confidence in either public or private security'*. Another police historian, Robert Storch in his article *'A Plague of the Blue Locusts'* reports seven instances of assaults on police in the 1840's, four in bordering counties of Lancashire and Yorkshire, plus one in the Potteries, all of them of an anti-police nature. Storch does make clear however, that though there were indeed many instances of assaults on police, invariably these were brought about by drunkenness as well as off-duty soldiers. In fact the largest of these riots in Leeds in the June of 1844, initially involved soldiers, but for reasons unknown a large number of civilians joined in turning it into a serious riot. He believes that a decision at the time by magistrates to suppress Sunday meetings could well have influenced the civilians involvement.

However such generalisations about the amount of crime and disorder and their causes should not be interpreted literally since the pace and scale of change across the country was uneven, and as Jennifer Hart has clearly pointed out, crime figures were not kept before 1857 and *'one cannot estimate at all accurately the amount of crime during this period'*. Reference to Howard Taylor, the author of *'Rationing crime: the political economy of criminal statistics since the 1850s'* confirms this statement for as he makes clear it was not until 1857 before there was a more comprehensive series of criminal statistics and even these, he explains, *'left much to be desired with anomalies between indictable crimes and offences known to the police'*.

For Cumberland and Westmorland, other than that reported, there is nothing to suggest that kind of turbulence described by Reith and others did actually exist to the same degree, and certainly nothing like the unrest experienced with their nearest neighbours Lancashire and Yorkshire. It would be true to say that there were reported instances of assaults on the Cumberland and Westmorland police during this period and especially so in the Whitehaven and Maryport areas, but it is clear from the court reports that drink was frequently instrumental in confrontations between policemen and members of the community, as several cases of assaults on police resulted from attempts to move drunks on, or where there had been some attempt to break up fights, and where not infrequently, one or other of the combatants turned on the policeman.

The aforementioned therefore gives a picture of the perhaps haphazard policing that was in place across the two counties and effectively protecting the lives and property of 195,492 people over this ten year span. Haphazard it may have been but nevertheless the various superintendents did show a considerable degree of professionalism, and the serious problems that they accounted over this decade were adequately handled, I believe, considering the small police presence.

The 'piece-meal' police forces of both Cumberland and Westmorland appear to have been relatively successful over this ten year term. However the introduction of the 1856 County and Borough Police Act brought about the need to appoint a Chief Constable who could offer both the experience and authority required to satisfactorily merge the two counties and establish one uniform, efficient, and professional police force.

It remained to be seen whether the 'new' force would prove superior to the 'old' ... and of course whether John Dunne was the man for the job. Of one thing we can sure however, that within the duration of Dunne's period as Chief Constable the conditions of many people in Cumberland and Westmorland would have greatly improved, with comforts and conveniences having been now put into place, improvements which of course had not even been thought of in the early 1850's. Though naturally we cannot thank Dunne specifically for that. However he and his men would certainly have had a lot to do with the fact that by the end of the century men were not stripping off their clothes and endeavouring to kick each other to death; dog fighting, cock-fighting, open gambling in public houses and houses of ill-repute though not entirely outlawed, were certainly far improved.

CHAPTER NINE

JOHN DUNNE

Cumberland and Westmorland

After years of this 'piece-meal' policing throughout the two counties of Cumberland and Westmorland, the first of January 1857 opened with the expectation of the dawn of a new police force for Cumberland and Westmorland, and as it happened the populace were not to be disappointed. Instead of small pockets of police in the major areas of Carlisle, Whitehaven, and Kendal, the public could now expect to see the newly formed county police forces actually policing over a far wider area, though with just an initial force of 74 men.

It is likely that the 1856 Police Committee really did believe at the time that appointing a total of seventy-four policemen would be a generous figure with which to police a population of 217,092 and a 'beat' exceeding forty square miles per constable, but nevertheless prior to 1857 there had been just 41 policemen to cover the same area, though they were assisted it is true with a few part-time parish constables, plus the occasional help of a number of felon societies scattered across two counties and of course they had being coping (partially anyway) with controlling some crime, reducing the number of vagrants, containing an epidemic, and dealing with continual Irish and navvy riots.

It was at the Carlisle Michaelmas Sessions of 1856 that the justices first received the report of the Police Committee on *'how the Police Acts may be best adapted to this county (Cumberland) and also to point out the number and descriptions of constables which it may be advisable to employ, and the salaries which they ought to receive'.* Their August report spelled out that following discussion with the police committee of Westmorland they would appoint the same Chief Constable for both counties at a salary of £300 per annum for Cumberland, and £150 per annum for Westmorland, *'to cover the whole of his travelling expenses, and that the county of Westmorland should not be called upon to pay more than a fourth of such salary and expenses'.* The same report specifically pointed out that the extra cost to the counties for combining the two forces amounted to just an extra one-third of a farthing in the pound (3000th of a £1) on the taxes, and the committee recommended the court to consider whether for the sake of saving so small a tax as this it was politic or just to maintain an invidious distinction between one part of the same county and another, especially so when no difference then existed in the rates for other purposes, for example, bridges and gaols. Their report outlined their estimates for a necessary police force, further stating that in their opinion the success of the new constabulary would benefit greatly from recruiting an experienced Chief Constable and thus action should be taken to recruit the best man for the job at the earliest date. To this end it was determined that to ensure a fair procedure acceptable to both counties the selection panel would be made up of three persons from Westmorland and six persons from Cumberland, any such selection being subject to the approval of the Courts of Quarter Sessions (September 1856).

For Allerdale above Derwent (in the event that the area was rated separately) it was agreed that the total police strength would be: 1 superintendent, 3 sergeants, 14 constables, (which would be made up of 7 first class constables, 6 second class constables, and 1 third class constable). For the rest of the county, Cumberland, which was made up of 29 sections or divisions, would be allocated a total of 31 constables (16 first class, 12 second class and 3 third class), plus 5 sergeants, 3 superintendents, and 1 shared Chief Constable. In the main just one unaccompanied constable was allocated to twenty-one of the sections, while the other areas, notably Penrith, Cockermouth, and Alston were allocated 2 constables and a sergeant.

The cost of the Chief Constable was shown as being shared equally throughout the whole area as £70 for Allerdale, £267.10.0 (£267.50) for Cumberland, and £112.10.0 (£112.50) for Westmorland.

The discussions with the Westmorland police to which the Cumberland committee referred had taken place in the October, after which the following was adopted at the Kendal Quarter Sessions on the 18th October 1856: that it would be in their best interests to link the two counties, and in deciding how the Police Act could be advantageously utilised it was resolved that they should appoint one Chief Constable to oversee the two counties. Finances again were considered important for it was further agreed that the costs of the salary for the new Chief Constable should not exceed £150 per annum for Westmorland. It is interesting to report that the committee in deciding such a salary actually got Dunne very much on the 'cheap' for the Home Secretary's guidelines on pay at this time were that Chief Constables should not be paid less than £250, or more than £500 per annum. Certainly no distinction was made when a Chief Constable headed two forces at the same time., as this situation was unprecedented. He was in fact the only Chief Constable during the creation of the numerous police forces in England and Wales that sprung up during the early years of Victoria's reign to establish with marked success two entirely separate autonomous constabularies in the same locality in an age when individual police systems and non-cooperation was normal.

The total cost of policing for Westmorland was agreed at £903.12.0 (£903.60p) per annum, plus the share of the Chief Constables salary at £112 per annum. Uniform cost was agreed at £6 each, with an extra £80 being allowed for horses for the two inspectors.

However what was particularly noticeable was like Cumberland the committee had not given adequate thought to the total areas each constable was required to patrol, and would be something that was to give the new Chief Constable considerable concern in the near future.

Back in Cumberland at the Carlisle Epiphany Sessions held on the first of January; following the reports of the joint Westmorland and Cumberland Police Committees, the justices unanimously decided that one John Dunne previously Chief Constable of Newcastle, should be appointed Chief Constable of Cumberland and Westmorland. A similar decision was made on the 9th January in Kendal when the justices resolved *'that this court approves of the election of Mr John Dunne as Chief Constable of the counties of Westmorland and Cumberland'.* The respective police committee would have felt that they had made an excellent choice, for not only was Dunne a highly experienced police officer with eighteen years policing, twelve of them at senior level, but he was unusual on two counts.

One, that he was a career police officer who had worked his way up through the ranks, but just as importantly at this time, he came from an upper-class background, rather than a military one ... well that was what was stated on his CV – we of course know a little differently. It was certainly unusual that he didn't stem from a military background as so many Chief Constables did, in fact we learn from Carolyn Steedman in her book *Policing the Victorian Community, the formation of English provincial polices 1856-1880* that in the majority of cases military experience was a pre-requisite for nineteenth century Chief Constables. David Wall writing in *The Chief Constables of England and Wales: The socio-legal history of a criminal justice elite* confirms this by stating that some 92.2% of Chief Constables had undergone military service, with most of them holding senior rank, i.e. Major, Lt. Colonel, and in a number of instances as high as Admiral as we learnt from McHardy the Chief Constable of Essex. As Carolyn Steedman further points out: *'very few men with experience of British policing were recruited into this rank in mid-Victorian years, in fact if anything there was an increase in the number of men with rural gentry backgrounds serving as county Chief Constables.'* A good example of this would be the fact that out of a total of 24 Chief Constables appointed nationwide between 1856 to 1880, twenty-two of them came from a military background which included eleven being shown as gentry.

William Chadwick, the one time Chief Constable of Stalybridge, Cheshire who besides having had 37 years experience, was but one of a small number of officers who had come up 'through the ranks' writes in his Reminiscences of a Chief Constable that:

> *'In the appointment of Chief Constables, influence appears to be a greater factor than merit. It is a question of having friends in court. In the English counties more than three-fourths of the Chief Constableships are held by 'outsiders' of the military class; while the English cities and boroughs favour the civil element in the proportion of eight to one, and in that proportion place practical ability before social standing in their appointing their Chief Constables' ... 'this state of matters raises a suspicion that in the counties the selection of gentlemen of social standing as Chief Constables to the disparagement of able men who have been trained to the work, is made for the benefit of certain classes, rather than in the interest of police efficiency. Those Chief Constables who have served their apprenticeship in the ranks, and gained their proud position by merit and ability, are better able to efficiently discharge the responsible duties of the office than those who have their duties to learn after appointment. The experienced Chief is naturally in close sympathy with his men, understands the difficulties and temptations they have to contend with from personal experience, and is able to point out the numerous pitfalls and stumbling blocks that surround the constable on his beat. He will also have an extensive knowledge of the criminal classes and their habits'.*

Dunne of course would have been only too aware of this situation but nevertheless was able to satisfy the Cumberland and Westmorland Selection Committee on both points ... landed gentry and policing background though with the former this was only with the help of a little subterfuge – better known as outright lying!

Presumably the panel of the Selection Committee were well aware of his experience and for that matter the excellent work he had done in re-organising both the Norwich and Newcastle police forces previously, for when they came to sift though the 123 applications, one glance at the name John Dunne brought a unanimous call for his instant appointment. No shortlist was ever drawn up, all the rest were placed on 'hold' pending his acceptance. Presumably they were unaware that Cumberland and Westmorland was not his only consideration, for he had also sent in his name as a candidate for Cornwall, Somerset, Devon,

Derbyshire, and Cheshire ... though clearly he decided that Cumberland and Westmorland was going to be his best option.

Thus at the beginning of January 1857 the then unmarried Dunne became Chief Constable at the previously agreed salary of £450 per annum, a sum incidentally which included all his travelling expenses, and a free hand to do what had to be done, thus making him the youngest Chief Constable in the country, at still age 31, as well as one of the most experienced. The average age of Chief Constables taking up such an appointment at this time was 39 and as far as experience was concerned he was now one of a small number in the country (5%) who had served as Chief Constable more than twice before.

The fact that his curriculum vitae declared that he came from 'landed gentry' would certainly too have been taken into consideration for as Carolyn Steedman succinctly points out *'it was easier to manage a man who shared the same social and governmental assumptions as the magistrates'* Little did they know!

So it was that the newly appointed Chief Constable began duty on the 26th January 1857. It was he that now had the task of setting the framework and standards for policing Cumberland and Westmorland. It is clear that Dunne wasted no time in settling down to business for the records show that on that first day of work he appointed the counties first constable, namely Robert Brown who had previously been serving with the Carlisle police. His warrant number was Number 1.

It is perhaps interesting to point out at this stage that until Dunne was appointed Chief Constable, Superintendent Sabbage (to whom I have earlier referred) was head of the Carlisle City police. However in the Liverpool Mercury newspaper report dated 7th January 1857, it was announced that the Newcastle -upon-Tyne Town Council had appointed a Mr Sabbage to be their new police superintendent of the Newcastle Borough Police force to replace Mr Dunne. Shortly afterwards Dunne appointed George E Bent to be Carlisle's new superintendent. One cannot help wondering how much influence Dunne had in Sabbage's move, and whether overall it was a somewhat political action to pave the way a little easier for him? Of course, Dunne could just have been repaying a favour, for as we are reminded by the earlier mentioned David Wall, it was common practice for candidates for Chief Constable to canvas support from members of the appointing body, usually by any means at their disposal. Who is not to say that Sabbage put in a good word for Dunne, if he would do the same for him in due course?

Dunne's first report to the Justices is dated the 4th April of that year from his new offices in Lowther Street, Carlisle, which he had selected as a suitable centre for his headquarters. It is obvious that Dunne did not consider that the Police Committees recommendations of strength for the new force was adequate for in this same report he suggested that the Cumberland force be raised to 75 and that Westmorland's numbers be raised from 14 to 20. He pointed out that the additional cost to each county (without any reduction for government grant) would increase from £4171 to £5110 for Cumberland and from £1068 to £1521 for Westmorland. These recommendations were approved, though not until a year later, with the extra costs involved accepted without argument.

His first moves were three-fold:

a) to survey the entire extensive area of the two counties in detail and determine what was required

b) produce a detailed handbook of the duties of the police of all ranks,

c) to advertise, interview, and select the first of the police constables for his new force.

Organised police, as explained, already existed in Carlisle, Kendal and Whitehaven, the first two of which would remain independent, though under his overall command, but Whitehaven not having the requisite civic status was subject for a 'take-over'. This did not turn out to be easy for the town's trustees fought tooth and nail and it was only after some dexterous application of his renowned charm (or should that be Irish blarney) that some level of initial operational liaison was eventually agreed upon. Within a short space of time Dunne's headquarters were established in Carlisle, the areas were split into divisions, in a manner as earlier determined by the Justices, necessary premises arranged, and firm contacts with local officials established. His strict codes of practice as outlined in his 'handbook for police' were implemented, and which as a safeguard also included the order *'no recruit shall apply for any other appointment or situation (non police employment) without the permission and sanction of Mr Dunne'.*

The initial number of constables, 31 for Cumberland, 14 for Westmorland, and 18 for Allerdale above Derwent were quickly recruited and immediately put through a training programme, though at this stage this amounted to little more than drill.

However, there was some theory too, for he laid great stress upon the importance of the police *'always giving their evidence in courts of justice in a fair and impartial manner without bias or prejudice. If they knew anything that may be favourable to the prisoner or defendant they were to state it candidly, and as readily as they would depose to anything they knew against him'.* He was of the belief that by following these simple rules, and by the 'faithful and fearless discharge of duty' the police would be in a different position from that the force had occupied prior to his appointment. It had taken him just two months to enrol and appoint his force, placing his men as approved by the Court of Quarter Sessions, which included re-appointing men whom he considered qualified and fit for service.

The position of the semi-independent police force of Whitehaven was clarified though not without a struggle, and perhaps understandably so when one realises that they had had a police force of their own since 1816. In fact by 1857 their police establishment actually consisted of one superintendent (George Goodman) one sergeant, and nine men with a police station at 19 King Street, where they also had a lock-up. In Peter Street close by they even had their own 'House of Correction' where delinquents were confined for up to fourteen days.

The Trustees who administered the Town were naturally desirous that their force under the new act should be maintained out of the general rates of the county, but Mr Dunne apparently leant to the view that the town could be formed into a separate police district under the Acts of 1840. Whitehaven in his judgement already had the proportions of the county constabulary it paid for and the eight constables who were the responsibility of the Trustees ought to remain as so many of their duties were solely in connection with the work of the harbour.

CHAPTER TEN

JOHN DUNNE

Cumberland and Westmorland
How the New Force was Recruited, Organised and Retained

It was, as previously stated, to take Dunne until March before he was ready to begin work in earnest. Strict discipline was imposed from the beginning and was something that he rigidly maintained throughout his service. Any flaunting of the rules brought swift retribution.

On the other hand his letter-book for this early period clearly shows that he would support any man who was in difficulties not of his own making. In addition, Dunne was obviously of the opinion that every man had the potential of achieving higher rank for his handbook clearly states that: *'all policemen would have the opportunity of promotion'*. However his philosophy was obviously at odds with the thoughts of some other Chief Constables for we learn from Carolyn Steedman that from the forces she researched, namely Buckinghamshire and Staffordshire, *'when a new police force was created a hierarchy had to be appointed, but after the formative period no man joined at any higher level that that of a third class constable'*. She went on to explain that in the English police forces, an officer would be the majority of inspectors and certainly all superintendents. In their case they were appointed, not promoted from the ranks. This officer class, she wrote, was composed of *'long-term men, a permanent contrast to the fluctuating lower ranks'*.

Dunne also showed concern as to the ability of his existing force to patrol satisfactorily the wide extent of the counties to be covered. In his opinion supervision was regarded as being insufficient and the area of the beat with each constable too large to permit of a systematic arrangement of patrol. This would certainly have been something he would have learnt in his early policing days under McHardy in Essex. With such a wide area to cover, the beat of each of his men was naturally of particular concern.

His initial force for the whole of both Cumberland and Westmorland shortly after his appointment amounted to just 74 men, and the total area to patrol covered 1,502,179 acres. The population at the time would have been 205,276 for Cumberland and 64,191 for Westmorland meaning that effectively each of these seventy-four policemen were expected to patrol an area of 20,299 acres each a seemingly impossible task. I think it can be safely assumed that all candidates at this time were not told of this little statistic!

In fact by comparing the figures prepared by Carolyn Steedman for Cheshire and Leicestershire police we learn that their effective police coverage was one policeman per 3028 acres for Cheshire, with Leicestershire one for 5371 acres. Interestingly the ratio in terms of police to population fares better for Cumberland and Westmorland, as this equates to one policeman per 3641 people. Cheshire for the same period is 3028, whilst Leicestershire's is an amazing 5371. Thus it was no surprise to learn that by the end of his first year Dunne had further persuaded the justices to allow the strength of his force to be increased to 104. Which probably indicates yet another strong case for the Irish blarney. However if we compare the median ratio for the whole country (from statistics returned annually to the Home Office) we learn that in 1857 there was one policeman to 1446 persons with a beat of 4360 acres, indicating that Cumberland and Westmorland were struggling even with an increased forces by the end of the year.

Dunne insisted that the qualifications necessary for service in the new police force amongst other things, included high character, physical power, great energy, and intelligence. In his opinion a country policeman would be called upon to judge and act for himself far more so than if he was in a highly populated town. He compared their responsibility as being equivalent to that of a sergeant in an urban community, though on a much lower salary.

Backing up Dunne's recommendations is the book *'The Register and description of Persons appointed'* covering the register of all policemen appointed for Cumberland and Westmorland during the period 1857 to 1865 and which makes for interesting reading. Besides requesting the name and date of birth of each applicant it also requested such information as trade, whether the applicant could read and write, and whether he had any previous public service or military background, and if so the length of such service. Finally the register asked, did the applicant have any police experience, along with the all important question, do you belong to an Orange Lodge or secret society? The continuous troubles with the Irish were obviously seen as an ongoing concern ... and secret society? One cannot see too many applicants answering 'yes' to that question. It is particularly noticeable that amongst the first of the twenty-four candidates accepted into the new police force 23 of them had previous police experience (one of whom had been a one-time superintendent with the Metropolitan Police) whereas only one is listed as a labourer. Overall in that first year 144 men were recruited from a variety of trades and professions, and which after taking into account those with previous police experience, the remaining recruits left were: 26 labourers, 5 shoemakers, 2 clerks, and 3 farmers, with the rest made up of a 194 variety of trades, namely; servants, butchers, carpenters, soldiers, saddlers, and surprisingly one schoolmaster, not overlooking the one listed as a 'gentleman' though these latter two lasted less than one year.

In order to appreciate the scale of Dunne's recruitment programme in 1857 it would be useful to compare his efforts with recruitment for a similar rural county, namely Buckinghamshire, Carolyn Steedman who as we have learnt has done considerable research in this area of early policing informs us that in her investigation it was labourers and farmers who showed the highest recruitment numbers totalling 56 or 33%, and with just two recruited who had previous police experience, which shows a considerable difference to Cumberland and Westmorland recruitment figures. Additionally we see similar comparisons when looking at Staffordshire recruitment figures, for here we learn that 35 labourers were amongst the earliest recruits with just three previously employed policemen.

Cumberland and Westmorland recruits were primarily home-based, (65% overall for that first year) though there were a fair scattering of recruits from Durham, Northumberland, Ireland and Scotland, and of course the previously mentioned from London. Interestingly no recruits from Newcastle where Dunne had previously been Chief Constable.

All Dunne's recruits were issued with a 125 page booklet entitled *'General Instructions for all ranks'*, which had been written by Dunne (though it showed close comparison to that originally produced for the Kendal Police) and besides giving a clear picture of their duties, whether superintendent, inspector, sergeant, or constable, (unusually it was to be some years before a deputy Chief Constable was appointed) also outlined their rates of pay, conditions of service, their authority, or power. In the introduction he wrote that the booklet was not to be understood as containing rules of conduct applicable to every circumstance, something must be left to the intelligence and discretion of individuals. And later he writes that *'according to the degree in which they show themselves possessed of these qualities, will be their claim to future promotion and reward'.*

He wrote that he expected his 'officers' (first time the word used for all ranks) to display initiative and common sense, and that the principal object to be obtained is the prevention of crime and *'to this great end every effort of the police force must be directed'*...along with *' when in any division offences are frequently committed there must be no reason to suspect that the police is not, in that division, properly conducted'.*

A further chapter headed 'Conditions of Service' states *'that each constable shall carefully abstain from the expression of political and religious opinions, in any way calculated to give offence '*. And also when on the beat, police officers were advised to *'not shoulder past respectable persons'*, and *'not to walk two or three abreast so as to obstruct passengers'*. He further stated that at all times a police officer was required to look clean and smart and if married his family had to be respectably maintained. And finally *'it is important that police officers should not form any objectionable connections. Constables,therefore, may not marry without the approval of the Chief Constable'.*

Of particular note is the section relating to cruelty to animals along with a leaflet from the relatively newly formed RSPCA, (1837) fully explaining the care all policemen should take when in contact with animals., which with the swine fever epidemic to come in just eight years time was going to prove vitally important. Turn over for those first few years was high, either because of the long hours or perhaps Dunne's insistence on strong discipline. In the majority of cases dismissal was down to drunkenness. By the end of 1857 out of the 104 men initially recruited 50% were dismissed for a variety of reasons. The years 1858, and 1859 faired little better for out of the 39 recruited in 1858, 19 were dismissed, and in 1859 out of 32 recruited 16 were dismissed. It took until 1860 before there was an apparent settling down, for only 3 were dismissed that year (out of a total of 34 recruited).

The worst year was 1865 (coincidentally the same year that Dunne was considering leaving) when 17 were dismissed and only 14 recruited. The dismissals overall were made up of many who were 'allowed to resign', though there were a number of instances of policemen being transferred to other stations. There was no system of appeal against the Chief Constables decision to fine, dismiss, or order removal – unlike today, where an officer could find him/herself suspended from duty on full pay for an indefinite period.

Note: 'allowed to resign' is more likely than not to be a euphemism for dismissal. Being 'allowed to resign' generally meant that a policeman could legally seek employment in another county force should he wish. Being dismissed simply meant that future employment in the counties was totally barred to him. 'Allowed to resign' meant that as with dismissal, a police authority was dissatisfied with a man. Though there were high numbers of policemen resigning in the Cumberland and Westmorland forces (or perhaps more accurately 'allowed to resign') in their first year of service, an average of 47% each year over a ten year period, actual dismissal is higher with an average of 51%. The figures for those dismissed with one or two years of service showed a marked increase to 56%

over the same ten year period, with those dismissed reducing to 41%. Length of service in Buckinghamshire, as declared by Carolyn Steedman, also bears comparison with Cumberland and Westmorland. For example in their first year in 1857, 47% of the one hundred and two newly appointed constables left. By the second year it was 15% of the intake and for the third year it was down to 13%. These figures showed a decrease of 7% for under one year recruits, and an increase of 6% for two to five years of service over the next ten years.

Complaints against the police for a variety of offences which warranted punishment in one form or another in Cumberland and Westmorland varied between 17 in 1860 to as many as 43 in 1863. It was still as many as 34 in 1865. Punishments normally consisted of a reduction in pay, though there are various instances of reduction in ranks, inspectors to sergeants, sergeants to constables, being a good example. Amongst some of Dunne's early recommendations included the creation of an intermediate grade between that of constable and sergeant consisting of a merit class when 25 men were distinguished by the wearing of an honorary badge plus receiving a salary increase to 21/- weekly (£1.10).

The first uniform as approved by Dunne consisted of one frock coat (with badge), one great coat (with badge), two pairs of trousers, one hat, cape, and stock, one lantern, one truncheon, one pair of hand-bolts, one belt and cape strap, and a small knapsack to contain a change of linen when employed away from home on special duty. Their uniform, Dunne decided, would be dark blue in colour, probably due to it being the same colour as the Metropolitan Police. There was also an allocation of a cutlass to all ranks, for use *'as and when necessary'*.

Salary in the initial stages was £175.0.0 per annum for a superintendent, 26/- a week for inspectors (£67.60 per annum), and 23/- a week (£1.15) for sergeants. Constables, dependant on whether they were First Class, Second Class, or Third Class, ranged from 20/- (£1.00) down to 17/- (85p).

Salaries for all were subject to a deduction of 2.5% for the obligatory superannuation scheme. All ranks further received 2/6d per week (12.5p) boot allowance. There is too a clear indication that subject to satisfactory work they could all expect an increase in their salaries after six to twelve months, three years, and again after seven years. These salaries bear some comparison with the national median figures for counties listed by Steedman. First year constables joining as third class constables enjoyed 18/- a week (80p) increasing to 20/- (£1.00) for first class constables. Sergeants are shown as having a pay scale of £1.2s.6d (£1.12) to 25/- (£1.25) per week dependant on whether they were third, second or first class, and similarly inspectors too show a variation of

£75.0.0 to £100.0.0 per annum, again dependant on first, second or third class.

These figures not only indicate that Dunne was keeping salaries a little below the national guidelines in the main, but more importantly he disapproved of placing sergeants and inspectors (and superintendents too for that matter) within a first to third class range, leaving this distinction solely for constables. Under the provisions of the Constabulary Acts, a superannuation fund was established *'for old and deserving officers'*. The fund would be supported by certain fines or portions of fines in cases where policemen were informants, and those inflicted on members of the force for misconduct, together with the aforementioned 2.5% from the pay of each member of the force.

Note: The term 'officer' is the first time that Dunne has used it in respect of all policemen. At this time it was common practice nationally to name only Inspectors and Superintendents as officers. As most of these recruits would have associated the term 'officer' generally as a senior military rank, the effect on these men to be similarly termed would have been enormous. Overall 1857 proved to be a busy year for Dunne, though one cannot say that it had not been successful in many ways. After a year of policing, initially with an untested and untrained force, current research indicates that by and large his forces had been relatively successful. Against a back-drop of ongoing resignations and dismissals of many of his men, he nevertheless managed to organise satisfactorily various police divisions across the two counties in a manner which had not been possible with his predecessors. It certainly appeared that Cumberland and Westmorland police committees were right in their selection of John Dunne as the joint county's first Chief Constable.

CHAPTER ELEVEN

JOHN DUNNE

Cumberland and Westmorland
Nature and Duties of the New Rural Police for the First 10 Years

John Dunne must have wondered exactly what type of people he had come to police in 1857, for there is a report in *The Times* dated 19th February 1857 just days after taking up his duties, of a blacksmith James Smith reporting to Halifax police that he had murdered the governor of Carlisle City Gaol. When asked what he had to say to the Halifax magistrates, after the superintendent of police had acquainted the bench with the facts of the case of course, the prisoner denied everything he had said a few days earlier. Under these circumstances and as the communications received from the police in Carlisle contained no information confirming the prisoner's original statement, the magistrates discharged him ordering him to pay expenses.

As it happened Dunne had to wait until 1858 before the first murder arrest in his counties, though he did inherit nine homicide cases within the first three months of taking up his post. It would be fair to say that Dunne started his career with the Cumberland and Westmorland police with some degree of disadvantage compared to many other constabularies. In his first report that Dunne submitted to the Justices in March 1857 (along with his quarterly report) he submitted details of the strength of his currently allotted police, linked to the population of his two counties, and compared them with that of twelve other constabularies.

As he was at pains to explain, the average number of policemen to population in these other forces was shown as one policeman to 1326 population and the area to be policed averaged out at 5.31 square miles per constable. However as his report made clear he had been allotted just 74 policemen for his two counties which together had a population of 217,092, and thus in comparison each of his officers needed to cover not only forty square miles each but could only offer a policing service of one policeman per 3000 people ... a seemingly impossible task. It is interesting to note however that in the report of the Police Committee to the Cumberland Michaelmas Sessions of 1856, besides determining the need for a Chief Constable, mention is also made of requiring in addition eighty constables or one constable per 1875 head of population. The Chairman (Edward

William Hasell) was obviously out by miles (literally). Such statements of Dunne are backed up by Carolyn Steedman for she reports that in Cheshire there was one policeman for 1835 of population with each servicing an area of 3028 acres. For Leicestershire she declares one policeman per 1783 head of population covering individually an area of 5371 acres. She goes on to point out: *'Should a constable have walked without stopping, and never having returned to his cottage or headquarters, he could not cover such an area, even in a working day of twelve hours, in which he could have been expected to walk at least twelve to sixteen miles'.* Which certainly proved that Dunne had a point. However in fairness, as she points out, he was not meant to. The rural policeman's beat was a well defined route that took in the farms, factories, shops and offices of his division. He kept to the road, not just because that meant faster walking, but because the Night Poaching Prevention Act of 1862 (25 & 26 Vict c.114) (in which Dunne would have had a hand) rendered his position of it untenable after that date.

In fact Dunne, or more accurately, his constables, were to have personal experience of the dangers of night poaching with a murder case in 1862 of a father and son who had, whilst salmon poaching, killed a river-watcher (or river-bailiff), the victim was Edward Atkinson. As Clive Emsley reminds us in his quaintly entitled article *'The Thump of Wood on a Swede Turnip'*, on his beat the policeman was on his own, and thus he had of necessity considerable discretion as to how he acted, how he interpreted the actions of others, and quite frankly, how he personally used the law. The policeman in Emsley's opinion, could employ a degree of violence on his beat to obviate the need for tiresome court appearances, though I can neither confirm or deny that such instances were part of the Cumberland and Westmorland policeman's modus operandi. Certainly the duties of the rural police in such districts differed much from the routine in many of the large towns, they being of a more comprehensive nature, thus each constable, not being under the eye of a superior, was left far more to his own discretion, and in consequence far greater responsibility was attached to him, something that was clearly obvious to Dunne. Hence the necessity of strict discipline, and the difficulty of always attaining the requisite degree of proficiency and sufficient numbers in a dispersed force. Not to be overlooked was the fact that besides the ordinary policing duties of constables, which more than anything else was the apprehension of criminals, rural policeman were also expected to serve summons, warn coroners of impending cases, summon jurors, convey prisoners to gaol, and generally act as peace officers. Nothing new their then for Dunne. Certainly as far as Cumberland and Westmorland were concerned many of Dunne's men were also expected to act as Inspector of Nuisances, which meant amongst their other duties, was also the tedious inspection of low lodging houses. As if this in itself was not enough they were further expected to act as Assistant Relieving Officers for casual vagrants.

The constables also had charge of the numerous lock-ups as well as the custody of prisoners temporarily confined in them. It was indeed fortunate that these specific duties were clearly outlined in Dunne's *'General Orders and Circulars'* along with instructions on how to deal with police assaults, something which Dunne clearly anticipated, though as it happened without too much fear. Assaults on police, if we are to believe Robert Storch (the author of *The Plague of Blue Locusts*) and others to whom I shall refer, that one would expect the policeman on his beat in the mid-Victorian era to have found this a regular occurrence, but in fact from the evidence I have gained so far from Chief Constables reports and the newspapers for Cumberland and Westmorland, this could not have been further from the truth. For example newspaper reports of 1857 record just nine assaults on the police and eight of them were by individuals under the influence of drink. Amazing when you consider this is the first year of the new force. Figures for 1858 were even better, with just five assaults reported for the year. In fact we learn from Dunne himself from his Criminal Returns for 1857-1870 that overall for the period there were just twenty-three assaults on the police for the entire fourteen year period, which certainly backs up the newspaper reports.

However such figures differ greatly from the findings of Robert Storch where he has argued that assaults on the new police in the northern industrial towns in the 1840s and 1850s were frequent and fierce. Nevertheless by comparing Robert Storch with Clive Emsley's report on the Bedfordshire police we learn that in the first quarter alone following the formation of the police in 1857, Bedford courts heard just five indictments for assaults on police, clearly indicating that in this area of the north-west such crimes were very much in the minority. Still we do learn of isolated cases in York especially where the police were regularly and violently assaulted by the police. Considering the large influx of Irish navvies during this period into Cumberland it is somewhat surprising that Dunne has not been reporting similar assaults on his men. Nevertheless as Emsley states: *'only isolated incidents of police violence were reported in the newspapers, and those few that did were predicable complaints from those of a liberal or radical turn of mind'*, which may well explain the anomaly.

It is interesting to learn just how different the criminal returns were in Cumberland and Westmorland in respect of assaults on police especially when one learns from Emsley that assaults on authority nationwide actually formed a significant percentage of early and middle nineteenth century assaults overall constituting about 15% of summary prosecutions in the 1860s alone. Overall this equated to a prosecution rate of roughly sixty-six per thousand.

With such low evidence of assaults on police in Cumberland and Westmoreland it is pleasing to note that for this same period the aforementioned David Wall was able to report a different picture, for he states that from his research he was clearly able to show that nationwide the police actually became more popular, and this was because the public saw them as that of a public protector.

Because of their involvement in the various emergency services, along with responsibilities for weights and measures, bridges, etc, they became an all purpose service upon which the public could rely. No reports of assaults on police during this time would be complete without reference to the historian Robert Storch as he shows comparative figures using a total of ten selected police districts, namely a mixture of rural and urban as his examples. This shows that over the same ten year period the highest period for assaults (0.700 per thousand of population) was shortly after the police came into power in 1858, with a low point (0.575) in 1861. By 1866 this had evened out to around 0.650. Both counties in Storch's report when declared separately showed substantial increases in assaults over this period, though Storch's analysis for ten districts actually shows a decrease, nevertheless what these figures and other do clearly show, is that in Dunne's counties, the opposite is in fact the case.

Dunne on taking office in the January had declared that *'crime detection should be the main objective of his men, rather than protection'*, thus an indication of the success of his new force over a short period would be appropriate. As far as the most heinous crimes are concerned, for the first ten years of the force Cumberland and Westmorland were faced with a total of seventeen homicides, which bar one exception were not theft motivated, and amongst which were some which in later years Dunne would record as being the most memorable. Though I would imagine that the Robert Irwin murder in the first year of his incumbency stayed in his memory for many a long year. In the years 1860 and 1861 alone Dunne's forces had five cases of murder to investigate, which comparing that with the 1860 figures of 141 instances of homicides nationally boded ill for the two counties. In fact nationwide, actual homicide figures in 1860 were 1.7 per 100,000.

Nevertheless regardless of that which he and his men would personally investigate over the coming years, it was nothing in comparison to those which he inherited, for as we learn from the *Cumberland Pacquet* for the 3rd March 1857 there were nine prisoners standing before the justices in March 1857 all on a charge of homicide. The first serious crime for the Chief Constable and his team concerned the death of an eighty-five year old retired farmer by the name of Robert Irwin, who had been found dead on Christmas Day 1857.

This case was to prove a test run for the many murder cases which were to appear before the justices over the coming years. For example the 1859 murder of Jane Usher by her husband Will Usher was to prove a turning point. Though Usher only received a sentence of fifteen months hard labour he was indeed guilty, though the jury pressed hard for a reduced sentence on the basis of the years of suffering experienced by Will due to his wife's heavy drinking. Nevertheless the verdict, and the well presented evidence submitted by the police, did proclaim that the police had put together a strong case for the prosecution.

Over the coming years, as we will see, Dunne attended and dealt with many serious crimes over his 45 year career with the Cumberland and Westmorland Constabulary, but without doubt the two most important criminal cases that he was to deal with over this time were within the first four years of taking up his appointment: namely the Ann Sewell murder of 1860, and the Charlton trial of 1861 The Ann Sewell murder was a case where both Dunne and his men could feel immensely proud of themselves, for not only did this case also receive nationwide publicity, but it was one in which the police (and Dunne in particular) had a strong hand in proving the case, and certainly confirmed Dunne's statement that the police's first duty was the 'detection of crime'. Ann Sewell was found in an Embleton farmhouse with her throat cut. A knife was in her hand and the police (initially) backed by medical opinion put it down to suicide. *"No"*, said Dunne, when visiting the crime scene *"knife in that hand could not have inflicted the wound"*. Later George Cass, the accused, was subsequently convicted of her murder. The Sewell crime was the fledgling force's first great murder mystery and thus a test of its reputation. Dunne took an especial interest in this case with good result. The fact that Ann was right-handed, and the knife had been found in her left hand was a pretty clear indication that she had not taken her own life as the physicians had declared. From the start Dunne felt that Cass was the guilty party and had kept the man under close surveillance for some two weeks after he discovered that the farmhouse door where Ann had been found could be locked from the outside as well as opened by means of a piece of iron used by Cass whenever he was late home. In addition Cass was in possession of additional money for which he could not account, coincidentally an amount similar to that which had been stolen from Ann. Cass was publicly hanged on the 21st August 1860, the first man to be hanged in Cumberland for five years.

The Ann Sewell killing was one of the first cases in the country where the evidence of the Chief Constable was to prove damning and to some degree set a precedent. The second murder to which I have referred was different in that it was a first for the police force involving both murder and theft. The victim was seventy-two year old Jane Emmerson, a crossing gatekeeper. The murderer was eventually to be discovered to be 32 year old William Charlton who had killed her in order to steal money and other possessions which he believed to be hidden in the woman's cottage. This case was interesting insomuch that it was one of the first instances where on the instructions of Dunne a plaster cast was made of footprints at the scene of the crime, and which in turn had a devastating effect on the decision of the court when it was discovered they matched Charlton's footprints. The jury found Charlton guilty of wilful murder, and he was hanged for his crime on the south wall of Carlisle gaol before a crowd of several thousand.

Obviously murder was not Dunne's only concern over these early years. Infanticide, though rare in coming to court, did see two such cases in 1862 and 1863. Infanticide was all too common not just in Cumberland but throughout the country at this time, but it was rare for the authorities to obtain a conviction. One particular case was interesting because if nothing else it threw light on the many poverty-stricken young single women who had illegitimate children in Victorian Britain and what could happen when they simply could not afford to keep them. The case to which I refer was that of Catherine Simpson where we have a young girl whose father was receiving relief from the Penrith Union, and her mother was in the Dunston Lunatic Asylum, thus there was no parental assistance. In court she admitted that she had smothered the child, named John, in the February of 1862, and had then planned to commit suicide. The girl's plea to the court was mainly one of pity for her plight, though her defence made a case for 'unsound mind', which the jury obviously took into account for she was found not guilty on the grounds of insanity. What was interesting about this case was the fact that Catherine was indeed guilty and under the laws of the land should have been taking the steps to the gallows, but the jury recognising that she was but one of many such unfortunate women, and took pity on her.

There was certainly recent precedent for the gallows in cases of infanticide for only in recent months a certain Mary Reid had been hanged in Dumfries, as well as a Constance Wilson at Newgate. This case of infanticide was not the only case to come before the Carlisle judge's, for in the August of 1863 Jane Byers was to appear on the self same charge. Again the defendant admitted killing the child but stated it was an accident rather than deliberate murder. And once again the mother was lucky, for the jury having heard all the evidence took the easier option and found her guilty of the lesser charge of concealment of birth, and she was sentenced to just twelve months imprisonment with hard labour.

As we learn from the historian Clive Emsley, cases of infanticide appearing before the courts in this era were not only comparatively rare in Victorian Cumberland, but nationally too. Though homicide might be one of the best reported crimes, infanticide was notoriously under-reported and rarely came before the criminal courts. An assizes jury was often reluctant to return a verdict indicating culpability on the mother's part. Emsley goes on to say that a new-born child murder, often described as infanticide, was overwhelmingly a female crime. Throughout the period 1770-1900 the all male juries and judges were often more moderate in their treatment of an accused than a strict implementation which the law would allow.

In his book *Crime and Society in England* Emsley makes mention of the small number of prosecutions for rape at this time with the majority of such cases being settled out of court. In most cases, whether it be magistrates or juries, both commonly dismissed accusations of rape or attempted rape. Again Cumberland must have been unusual in not only hearing such a case at the Midsummer Quarter Sessions in 1858, but actually finding a prisoner guilty of the crime and sentencing the man to twelve month's hard labour.

According to Dunne's Analysis of Criminal Convictions for the period 1857-1866, we learn that overall for both the combined counties, the total of indictable offences amounted to 1730 (1421 for Cumberland, and 309 for Westmorland), jointly an average of 173 per annum. For criminal cases handled summarily the figures amounted to 21,750, jointly an average of 2175 per annum (Cumberland, 18,345, and Westmorland 3405). Separating the two counties for the purposes of statistics, we learn that over this ten year period indictable crime actually decreased by 29% for Cumberland and 39% for Westmorland. For cases heard summarily the opposite was true, namely Cumberland increased by 50% and Westmorland by 37% In comparing Cumberland and Westmorland's crime figures to those declared nationally, indictable offences in 1857 were shown as 90,000 and by 1867 were down to 83,000 equating to an 8% decrease in crime overall as against Dunne's declared decrease of 29% which indicates that either the Chief Constable was doing a far better job, or as Howard Taylor would have us believe, (in his article *Rationing Crime: the political economy of criminal statistics since the 1850's*) such statistics as were available for this period should be taken with *'a pinch of salt'*. Based on the evidence of newspapers, crime figures and Chief Constables reports for Cumberland and Westmorland over this period I would prefer the former as at the time the total number of forces in Britain averaged 220 this would have equated to an average of 409 crimes per force, per annum. Crime however was not only Dunne's only concern, especially during the years 1865/6 for it was the serious attack of cattle plague that was to take up a lot of police time.

Better known as Rinderpest, this is a contagious disease that principally affects cattle, but occasionally can affect sheep, goats and pigs, though as far as the 1865 outbreak was concerned only cattle were affected. In 1865, 50,000 cattle nationwide were slaughtered due to the disease. Since 1877 there has been no further outbreaks in Britain. We learn from the Chief Constables report of the 4th July 1866 that in Cumberland and Westmorland throughout the entire period of the plague a total of 7632 cattle had been destroyed on his orders. His report went on to say that in order to properly control the problem he had had to borrow from Lancashire a further thirty constables but only after he had been obliged to write personally to the Under-Secretary of State on the 3rd January of that year stating that he could not cope with the problem with his existing force. Regardless of the urgency he still had to wait a further three months before the request was honoured. Such was bureaucracy then, as now. (Note: The Chief Constable of Lancashire at this time was a Captain William P Elgee (1859-1868) who it is thought wasn't too happy with dealing with a Chief Constable who had come up through the ranks.) Coincidentally a further letter of Dunne's dated 3rd April 1866, as part of his quarterly reports to the Police Committee states: *'that the loan of these extra men had also assisted him greatly in reducing crime'*, for he had noticed a general absence of crime due to the suppression of vagrancy.

Prior to Dunne's appointment in the January of 1857, vagrancy had been high on the list of Cumberland's most senior policeman, the aforementioned Superintendent Sabbage, and this as we shall see was also an area which required ongoing policing, and which in Dunne's view formed a very serious part of his crime figures. His instructions and the actions of his men were to prove quite successful over this early period. For example in an article in *The Times* Dunne is shown drawing attention to the beneficial effects which had been produced by dealing rigorously with tramping vagrants. In 1866, upon his recommendation, the magistrates of Cumberland had agreed to give all tramping vagrants a months imprisonment when convicted of offences against the Vagrancy Act. The expediency of adopting this course apparently first commended itself to the magistrates after the cattle plague of 1865. The report goes on to state that when the Rinderpest prevailed in Cumberland the 'tramps' were rigorously dealt with, and the police deterred them as far as possible from coming into Cumberland.

The result was found to be a great reduction in crime, and at the suggestion of the Chief Constable the *'rigorous application of the law had been adopted during the whole of last year'*. The returns presented in 1867 by Dunne showed that the daily average number of vagrants in Cumberland was 122 (the previous year it had been 134) whilst in Westmorland this had dropped from 35 to 28. However that only gives an indication of the picture in 1866. In 1863 for example, in his reports to the Justices he showed daily averages amounting to a total of 331 covering both sexes and ages ranging from under sixteen to over sixty-five years. By 1864 this was reduced to a daily average of 312, and by 1865 to 298, thus his declared average of 122 by 1866 certainly showed a considerable improvement.

Over the years there is no question that Dunne and his men were successful with their policy of reducing the number of 'vagrants', which in turn also affected the annual crime figures. However it should be noted that the numbers of 'vagrants' arrested does not give a clear indication of the individuals background. Many could quite easily have been out of work craftsman, or soldiers returning from the wars. There would need to be far more research into this subject to clarify the true picture of the word 'vagrant' as it was applied in Dunne's days.

Throughout these early years there is clear evidence to prove that regardless of the ongoing problems of loss of policemen for varying reasons, the relatively high crime rates, together with the need of prevention, not overlooking the devastating years of 1865 and 1866, thanks to the Cattle Plague; the Cumberland and Westmorland Police were also expected to cover a multitude of additional services. Dunne certainly was concerned over the full extent of their duties, believing that many of these extra duties were to the detriment of their normal policing duties, namely law and order, and a letter to the Home Office of 1866 of his clearly shows this concern.

Dunne was not alone in these concerns for as we learn from Carolyn Steedman, between 1856 and 1880 forty of the 43 English administrative counties continuously used the county police forces to act as their inspector's of weights and measures along with collecting the county rate, survey roads, inspect bridges and survey market trading let alone acting as impounders of stray cattle. In addition we are reminded that 35 of these county forces were employing their police as assistant poor law relieving officers for periods lasting over ten years, and 33 counties used them as inspectors of common lodging houses, again for ten years or more. Inspectors of Nuisances were employed in just 9 of the counties. When one learns that the Cumberland and Westmorland Police were jointly involved in all of the aforementioned than one can well understand Dunne's concerns. No record has been kept of their fire-fighting duties, (though the newspapers of the time regularly report on their attendance) so we are aware that this would have been yet another normal duty at this time, and of course one must not overlook the time needed for the constables would have spent writing up their reports, without the aid of typewriters. (Remington didn't begin production of its first typewriter until 1873). Thus this first ten year span (1857-1867), based on a variety of policing aspects, clearly show that policing was not as Storch or Vorspan would have us believe i.e. one of continual assaults on police, or for that matter an ongoing fight with the working class over their social interests. In Dunne's case it was more a case of a fight against bureaucracy. Not exactly something he was unused to.

Policing under Dunne for this period needed to concentrate on normal everyday crime and disorder, with the accent on rural rather than urban activities, for example theft was predominantly associated with agriculture (as was the case too in Bedfordshire) and homicide with domestic problems, rather more than theft. Vagrancy, was certainly high on Dunne's agenda (as it was in Sabbage's day) but then so was cattle fever when it reared its ugly head in 1865/6. As to be expected policing in a rural district had considerable difference between it and an urban society. In the first instance it could be said that more responsibility was attached to a rural policeman as he didn't immediately have the advantage of a superior on his doorstep, as well as often being left to make a decision based on his own discretion. It could perhaps be said that policing in a large urban area could be considered far more dangerous, but to that one could respond that walking a beat in pitch darkness in an area where poaching was particularly relevant could be equally as dangerous, as Dunne had proven on more than one occasion; in fact the Chief Constable reported in 1871 that during the period 1862-1871 there had been 953 cases of offences under the Salmon Fisheries Act, 1861, including assaults on a number of bailiffs on the Wye, Eden, and Derwent who had been shot, or murdered between 1860 and 1861.

Overall for this first ten year period Dunne's biggest problem was his lack of staff compared to many other forces, and which is borne out by the need to borrow men from a neighbouring force during the cattle plague. By 1866 Dunne had managed to increase his meagre force of 74 to 106 which at least meant he could now ensure one policeman per 2542 head of population, not a massive increase when compared with some other forces, but was certainly an improvement on his earlier figures. However, with such a small force, it would be difficult to argue that the Cumberland and Westmorland police force had not been relatively successful in their first ten years of operation.

CHAPTER TWELVE

JOHN DUNNE

1857- Not all plain sailing

Notwithstanding the fact that Dunne had the unenviable task of setting up, not one, but two new police forces entirely from scratch, and which was clearly not only totally inadequate for the two counties and the numbers of population, but all the time he was undergoing vitriolic 'barbs' from certain members of the community, and one newspaper (the *Cumberland Pacquet*) in particular. I suppose in retrospect he could consider himself lucky that he had to wait until early April of 1857 before his first serious problems arose. And these came from the west coast – Whitehaven.

As we are aware Whitehaven had until now enjoyed their own independent police force with a strength of eight men all clearly employed with the sole objective of protecting the interests of the Port's Board of Trustees i.e. the docks area, and the vast numbers of ships and the ongoing movement of their contents with protection of the town itself and its large populace clearly coming a very poor second in responsibility. Obviously this was not exactly a state of affairs that could continue under Dunne's new regime ... almost his first words upon taking office were the need for law and order,and the protection of people and property, thus Whitehaven's current priorities didn't exactly fall into that pattern, and something had to be done about it.

However such changes did not exactly come about in quite the way that he would have planned. The first inkling of problems to come stemmed from a meeting held by the Trustees of the Town and Harbour of Whitehaven when they declared in the April *'That notice be given to the Chief Constable of the County, and the Superintendent of Police of the district of Allerdale above Derwent of the intention of the Trustees to discontinue the eight additional police appointed by the said superintendent at the request of the Trustees and at present paid out of the Lamp and Paving Rate of the town of Whitehaven'.* However rather than dismiss their eight constables forthwith it was agreed *'that the question of interfering with the police arrangements be deferred until the Solicitor of the Trustees had communicated with the Home Secretary and obtained the opinion upon the propriety or legality of any change'.* After which the inevitable committee was then appointed to confer with Mr Dunne, Chief Constable, requesting the least inconvenient mode of carrying the above resolution into effect. Dunne did not 'rest on his laurels' in thinking about his reply for almost immediately he responded, both directly and through the *Cumberland Pacquet* newspaper, that he was convinced that their decision was invalid as the Trustees had not taken into account that the 1856 law actually allowed for the consolidation of both a borough and divisional police force, and thus that there was no need for any amalgamation of the two forces, as such an amalgamation automatically existed. In his reply on the 20th April he went on to say that:

> *'The police of Whitehaven are supported out of local rates and revenue and have been consolidated with the County Constabulary (since the outset) and have been entirely under the supervision and control of Mr Clarke, the county superintendent,therefore there was no separate police force at Whitehaven at the time of my appointment and consequently it was not necessary to give the notices prescribed and thus they are performing their duties strictly in keeping with the law'.*

Clearly this did not satisfy the Trustees for at their meeting on the 12th May, they agreed that *'A copy of the notices to be served upon Mr Dunne, Chief Constable, and Mr Clarke, Superintendent ... of the intention of the Trustees, to discontinue the eight policemen paid by the board'.* On the motion of Mr Clarke, seconded by Mr Poutson, it was adjudged and ordered to be signed. Dunne's reaction to this was simple, he put the borough of Whitehaven into a further separate police district of Cumberland, and set about appointing a totally new police force (which did not include the eight relinquished policemen).

Over the coming weeks, and with the assistance of the current superintendent he appointed one inspector (at 26/- per week) one sergeant (at 23/- per week) and a total of twelve constables at differing levels of experience. We later learn that as far as the original police constables were concerned their services now appeared to be superfluous for the Trustees in their wisdom had decided not to pay their wages NOT because they considered their services unnecessary for the preservation of order and protection of life and property, but solely with the view that they should be supported out of the general rates of the county. No doubt these same men were delighted when Dunne reappointed them. Still, by September 15th the editor of the *Cumberland Pacquet*, who clearly has been influenced by the Whitehaven Trustees is writing an editorial headed *'Our local police force'*, and with numerous instances of sarcasm. It read:

> *'For two to three months there has been a growing spirit of discontent in management of public affairs in town (Whitehaven) respecting the state of the police force. Two years ago the police were in the pay and solely under the*

control of the Trustees of the Town and Harbour ... There were no rural or county constabulary. Reasons show little public reason to be gratified with the change which has been in operation sufficient time to justify all the arguments and assertion that were urged against it. Formerly we had an efficient force in Whitehaven ... with the co-operation of the parochial constabulary its influence was felt throughout the entire district. Management was an efficient superintendent, who knew all that was needed to know about the area. (Mr Clarke) He knew the value of having a force composed of officers of experience like himself... he employed and dismissed men. In eight to ten years he got on well with superiors (the Trustees) He obtained men from other forces with plenty of applications on his books. The best of his men were Sergeant Wood and Acting Sergeant Douglas' ... The first change introduced was the formation of divisional police force each under the management of a Chief Constable. Allerdale Ward above Derwent was one of those with some twenty-five or twenty-six men including eight provided and paid for by the Trustees of the Town of Whitehaven. This, though a blow to the distinctive status of the town, did not in any material degree impair the efficiency of the force. Next came the passing of the County Constabulary Act which rendered it compulsory on counties to adopt its provisions for the establishment of a general force under a single Chief Constable. The magistrates agreed to combine for police purposes.(Cumberland and Westmorland)) but the circumstances attending the junction are somewhat foreign to our present subject'. 'Mr Dunne of Newcastle was selected from a number of applicants (no mention of large number of applicants) at a salary of £400 plus travelling and office expenses. That he is fully competent to receive the money is unquestionable and that he imagines himself a man of considerable importance is equally so if we may judge by the manner in which he has treated, or wished to treat, the Trustees of Whitehaven and the magistrates of the division...but we have serious doubts whether those who are anxious to have an efficient police force can fairly pronounce him to be the right man in the right place'. (certainly plenty of sarcasm there then) 'Of this appointment...his voluminous report to the first quarter sessions afterwards and his proceedings for the purpose of obtaining possession of the eight men employed by our Trustees we shall have occasion to speak at length in future articles. Defeated in his attempt against the Trustees, he in conjunction with his friends on the bench obtained the sanction of the Secretary of State for the formation of Whitehaven into a special district for rating, in order that we may be saddled with the maintenance of the men, whom the Trustees had discharged'.

We apprehend however that such an order would not be retrospective and therefore it is desirable to know who paid or who will have to pay the men from the time they were discharged by the Trustees till the issuing of the order from the Home Office ? But to come to a more important subject. With the appointment of Mr Dunne he was invested with the sole power of appointing and dismissing all the men in the police forces of the two counties. There is no court of appeal, Mr Dunne can coolly inform an efficient officer that he has no further need of his services and fill the vacancy by the appointment of a friend of his own whose only recommendation is a desire to pocket the remuneration.

We should be sorry to be forced to the conclusion that Mr Dunne would knowingly be guilty of conduct so improper in a public officer, but we have heard complaints made publicly within the last few weeks that he has been, and know from observation that some of the best and ablest officers have been dismissed or removed and their places filled up by men of neither experience or ability. A letter now before me states that there was recently a vacancy for a sergeant in Whitehaven. There was an experienced man also who for years had efficiently discharged the duties without the pay of a sergeant. Common sense would have said that such a man ought to have been promoted, but instead of that Mr Dunne sent a man who had never previously served in a police force. It is currently reported that the man was frequently guilty of flagrant breeches of duty, and yet two months did not elapse before Mr Dunne promoted the raw hand to an inspector-ship and filled his place by another stranger. We wonder whether the breeches of duty were reported to Mr Dunne, as if not, Mr Superintendent Clarke's was guilty of gross neglect ? If they were reported then Mr Dunne has been guilty of such a flagrant breech of duty as we should not like to characterize by a fitting term. These are subjects on which, notwithstanding frequent applicant to Mr Superintendent Clark and the magistrates here, we can obtain no information.. Mr Clarke, perhaps, as is duty bound declines positively to furnish any official information and refers us to Mr Dunne. Perhaps that gentleman can explain the circumstances connected with the above appointment. On the general state of our police which we believe to be both short-handed and generally inefficient, we shall have more to say bye and bye.'

Rather than reply to such an abusive letter Dunne chose to deal with the complaint his own way. This was by way of a parade of his men just five days later though by the way the parade was reported in the *Cumberland Pacquet,* clearly it didn't go down too well with the editor.

His report in the 22nd September edition went as follows:

> *'Inspection of the Police'. 'Tuesday last Magistrates of Whitehaven and neighbourhood were invited by Mr Dunne the Chief Constable of Cumberland and Westmorland Police to witness an inspection of the police force of the Whitehaven Special District. Ordered by Mr Dunne in consequence of certain complaints being alleged to have been made by the justices on the bench respecting the inefficiency of the force- the fact that some of them being kept without uniform an unreasonable time after their appointment, and to the effect that the Chief Constable rarely took the trouble to visit the district'. 'Mr Dunne at the same time took the occasion to allude to an article which had appeared in one of the newspapers (the Pacquet) on the state of the force and the shortcomings of the Chief Constable. Six magistrates were in attendance. The men, to number eighteen including Superintendent, Inspector and three sergeants were drawn up in the Town Hall Yard. A sergeant who had been in the army and had experience of drilling, and at one time was in the Newcastle police, was engaged in putting the men through their facings'. 'Drawn up in two lines the force appeared formidable, but it was questionable whether standing erect and clapping hands will make them more efficient in quieting disturbances among the drunk and disorderly characters of Strand Street, Mark Lane, and Quay Street, or enable them to make head against the bellicose fish wives in the Market Place. The sergeant then put them through a demonstration of drill.' Mr Dunne appeared and asked each man how long he had been in the force, the nature of their previous service etc. Supt. Clarke, Sergeant Wood and five men were all out of the sixteen constituting the Whitehaven force who had served under the Trustees. The rest were new men appointed by Mr Dunne and were strangers to the town and neighbourhood. Two of them had not been in the Police Force before . In reply to questions from Mr Dunne, Superintendent Clarke stated that Mr Dunne had asked him whether he could recommend Sergeant Wood for promotion to Inspector…he replied that he could not.. He did not think Wood competent. Dunne asked each man if he had any complaint, were wages paid OK and had he received his full uniform. As to be expected all answered in the affirmative. The men were subsequently dismissed and the magistrates adjourned indoors, having said they were happy with what they had seen and heard. Mr Dunne admitted that Whitehaven might have been as low as twelve men but never as low as ten. He apologised for not visiting Whitehaven more regularly, but insisted that Superintendents and Inspectors report more often and lay open their journals and documents before the magistrates. If they did not do so that was their fault not his. Some discussion*

about completion of forms and he said that not completing them was the fault of the Superintendent not his. Stated that he had had to dismiss Sergeant Agassiz, as he was regularly the worse for drink (In fact this sergeant had been promoted to Inspector on the 18th August and transferred to Penrith).

No doubt this article gave the editor of the *Cumberland Pacquet* a great deal of pleasure, but quite what it did for the police/public relationships is debatable!

By the end of the year we are reading of an ongoing argument between the Trustees and the police (and somewhat naturally John Dunne in particular) over the use of rooms for the police at the Whitehaven Town Hall, though no proposal was being made for any alternative premises. The Trustees stepped back rather rapidly when it was determined that if the police gave up the use of these rooms they would at the same time be unable to make use of the fire-fighting equipment which was stored there, and thus there would be no one, and no equipment available in the event of a fire ... Score: Dunne two, Trustees zero!

By the January of 1858 Dunne is still in the headlines, this time for his dismissal of Whitehaven's long-standing superintendent Mr Clarke. In fact Clarke himself tried to cover his tracks in the following letter printed at the time in the *Cumberland Pacquet*:

Letter from Joseph Clarke. Late Superintendent of Police, Town Hall, Whitehaven January 14th. 1858

Sir.

Your love of fair-play I feel assured will induce you to favour me with a small space in your columns in order to refute a charge made against me by Mr Dunne the Chief Constable, which charge is totally devoid of truth. In a letter which appeared in your last paper addressed by Mr Dunne to Mr Musgrave, the Secretary of the Trustees at this Port, I am charged with having neglected to communicate to Mr Musgrave in accordance with Mr Dunne's request, the consequences which might ensue if the police were deprived of certain apartments in the Town Hall. This charge I utterly deny and appeal to Mr Musgrave for confirmation of the statement I am about to make ... On receiving Mr Dunne's orders I waited upon Mr Musgrave and told him the message I had been deputed to deliver and which I had no doubt that gentleman will yet distinctly recollect. I am at a loss to comprehend why Mr Dunne should continue to exhibit so bad a feeling towards me, seeing that the end that he has so long and zealously laboured to obtain has at length been consummated. If however in pointing out my short-comings, whatever they may have been he will adhere to the truth, I am not afraid. But I shall be able to meet these charges in such a manner as will satisfy a reasonable public, but if he persevere in making accusations as that which I refute, and others which have gone before, I am determined not to have them showered upon me without exposure.

Clearly Dunne could not leave such a letter unanswered, and in the *Cumberland Pacquet* of 26th January 1858, though not without a certain degree of sarcasm from the editor for in a preamble to printing his letter they state: *'The readers of the Pacquet know of our opinion on the questions at issue between Mr Dunne and the Trustees and the late Superintendent of Police here, and we must say that the long story which in fairness we publish today at Mr Dunne's request does not materially alter that opinion'.* Dunne's letter in this newspaper reiterates all that has gone before, but with one addition. where the ex-Superintendent Clarke states *'baseless accusations which have gone before'.* Dunne responds:

Much has been said about the reference I made on a late occasion. To the dismissal of PC Taggart. I enclose you the correspondence in connection with this case, which will prove that my statements were perfectly correct, and I shall feel thankful if you will have the goodness to publish it, because this particular case was made the subject of comment in your paper dated the 29th December last With regard to the other circumstances mentioned, I can only say that the public books and documents will prove them to be true. I am held responsible for the internal organisation, economy and efficiency of the force and from first to last my sole and only object has been to do what I conceived to be absolutely necessary to have those points properly and effectively carried out and I must emphatically and conscientiously declare that in the discharge of these duties, I have never for a moment allowed myself to be influenced by any personal motives or private feelings whatsoever.

With many apologies for trespassing so much upon your time

Signed J Dunne

21st January 1858.

Ex-Superintendent Clarke, rather than be permanently removed from Whitehaven, chose to later accept the position of Inspector of Nuisances at a lower salary. In the July by way of 'sticking up two fingers' at Dunne, the Whitehaven Trustees made a presentation to Joseph Clarke of a purse containing £146.8s 6d (£146.42) clearly not an insignificant sum as today that would have been worth around £21,000!

By August 10th ex-Superintendent Clarke had gone on to be further promoted when he was also appointed Inspector of Cargoes for the Whitehaven Trust at an additional salary of £50 per annum. (This letter included extracts from letter book page 200, letter 487 and letter book page 261, letter 488 reference PC Taggart). And if Dunne thought that was the end of his troubles in Whitehaven, he was sadly mistaken, for just one week later the following article appeared in the same newspaper: *Cumberland Pacquet* February 9th 1858 Article headed '*Chief Constable*' again...

> *I perceive that Mr Dunne's trumpeter at Carlisle, if that official do not discharge the duties himself of so important a functionary, has been again lauding him in unmeasured terms as a disciplinarian. a man who is scrupulously careful as to keep all his pauper- clad underlings at their posts, and to exact from them a zealous and faithful discharge of their duties. I need not tell you that Mr Dunne aspires to be a marvellously great man and I witnessed in this locality a few weeks ago an instance of show-off which now and then manifests itself in men who are big with their own importance and have within their grasp a little brief authority. At the Brougham coursing meeting, where some of our county aristocracy and a large sprinkling of the squirearchy were congregated, there, as a matter of course, was Mr Dunne and from half a dozen to half a score of the county constabulary, not in the capacity of thief-takers but as so many liveried attendants on the great man. I will pass over the conduct of the county-paid police which in not a few instances to many of our honest grey-coated yeomanry was rude and uncivil in the extreme to inquire upon what authority the head of the force ..this rigid disciplinarian -durst presume to take, from their several allotted beats some half dozen or half score policemen to dangle at his heels at a public coursing meeting? I may possibly be told that they were present to prevent order and to keep back on the crowd, and if so I have merely to remark that the great over-paid has yet to learn some important parts of his duty. The police are not paid to attend coursing meetings nor has the head of any force any right whatsoever to withdraw them from their stations for purposes so palpably useless, save perhaps that of ministering to the empty vanity of their Chief. Letter of the 6th February signed by 'A Looker-on', at Knipe Scar, Shap.*

This time John Dunne, deigned to reply – possibly there was little he could say in his defence. And one week later on the 16th February yet another letter in the same newspaper. Headed ... '*The Costliness and Injustice of Red-tapism*'. And which complained that Superintendent Oakley (the replacement to Supt Clarke) is totally incapable of fulfilling the obligations of a Weights and Measures

Inspector when *'the perpetrators of so many robberies and serious crimes that have taken place in this town and neighbourhood have not yet been found out'*. It went on to say that:

> *Nothing was being done by the police ... order and regularity out of question ... disorderly state of police.*

And if just one letter was not enough, on another page was one headed *Chief Constable Dunne and his acute staff'*. It read:

> *It affords me great pleasure (says a correspondent in Keswick) to add another to the several proofs which from time to time have appeared in your columns of the deep penetration of the Chief Constable, and of the acuteness of the men he selects to parade the streets of this and of other towns in West Cumberland. A tale I am about to narrate presents the public with such a specimen of gross stupidity as will satisfy the rate-payers of West Cumberland of Mr Dunne's unfitness to select men of even such common capacity and observation as might be supposed competent, to fit them for the post of police constables. Be this as it may, and let the public by whom he is paid place ever so small an estimate upon his merits, one thing is evident, to wit, that he has had no moderate opinion of himself, in short he seems so completely absorbed in himself that public sentiment cannot by any possibility displace the manifestly high opinion he entertains of No.1.and therefore let what will betide the Chief Constable as perfectly at ease and happy. Let me however proceed with my tale. An accident occurred here last week which rendered the services of the county coroner necessary, and one of Mr Dunne's staff at this place, whose name he shall himself by and make known to your readers, was despatched to Whitehaven to appraise the official of what had taken place. In order to perform his journey he bestrode a prime chestnut roadster belonging to one of our inn-keepers, with 'switch-tail' and a 'white star' on its forehead, points one might have thought sufficiently conspicuous to have awakened the attention of even of an official of Chief Constable Dunne's choice, after an acquaintance over a journey of no less than twenty-seven miles. The chestnut and its rider reached Whitehaven in safety and the Pack Horse Inn in Lowther Street was selected as quarters for the night. So far all was right, but the morrow brought with it divers troubles to the journeyman constable... In the morning he arose a new man refreshed with a nights repose and the good things of the Inn, and being as he represented himself, 'quite at home' among horses, he volunteered to saddle his own kit and was accordingly permitted to discharge the duties of ostler. This done, he forthwith mounted the horse of his choice and set off for Keswick. All went well, as I have been*

informed, their arrival at Cockermouth, but here a discovery was made by the stable boy who attended to the chestnut on its way to Whitehaven the previous day; and after putting sundry questions to the rider; where he had 'swopped' horses, what 'boot' he had received, particularlizing the points of the two animals, descounting on the star-faced, switch-tailed chestnut and the dark bay 'cut- tailed' cob then before them, before he at length succeeded in convincing the acute and sharp-sighted constable that he had not brought back the same horse which he rode the previous day. The man 'at home among horses' being sadly taken aback, and not knowing what was best to be done in his awkward predicament received on addressing 'mine host' at the Pack Horse Inn, which he did in the following terms… Letter 13th February 1858, ex Cockermouth. Dear Sir. You will much oblige by sending the horse that I rode to Whitehaven on yesterday, as the mistake in taking the wrong horse this morning was not discovered until I came to Cockermouth where he remains for returning at your earliest convenience. Signed. William McKee Johnson, Police Constable, and addressed to Mr George Pack, the Pack Horse Inn, Whitehaven. The letter continued: Very cool, this, and quite equal to what might have been expected from Mr Dunne himself Your horse remains for returning by 'earliest convenience' and 'you will much oblige not to delay', meaning of course, not to delay returning the chestnut, and that the bay cob will be sent back at the constable's earliest convenience! This man 'at home amongst horses' will in all probability have discovered ere this, that he had not been permitted with impunity to take a gentleman's horse out of a stable, and ride it fourteen miles even though he premise to return it at his 'earliest convenience'. Very proper, say I, that men should have to pay for such doltish stupidity as is betrayed in the above affair, but what a brilliant specimen of a 'thief-catcher' as you have termed the police has the county in Police Constable William McGee Johnson, and better still, what proof he exhibits of the Chief Constables competency to select men for the constabulary force… men who have just sufficient penetration to distinguish a cow from a donkey, but who are utterly unable to discriminate between a star-faced, switch-tailed chestnut horse, and a dark bay, cut-tailed cob pony. The original letter of which I have been kindly permitted to take a copy has just been deposited in Mr Crosthwaite's Museum at this place, as a curiosity.

Once again Dunne deigned to reply! By June 8th we are learning that Dunne's replacement for Supt Clarke in Whitehaven, namely Supt Oakley, has been suspended and reduced in rank for intemperance while on duty. Immediately the *Cumberland Pacquet* sided against Dunne, and even the magistrates were asking him to give Oakley another trial, as this was the first time he had been in trouble. Dunne was having nothing of it for by the 15th June the same newspaper is reporting that the new Superintendent of Police for Whitehaven is Mr Warwick who had been serving in Penrith, whilst Oakley had been removed to Carlisle. Dunne was clearly proving that discipline was amongst his priorities for in the same newspaper there is a report of Dunne bringing one of his constables, Jefferson Robinson in front of the magistrates for drunkenness … which in itself was unusual, however as he stated at the time: his only object in bringing this case before the magistrates was to have a full investigation and afford to the public protection against any inappropriate acts of a policeman while in an unfortunate state of intoxication. The policeman had been in a gross dereliction of duty in acting as he had done and he (Dunne) could only say he regretted it very much for the sake of the credit of the force on public grounds. Such a man was totally unfit to hold the responsible position of a constable, and he felt it his duty to dismiss him from the service. I am rather surprised that the newspaper did not query why he had not done the same with Supt Oakley. Complaints about the newly formed Cumberland and Westmorland Police seem to continue unabated throughout '57 and '58.

The next item which the *Cumberland Pacquet* were proud to relate was on the 15th June when they published a letter from someone signing themselves 'Fair Play' Headed *'The County Constabulary'*

> *Sir, Can any one of your readers inform me what the duties of the rural policeman are and whether they are disturbers or guardians of the peace? From what I have seen of some, I am inclined to think that they hold the former position, and care very little for the public good. I am much strengthened in the opinion by the fact of having only the other day been standing in the street in Cockermouth with a few friends laughing and chatting away, when a policeman came up and very coolly informed us we should not laugh at him and if he ever saw the like indiscretion again on our parts, he would take out a summons against us. He also gave us to understand that the street was his own and in it he would not be insulted. I should feel obliged if any of your readers can inform me whether or not laughing in the street will amount to an assault? If so I shall in future be more demure when the ghostly minions of the night stalk past.*

June 29th The response to this came not from Dunne, but by Superintendent Brown who headed up the Derwent Division. His letter stated:

> *'After investigation the allegations were found to be totally false and without foundation and must have originated from some malicious and evil design for the purpose of bringing the service into disrepute'.*

It was to prove to be one of many of such false allegations. Almost immediately there was another letter complaining about the police and their workings of Weights and Measures, which considering it was an area in which the police were discovering vast numbers of breaches of the law, the letter could only have come from a dissatisfied shopkeeper. Then there was the letter complaining that tailors are being brought from London to measure police for their uniforms with the proposal – why not a local tailor? Probably a good point!

By October 19th we find a letter signed 'A Passer-By' which has to be another false accusation for though this complaint is about farm servants and farmers sons etc, accosting respectable females in Gosforth, goes on to say that the town's one and only policeman is *'never around when you need them'*. As usual the editor of the *Cumberland Pacquet* adds his 'two penn'orth' by stating: *'What is the use of lock up and magistrates rooms if there are no policemen?'* Or if there are they won't do their duty comparing Gosforth with Whitehaven. Just one week later the same editor is mentioning the fact that the police are now taking some notice of crowds in Whitehaven ... by arresting a young lad for trying to accost a girl. And one month later we hear the same solitary Gosforth policeman (John Crosthwaite) is retiring and the editor is writing: *'highly commended, excellent PC !'* And, yet again later in the year Dunne is in trouble once again in Whitehaven, this time for dismissing one of their constables, apparently without the permission of the local populace, PC 69 Thomas Warwick, was the subject of their letters, enquiring as to why such a hard-working young constable should have been picked on and cruelly treated by his Chief Constable. This time Dunne did respond to what was once again nothing more than a malicious letter and explained that Warwick had not only been found sound asleep at 1.30 am whilst supposed to be patrolling his beat, but in addition his superintendent had reported him for insubordination, inefficiency, and *'unworthy of confidence'*. Dunne advised the many readers of the *Cumberland Pacquet* that there had been a thorough investigation of the facts, and he was entirely convinced that the man should have been dismissed. Strangely enough not another word was written on the subject.

Possibly the most embarrassing and damaging letter ever to be written about Dunne and his officers was that which appeared in the *Cumberland Pacquet* on the 4th January 1859. This was headed: *'Chief Constable and his staff'*

> *'I observe a paragraph that is going the rounds of the local press to the effect that on Christmas Day Chief Constable Dunne entertained all his superintendents and inspectors of police to the counties of Cumberland and Westmorland to dinner at Carlisle. Really, Mr Editor, it sounds very grand*

this, and is no doubt an excessively graceful act of condescension on the part of Chief Constable Dunne, if he has, at his own expense, giving these, his subordinates, not only a dinner, but also lit up the sun of their future lives, by allowing them to eat at the same table as himself - a thing they will no doubt treasure up as the one great event of their lifetime. Yes, each subordinate as he saw his portly superior seated at the head of the festive table, must needs have had dim visions of a future Chief Constableship floating in their bewildered brain. Let me however turn to the thought which prompted me to invoke your aid. It is this... Has Mr Dunne paid the entire cost of this feast ? Has he paid all the subordinates railway fares from the uttermost portions of each county to Carlisle? Or has the counties to pay them? The thought that Mr Dunne would ask all those men to dinner and put them to the cost of their own railway fares, cannot for a moment be entertained. It rests therefore with Mr Dunne, or the county, and I trust someone will enlighten us on the above points, if not I shall proceed to calculate the cost the county will be put to by this freak, which it seems to me would have been quite as well let alone. Surely £400 a year and expenses, is enough for any Chief Constable, without this show of homage. By the bye, I would like that item 'expenses' detailed, and classified at the end of each year'

Letter signed 'a rate-payer'.

Thorough research of the *Cumberland Pacquet* for some weeks after the publication of this letter did not produce any evidence to the fact that Dunne replied to such an accusation ... which is perhaps more to the pity, as we shall never know the truth. However by the end of the year things seem to be taking a turn for the better as it now appears that Dunne and his men are at long last being accepted by the populace and the people of Whitehaven in particular., for in the *Cumberland Pacquet* of the 13th December 1859 the Trustees of the Whitehaven Town and Harbour Trust seemed to have had a change of heart for it is reported that they have given a vote of thanks to the Chief Constable. In fact the secretary had written forwarding their resolution passed by the board at their last meeting tendering their thanks for the efficient measures taken by the police for the preservation of peace during the late election of trustees. Which at least was a step in the right direction. Dunne replied:

'Thanks for the complimentary letter and promises to circulate such news to all his men as will be gratifying to them'.

Interestingly the letter was tempered with a request for some additional help from the Chief Constable, namely referring to the problems on the streets of Whitehaven for example: beating carpets at improper hours, causing obstructions in the streets and footpaths, laying down ashes and 'night-soil'. Dunne immediately replies agreeing to help and to confirm this sent a copy of his instruction which he had given to his superintendent in Whitehaven and a second letter from Dunne recommending all parties should be cautioned and if that doesn't work take them before the magistrates.

From this point on the relationship between the police, and especially so Dunne, was to improve significantly and there were little more complaints that the newspapers considered worthy of publishing for the remainder of his forty-five years service with the Cumberland and Westmorland Police. The view of many of the public can be summed up satisfactorily in a letter of the 16th April, signed A Trader. It stated:

'I believe I express the sentiments of my fellow townsmen when I say that a very good feeling exists between the inhabitants of the town and the police, and pray why not? The men, as a whole are courteous and obliging, their appearance speaking highly for the care and attention paid to their discipline. I have always found any complaint promptly attended to and every assistance freely rendered at any time and surely no one would find fault with the detective department if they take the trouble to read the police reports in any of our local papers.'

There is a further illustration of the publics' warmth to the new force in 1863 This is in respect of a letter written to the *Cumberland Pacquet* on the 1st December accusing the police of various assaults on the public over the years. It was a relatively long letter by a person who entitled himself Justitia, and the complaints were dealt satisfactorily within the same newspaper by Superintendent Little. However the respondent had specifically written about the unruly crowds at the trial of the Brocklewath salmon poachers,where three men had been found guilty of killing an Edward Atkinson. Due to the crowds disapproval of the penalties handed down ... two terms of 10 years, and one of 12 months the crowd clearly thought the death penalty would have been more appropriate.

It was, according to the correspondent, the lack of police presence and attention to which he was referring. However as Superintendent Little made clear, this was not the case. He wrote that:

'When the coach left, mob hooted and yelled and pelted High Courts Judges carriage. Afterwards when the police who had escorted the judge were returning to the court, the mob wreaked their wrath upon them and made several attacks with stones and all sorts of missiles. On their march to the courts a young lad named Holliday was taken into custody by a policeman

named Scott, charged with being one of the mob who were assaulting the police. Upon enquiry, the explanation of Holliday was that he was forced against the police by the mob and as it appeared that this might have been so, he was allowed to leave, instead of being locked up all night and subsequently taken before the magistrates. The policeman was however summarily summoned before the borough magistrates at Carlisle for taking Holliday into custody, and was fined 1/- (5p) .On that occasion there would have been from 6,000-8,000 persons comprising the mob. There were about sixty policemen on duty, and if the Chief Constable had done what many persons present urged him to do, namely allow the police to clear the streets of the mob, what would the consequences have been?

No doubt many persons would at least have been greatly injured and wounded, and the results would have been most serious. In place of doing this the Chief Constable marched the police into the courts, had the front doors shut and quietly got them out through some other passages to their quarters. Therefore I maintain that it was through the caution, discretion and foresight of the Chief Constable that what could have turned out to be a most terrible conflict between an excited mob and a body of police, smarting from the insults and assaults that had been heaped upon them, was avoided'.

Finally in the same report Little states that some 21,260 prisoners and cases of different description had passed through the police hands since their introduction some years earlier, and as 'Justitia' had additionally complained about the police 'Merit' badges., he completed his report by pointing out that

'in every well regulated force there is this badge. Believes there are eight officers in Cumberland and Westmorland who have a Merit Class, and before a man can receive this badge he must earn it by some extraordinary energy and efficiency in the discharge of his duties, coupled with an exemplary conduct during his service. Our men who have this badge have so distinguished themselves'.

Nothing further was heard from 'Justitia'. It had taken Dunne close on three years to get to the stage where he and his men were accepted, which for him was something of a record considering his previous employers had only enjoyed his services for approximately two years each perhaps if they had given him a little more time? Over the ensuing years however it was more likely than not that it would be the magistrates or justices who would receive the bad publicity much the same as today.

One such instance, out of many stands out and that was the letter of the 17th February 1863 headed *'Speedy Justice'* It read:

'We had a forcible illustration at our Police Court (Whitehaven) on Monday last of the truth of the old adage that 'things done in a hurry are seldom done well'.

On that occasion several cases of larceny were dismissed because the prosecutors did not happen to be in court to a minute at 10 o'clock, a course of procedure which I need hardly say has caused much disaffection among all the parties concerned- except the prisoners, who doubtless would appreciate very highly this latest and most extreme application of the ticket-of-leave system. I would not for a moment discourage punctuality, but if unseemly haste be objectionable in one place more than another,it is I would suggest be in a court of justice. Beside, sir, justice as we all know, is blind and might therefore be all the more guarded against being in too great a hurry, but should she stumble, or perhaps even fall and hurt herself. I am sure that on reflection the gentlemen who were on the bench at 10 o'clock that Monday will feel that setting at liberty people charged with larceny, without any examination, is a very grave matter, being most discouraging alike to prosecutors (i.e. the police), indeed, the sooner the police force is disbanded and the great cost of their services saved, the better, if the detection of criminals is to be nullified - as in this instance. I have known judges at Assizes strike a civil action out of the cause list because the parties were not ready for trial, when their case came on its proper order, but who ever heard of a judge discharging a prisoner because the prosecutor, or one of the witnesses was not in court at the moment he was called.

The letter was signed 'The Public Eye' and dated 14th February 1863.

So, as seen those first few years were not without it's problems. As we will learn the next ten years would prove to be rewarding to him and his men, though it would have been less so without the help of the magistrates, judges, and indeed the public. Perhaps those years of 'discomfort' would prove worthwhile overall.

CHAPTER THIRTEEN

JOHN DUNNE

1857- 1860

Including the trials of:
William Graham, (1857) Jacob Skelton, (1858) William Usher, (1860)
George Cass, (1860) Thomas Sowerby, (1860)

If Dunne thought he had been busy on his earlier postings, then he was in for a big surprise. Notwithstanding the need to recruit his new forces from scratch, set up police stations throughout the second largest (combined) counties in England and Wales, and constantly respond and act upon the malicious letters that appeared to be coming in all directions, on top of all that he still had to undertake the job that he had actually come to do ... namely create law and order, in counties where little until now existed.

Unlike Newcastle and Norwich; Cumberland and Westmorland were areas where the main routes were mere stony paths, where villages and hamlets were isolated and people rarely ventured beyond their village boundaries and certainly in the main never more than a dozen or so miles, and that was done either by foot, or just occasionally, depending upon your purse, a horse. It would not have been uncommon at this time for people to walk as much as 40 miles in a day – indeed, as Dunne had already discovered, this could often be the amount his newly recruited police officers could be expected to do, and not just once, but regularly.

Clearly it was not an easy life for the populace, more often than not their houses would be damp and bitterly cold during the invariably harsh northern winters. Central heating, gas and electricity were in the early 1850's still a long way away. This of course was still the time when the woman remained at home, both cooking and looking after the house, and invariably rearing as many as a dozen children, unless she lived near the larger towns and cities of Carlisle, Kendal, Whitehaven, Apppleby etc, when working from 6am to 9pm in the many factories, and bringing up a family, would be the 'norm'.

No doubt Dunne would have been well up on the law as it stood at this time, as well as the need to implement the continuously changing laws ... still one wonders if the 1847 Town Police Clauses Act (section 28) ever came to be used. Namely that you could face fourteen days in jail for kite flying, as they were believed to spread diseases. (Is that law still in place?) The same Act also declared that it was illegal to beat or shake any carpet or rug in any street (except before 8am). There was also the law stopping you keeping a pigsty in front of your home with a maximum penalty of £1,000. Simple solution, move the pigsty to the rear of your home! It was also against the law to make a slide in the snow, with a penalty of fourteen days in jail for doing so. Can't imagine the latter law getting very far, otherwise the detention centres would have been full with criminals (all under the age of twelve).

Naturally there were far more serious laws to deal with over the coming years, homicide, theft, cattle stealing (it was the countryside after all), infanticide, manslaughter, even the odd case of highway robbery – as we shall learn. In fact the first of this latter crime happened within days of Dunne taking up his duties, and in Westmorland rather than Cumberland. That was when a certain Richard Metcalf, an ostler at the Crown Inn in Kendal was assaulted on the Milnthorpe Road; he was stopped and ordered to hand over his money and possessions. However despite his horse's reins being cut (a common practice at the time) he managed to escape with both his life and his possessions. Of the robber? Nothing more was heard.

The 1850's experiment known as ticket-of-leave for releasing convicts from prison (the forerunner of parole) also heightened the fear of crime at this time. *The Times* newspaper around this time was stating loudly that:

> *'We protest in the name of the British public against the system of turning out criminals upon society, under the name of ticket-of-leave men, to rob us in the public streets by day, to break into our houses at night, to assault and throttle unoffending persons'.*

In a word to keep the country in a state of constant alarm. And the parliamentary publication *Hansard* was this year (11.5.1857) stating that:

> *'Society has been horrified and frightened by the uncertainty of life and property created by the ticket-of-leave men throughout the country and the terror had proceeded so far that people had been afraid during the late winter of walking through the streets of London'.*

Unfortunately it was to be another twelve years (1869) before the Habitual Criminals Act came into being which ensured that all ticket-of-leave men (and others) were recorded as to their movements.

The good news for Dunne was that there was only one murder on his 'patch' this year. or put more accurately the crime had actually been committed prior to his arrival, but nevertheless the trial, and his regular attendance at the court rooms in Carlisle, would take up a lot of his valuable time . The criminal was a man named William Graham, and his crime was the alleged murder of Thomas Simpson in the December of 1856. The trial of William Graham was held during the early months of this year, and possibly was one of the first instances where Dunne would have appeared at the assizes. In 1856 he and his two brothers, Henry and Joseph, were involved in a fracas with a keeper on Charles Featherstonehaugh's estate (Staffield Hall) outside Penrith, during the course of which the keeper was bludgeoned and died. All three brothers were arrested, but Henry and Joseph were not in the end charged with the keeper's death. Upon his arrest William was first held in Penrith gaol, and later moved to Carlisle to await his trial. An earlier inquest jury had found William Graham guilty of murder, but the later trial jury surprisingly found him guilty of the lesser charge of manslaughter a finding that may have been affected by the general claim that William Graham had been drunk on the night of the affray. His punishment was to be transportation for life, though it was to be a further eighteen months before he found himself aboard the Edwin Fox en-route to the Swan River Colony (as Western Australia was then known).

He was not alone as in total there were 280 convicts, though only one heralded from his home county. Patrick Davey, aged twenty six, sentenced for robbery with violence. From researching this case I came to discover that during the whole period between 1788 and 1868 (when transportation to Australia ceased altogether), there were but 300 incidences of transportation (out of a total of 130,00 odd male convicts) for poaching offences. William Graham then, was comparatively speaking, amongst a select group whose offenders most often received sentences of seven or fourteen years depending on the offence, the former the most likely, although after 1828, if three or more persons assembled for the purposes of poaching and if one of them carried an offensive weapon, they were liable to fourteen years transportation. In William Graham's case although the offence was connected with poaching, the transportation order was for manslaughter – hence for life. In fact Graham lived until 1891 to the age of 61, thus spending 38 of his remaining years in Australia, mostly as a ticket-of-leave settler. (from 1861).

Graham, of course, was not the only convict transported on a long voyage away from Cumberland and Westmorland both before and after Dunne's arrival. Prior to his arrival in 1857, there had been some twenty convicts transported from the joint counties during the period 1850-1856, though not all heralded from the Carlisle Courts. As stated there was a total of twenty in all of which just ten were despatched from Carlisle, with the remainder from the courts of Appleby, (6) Kendal (1) and Cockermouth (3).

By comparison during the years 1857 through to 1868 there was a total of fourteen criminals transported from the two counties, one of which Henry Smith had been given a sentence of fours years transportation in 1852 for larceny and had been incarcerated until 1859 until his transportation order arrived for the Sultana which subsequently arrived in Western Australia on the 19th August 1859. Considering he had been in prison then for seven years and to all intents and purposes completed his sentence, no doubt he had good reason to complain to the authorities upon his arrival in Australia! Fortunately for Dunne there was to be only the one murder/manslaughter trial for him to contend with during that first year in office, which perhaps was as well considering how full his days would have been.

Naturally throughout his time in office there was an ongoing onslaught of new laws and acts coming into being all of which had to be understood, and then relayed to some, if not all, of his serving forces. For 1857 alone there would have been numerous new acts one of which would have been the Burial Act.

The purpose of this Act was to regulate burial grounds and determine where and how deceased people could be buried as well as providing for the exhumation of remains.. The Act also made it illegal to disturb a grave (other for an official sanctioned exhumation). Strangely enough the Act did not make it illegal to steal a body as it was only the opening of the grave which constituted an offence, not the removal of the contents., though I have yet to find a court case during Dunne's years in respect of this Act, thus I assume it would not exactly have been a 'popular' pastime.

Another new law for this year was the Obscene Publications Act.This was the Act which for the first time allowed police to search premises, but not people, where (sexually explicit) publications were on sale, and Customs Officers and Post Office officials were allowed to destroy consignments, and to prosecute offenders. I'm inclined to think that the Victorian definition of 'sexually explicit' could well be different to the current definition, especially at a time when the Victorian's were still covering up the legs of tables and pianos for fear of causing offence.

The Act which would have given Dunne the most work this and in coming years would certainly have been the Industrial Schools Act. This gave magistrates the power to sentence children between the ages of seven and fourteen years old to a spell in one of these institutions. The Act dealt with those children who were brought before the courts for vagrancy OR in other words being homeless. In 1861 the Act was extended further and different categories of children were included namely: *any child under the age of fourteen found begging or receiving alms (money or goods given as charity to the poor), any child apparently under the age of fourteen found wandering and not having any home or visible means of support, or in company of reputed thieves, and any child apparently under the age of twelve who having committed an offence punishable by imprisonment or less, and any child under the age of fourteen whose parents declared him to be beyond their control.* To some degree the Act was quite difficult to impose for many children did not know their true age, especially if it was advantageous for them not to know. In any case it was not until 1875 before it became compulsory to register births.

There was an alternative to being sent to those of these institutions at this time, and that was the lesser known *Akbar Reformatory Ship* which was based in Liverpool. The Akbar was a reformatory school ship (solely for the reform of Protestant Boys) and which was moored in the River Mersey in the 19th century. Boys were sent to the Akbar for training after serving short prison sentences for committing crimes. It was hoped that the training they received onboard ship would help to reform their character. I imagine this reformatory and many others came about following the introduction of the Youthful Offenders Act of 1854. Previously young offenders had been incarcerated in adult jails, now this Act granted permission for the establishment of reformatories for children and young people. Until 1899 they spent the first fortnight of their sentences in prison, but the Act was nonetheless a great step forward ... (Though I bet the lads didn't think that if sent to the Akbar !!).

Some indication of the crime problem that was in existence at the time Dunne joined the force can be garnered from the reports of the Quarter Sessions for the 6th January 1857 when it was reported that in the last quarter alone there had been a total of ten persons committed for trial (out of a total of 294 arrested for various misdemeanours, which included 83 for being drunk and disorderly), 2 were for manslaughter, 5 for felony, 9 were assaults on police officers, and 3 for various misdemeanours. Whereas at the Cumberland Epiphany Sessions later that month the Chairman E W Hassall was reporting that *'there were more prisoners before him than there had been in previous years and that over the past seven years there had been an average of 31, today alone he was seeing 31'.*

No doubt Dunne was pleased to learn that by March at the Cumberland Spring Assizes this number had reduced down to 21, though in truth one of those cases involved the aforementioned trial of William Graham, and also that of Patrick Davey (the fellow that accompanied Graham on his long journey to Australia) It was not until the Wigton Petty Sessions in May that we learn that at long last Dunne had managed to put in place a number of superintending constables across Cumberland and Westmorland, and which no doubt would have assisted his work load enormously.

He had already three superintendents in place at this time, namely John Allison stationed at Carlisle, Joseph Clarke at Whitehaven and Robert Brown at Cockermouth. Now he had a John Little at Wigton, John Donald stationed at Brampton, Thomas Warwick at Penrith, Robert Parks at Appleby and Edward Hibbard at Kendal. In total he had interviewed a total of 367 applicants, and which he stated later to have been made up primarily of military and naval officers (colonels to ensigns) titled gentlemen and persons filling every position in public and private life. It need hardly be said that all of Dunne's choice came from a background in policing, and even then only after a high degree of questioning on their background and experience. In addition to the appointment of his additional superintendents, no doubt he was also delighted to learn that he now had a clerk in place at £75.00 per annum.

Life could only get better for him now. Indeed it could. For in July Dunne had the first of his obligatory visits by the Government Inspector of Constabulary, Lt.Col. Woodford, who reported his approval of the system and discipline in place, though he commented that increased numbers in his force would be desirable. He backed up this statement by writing that

> *'constables vastly disproportionate to their extent and to the character of certain classes of the population, that some of the large villages (on cross roads) were entirely without the protection and advantages of a resident constable, and the lock-ups in Longtown, Keswick, Kirkby Lonsdale and Kendal he considered unfit for use'.*

Though that was hardly Dunne's fault. Shortly after he referred the problem of the lock-ups to the Police Committee. Woodford's Report also included a communication from Whitehall signed by a W.Massey which stated that Sir George Grey the then Home Secretary had been gratified to learn from this report the degree of efficiency which has been maintained from the first establishment of the police force in these counties, but as at present informed he does not feel justified in granting a Certificate of its efficiency in point of numbers prior to its increase on the 3rd July last, as the Inspector of Constabulary is of the opinion that the total number of men previously appointed was by no means adequate to a full and efficient discharge of its important duties.

From that period the Police of the two counties has been fully entitled to a Certificate. Interestingly, shortly after this inspection, and no doubt on the recommendation of Col.Woodford, Dunne appointed a Mr Oakley to the position of Superintendent of the Cumberland West Ward. Nothing unusual in that you might think, until you learn that Oakley had previously been an Inspector of Constabulary working alongside Woodford and early in 1858 Dunne took possession of his newly built police station in Earl Street, Carlisle until now he had been sharing the premises of the Carlisle City Police. His cup was 'truly running over'.

The year 1858 started off a little differently as it is noted that this was the year of the 'Great Comet' (Donati's) when Penrith, as well as the country generally, was placarded with large posters, bearing the following *'Will the great Comet, now approaching, strike the earth?'* The people seemed terror-stricken at such a prospect, but when the day and the hour came the earth passed through the tail of the comet without inconveniencing any inhabitants of this earth or so the Cumberland Patriot reported at the time.

The arrival of 1858 presented Dunne with yet another lengthy attendance at court, for yet another murder trial, this time it was of a certain Jacob Skelton accused of murdering his father-in-law The scene of death this time was Fenton a small hamlet some seven miles to the east of Carlisle. Here, 85 year old Robert Irwin a retired farmer had lived for some months with his only daughter, Mary Ann, her husband Jacob, and the couple's three sons. Irwin was believed to have savings amounting to some £260, in fact local gossip had it that the amount could be even greater. Under the constantly recurring headline: *'The Fenton Murder'*, Jacob Fenton was variously described as one who had been to prison for stealing, and someone who had left various places *'under discreditable circumstances'.* Perhaps that had indeed been the case, but not only was their insufficient evidence right from the onset to establish that there had definitely been foul play but there was little to suggest either that the prisoner was much more than a poorly-educated oaf of a man whose main fault was his unlikeable temperament. At his forthcoming trial the judge's summing up was balanced and fair and far from detrimental to the prisoner. The jury was undoubtedly swayed by his thinking and what they had heard beforehand. Skelton was not a likeable individual but the jury obviously felt he merited the benefit of fair play. In fact they were only out ten minutes before returning with a verdict of not guilty.

Notwithstanding the many trials (and tribulations) that Dunne is suffering at this stage by early 1858 Dunne is somehow also getting a number of glowing reports, and not just from the Constabulary Inspectors but nearer home too, this time the Police Committee who are declaring *'that the general duties of the police force have been performed to their entire satisfaction and the rules and regulations now in force appear to have been properly carried out*'. Dunne's own report for the same time (April) declared that the '*general state of each county has been remarkably quiet and orderly. Peace has been undisturbed and the criminal returns will show that notwithstanding the general dearth of unemployment and in some instances the great distress which prevailed during the winter, very few serious offences have been committed and crime has seriously decreased*'.

Clearly, as far as Dunne was concerned his criminal returns for the past three months did not include one instance of murder, preferring to put a veil over that sorry affair, and especially so when the result was not exactly in the polices' favour. His report however did show one especial positive contribution and that was in respect of his weights and measures inspectors, for he was able to report that out of a total of 17,493 inspections just 360 were found correct. Which clearly gave an indication to the public just how incorrect and crooked were the majority of shop-keepers at this time. No indication is available unfortunately of how much was collected in fines, but at £5 a time it would clearly have been substantial, and once again Dunne would have been able to show an actual profit from his men, which would not have gone unnoticed by the powers that be.

Based on this success Dunne decided that such examinations should be a regular basis, for by September he is announcing in the papers that shopkeepers should be aware that a further inspection will be taking place shortly, and regularly thereafter. Presumably because of this success, or at least in part, he was able to announce at the same time the appointment of the two counties first Deputy Chief Constable, namely Superintendent Edward Hibberd of Kendal. It is now becoming noticeable that within a year of taking up his appointment he now had an executive team in place not only consisting of a DCC but also a loyal group of Superintendents based across the counties. Now all he needed was sufficient police officers to actually cover the vast area. Still there had been some improvements by this time for we learn that his force now consisted of 180 in total, which besides constables and inspectors also included 10 sergeants and 8 inspectors.

Unfortunately not all Dunne's police force could be considered satisfactory, as we have already learnt he regularly lost a high proportion of his men each year through drunkenness and laziness, but there were also the instances of untrustworthiness too.

One such instance was that of PC William Colman, of Kendal Police who clearly considered himself above the law when he stole nine books from Kendal railway station in the January of 1859. He quickly discovered that he would be treated no differently to many other miscreants appearing before the justices at the Westmorland Spring Assizes when he 'went down' for six months. No doubt the inmates of Kendal Prison welcomed him with open arms.

Without the benefit of nationwide data on homicide at this time, Dunne by now must have been thinking that he had inadvertently discovered the 'murder capital of the country' especially so when the file on a certain William Usher suddenly appeared on his desk in the November of 1859 that in itself was bad enough but was soon to discover that his force had two more murder cases to solve and bring to court before 1860 was out would definitely have confirmed his suspicions.

The first case that of William Usher whose crime was one of wilful murder of his wife, Jane Usher in the November. The first anyone knew of this murder was on the 15th November when residents in the neighbourhood known as the Ginns, in Whitehaven and located close to the town centre, learnt of a violent crime in their midst. Only earlier that same day neighbours had observed the victim, 34 year old Jane Usher out on the street. She was friendly and cheerful as usual and well known having lived in the area most of her life before and after her marriage. She had relatives in the vicinity and three healthy boys of her own, aged 6, 4 and 16 weeks. But Jane Usher had one great drawback, she had a serious drink problem. This as would later be established had already blighted her marriage to a man twelve years older than herself, William Usher, the father of her children, who was as introvert as she was extrovert. For some considerable time Usher had suffered his wife's drinking with a certain degree of restraint but at some point something snapped in his head and he savagely struck his wife until she fell and struck her head on the chimney corner. The trial itself took place in the March by which time Usher had had time to think and even consider legal guidance. Nevertheless he pleaded not guilty to the charge of murder even though early indications were that the odds were stacked against him. A post mortem had revealed external and internal bruising. But it wasn't felt that the victim had died from falling against the chimney corner, more likely from a blow, or possibly from a man falling upon her. At his trial and acting upon advice from his defence layer Usher changed his plea to manslaughter and was subsequently sentenced to fifteen months at hard labour.

As stated this was not the only murder case to land on Dunne's desk this year. Before the trial of Usher was over Dunne once again found the paperwork for yet another murder on his 'patch' this time the victim was an Ann Sewell who had been found with her throat cut on the 26th March. However this case would prove especially important to Dunne, for in the first instance it was his observations alone which determined the outcome of this murder, the whole plan of operation was determined by Dunne, and in addition it would be the first (but certainly not the last) time that he would bring in the services of an eminent analytical chemist to assist in the prosecution. It would also prove to be the first time for Dunne that his presence would be required at a prisoner's execution – in Cumberland at least.

The facts of this case were as follows: On Monday 26th March of that year, Thomas Fearon of Beckhouse, a secluded hamlet in the Vale of Embleton, went off to Cockermouth market in the early morning with his widowed mother Isabella. Thomas Fearon was one of a limited number of better-off farmers who actually owned his 290 acre farm at Beckhouse, where he employed a hired man full-time along with two day labourers and a female house servant. On this occasion the house had been left in charge of the female servant, an attractive girl of 26 named Ann Sewell, whilst the men went about their everyday tasks. By 5pm Mrs Fearon was back home again only to find the house locked up and the whole place apparently deserted. She immediately went to a neighbour's house and requested the assistance of the servant there, Sarah Earle. The servant girl managed to get into the house through a window and quickly saw Ann Sewell lying on her side in the kitchen passage. She was still in her clogs and working dress and the house seemed undisturbed, and everything fine. However a closer examination soon revealed the true horror of the situation. The girl's throat had been cut and she was lying in a pool of blood, and in her hand was a long-bladed kitchen knife. Ann Sewell's throat was so violently cut that the spinal cord had been entirely severed. She certainly couldn't have held on to the knife afterwards in this event. And, importantly the knife had been found in her left hand. Sewell was right handed. In fact it was John Dunne who was first to notice the anomaly, and immediately stated that it was impossible for the girl to have taken her own life as the knife would have been in her right hand if she had considered taking her own life. Later at the criminals trial it would be the evidence of Dunne, along with the prisoners own statement which would seal Cass's fate. It did not take long to determine that Cass was something of an unsavoury character. He was known to drink rather heavily, at least whenever he had money though he was currently in debt to his employer. It was also reported that a Whitehaven girl, Jane Atkinson, had had a child by him fifteen weeks previously and that Cass had a violent temper. Notwithstanding the aforementioned, Cass was placed under close surveillance at the personal instigation of John Dunne.

Not overlooking the three previous murder trials in the two counties recently the Sewell murder had to be the force's first great mystery, where it was not immediately obvious who the assailant was, and thus to them it would have been considered a test of its reputation. Dunne himself once again took an especial interest and with good result too for though Cass had been a prime suspect almost from the start, there had still been little to make a charge stick: the corpse had been discovered within a house locked from the inside and the suspect had neither key nor blood upon his clothing; and of course fingerprinting still remained an unknown phenomena, with Cass not saying anything. Finally George Cass was arrested on 6th April, 1860 charged with Ann Sewell's murder and placed in a police cell at Cockermouth, where shortly after he made a written statement admitting to the offence. The trial itself began on the 2nd August 1860 and was of fairly short duration. Cass pleaded not guilty, probably hopeful that he might be found guilty at least on the lesser charge of manslaughter but that was to no avail. By this time the case had already engendered so much horrific publicity (as in previous trials of course) that it seemed doubtful if there was a single juror who could have been found throughout the length and breadth of Cumberland who would have been without some kind of prejudice. And yet, as the judge, Baron Martin emphasised in his summing up, without the damning statement of the accused *'there would have been no evidence to go to trial at all-on the other hand, if they the jury believed the statement, then the accused was guilty of murder'.* There was little doubt in the jury's mind. They were out just half an hour before returning with a unanimous verdict of wilful murder, but with a rather surprising recommendation to Mercy. Though such recommendation did him little good. On 21st August 1860, the date set for the execution he walked with a firm step to the scaffold on the front wall of Carlisle Gaol and is reported to have kept his eye steadily on the cross beam above him before being hooded and haltered and launched into space. Several thousand saw him go. Being stout and strongly built he dropped heavily and expired fairly quickly, the first man to be hanged in Cumberland for five years.

Now Dunne could take a breather from such time-consuming trials ... or could he? Clearly not for within just fifteen days following the killing of Ann Sewell, Dunne had yet another violent slaying on his hands to contend with. The third that year and all within four months of one another.

This time the victim was a man named Simon Manessa and the culprit quickly determined as one Thomas Sowerby. Simon Manessa had been discovered on Tuesday the 10th April by a George Pattinson The victim had clearly received a violent blow to the head-as the back of his skull was smashed in and a broken ash sapling lay nearby coated with blood. There was also blood in the nearby stagnant stream, and a hat floating on the surface of the water with blood on the stone wall close to the body. Pattinson decided this was a matter for the police. They were quickly on the scene and to their credit, conducted a thorough on-the-spot investigation under Superintendent Carson with some result. The investigation was all the more impressive considering that Cumberland had until recently not normally been a place with a high homicide rate, in fact it was only in the past few months that that image had changed dramatically, in the main the officers involved were more likely to be dealing with brawlers, drunkards and thieves. However the calibre of the new Cumberland and Westmorland Constabulary had already become quite evident in the case of George Cass and they were not destined to be found wanting throughout this latest tragedy . A number of people were questioned and shortly the police arrested a man who gave his name as Grey, though shortly after admitted his true name was Sowerby The police now had their suspect in custody but initially had no idea who the victim was. He was a man of some 50 years of age with dark hair and quickly established that he had only arrived in Penrith the previous Saturday, advising those he encountered that his name was Simon Manassa. By the following Saturday Sowerby was expressing a wish to make a confession. At his trial the following August the prosecution were eager to find him guilty of wilful murder. However, it would be true to say that weather conditions at the time had almost certainly played a part in the victim's death, possibly in part due to his already run down physical condition. In addition there was no evidence presented to prove the accused guilty of robbery which was of crucial importance in the determining of his fate. The Jury returned a verdict of manslaughter without even retiring but the judge had been toying with the idea of an extended period of penal servitude and only a recommendation to mercy spared a longer sentence. As it was, he was probably fortunate to receive no more than eighteen months hard labour which he appeared to accept unconcernedly.

In later years it was discovered that Dunne himself may have had his own ideas about Thomas Sowerby and the true magnitude of his crime. Extensive press clippings on the Townhead killing appear on a day-to-day basis in a scrapbook kept by Dunne and which survives to this day in the Carlisle archives. He had obviously followed the case closely and may well have been disappointed at the eventual paltry sentence. It is noted that even before the trial Superintendent Carson the man who had been responsible for bringing Sowerby to justice was promoted by Dunne to Merit Class with the award of a medal confirming this. The award stated *'that this distinguished honour had been done Mr Carson in consideration of his general exemplary conduct coupled with his efficiency, zeal and promptitude in apprehending and bringing to justice the prisoner Thomas Sowerby, charged with the Penrith murder'*. In this day and age such an award before a court decision would clearly be considered somewhat biased, and it is even arguable considering the outcome of the case, whether he would have still have received this award after the hearing, rather than before.

Though Dunne would not have been involved in any more murder trials as such this year, death in all its forms still appeared as a regular agenda item at many of the magistrates and crown courts throughout this and most years.

Uppermost of these was the crime of *'concealment of birth'*. For reasons unknown Victorian Cumberland and Westmorland had the dubious honour of having a single parenthood figure running at over 10% (as opposed to a possible rate of 4.2% in London), and which was equalled only in neighbouring Westmorland and Norfolk. Why there should have been quite so much illegitimacy in Cumberland and Westmorland is uncertain though in recent years the living conditions of farm servants have since been held up as a possible cause, along with the size of the primarily agricultural counties. Consideration too has been given to cultural norms with prospective brides supposedly permitting their boyfriends free licence on the strength of a promise of marriage only at times to be betrayed. But the major cause may simply have been the abundance of girls employed as farm labourers or domestic servants (or both), often in quite isolated areas, bored and uneducated to begin with. Yet the whole business has still to remain something of a riddle for not all the girls who fell prey to unwanted pregnancies were necessarily living in cramped isolated circumstances either, on farms or in towns, and many were far from gullible.

It follows that due to the embarrassment of such a condition Cumberland seemed prone to many cases of *'concealment of birth'*, though it would be true to say that the magistrates, mainly, dealt kindly with such cases. These cases could, and often did end up as a crime of infanticide, which seemed to run on a par with *'concealment of birth'*.

And how was Dunne doing by this time in countering the crime problem. Well one supposes that the observations of the Chairman of the County Quarter Sessions in the October answered this, for he declared: '*that the average number of prisoners for the past ten years was twenty-five (per year)*'. He went on to report that 17 prisoners had been tried by the magistrates under the Criminal Justice Act during the last quarter and 13 went for trial at these sessions ... numbering 30 in total, which he declared was above the average for the past ten years, though the number of 13 was below the average of prisoners tried at the quarter sessions and in his opinion there was reason to hope that the higher class of offences in this county had diminished.

One must imagine that Dunne would have been quite surprised at such a statement considering the number of murder trials he had already sat through in his first three years as Chief Constable. Though I doubt he was prepared to argue the point with the chairman. Interestingly enough at the same time as such statements were being made the County Business and Finance Committee were sitting in judgement regarding the expenditure that Dunne had incurred of late in bringing various criminals to justice, and demanding to know why he had spent so much, especially so as far as the two recent murder trials were concerned. Dunne responded that it had been the magistrates who had given him his orders. The chairman of the committee wanted to know: *'How far the Chief Constable was to be permitted to put the county to cost in any particular cases...such as the recent ones...he believed there should be some steps to define what was the line of duty as a general rule for the Chief Constable to pursue in bringing offenders to justice'.* Dunne stated *'that he wished it distinctly understood that he never incurred the expenditure without first consulting the magistrates as to its propriety. In this case he had all the circumstances connected with it before the Penrith bench and what he did was in accordance with their wishes and what had been done had been at their request'.* The response he received from Mr Brisco (Clerk of the Peace) was that if the magistrates had acted illegally they must bear the brunt. However the chairman declared that he hoped that the Police Act would give them the power to allow what was reasonable, for the magistrates had been very anxious to bring the offenders to justice. He could not help thinking that the ends of justice would be very often defeated if the magistrates were not to take upon themselves to act as they did in these two very important cases. The matter was referred to the Police Committee.

On a totally different track the same committee decided to discuss the salary of the Chief Constable. The chairman declared that the Chief Constable's salary had been fixed at £300 plus travelling expenses (£150) but with the understanding that after a certain length of time the question again should be taken into consideration. Once again they did not feel it was their duty to decide and this too was referred to the Police Committee. The aforementioned Brisco, who normally voted against Dunne in pretty much all policing matters actually for once sided with Dunne and stated that: *'whilst hearing testimony to the good efforts of Mr Dunne's rule in what he determined one of the worst districts of the county thought it was time enough to consider the question when Mr Dunne (himself) applied for an increase in salary'.* Clearly we learn from that, that it was not Dunne himself who was applying for an increase, rather his employers. Still that being said, after taking into account that which he had undertaken, apparently so successfully if all the reports were to be believed, his first three years in position had all been worthwhile. It just remained to be seen whether future years would continue to be equally as successful.

CHAPTER FOURTEEN

JOHN DUNNE
1860 - 1866

Including the trials of Jane Davidson & William Horsley (1861), William Charlton, (1861) Robert Robinson, William Robinson, & Hugh Earl, (1861) Jane Byers, (1863) Agnes Pattinson (1863) and The Swine Fever Episode (1865-1866)

By 1861, as we know, Dunne has some four years experience of policing the two counties of Cumberland and Westmorland. He appears to have settled in well, a strong and well respected police force is in place, (116 now) and though he still has an approximate loss in man-power of 30% each year which he needs to constantly up-grade, at least the figure is dropping and clearly his constables are staying longer, and in the process becoming a more experienced force.

According to the latest census the population nationwide is growing, (23.1 millions) which includes Cumberland at 205,276 (over 12,000 Irish) a strong force as Dunne was only too well aware was an essential part of the two counties infrastructure.

Dunne of course is now well established with his headquarters in Lowther Street, Carlisle, with his number one aide being Thomas Fowler who according to the Directory and Gazeteer of Cumberland for1861 is both his secretary, and a superintendent. Interestingly the same directory lists a William Douglas as a detective inspector for the two counties who is clearly the only detective appointed. This would have been something of a radical appointment for Dunne, considering that London's Metropolitan Police did not set up their Criminal Investigation Department until 1877. Local newspapers for the time have made no mention of this appointment, which indicates that Dunne was perhaps unsure of his ground, and was taking each step carefully. New Acts coming into being would have been a constant 'pain'.

The most important for this year would unquestionably have been the Offences against the Person Act which rationalised all offences dealing with physical status (and it is still the basis for much law today). Abortion was made illegal, buggery was no longer a capital crime, the intention behind the murder became as important as the act (manslaughter, self-defence etc). This Act also reduced the penalty for abortion from execution to life imprisonment. Also under this Act the age of consent was twelve (which reflected the Common Law) it was a felony to have unlawful carnal knowledge of a girl under ten, and it was a misdemeanour to have unlawful carnal knowledge of a girl between the ages of ten and twelve.

In addition the 1861 Act had made the penalty for indecent assault or attempted rape of a girl below the consensual age, two years imprisonment. Girls over the age of thirteen and the poor had little protection under this law. Nothing still about not publishing the name of the victim, that law was to be many years hence.

The Act also covered the death penalty which was now limited to murder, embezzlement, piracy or to acts of arson perpetrated upon docks or ammunition depots. (this incidentally also included England dropping the death penalty for male homosexual acts). This Act was indeed quite extensive for there was also a special section in respect of whipping. None of the statutes made any provision for whipping as a penalty for persons over the age of sixteen years and as whipping under the common law for misdemeanours was already falling into disuse at this time, the effect of this Act was that with four exceptions whipping was abolished as a penalty for adult offenders. (the exceptions were mainly confined to the Vagrancy Act and the Treason Act). However whilst whipping of adults was now curtailed, it was still recognised by Parliament that corporal punishment was more often suitable than imprisonment as a penalty for young offenders.

This Act was modified slightly in 1862 to allow for offences of robbery with violence to be punishable by flogging (or at least as part of the sentence), and now clearly indicated that no offender could be whipped more than once for the same offence (presumably just given a few more whacks on the first occasion) and that the practice of whipping in public should be discontinued. Clearly that and public hanging were not considered a suitable sight for the public any more. In fact it was an 1847 Act which allowed justices to deal summarily with offences of simple larceny committed by persons under fourteen years of age, and in addition provided that boys so dealt with might be ordered to be once privately whipped, either instead of, or on occasions, in addition to imprisonment.

As evidence of this the *Cumberland Pacquet* was reporting in their July 9th newspaper the case of a girl of twelve stealing a skirt the magistrate recommended that the father *'take her home and give her a good whipping and confine her to her room for a week on bread and water'.* Clearly this wasn't the same magistrate who just weeks earlier had punished the same girl's stepmother for beating her!

This year also saw the introduction of the Accessories and Abettors Act, which meant that from now on an accessory to an indictable offence would be treated in the same way as if he/she had actually committed the offence themselves.

And also importantly for this year was the Malicious Damages Act, which clearly showed the growing awareness of public roads and railways for this act was mostly concerned with damage to property in the transport sector of society. It forbid wilful damage to railways, roads and lighthouses.

Other Acts for this year were the Anti-prize fight Act which made it illegal to even transport someone to the scene of a prize fight, let alone the prize fight itself, which for the local populace led to a rapid decline in the then popularity of the sport. Fortunately, for them however, at least cock-fighting was still as popular (though illegal).

The Act which in all probability made the biggest impact on Dunne this year would almost certainly have been the Larceny Act as this covered a multitude of sin's (pun intended) and would have involved a massive change in understanding for both the police and especially so the magistrates. This Act was not confined to simply theft from the person, it also covered cattle, *'written instruments'*, mines, burglary and housebreaking, factories, ships, embezzlement; thefts by tenants or lodgers, fraud, obtaining money by false pretences, the receiving of stolen goods as well as the action to be taken by the authorities in respect of the apprehension of such offenders and the proceedings which followed. One can imagine Dunne and his senior colleagues (at least) having many sleepless nights digesting and understanding that lot!

On the positive side for Dunne this year was the announcement on January 8th, that his salary had been increased by a further £100 (to £400, plus £150 expenses). The grounds for the increase were based on the salaries of other Chief Constables, the number of the force, the extent of the district and other unspecified circumstances. This increase at today's rate would have been a massive third on his then salary, (around £20,000, bringing his actual salary to £80,000 plus £30,000 expenses). Unfortunately it was still to be some time before the lower ranks would see an increase in their wages, and it would never ever be as much as one third in one foul swoop. Still it would be true to say that Dunne did have his men's interests at heart where money was concerned for in the May at the time of the latest inspection by the Constabulary Commissioners, that the Class of Merit was introduced which warranted an increase in salary of 1/- (5p) a week (or £10 a week in current wages), plus being allowed to wear a specific 'Merit' badge. And by July Dunne is recommending to the magistrates that there should be a gratuity of £3 to his men for specific instances of outstanding duty or bravery. This was immediately overturned by the magistrates who stated that that was too small an amount – it should be £10.00!

Three cases of murder for Dunne during 1861, though only one which would warrant his attention at the scaffold at Carlisle prison. The first of interest was that of the murder of William Horsley in the Pack Horse Inn, Carlisle in the April, which once again made the headlines of the local papers. Indeed had Mrs Davidson lived to stand trial the whole thing would almost certainly have become a cause celebre and she would probably have been the first women (and probably last) to have been hanged in Cumberland that century.

Once again an interesting case for Dunne and his team, but one which for them had the wrong ending. Mrs Davison was a native of Scaleby village who was then in her forties though still an attractive woman. Unfortunately for her she became infatuated with her daughter's new husband, William Horsley, and being himself of a weak disposition also fell hopelessly in love with her. Regretfully this was not to be a romance that was to go anywhere, eventually leading to Jane Davidson strangling her amour and taking sufficient arsenic tablets to kill herself. Following the evidence of all those involved, the inquest came to their decision within just ten minutes. *'Wilful murder of William Horsley against Jane Davidson and self- murder against the same Jane Davidson'*.

Death, as we have learnt played a large part in the life of a rural policeman, not only the various cases of murder and manslaughter which has been related, and not overlooking the many cases of infanticide, but the normal everyday instances of accidents, and misadventures. Yet their was another serious area too, that of suicides (or attempted suicides) which took up a lot of their time.

These days we tend to forget that suicide was a criminal offence throughout England and Wales in the Victorian era and many people would have been sent to prison for attempting to take their own lives.Though in truth many of the courts in Cumberland and Westmorland during the 1860's especially, appeared to favour a more sensitive means of dealing with such 'crimes'. Which was just as well for just by looking in virtually any local newspaper during this period would immediately confirm that the two counties had more than their fair share of suicides and attempted suicides over the years. Many did succeed in killing themselves, but there were still those who did survive and found themselves before the courts yet invariably only going to prison for a short token period. And there were others who were more likely to be freed on payment of a small recognizance or even just bound over, assuming of course that they weren't deemed unstable. Yet there were some local verdicts which bordered on the ridiculous in respect of those who had actually succeeded in their endeavours . For example: *'deceased committed suicide during a temporary fit of insanity induced by drinking through the week'.* No mention of course of possible reasons such as sheer misery of everyday living which led to abuse of alcohol prior to ending it all, or indeed chronic alcoholism and damaged brain cells as a result of the rampant liquor trade which had continued unchecked for many years, not just in Cumberland and Westmoreland, but throughout the whole country. Though as the majority of suicides induced by alcohol were attempted by the poorer classes then that is perhaps understandable for this period. Nevertheless the fact remained that suicide and attempted suicide had long been a grey area which is as poorly understood in the 19th century as it often is today.

'Navvies' ... the very word would probably have conjured up a variety of problems in Dunne's mind, never good ones either as the word invariably meant Irish, fights, murder, manslaughter etc, and taking up the time of too many of his men on far too many occasions.

One such incident amongst many would have been what became known as *'The Brutal Manslaughter at Penton'*, and I am indebted to the Carlisle Journal of July 26th 1861 for the recording of the under mentioned story.

The story relates to a certain John Donnelly who was found dead at Penton on the Sunday morning under circumstances which left little doubt that he had it had been one of brutal manslaughter. Penton is a small hamlet of a few scattered houses, about six miles beyond Longtown, and situated on the borders of the wild and sparsely populated district of Nicholforest, a region rendered famous by many a border raid and foray in olden times. At Penton itself there was a large gathering that night of navvies, and the Penton Bridge Inn was once again filled with drinkers. And, of course as they became drunk, then quarrels took place and the use of the fists being with them the most forcible argument, many fights took place in the course of the evening, What was later determined was that it was in this atmosphere that the deceased John Donnelly a Scotsman had gone into the public house, and when drunk had apparently accused some of the customers of stealing a shirt he had just bought … for this statement he was immediately knocked to the ground. The navvies by this time were swearing profusely and anxious to get at him, however the publican anxious to avoid damage and bloodshed inside the pub suggested that the fight should continue outside. All the men then went outside, and this was the last time that Donnelly was seen alive by any of the witnesses who were later examined. The post-mortem examination of the body showed that the neck had been broken. In addition his neck was severely bruised and swollen, but more to the point his spine was broken with the upper part having been forced to the left side . Their was also external injuries on the right of the body. There was no doubt that Donnelly was first knocked down by a blow of the fist and whilst on the ground and unable to defend himself he was violently kicked in such a brutal manner as to cause his almost immediate death. According to the newspaper report it was thought that the police had a good deal of evidence to bring to the magistrates the following Monday, although they had met with considerable difficulty in obtaining this evidence, no doubt on account of the fear by those who could give it that if they did so the consequences might be serious to them from the future violence of the navvies. The offender Flanagan, though was eventually caught and was later sentenced to a short term of hard labour in Carlisle gaol.

Just one of such violent episodes that was to regularly occur throughout Dunne's time. On the morning of Friday 22nd November 1861, Carlisle was startled to hear news of yet another horrific murder that had been committed during the previous night this time at the Botcherby level crossing located on the Newcastle and Carlisle Railway. The victim this time was Jane Emmerson, an elderly lady, 72 years of age, and who was the crossing gatekeeper. It was her duty every night, after the last train had passed at 10.30pm, to close the gates across the line, and to take into the house two lamps. Between 10.30 and 4am she had nothing more to do. It was about 6.30 on the Friday morning when she was found dead beside the line, within a few yards of the cottage porch. Jane Emmerson was found lying with her face covered with blood, one eye been driven in with a sharp instrument, and there being several cuts on the face, one of them apparently inflicted with a stone. Importantly as it happened a man's footprints were traced from the posts of the south gate, and leading across to the window. The County Constabulary, under the personal direction of Mr Dunne, made every endeavour to discover any circumstances that might lead to the apprehension of the murderer, and in this they had the co-operation of the city (Carlisle) police, as it was believed he was connected to the city. As mentioned, both on the ground, from the south gate, along the line, and across to the cottage window, and also on the door, there had been founds the marks of a man's footprints. Closer examination showed that the 'sparables' or nails in the shoe soles were arranged in a peculiar pattern, and it was at once seen that if the shoes worn by the murderer could be traced it was important that there should be irrefutable proof of their corresponding with those footprints. In those days, fingerprinting as a means of identification remained an unknown phenomena and there were no obvious clues, except for a number of footprints. In this respect the killer had been decidedly careless, even to leaving the mark of his shoe nails on the cottage door. Thus at 1pm on Sunday 22nd December 31 days after the murder, the man upon whom suspicion had fallen was arrested, at his house in Harrowby Street, London Road Terrace, Carlisle. William Charlton, the man in question, was an engine driver on the Newcastle and

Carlisle Railway, 35 years of age and a married man, with three children. He was brought before the County magistrates at the Court House, in Carlisle, on Saturday 28th December. At the later inquiry it was revealed of the steps taken to secure evidence connecting the footprints with the case. The police official most actively employed had been Inspector Alexander Taylor and he testified that, on discovering the footmarks, he immediately protected them with buckets and pails from the station until the arrival of Mr Joseph Pickering, a Carlisle sculptor, who took casts of the footprints with plaster of paris.

This is the case where Dunne engaged the services of a local artist to take accurate plaster casts of footprints found in soft earth, an unheard of procedure that eventually was to prove the case. At the later trial the jury returned a verdict of wilful murder against William Charlton, but strongly recommended him to mercy. The Judge elicited that this recommendation was founded upon the prisoner's previous good character. The Judge, in passing sentence of death, warned the prisoner that he could give him no hope of the sentence being commuted. and in fact the sentence was accordingly fulfilled at midday on Saturday 16th March.

As it happened this was to be the last public execution in Carlisle, and was carried out at the usual place, on the prison wall, southward from the entrance. The execution was witnessed by a large crowd, estimated as numbering from six to eight thousand people. During these early years another crime area which was to cause some concern to Dunne, would be what became known as the Garrotting Panic of 1862, though in truth it was really London that was panicking, rather than these rural areas. Garrotting was a method of robbing people which was seen as more convenient than knocking the victim down and having to struggle with him in the street and run the additional risk of being caught. It took its name from the manner of inflicting capital punishment in Spain by means of a collar which was tightly screwed round the neck of the criminal whilst seated with his back to an upright board, to which the apparatus was fixed. However on the streets of England this was done by one criminal attacking a person from behind and pressing his hands round the victims throat until suffocation or unconsciousness ensued, and at the same time his partner in crime would be rifling through the victims pockets and this would be done so quietly and noiselessly that often a victim could be robbed on a busy highway without any passer-by being aware of the crime. The special Act of Parliament (Garrotting Act of 1863) which was empowered following these attacks authorised the judges to order persons convicted to be whipped – which fortunately had the effect of almost stopping the attacks altogether.

Such a crime was as stated not simply confined to London. Cumberland had its problems too. For example: On 9th April 1863, Andrew Brotherton left Lochmaben in Dumfriesshire to travel to Whitehaven on business. Andrew's visit was not destined to end happily. He finished his business quickly and that same evening went drinking with two acquaintances named Gibbon and Wales. Indications were that a considerable amount of pub crawling had ensued by the time Andrew encountered two local misfits, Sam Mooney and Jim Doran, Brotherton even buying the twosome a drink apiece in passing and appearing to find their company congenial enough. Andrew later went off to search for accommodation for the night and in so doing met again with Mooney and Doran and asked them if they could show him a suitable place where he might spend the night. Andrew later claimed that Mooney put his arm around his neck and under his chin and effectively choked him. He came too later and found himself lying on the ground less a sovereign, half a crown and his keys. He was not too drunk to call upon the police for help and Mooney and Doran were soon arrested. It was to be a further year before the trial took place when the jury returned a verdict of guilty, whereupon they were sentenced to a penalty of six years penal servitude. A penalty which clearly reflected the fear that the *'Garrotting panic'* had affected the judiciary and the public. This *'garrotting panic'* was in reality a response to the new phenomenon that the public had recently been obliged to come to terms with, that is the return of released prisoners into the community, which of course until the early 1860's had not been something that was often experienced, given that most offenders had in the past been transported to Australia.

The end of transportation meant the releasing of prisoners into the public arena, and crimes committed by these released prisoners, known as 'ticket of leave men', were a staple of the Victorian media. In truth the increased interest in cases of garrotting only came about after the MP Hugh Pilkington was seriously attacked on the 17th July 1862. Up to that date only fifteen cases had been reported nationwide. However the moral panic of the time, was not caused by an increase in garrotting, on the contrary the rapid increase in the number of garrottings recorded was actually caused by the newspapers reporting.

It was this 'crime wave' which resulted in more policing and the redefining of minor crimes as more serious offences along with tougher sentencing in the courts. It also helped to produce a number of legislative changes. An Act was passed which temporarily reversed the long-term movement away from corporal punishment by reintroducing flogging, along with imprisonment for all robbery with violence. A year later, stricter sentencing policies were introduced in a further Act. The trend towards greater severity continued in the Prisons Act

1865 and the Habitual Criminals Act 1869.

The panic reached its peak in November of this year following the trial of 23 alleged garrotters at the Old Bailey, after which it gradually faded in intensity. It had lasted for less than six months. However the consequences for penal policy were to prove far reaching.

Another area of ongoing concern for Dunne and his men was of course poaching which was clearly more serious in rural areas than urban ones. Thus Dunne was probably pleased when the Poaching Prevention Act was introduced this year. Until 1862 rural constabularies had refrained from involving themselves too closely with poaching incidents. Most Chief Constables (and Dunne would not have been the exception) felt that their forces would have been even more unpopular if they had acted as a gamekeeping body paid for out of the county rates. In fact the one-time Chief Constable of Lancashire Lt Col John Woodford. (now inspector of constabulary) had specifically ordered his men not to become involved in game law offences because it was commonly believed that *'the police have surrounded country houses at night and that patronage blended into the rural police system'* so it is possible that Woodford passed on these views to other Chief Constables later. This new law stated that: *'It shall be lawful for any constable or peace officer in any county, borough or place of Great Britain and Ireland, in any highway, street or public place, to search any person whom he may have good cause to suspect of coming from any land where he shall have been unlawfully in search or pursuit of game, or any person aiding or abetting such person, and having in his possession any game unlawfully obtained or any gun, part of gun (or nets or engines used for killing or taking game) and also to stop and search any cart or other conveyance in or upon which such constable or peace officer shall have good cause to suspect etc'.* Thus the police were now officially brought in to help eradicate poaching.

Coincidentally, Dunne was to find himself very much part of a trial of three salmon poachers at around the same time that the new law on poaching came into effect this year. This was the trial of Robert Robinson, blacksmith aged 50, William Robinson blacksmith aged 22, and Hugh Earl, blacksmith aged 40 all being accused of killing a certain Edward Atkinson. The charge of wilful murder was in relation to a crime allegedly committed in the vicinity of a place known as Brocklewath, which was located on a small island in the River Eden, a reasonable distance across the fields from Cumwhitton and just two and a half miles up the river from Wetheral. It was footprints which again assisted the police but they also had the benefit of several local witnesses on this occasion. The Robinson's and Earle were in custody quite quickly having scarcely had time to dry their clothes. At the subsequent trial of the three it was held that William Robinson had struck the fatal blow with a large hedge-stake,assisted by Hugh Earle, the stake being produced in court. The judge himself directed in his summing up that should the jury decide upon a verdict of guilty, than this should appertain to manslaughter rather than murder, presumably with especial mind to the non-appointment of the watchers and the spontaneous nature of the assault itself. After that it was soon over. The jury, drawn in this instance from beyond the immediate Cumwhitton area, brought in verdicts of guilty in respect of all three but in each instance they were found guilty of manslaughter rather than murder, Robert Robinson being strongly recommended to mercy. Robert Robinson received a sentence of twelve months imprisonment with hard labour. William Robinson and Hugh Earl each received ten years penal servitude.

On the 15th April Dunne through the pages of the *Cumberland Pacquet* reported that:

> *'With regard to the murder of Jane Emerson at Durran Hill on the 21st November last and of Edward Atkinson at Brocklewath on the 15th January last it is but an act of justice to the officers of the county constabulary who were engaged in investigating the intricate and difficult circumstances of these cases to state that it was entirely through their indomitable energy, zeal and efficiency that the offenders were apprehended and brought to justice and I therefore feel it my duty to recommend that in consideration of their services, gratuities of £3 each be granted to Mr Superintendents Carson, and Taylor, Inspector Douglas for the former (Durran Hill) and Mr Superintendent Carson, Taylor Fowler and Constable Cowman in the latter, under the provisions of the Act 22nd and 23rd Victoria Cap 32.Section 24'.*

The newspaper went on to state that the magistrates had unanimously agreed to the award, and also went on to state that the chairman of the bench that day had also stated:

> *'that some recognition was due to Mr Dunne from this court of his valuable services. He thought that the thanks of the court be given to Mr Dunne as well as the proposed gratuities being paid to the Superintendents'.*

All agreed except Dunne's arch-enemy Mr Brisco who thought it would set a bad example if Mr Dunne was congratulated every time something came before the court, after all he was a paid officer and only therefore doing his duty.

And following the poaching case, the newspaper reported that the Chief Constable had drawn up certain rules for the government of the Police Force, which had been approved by the Court of Quarter Sessions and by the Secretary of State. The new rule stated that: *'Constables are positively forbidden to assist in watching game preserves, or to lie in wait for poachers. If it should come to their knowledge that armed men, whether in large or small numbers, go about at night for the purpose of killing game or fish, or for any other unlawful purpose or that they hear of an intended combination of the kind, it will be their duty to acquaint their superior officer forthwith in order that steps may be taken to put a stop to a proceeding so fraught with danger and so prejudicial to social order . If in the cause of their ordinary duty at night they should come upon men poaching or fishing in presence or receive information of it under other circumstances, they will acquaint the proprietor of the land or his gamekeeper in order that proceedings may be taken if it is thought fit'.* When the motion was put to the Police Committee it was immediately approved. Perhaps the earlier death of Edward Atkinson had not been entirely in vain after all. Another area which Dunne and his force would regularly would be obliged to contend with would be the numerous mining accidents and disasters which occurred throughout the whole of his career.

The mining areas, predominantly in Cumberland, were located in Cleator Moor, Whitehaven, Lamplugh, Seaton,Brampton, Flimby, Workington, Lowca, Alston, Egremont, Beckermet, Keswick, Carlisle, Braithwaite, Millom, Langwathby, Caldbeck, Coniston, and, as stated their were regular incidents which involved the police, almost on a yearly basis. 1863 was no exception when three men and a boy were killed at the Cleator Moor mine, and then again 1864 there is report of yet another death. And it wasn't just mines either, for in 1864 we learn of a serious explosion at Low Wood, near Windermere, where three men had been killed and five seriously injured. Again not an uncommon occurrence.

The explosion on this occasion was thought to have been caused by a certain Matthew Whittam an employee who was apparently cleaning a cylinder in the glazing house containing one hundred weight of gunpowder. According to the newspaper reports of the time he had been frequently warned about the danger of causing an ignition but apparently ignored the warning. He suffered for it, for he was one of those killed. Throughout this time we are still learning of murder cases again, almost on a yearly basis.

In fact in the August we learn of a young woman, namely Jane Byers finding herself in front of a judge charged with the offence of wilful murder, this time of a female child in the Brampton area the previous February. She pleaded not guilty to the charge. This time though the case against her was more telling than most. Jane's daughter had borne distinct evidence of violence. Up to now no woman had been hanged in either Cumberland and Westmorland during this century, still there had to be a first time. Jane Byers came from yet another poor family She had almost got away with her crime until 26th February 1863, when a slater, Robert Eilsdone, was taking states from the roof of an outhouse at Beckriggs, near Brampton. He happened to peer through a hole in the roof and saw what he assumed to be a bundle of rags. He went into the building and immediately saw a child's foot protruding from the bundle, whereupon the local police were called and investigated. A child's body was found which had been wrapped in cloth with a piece of it knotted around the neck so tightly as to have almost severed the head from the body. The doctor who subsequently undertook the post mortem found the body badly decomposed Jane Byers was quickly apprehended and soon found herself before the judge at the next assizes. In the judges summing up he contended that there was a preponderance of evidence to show that the child had breathed but insufficient for a verdict of wilful murder though he felt that there were strong grounds for suspicion. The jury thereupon consulted briefly and then retired. Within about ten minutes they were back with a verdict of concealment of birth, such announcement being met no doubt with Jane expressing a large sigh of relief, at least she was not going to be hung whatever the sentence. The judge sentenced her to twelve months imprisonment with hard labour.

Not all such mothers were so lucky, for their was the case of Agnes Pattinson who was actually sentenced to death at Appleby Assizes in the August of 1863, for the wilful murder of her infant child in Windermere in the April. According to the trial report she was admitted into Milnthorpe Workhouse for confinement in the February, with the child being born on the 13th March. Records showed that she left the workhouse on 1st April, when the child was then healthy and well. On the 2nd April at 7pm Agnes was met near Windermere Station by a man named Park who noticed her carrying a small bundle, but no child. It wasn't until the 13th April that a railway porter discovered a bundle which upon investigation he discovered contained the body of a dead female infant. Examination later determined that a triangular bit of bone, about half an inch across had been driven into the brain, the skull having been fractured. The Inquest determined that this would have been the cause of death. It was these injuries which ensured the arrest of the child's mother, namely Agnes Pattinson, whereupon she was taken into custody. At her subsequent trial she told the jury that she did not like the idea of going to the police to report the death so simply left the body where it was found ... as near to the police station as possible. That explanation wasn't enough however for the jury found her guilty though recommended mercy. Rather than treat her gently as had been the case in so many trials of young girls on similar charges this time the judge donned the black cap and passed sentence of death, directing her body to be buried in the grounds of the gaol.

This being one of the only times for years that a charge of murder had arisen in Westmorland, and even more so the penalty of death, the fate of the young woman certainly caused quite a stir in court that day. All was not lost for Agnes however, for just one week later Mr Ridge, Governor of Appleby county gaol received a registered letter from the Secretary of State's office, containing a respite of the sentence of death passed on Agnes Pattinson ... *'until further signification of Her Majesty's Pleasure'*. After that there was no further news of Agnes who no doubt was incarcerated for many a long year.

Newspapers then, as now, were not in the habit of reporting when prisoners were released, so it will always be something we shall never know. Naturally reports on the constabularies of Cumberland and Westmorland continued as usual and it is from these that we learn that the population of the two counties has now increased to 224,638 persons and the acreage remained at 1,482,863.

There are now 113 constables under Dunne's command each of whom is still expected to patrol an area of 13,122 acres and police 1,987 people – daily. Still this didn't stop Colonel Woodford reporting: *'That the men looked remarkably well and stated that in his opinion the establishment had been maintained at all points in a highly satisfactory state of discipline and general efficiency'.*

Another area which I have touched upon in the past is the number of tramps and vagrants which plagued the lives of the Cumberland Constabulary, also on an ongoing basis. This was brought to light somewhat that year at the Cumberland Quarter Sessions in the October when in the Chief Constables report we learn that the daily average of vagrants and tramps in Cumberland under sixteen years was 14 males and 11 females. For those sixteen years and above there were in total 184 males along with 45 females. Westmorland was considerably less with just seven in total (4 males and 3 females). For those sixteen years and over there were just 55 males and 15 females.

His comparison with the previous year's totals show a daily increase of 21 in Cumberland and 10 in Westmorland ... which was not exactly the improvement he had hoped for. However Dunne was able to advise that these figures had been ascertained by careful daily and nightly supervision of lodging houses, a supervision which had been the means of leading to the detection of several offenders who had already absconded from other districts. He pointed to this as being one of the many advantages arising out of the police acting as Assistant Relieving Officers and ventured to recommend the subject to the favourable consideration of those Boards of Guardians who had not yet availed themselves of the offer of the police to act in that capacity.

Dunne had at least a little help in respect of his tramps and vagrants with the introduction of the 1864 Vagrancy Act. This was an Act for the punishment of idle and disorderly persons, and rogues and vagabonds, in England. For this the police would now have some help in clearing the streets of desirables for it stated : that any person whatsoever was permitted to apprehend any person who shall be found offending against this Act and forthwith to take and convey him or her before some justice of the peace, to be dealt with in such manner as is herein before directed, or deliver him/her to any constable or other peace officer of the place where he or she shall have been apprehended to be so taken and conveyed as aforesaid. It would remain to be seen whether this change would indeed help Dunne in the apprehending of such individuals.

It was in 1864 that Parliament brought about another Act which was to put even more pressure on Dunne. This was when they passed The Contagious Diseases Act, forcing the compulsory registration, licensing and medical inspection of British prostitutes. The new law made any woman suspected of prostitution in a garrison or naval dockyard town subject to 'inspection' by the morals police for venereal disease. These days the very words 'moral police' conjures up visions of Arabs (and others) rounding up their own people who they think of as committing any offence under their strong religious laws, however back in 1864 though this was offences against the new Act, the results would be much the same, for this Act allowed police to arrest women simply suspected of being prostitutes, under the justification of preventing and controlling venereal disease.

In actual fact, the fear of venereal disease was greater than actual infection and the legislation was aimed at protecting male clients and therefore their chaste wives. These sexual double standards saw prostitution and unmarried mothers as the targets of social reform rather than their male partners in 'sin', Cultural anxieties about a loss of social control and prostitution were personified in the 'fallen women' and prostitution was inevitably used as a measure of poverty, public health and social morality.

Its unintended consequence was that any women who happened to look like a prostitute (in the policeman's eyes) would be subject to this law. Which of course ensured for the next few years at least, that many an innocent working girl, be it shop assistant, domestic servant or agricultural worker could easily find herself the subject of an arrest, and worse an intimate medical inspection.

Men, not surprisingly were not subjected to this ordeal even though they were equally responsible for spreading the disease. However the Acts were later repealed due to public pressure over the double standard nature of these laws (1866 and 1869) ... though not before many a girl had suffered untold indignities upon her person. The new Act even made the statement of what to do in the case of a woman who was menstruating at the time of the arrest. This stated that she should be detained until an examination is possible. Doctors who then perform such examinations could be said to have raped their patients, and if they alone decided a woman was diseased then she could be held in confinement and treated with mercury until deemed cured. Even women who refused to submit to examination could be imprisoned with hard labour. Newspaper reports over the next few years nationwide regularly reported instances of police taking extreme measures over this new law, though it would be true to say that there were very few instances of arrests under this Act appearing in Cumberland newspapers.

It is not too surprising with so many changes to the law coming about at this time that Dunne should find the need for more men. By the July Midsummer Sessions we learn that he is applying for an additional ten men for Cumberland and three for Westmorland such men to be distributed at, Millom, Bootle, Cleator, Oughterside, Silloth, Flimby, Upperby, Penton, Brampton, Plumpton and Skelton, and for Westmorland at Ravenstonedale, Grasmere, Greyrigg and Kendal. He made clear in his request that this was not a requirement solely from him but had emanated from the residents themselves.

However he did point out that since 1856/7 there had been no permanent increase in men, although there had been a large increase in the population. From newspapers of this date we learn of yet more details of what was then termed his General Orders. The following which related to ticket-of-leave prisoners was clearly to be of direct interest to the populace for the *Cumberland Pacquet* were happy to print it in full. Dunne's instructions were:

> 1. All convicts to whom licences are issued to be seen by the police on discharge, whether they are placed under the Prisoner's Aid Society or not.
>
> 2. All convicts, who on discharge go to any city or town having a police of its own, must report themselves within seven days of their discharge to the superintendent or head of such police, and if discharged to any county must report themselves to the Chief Constable of such county or the Chief police officer or superintendent of the district.
>
> 3. A notification of the discharge of every convict on license (together with two photographs for the purpose of identification) will be sent to

the Chief Constable of the city town or county to which he goes one day before he is discharged. (This would probably have been the first time that photographs were being used by the C & W Police for the purposes of identification of criminals).

4.You will give the necessary instructions to every prisoner on discharge and forward the notification and photographs as soon as the arrangements for taking them are complete, the day prior to the prisoners discharge.

5. You will warn the prisoner that he can only receive his gratuity on production of a certificate on his gratuity letter that he has been seen by the police and that if he failed to report himself to the police as he is required to do, the Secretary of State will be informed thereof and his licence will be liable to be revoked.

No doubt this order came about following the recent Vagrancy Act where he was clearly hopeful that numbers of vagrants would be severely reduced thanks to both the police and in some instances members of the public.

By October at the Cumberland Michaelmas Quarter sessions Dunne's request for more men was honoured when a further fifteen was added to his force. This now meant the police of Cumberland and Westmorland could offer support by the means of one policeman to 1758 head of population. Dunne though clearly happy with that decision still felt the need to point out *'That with the exception of Westmorland this county would still even after the proposed addition of fifteen men stand one of the lowest, if not the lowest, both in the cost of the police and proportion of officers to the number of populous second to none they believe in the organisation and efficiency of its force'.*

Based upon his recent requests Dunne probably needed all the help he could get especially with the introduction of the Locomotive Act of 1865. Though their had been innumerable instances of fast driving, jay walking, drunken driving and the like over the years ... not unlike today but at this time solely involving horse and buggy, this Act recognised the fact that there was now the possibility of mechanically driven vehicles on the road thus the new act.

This in turn brought about the first speed limit ever on the streets of Britain which was to be 2 mph in town and 4 mph in the country. In addition the vehicles were obliged to have three attendants, one to steer, one to stoke the engine and one to walk 50 yards ahead carrying a red flag to signal the driver when to stop. Regretfully there is no report of who was the first police officer in Cumberland to issue a speeding ticket.

1865 was as it happened to prove a particularly significant year for Dunne, for as history now informs us this was the year that Rinderpest (or Cattle Plague) was first discovered in Cumberland (it fortunately never affected Westmorland), and as we shall learn it was Dunne that was to play such an important part in stopping the disease.

However in the April of this year there were, to Dunne, far more important things on his mind of a personal nature, for he put his name forward for the appointment as Chief Constable of Gloucestershire. Quite why he did so is not recorded, but it is unlikely it was for the money,though it could have been the fact that Gloucestershire had a far bigger force, and anyway he had already spent more time in Cumberland and Westmorland than he had done with other postings, which for him was something of a record. As it happened he wasn't offered the post,though of the eighty- seven candidates who put their name forward Dunne was one of the few who was in the final selection ... though was unsuccessful in being appointed. However when one learns in the June that the man who did get the post was a certain Captain (later Admiral) Henry Christian lately the captain of the Royal Yacht and earlier the captain of H.M.S Euryalus, and who had been recommended for the post by no less a personage than Queen Victoria herself, than perhaps we can understand why Dunne once hearing of this applicant immediately withdrew his application.

Clearly it helped if one had friends in high places...and who was higher than the Queen? Dunne, if nothing else certainly knew when he was clearly beaten. Still in fairness to Christian, he did stay in the post until 1910, a period which equated to 45 years, exactly the same as Dunne would stay with Cumberland and Westmorland now he had been beaten at the post.

It is at this point that I would like to beg the question, would Dunne have met his intended bride of three years hence if he had actually moved to Gloucestershire? So as it turned out Dunne was remaining in Cumberland, and within three months was taking on one of the biggest responsibilities of his career. Namely the Swine Fever epidemic which spread across the county. September 12th 1865 was when there was a first report of an outbreak of cattle plague in Cumberland, though it wasn't taken especially seriously at first as it only affected one farm. However by October the powers that be were starting to recognize the potential of this deadly disease, following outbreaks on other farms, and the first order affecting the agricultural community was issued on the 31st of this month when it stated that cattle were to be excluded from all markets until further notice. Then it went quiet for a while, with everyone hoping that the disease had gone away ... until the 5th December when it came back with a vengeance. By early January reports in the newspapers stated that the disease was now affecting some 38 counties, with 62,469 cases reported. Clearly Cumberland were not alone. Dunne and his men were to be at forefront of tackling the disease from the beginning.

At the January Quarter Sessions he reported to the justices that: *'No doubt the public should have the fullest benefit of the services of the police without any extra charge being made for their time and labour in connection with the duties involved in this subject. Nevertheless some special expenses must necessarily be incurred, and as these expenses are quite exceptional to those embraced in the regulations I shall be glad to know what way they will have to be reimbursed. Also whether the horses hired at the request of the Penrith magistrates shall be continued?'* He went on to report that: *'53 people have been summoned for removing cattle and other offences against the Order in Council. The superintendents and other mounted officers are upon almost constant duty. Strenuous efforts are being made to induce the owners of cattle and other animals to conform to the regulations and I am confident that every one of our men is activated by a most anxious desire to exert himself to the utmost of his power to endeavour to check this calamity'.* And … never one to miss an opportunity he also made application for an increase in policeman's wages.

Regardless of prayers and all manner of attempts to stop the disease, by February there were no signs of any decrease … in fact if anything the situation was getting worse. Sir George Grey the out-going Home Secretary wrote to Dunne and advised him that: *'the police would be entitled to the usual government allowance for aid given in suppressing the plague'* which in part went some way in answering his question to the justices in the January.

Later that same month Dunne was attending a Cumberland County Meeting in Carlisle where he proposed the formation of a fund in guarantee of the voluntary rate so that immediate action might be taken. He stated that it would take considerable time to collect a voluntary rate and it would be the 1st March before they could get any assistance from Parliament. The names of a certain number of gentlemen should be put down for a guarantee fund so as to enable them to get to work tomorrow and destroy every affected animal in the county. He would be glad himself to put his name down for £100 to a guarantee fund and there were many other gentlemen here present who could better afford to do so than he. If £10,000 were now guaranteed that would be all that would be required to meet all the present cases, and he was sure the farmers would be ready to accept a reasonable value for their stock. Sir R Brisco responded that in reference to what Dunne had said he was afraid was perfectly impracticable. If they would consider the sum of money required to be guaranteed and assuming that the county would not respond to the call, he should like to know where these guarantee gentlemen were. For his part he would not guarantee one halfpenny after what he had seen the county was disposed to do. He had no more confidence until he saw the money down upon the table. Until then he did not believe they would conquer the disease. Subject was then dropped.

Not to be outdone however Dunne next approached a meeting of magistrates and farmers in Penrith where this time he proposed that the Penrith farmers should form a Rinderpest Preventive Association Committee and that they should agree to buy up half their estimated value any cattle pronounced to be suffering from the plague in Leath Ward. This time his proposal was unanimously accepted and a Guarantee Fund was opened. Many attending put their names down for £50 a piece which included Dunne himself.

By the 27th February the Government were at last sitting up and taking notice of the serious problem that was affecting a high proportion of the country, for almost without parallel they swiftly brought in the Cattle Diseases Preventive Act, which amongst its many resolutions stated that *'Chief Constables and all their officers and men be appointed officers for carrying into effect the provisions of the Act ...and that the Chief Constable do as speedily as possible cause all animals condemned by an inspector as affected with the cattle plague to be slaughtered in accordance with Section 12 of this Act'.* Within a week this order was in effect and as far as Cumberland was concerned with a vengeance.

According to newspaper reports of the time *'Police began work on the Monday morning and continued through to Tuesday 3pm, at which point there were no remaining diseased cattle in Cumberland'.* A total of 778 cattle were destroyed. Throughout the entire operation the Chief Constable was in attendance and in full command. In addition to the slaughter each and every farm was thoroughly disinfected. Over the next two weeks a further 1,000 cattle were condemned and at Dunne's recommendation more cattle plague committees were set up across the county... each of which offered financial assistance to the farmers.

Due to the pressure on his own police Dunne was obliged, for a short time at least, to call upon the services of the Lancashire Constabulary for the loan of some of their officers. This in itself was unusual as county constabularies were not in the habit of loaning out their men to other counties, and initially he received a downright 'no' to his request to the Lancashire Chief Constable. However by the simple expedient of bringing this problem directly to the eyes and ears of the Home Secretary he was able to obtain an order authorising the loan of the men. No doubt Lancashire's Chief Constable Captain William Elgee was not exactly pleased with the order, but nevertheless complied. A total of thirty were requested and subsequently worked with his own men, which as it happened was not just for the slaughtering of the animals, but with help in keeping a cordon around the county to ensure no further movement of cattle was allowed.

As he was to later discover through his own crime figures, the fact that they were either fumigating or stopping tramps and vagrants either in or coming into the county actually reduced the crime rate. Having said that, at the same time as the cattle plague was causing untold havoc across the county, the Chief Constable was discovering that the plague was in itself throwing up a considerable number of offences against the Cattle Diseases Preventative Act with many farmers still attempting to sell their cattle to other farmers or moving them outside the infected area.

In all instances it was Dunne himself who instituted the prosecution of the individuals and thus attended court in all cases to give evidence. The first of these cases were being held as early as January 2nd of that year, but they were to continue to be the largest number of offences appearing before the magistrates for many months. There was even an instance of a cattle inspector himself appearing before the magistrates in the April when John Armstrong was charged with keeping alive and curing certain cattle which his co-inspector Mr Howe had condemned as affected with rinderpest. Their were a total of seven charges in all. For these offences he was fined 20/- (£1).

By the October Dunne was reporting to the Justices that it was now some four months and nine days since the last case of cattle plague in Cumberland. A total of 7,632 cattle had been destroyed and 642 farms disinfected. For some months an entire cordon had been placed around the county and Dunne's system of slaughtering infected cattle, disinfecting the farms, and ensuring that cattle were not moved, seemed to have worked. Ever since then whenever their has been similar such animal disease, be it foot and mouth, pleuro-pneumonia, swine fever and any other cattle disease, the 'Cumberland' or 'Dunne' system has been brought into being, and it is still used today as the basic principle of control, as much as it was used then to tackle the diseases. Overall it had cost the county £31,000 but it was money well spent as it was to be many years before it or similar such diseases were to hit the county.

Obviously law and order was still being accomplished throughout the period of the disease, in fact the year had started off with a strike of masons, joiners, shoemakers, tailors and weavers which warranted a certain amount of riot control by Dunne's officers.

In the January Quarter Sessions there had been a total of nineteen prisoners for trial which according to the judge showed a diminution in crime, which at least was some pleasing news for Dunne at this stressful time.

Other good news for Dunne this year was the announcement in the April that his request for an increase in pay for his men had been approved exactly as he had requested ... and as he pointed out it was not before time too, as many of his men had already left to join other forces where the wages were considerably more than he was then offering.

One such officer was Superintendent Little who was applying for the post of Chief Constable of Oldham, though as it transpired, unsuccessfully. Now each and all of his men would receive an average 2/- (10p) per week extra in their pay from now on, which may not seem much in this day and age but it was the equivalent of £20 in today's money. One month later officers attached to the Carlisle City Police were also putting in a request for increased wages !

CHAPTER FIFTEEN

JOHN DUNNE

1867 - 1876

Including the trials of John Little and James Dalgleish

On the assumption that Dunne did not wake up with a severe headache on the 1st January 1867, one can be sure that he soon got one once he arrived at work early that morning. One of his hand-picked and trusted superintendents, namely that of Daniel Munro was reported missing, and more, their were reports of some £60 (equivalent to around £12,000 these days) missing from his office.

Investigation soon determined that not only had Munro stolen the money, but additionally he had also absconded to Edinburgh it was believed with a young woman with whom he had apparently been having an affair ... leaving behind a wife and young family. Without the then benefit of inter-county/country relationships with other police forces their appeared to be little chance of finding the man, even after Dunne posted a reward of £20. All to no avail, for Munro and his girlfriend were never seen again.

The next item of significance for Dunne within the first week of this new year was finding himself a victim of a train crash. Returning from London on the 8th January, and comfortably ensconced in his first class compartment; Dunne suddenly found himself being thrown from one side of his compartment to the other. Other than a few bruises he had been fortunate to get away with little more. It soon appeared however that his train the London to Carlisle somewhere between Southwaite and Calthwaite and whilst travelling at high speed, had suffered a broken axle and become derailed. A number of people were injured in the accident, but fortunately none seriously... no doubt this event would be yet something else that Dunne could relay to his friends over dinner, along with many other unusual circumstances that had happened to him over the years.

Upon his return to Carlisle one of the first items on his agenda was his required attendance at the January Cumberland Quarter Sessions. According to the *Cumberland Pacquet* however, rather than him giving his police report as was normal on these occasions, or giving evidence, he was needed simply to hear a speech by the justices about: the *'efficient services of the 'indefatigable Chief Constable'* during the cattle plague and where it was generally expressed that his energy and zeal demanded some compensation. It was resolved that the consideration of the remuneration justly due to the Chief Constable for his exertions in the suppression of the cattle plague be referred to the Police Committee and that they report at the next assizes'. So it looked as though Dunne was in for another pay rise!

As it happened the January train incident was not to be the only train accident involving Dunne at the early part of this year, though this time fortunately not with him as a victim, with the accident itself being considered quite bizarre. The London and North Western Railway was on its way from Lancaster to Carlisle along the edge of the Lake District, at the point where it runs through the Tebay junction, Shap, (famous for its granite) and Clifton before reaching Penrith, where tourists changed trains for Keswick. It was along this lonely rocky line at about 11.20 pm on the night of 26th February that a goods train having successfully climbed the Shap incline, came through Clifton. It was then that the town of Penrith as well as the district for miles around were startled that night by what was initially presumed to be an earthquake. For miles around several window panes were broken, doors thrown open or closed violently. It was quickly discovered that this was not an earthquake as first thought, but an explosion of a wagon load of gunpowder, on the railway close to Yanwath Bridge.

Apparently the wagon had left the rails and 'jumped' onto the line coming in the opposite direction. As luck would have it their just had to be a another train coming from the opposite direction at the precise same time, which was to bring about a crash along with an explosion as a result. The explosion for those who saw it would have been quite dramatic for part of the Yanwath Bridge was lifted, the railway walls were levelled, and the top of the wagon was blown as far afield as the water trough situated on the east of the village. The engine of the ongoing train was what today we would class as a total write-off, but most unfortunate of all was the fact that this time their was to be loss of life for the engine driver and the fireman were killed. Some extent of the damage can be gathered by the knowledge that the explosion caused a fire that took three days to extinguish. Apparently what had happened was that one of the wagons on the goods train was filled with some four tons of gunpowder and it just happened that it was that one that came to a halt slap bang in the middle of the up line. Before the train guards could do anything to give notice of the danger they heard the roar of an approaching train on the up line. It was another goods train. The driver of that train, seeing no signal and supposing the line clear, came along at full speed-straight into the gunpowder wagon. Instantly there was a shower of sparks and a vast, all encompassing explosion that shook and rumbled hundreds of feet into the air and deep down into the earth. As soon as they had recovered the four survivors which included the driver and fireman of the train from the south, along with the guards of both trains quickly took measures to stop further traffic north and south of the blockage.

No doubt that was yet another incident that would take up hours of Dunne's time in producing reports to the coroners and justices. In fact the inquest on the 5th March determined that the driver and fireman had been accidentally killed ... and a short after-thought here ... there actually had been a minor earthquake just four days earlier, on the 23rd which had affected the towns of Windermere, Bowness, Grasmere, Ambleside, Coniston and Hawkshead. So it is quite understandable that the local populace would immediately think 'earthquake'.

Of particular concern to Dunne and his constables this year was possible problems with the Irish Fenian movement. The problem had of course been around for some years, especially so in Ireland where the leader John Mahoney had fled to America firstly to avoid arrest, but also importantly to try and gain support in the desire to separate Ireland from England. However there were concerns in England that members of this movement would gain support from the large Irish community and their could quite easily be an uprising. Indeed their had already been attempts for an uprising in Ireland in 1866, but it had never taken place as the Government had already been aware of it. Though the fear was mainly confined to London, correctly so as it happened, nevertheless Cumberland police were on alert and the *Cumberland Pacquet* was already writing of '*Fear of Fenians*' as early as February. In fact later that month suspected Fenians were arrested in Whitehaven, though later released due to insufficient evidence. The matter was actually raised at the July 9th Cumberland Quarter Sessions when the justices enquired of Dunne what contingency plans he had in hand for a possible attack on the militia in Whithaven. Dunne appeared to know more than he was saying, for he simply replied that '*he had everything in hand in the event of an attack, and in any case their was nothing that the public needed to concern themselves about*'.

Not so in Manchester however, for later that year, on the 18th September a group of armed Irishmen freed two Fenian prisoners from a prison van on Hyde Road, Manchester. They had been arrested during an attempt to attack Chester Castle to gain weapons and ammunition, clearly showing that the justices concern about an attack on Carlisle Castle earlier that year was not entirely unfounded. During the escape attempt a policeman Sergeant Charles Brett was accidentally shot dead. Three Irishmen, William Allen, Michael Larkin and Michael O'Brien were convicted for the shooting and hanged in public outside the New Bailey prison, Salford on the 23rd November. (The last public hanging in England as it happened).

Few believed that they were guilty and major demonstrations were held in England, Ireland and the United States. The executions served as a spur to those seeking Irish independence. Friedrich Engels (the father of the Marxist theory alongside Karl Marx) was himself living in Manchester at this time with an Irishwoman, Lizzie Burns. After the execution he noted prophetically that the executions had *'accomplished the final act of separation between England and Ireland, the only thing the Fenians still lacked were martyrs ... They have been provided with these'.* In December this same year several Londoners were killed when a bomb planted by the Fenians exploded at Clerkenwell Prison.This not only caused a wave of anti-Irish feeling in London but elsewhere in England.

Clearly Cumberland was on 'red-alert' for a while yet, and rightly so, for in the November following the executions of the three Fenians, Irish uprisings were expected in various sectors of Cumberland and extra police officers were posted at Cleator, Harrington and Millom all armed with revolvers and cutlasses, and according to the *Cumberland Pacquet*, *'ready for any emergency'.* The report went on to say that: *'both Dunne and Superintendent Little were on constant duty and were at all times in communication with each area, making such general arrangements so that any problems that could have arisen would have been effectively overwhelmed and crushed at the slightest attempt to disturb the public peace of these neighbourhoods'.*

Their was a further fear of uprising in the December, again at Cleator Moor and once again Dunne was on hand with a large contingent of his officers armed and ready for any such problems. However like the earlier scare, the Irish contingent based in these towns thought better of causing havoc, and Dunne and his men were fortunately not required. Even New Year festivities were not sacrosanct, as the Whitehaven Town and Harbour Committee were concerned that a Fenian attack was imminent, though this time rather than call upon the police for assistance, they requested and received two companies of soldiers from the 70th Regiment, who were barracked temporarily in Whitehaven. Nevertheless following questions at the next Cumberland Assizes it was thought appropriate to be fully prepared for such emergencies in the future, and Dunne was charged with recruiting a minimum of one thousand special constables to be available purely in times of emergency.

The cattle plague problems that had caused so many problems over the previous two years appeared to be making a comeback in the March – which immediately caused panic in Cumberland, not least of all in Dunne's office, where he would have been anticipating yet another draw upon his men and finances for the ensuing months. As it happened it was unfounded as the attack on the 19th was confined to just one cow in Lanercost which was suffering from the disease, whereupon Dunne issued orders that it was to be immediately destroyed. This would have been particularly disastrous for this farmer as it was the only cow he owned. Fortunately as it happened this was to be the only case of the disease this year (and for many years to come) for on April 9th the cattle plague restrictions were at long last lifted.

One week later at the Cumberland Quarter Sessions it was reported that the Police Committee wished to thank Dunne for all his work during the Cattle Plague. They clearly were concerned about losing him for their report also included a recommendation for an increase in his pay. In fact the Home Secretary actually approved an increase in his annual salary from £400 to £500 per annum. The run-of-the-mill constables had to be content with a new uniform.

Up until now romance and emotion, to be the best of the writers knowledge, have played little or no part in Dunne's life and career, but soon all that was to change. Dunne himself would by this time have been considered an eligible bachelor. He was on an excellent income, the equivalent these days of £100,000 per annum (plus expenses) and in consequence had moved from his bachelor quarters at his offices in Carlisle to an extensive two storey house, Moorhouse Hall, in Warwick, Wetherall, complete with accompanying cottage for his household staff. Dunne was clearly coming up in the world. Perhaps now was the time for him to consider matrimony after all he was 42 years of age, and if he was to consider marriage and a family to perpetuate the family name than clearly he should not be leaving it much longer. His bride to be whom he would regularly be seen escorting this year was a certain Mary Barnes one of four daughters of Dr Barnes, an eminent GP living at Bunkers Hill, Carlisle, and justice of the peace, whom Dunne would have known well due to his regular attendances at Quarter Sessions over the years. In all probability Dunne would have made the acquaintance of Mary at one of the regular formal dinners arranged by magistrates and justices and at which he would have been obliged to attend and in all probability actually introduced to Mary by her father.

Mary by 1867 was 37 of age, and in all probability at this age in the Victorian era would have convinced herself that she was to remain 'on the shelf', and spinsterhood with no family of her own was to be her future, though her lack of finding a husband would have had nothing to do with lack of dowry for she was an heiress in her own right.

Her meeting with Dunne this year was to change everything for her. The Barnes were a wealthy family. They already owned and lived at Bunkers Hill, named by the original owner, the 11th Duke of Norfolk after the major engagement at Bunkers Hill, in the Charlestown peninsular (South Carolina) during the first major engagement of the American War of Independence in 1775. It is interesting to note that there was a William Barnes linked to Bunkers Hill in North Carolina USA in the early 1800's had to be a family member. The Barnes family actually purchased the house in 1832. Thomas Barne's wife Anne, was the daughter of John Ismay and had been born at Bromfield, near Aspatria.

The Ismay's were 'big' in Whitehaven, for her father and other family members were founder directors of the renowned shipping company the White Star Line (Isaac Fletcher M.P for Cockermouth was one) ... later to become infamous as owners of the R.M.S Titanic in 1912. (though in truth they had had an earlier disaster in 1873 with the sinking of the SS Atlantic and the loss of 535 lives, near Halifax, Nova Scotia).

This romance, and subsequent engagement were to continue though until their expected marriage in October of 1868 – but that is still to come.

As in previous years there were numerous new laws through 1867. One of these was The Police Town Clauses Act which due to its extent would have taken considerable understanding today, as much as it did in 1867. Dunne must have read it however for in the Cockermouth magistrates courts in the June he was arguing with this court over the police right to arrest and remand anyone caught throwing stones. Magistrates agreed eventually, and the offenders, two young boys were imprisoned for seven days. There was also good news for the Repeal of the Master and Servant Act actually relieved the police of their, until now, responsibility to intervene in conflicts between employers and individual employees.That would have freed him up at least an extra minute a day!

Unfortunately the 1867 Criminal Law Amendment Act swiftly brought back that gained minute which amongst other things permitted evidence noted down by the police to be read in court. Even prisoners on trial for felony were now allowed to call witnesses for the first time.

One big law that came into being this year and caused considerable controversy would have been the Vaccination Act. This was the law that stated that for the first time parents were compelled to have their children vaccinated against smallpox within the first ninety days of its life. Those who objected would be continually badgered by magistrates and fined until the child turned fourteen.

The law was passed on the assurance of medical officials that smallpox vaccinations were safe. Non-payment of fines for skipping smallpox vaccination resulted in harsh penalties, which on summary conviction would be as much as

20/- (£1) The 'vaccinators' were paid 1/- (5p) to 3/- (15p) for each child dependant on how far they had to travel.

And hanging, drawing and quartering was abolished this year ... not that there had been any instances of this punishment for many a long year – still in force though for high treason. And, though transportation had to all intents and purposes been discontinued some ten years earlier it was in fact only this year that the last transport ship sailed for Australia, The Hougoumont carrying a number of Fenians.

The tenth (and as it happened the last) report of Lt Col. Woodford (Inspector of Constabulary) was in the September. Besides announcing his pleasure at the actions of the police during the recent cattle plague he additionally pointed out the difficulty the force had been experiencing over the last year or two in *'procuring and retaining the services of men properly qualified to discharge the duties of police constables'.* He went on to say that *'the difficulty has been met in the part of the county magistrates and generally that of the town councils of boroughs where it was felt requisite by authorising an increase in pay'.*

It was in the November that Dunne was to hear the sad news that his long-term friend Colonel Woodford had died suddenly at his home,The Cliff, in Preston. And, quite why Dunne had left it so long to complain, but it was not until the October that we are learning that in a letter addressed to Mr Nanson, the Town Clerk of Carlisle, he is complaining about their Chief officer in Carlisle (George E Bent) entitling himself Chief Constable. As he explained the law as it then stood only allowed for Bent to term himself superintendent of police. Dunne pointed out that when he was head of police in Newcastle he was entitled superintendent of police as indeed was his predecessor ... Strangely enough the complaint originated from the Inspector of Constabulary himself. Considering that it was Dunne himself who appointed Bent Carlisle superintendent back in 1858 shortly after his own appointment, it is difficult to understand why he left it to someone else to complain especially so when he had experienced similar occurrences in the past.

In the December Dunne was to learn that Bent's predecessor John Sabbage (he who Dunne had helped to obtain the post of Chief Constable of Newcastle in 1857) had died suddenly leaving the post open again. This time the salary was being advertised at £300 per annum, plus an extra £50 for a horse.

In the December Newcastle was in the news again when their were reports of a serious explosion where five people were killed and many injured. No doubts this would have brought back some sad memories to Dunne.

By 1868 there were two major incidents that warranted Dunne's undivided attention, one of course was his requirement to attend a marriage ceremony in London in the October (his own), the other was the major fire at Greystoke Castle, the home of Henry Howard which occurred on the 5th May of this year. A maid had apparently left a lighted candle in a cupboard full of linen and the consequent fire destroyed large parts of the castle. Many of the treasures and works of art were lost for ever, It was rebuilt by Henry Howard (the 18th Earl of Suffolk) using labour and materials from within the estate,. It is believed that the maid received her 'marching orders'. The fire actually blazed for days, and the volunteer fire brigade under Dunne's direction were in attendance throughout.

1868 wasn't exactly a good year for the Earl as in the General Election of this year he was defeated, and needed to stand down from his position as MP for Amesbury (Wiltshire). On the other hand, like Dunne, he too chose 1868 to get married (at age thirty-five) to Mary Eleanor Lauderdale, daughter of the Hon. Henry Amelius Coventry. They went on to have six children ... so it wasn't all bad after all. History doesn't tell us if Dunne was invited to the wedding.

The other major incident was Dunne's own wedding which took place on October 1st 1868 at All Souls Church, Langham Place, London, and was conducted by the Rev. Henry Woods M.A Rector of Tidmarsh, Berks. Mary Barnes is listed as the eldest daughter of Thomas Barnes M.D of Bunkers Hill, Cumberland and Tring Park, Hertfordshire. Following a rush back to Cumberland that day the marriage was celebrated in his home town of Warwick that evening. According to the *Cumberland Pacquet* dated 13th October:

> *'The celebration of the marriage of John Dunne Esq Chief Constable and Miss Barnes of Bunkers Hill which took place on Thursday 1st October last was celebrated on the same evening at the Queens Arms Inn, village of Warwick, near Moorhouse Hall the residence of the bridegroom who with his wonted generosity and kindness issued a cordial invitation through Mr Bell to all the house-holders of the village to partake of a supper on the happy event. The chair was occupied by the worthy host and the vice-chair by Mr G Johnston of Moorhouse. The company assembled enjoyed themselves with the greatest hilarity. Supper over the host of the house in a very graphic and complimentary speech proposed the health of the happy pair which was responded to by the whole company with the heartiest cheers. The Misses Bell spared no pains in decorating the room for the special occasion.'*

No mention of *'throwing the stocking'* an old Cumbrian habit where the couple sit in their matrimonial bed, and the guests throw the brides stockings at them ... their way of giving good luck apparently. Frankly Dunne had every reason to be happy, not only had he married a charming daughter of a well known and respected family, but as earlier stated, a wealthy family at that, for it would have been around this time he would have determined exactly how wealthy his new bride was.

As is noted the Barnes declared their homes as Bunkers Hill and Tring Park, Hertfordshire, which initially indicates that the family at least owned two homes. However Tring Park was not then their property at least not in its entirety, though their was a part ownership of the manor in the name of Ann Barnes, Thomas Barnes wife. Tring Park, mansion (and 3,643 acres) was a large property built to a design of Sir Christopher Wren in 1685, and was well known to at least two frequent visitors, namely Charles II, and William III.

Its background was quite impressive. Sir William Gore Lord Mayor of London bought it in 1705 and it then remained in the family for two generations. In 1786 it was sold to Sir Drummond Smith, a London banker who refurbished the interior in Georgian style and at the same time remodelled the park in the fashion made popular by 'Capability Brown'. William Kay, a Manchester textile magnate then bought the estate in 1823, (for £90,000) and in 1838 Nathan de Rotchshild began renting Tring Park simply as a summer residence. When the property was sold in 1872, Lionel de Rothschild bought it as a wedding present for his son Sir Nathaniel (later Lord) Rothschild.

Interestingly, and possibly appropriately William Kay himself had Cumberland connections having been born at The Mains, Wigton which would well explain the Barnes family link to the Kay's for William Kay was a brother to one of the Ismay family, thus an uncle to Ann Barnes. The background to Ann's part ownership of Tring Park was that when Sir Drummond Smith died in 1823, he died without issue, thus the manor was sold to the aforementioned William Kay, and when he died in 1838 half of the estate under his will went to his son William for life, with the remaining half to the male heirs and to the testators nephew and niece, namely Robert Nixon of Aylesbury and Ann, only daughter of John Ismay ... who as we have now learnt was to become the wife of Thomas Barnes.

Naturally before the introduction of the Married Women's Property Act in 1882 any property owned by a wife would automatically have become the property of her husband upon marriage, Thomas Barnes was thus perfectly in his right to name Tring Park as his possession, even if only in part. Though by

1870 the government of the day had actually brought into being the Women's Property Act initially it was somewhat ambiguous and it was not until 1872 that the government clarified the act by ruling that such property would be confined solely to single and widowed women. Dunne (and Barnes) would undoubtedly have breathed a large sigh of relief.

Weddings apart, Dunne, thanks to his new wife, was now part of an exceptionally wealthy Cumberland family, and to celebrate his new position in the community bought Moorhouse Hall, which until now he had been renting. Such a marriage for Dunne would have given him an opening for a whole new range of friends and acquaintances, and of course Mary would have felt herself lucky not only to have found love so late in life, but also ongoing security.

However as much as Dunne would probably have liked to have spent more time with his new bride, the job of policing the two counties needed to go on. Earlier that year he had been surprised to learn of the resignation on Jan 28th of John Hibbert the superintendent of police for Westmorland who had been based in Kendal. He had been fortunate in obtaining the post of Chief Constable of Salford, near Manchester. No doubt Dunne would have given him a few tips about policing in this area. In the meantime Dunne had the task of finding a replacement for the ambitious superintendent and decided on a novel way to temporarily 'fill the breech' by proposing that two members of the Town Council should provide extra support to the town by pounding the streets until a replacement was found. Considering that these councillors were under no obligation to Dunne to undertake such duties, it does at least give us a good indication of the esteem that such individuals had in his command. It was, as stated, only temporary for just four weeks later Dunne had moved superintendent Bird from Wigton to Kendal, and promoted him to superintendent of police for Westmorland.

In the February Dunne received the news that Carlisle Gaol, for the first time in its history, was full with 150 prisoners, (with 122 of them being Roman Catholics) indicating either that he and his officers were doing an excellent job, or crime was on the increase.

Amongst the inmates on remand at this time was another girl accused of concealment of birth, and a certain Mary Hindson aged eleven years convicted of stealing a dress two jackets, gold ear-rings. She was later sentenced to imprisonment for a fortnight followed by a spell in the reformatory. Later in the April the judge at the Cumberland Assizes was at pains to point out that the average number of prisoners which had been disposed of in past seven years was seventeen and at this trial there were ten awaiting judgement, PLUS the nine which had been disposed of under the Criminal Justice Act making nineteen in total or in other words far more than the average. Rather than blame (or congratulate) Dunne the Judge reckoned it was *'the strictness which had been observed in committing tramps that had caused this and hoped it would have the effect of reducing crime'.*

Another inmate at this time, on remand for burglary, was a certain George Washington. No, not the American president but a black man, the son of a slave – hence the name (though the name could also be linked to the fact that the port of Whitehaven was once the home of Mildred Washington the president's grandmother) who had clearly got himself in a spot of bother. Rather than appear before the judges he and a fellow prisoner decided to affect an escape. They were only semi-successful however for one prisoner broke his ankle in jumping over the prison wall, and Washington was caught within a few hours. No doubt a black face amongst so many whites didn't exactly help his attempt. For his pains George Washington, then aged twenty-five years got six months hard labour for escaping whilst on remand. However his fellow prisoner, a white man and who had also been on remand, received no sentence whatsoever. Just to add to his pains, one month later Washington was up before the judge on the original charge of burglary, and received a sentence of ten years.

This was the year that Parliament in the May passed the Capital Punishment within Prison Act ending public hangings and directing that all future executions take place privately within prisons ... which was one form of entertainment that the people of Cumberland and Westmorland would not be enjoying any more.

Other major changes to the law was the fact that no more convicts would be transported to Western Australia, from now on convicts would have to be satisfied with a jail sentence – invariably with hard labour.

Another Act this year was the Pharmacy Act which at long last restricted the sale of opium ... though as to be expected the sale and consumption still continues, illegally, even to the present day.

Of perhaps more importance to Dunne was the knowledge that there were now telegraph links between police stations, though initially this was only in London. Within a year or two, Cumberland was to be linked to this important service. Whether he would have been so keen at the news in the April that the Police Committee were planning to install a library in the police station, specifically for the use of constables, and hopefully as an aid to their further education, is not reported.

Probably the only major incident of consequence in 1868 would have been the strike of some four hundred miners at Flimby Green during the July, which thanks to the usual fighting and squabbling expected of miners would take up a great deal of police time.

However 1869 was a little different insomuch that there was yet again to be some major trials for Dunne to contend. The most important of these so easily could have brought its perpetrator to the scaffold. This crime later became known as the Raffles Shooting and it took place in the January. The story goes that during the evening of Saturday 30th January 1869, a farm labourer by the name John Ward was making his way home to Great Orton, following a visit to Carlisle. His route took him via the area known as Raffles, though the area then was no more than a small village with just one public house, the predecessor of the present Horse and Farrier. He was no more than a few hundred yards beyond the turnpike when a gun went off and his right shoulder was peppered with small shot. He swung round only to receive another volley – this time in the chest. It was already fairly dark but he later reported that he saw a short man wearing what he remembered as a frock coat and standing just a few yards from him. In considerable pain, he struggled to the nearby pub where he received first aid before he was removed by cart to the nearby infirmary. Thanks to the local police they had a man answering the description in custody within just three days. He was named as John Little and was reported in the press as being aged thirty-five years, and employed as a butcher in Crofton. The evidence against Little was soon found to be overwhelming so much so that it took the jury only ten minutes to find him guilty without them even leaving the courtroom. Mr Justice Lush firmly advised Little that had Ward died, then the juries decision would have meant finding himself a place on the scaffold. Instead he received twenty years penal servitude clearly indicating even in 1869 the menace of firearms was recognised.

In fact it was within the law for any man, woman or street urchin even at this time to carry a gun for it was not until 1870 before a licence to carry one was introduced.

Six months later another crime was perpetrated in Cumberland once again involving poachers and poaching, and additionally inadvertently caused the death of the water bailiff. However though a great deal of time and effort was exerted by Dunne and his senior officers in the hopes of obtaining a conviction for murder, or if necessary the lower charge of manslaughter this was not to be the simple murder case that he had at first anticipated. The jury in this instance determined that there was insufficient evidence to convict two of the criminals and they were discharged by the judge, the remaining defendant Hodgson received just five years.

March of this year saw the introduction of a new Inspector of Constabulary to replace the late lamented Colonel Woodford, who had died in the November of 1867. The new man was a certain Captain Elgee (yet another of military rank) who was responsible for all constabularies in the north of England. His first report on the state of the joint constabularies of Cumberland and Westmorland was detailed in the *Cumberland Pacquet* for the 9th March and reported verbatim:

> *'In my report upon the counties of Cumberland and Westmorland I have referred to the measures the justices have taken for the suppression of vagrancy by rigidly enforcing the provisions of the Vagrant Act and which according to a statement kindly furnished me by the Chief Constable have been attended to with favourable results. Undoubtedly a considerable amount of crime especially in country districts is committed by persons on tramp and were the course pursued in Cumberland and Westmorland generally adopted and the law in respect of vagrants and tramps strictly administered I am of the opinion it would be found to operate beneficially in the suppression of professional vagrancy and the diminution of crime.'*

He went on to report that in the year ended 30th June 1868 a total of 288 tramps had been apprehended in Cumberland of which 173 had been committed to prison, whilst in Westmorland 166 had been apprehended with 124 committed to prison.

He declared that the Cumberland Police force now consisted of, seven superintendents, seven inspectors, eight sergeants, eighty-seven constables and thirteen 'additional constables' ... (i.e. sworn in but only called upon to assist in times of emergency). In Westmorland the force now consisted of two superintendents, two inspectors, one sergeant, nineteen constables, plus two 'additional constables'. In other words Dunne's constabularies now totalled a force of 133 (109 Cumberland and 24 Westmorland), plus of course the fifteen in total 'additional constables').

However, we are reminded that besides the normal duties of controlling crime this force still had responsibility in a number of other duties: assistant relieving officers for relief of tramps and vagrants, inspectors of common lodging houses, inspectors of roads, acting as 'High Constables' at petty sessional divisions and in a limited number of areas, inspectors of nuisances. He further noted that in his opinion there was still insufficient police in the towns of Wigton and Cockermouth, and recommended the appointment of at least two further police constables.

Few additional laws for Dunne to 'take on board' around this time,; one was the Contagious Diseases Act which clarified the law regarding arresting female prostitutes. Once again, as in previous laws there was no law that allowed for the arrest of the male customers. Of more importance, and one which would bring in far more paper-work for his men (a complaint that is still being aired to this day) was the Habitual Criminals Act of this year. We are already aware of the 'ticket of leave' scheme, where prisoners were often released early. People were still concerned that they would re-offend. Now these 'ticket' prisoners had to prove that they had a job otherwise they would be immediately sent back to prison. The act was also designed to allow for the suppression of crime by old offenders and authorised their summary apprehension upon any suspicion that they may be intending to commit a crime. At the same time as this act was being enforced the government brought out the Imprisonment for Debt Act. (better known as Debtors Act 1869) Until now many people in debt were sent to prison until they could pay off their debts.This was the act that stopped that for most people. What the act didn't cover was debt incurred involving court costs and penalties earlier awarded. The act was in all probability brought about due to the fact that even then the prisons were close to being full, with national crime being reported as up by 1.98% on the previous year.

Still for Dunne this did mean one group of people were not now eligible for arrest. One door opened, one closed! The long awaited Gangs Act was also passed this year. For years there had been a cruel ongoing use of child labour hired by groups of itinerant gangs. These gangs could be anything from a dozen to a hundred and comprised of men women and children. They were hired out by a gang master as mass labour for the harshest tasks-stone and weed clearing, potato planting, ditching, turnip havesting etc. The Gangs Act was meant to control these gangs ... up to a point ... by forbidding the use of any child under the age of eight. Not that the act helped much, for many children as young as six were still put to work on the quiet and paid a mere shilling (5p) a week.

It would be true to say that children under thirteen still made up about a tenth of the workforce in textile factories. Over 40,000 of them toiled in cotton mills and almost 25,000 in woollen mills with similar number of thirteen to eighteen years old. Around the same time as the poaching case(s) were ongoing Dunne was 'flitting' between Carlisle and Whitehaven thanks to an ongoing argument with his arch-enemy Brisco. This was thanks to Brisco complaining that Dunne had been employing his men in quite large numbers in Brampton and Longtown, during the elections of that year, without apparently having the authority to do so. Dunne responded that without inferring any political prejudice it was initially the Liberal Party of Whitehaven who had requested him to supply a large body of police to man their polling stations. As he understood it the local police were overpowered in these two areas. In addition Wigton Police station were also having problems. In order to deal with the problem he initially referred to Superintendent Bent of Carlisle Police for help with more men. His answer was to refer him to the mayor for the necessary authority. No help being forthcoming in that direction he went to see one of his own magistrates who immediately gave permission for the extra police to be supplied. As it happened they were urgently needed to control the angry crowds, and in fact many people were injured during this incident. His prompt action quickly sorted out the problems, though as it turned out it didn't do a lot for Dunne's future relations with Brisco.

More than anything else this year, the one concern that Dunne would have had uppermost in his mind was a possible re-occurrence of the cattle disease. His fears were founded when in the October the local newspapers were reporting another instance of the disease, though this time it was in Westmorland, rather than in Cumberland ... which was a first for them The Kendal Mercury reported:

'We regret to learn that Westmorland which has hitherto enjoyed a happy immunity from the various phrases of destructive maladies peculiar to homed stock has become a scene of an outbreak of cattle disease. According to a report upon which we may place every possible reliance, it is stated that what is known as the foot and mouth disease, now prevalent in the neighbouring counties of Lancashire, Yorkshire, Durham, and Northumberland has manifested itself in the Eastern Division of this county. Several cattle have been seized in the neighbourhood of Newbiggin and Kirkby Stephen'.

The article continued:

'For the source or cause of the disaster we have not far to look. On Friday in last week, a peripatetic drover came out of Yorkshire driving before him between one and two hundred head of cattle, which he pushed on to Appleby and there disposed of it. It has since turned out that these animals were affected with the new contagion and hence distributed as they have been over the hitherto pure and healthy farm-steads of this county. It is easy enough to divine the cause of the present unwelcome bearer of sickness to our herds and of trouble to our agriculturists. To make matters worse, Brough Hill Fair was held on Thursday and yesterday when an immense gathering of horned cattle took place and where it would be almost too much to suppose that the contagion did not receive a still further stimulus in its career of devastation. Up to the present time however, we have not heard of any fresh case of outbreak. The magistrates are using every conceivable precaution to ward off the impending danger and the various approaches to the county are under

> *strict police surveillance, the instructions from the Chief Constable being most emphatic and most comprehensive. As may be conjectured the fatal presence has caused no slight dismay to the minds of the farming community generally in the immediate neighbourhood of the outbreak.'*

However the movement of cattle meant that Cumberland were not to miss out on the disease for the Carlisle Journal additionally reported that:

> *'The foot and mouth disease continues to spread in Leath Ward in this county. Mr Edward Carlisle, the Inspector for Leath Ward has been during the past days called to two or three places that have been infected since our last visit. The disease still exists on the farm of Mr Stephenson, of Dacre and also on the premises of Mr Noble of the same place. Six fresh cases were reported from Dalemain, the other places are Mr Stamper, Lamonby, Mr Hodgson Norman, Mains, Kirkoswald, Mr Brunskill, Blencairn, and Mr Clarke, Busk, Rernwick In no case has the disease yet proved fatal.'*

Fortunately the disease in both counties was quickly remedied thanks mostly to Dunne's trusted methods. Nevertheless after three years now of the disease taking over the lives of himself and men, it is doubtful that Dunne rested easily, no doubt anticipating a further outbreak at any time. Mind you the news that Mary Dunne would have been announcing her pregnancy around May/June this year of this year would have cheered him up a bit .

The big news for Dunne (and Mary) in 1870 would have been the birth of their first child ... a daughter, namely Henrietta Julia Mary who was born at home in the January. Quite where the name Henrietta (or the male version Henry) comes from it is difficult to ascertain for it certainly didn't stem from either the Darby Dunne side of the family or what Dunne would have us believe as his ancestors, the Brittas side. Julia however would have been the name of Dunne's mother, and of course Mary is self explanatory. One can be sure that Mary would have utilised the old and aged custom in Cumberland of celebrating a Wives Day (or Wiving) where she would invite her female friends to tea to show off her new born. Mary at now 40 years of age would in all probability not have had an easy birth, but this was not to stop her having more children for later that year in the September she would have been happily (?) telling her husband that she was indeed pregnant again, this time with the birth forecast for the April of the following year. Becoming pregnant so soon after the birth of their first child could have presented a few medical problems for her to contend with, but from a financial point of view would simply for Mary, have meant employing a nanny a little earlier than she had perhaps first considered. Annoyingly for Dunne perhaps at this time was his obligation, also in January, of attending the Cumberland Assizes in the January, for yet another manslaughter trial, The victim this time was a fellow named Henry Kendal who had died violently in a fight in the January. The accused was 25 year old Wilson Towers. Towers was tried the following month but everyone immediately concerned had been so drunk that it was impossible to say whether he had knocked Kendal down or not. The cause of death was given as concussion of the brain and there were no other marks on Kendal's body deemed serious enough to cause death. Towers was not surprisingly found not guilty and was simply bound over to keep the peace.

One assumes that Dunne was not too happy with the outcome of this trial Interestingly the tiny village of Armathawaite was in the news this year when the *Cumberland Pacquet* was reporting an accident on a velocipede – literally one of the first cycles to have been seen on the roads of Cumberland. It was not just the curiosity of the strange four wheeled vehicle that made it newsworthy it was more the case that the rider had somehow managed to get his feet entangled in the mechanism and in the process badly damaged his foot. It fact the injury was so bad that the cyclist actually died of his injuries the following day meaning that in all probability this fatal accident would have been the first of its kind in the country. One can imagine the police constable's problems in writing up, for him, the very first fatal wheeled traffic accident.

The year 1871 was yet another important date in Dunne's life. In the first instance the birth of his second child a long awaited son in the June, would have made him especially happy. Once again the child was born at home Moorhouse Hall. The child was baptized on the 25th June and given the name Francis Plunkett Neville; named after a member of Dunne's assumed 'Brittas' side of the Irish family, and a certain Major General Francis Plunkett in particular. Coincidentally the child's namesake died himself just three years later in 1874. Regretfully the birth was tempered somewhat by the death on the 3rd February of Mary's mother Anne, at the low age of just sixty-nine.

In the January (10th) Dunne would have found himself, along with a number of his men fighting an enormous fire at Slater's Cotton Factory in Carlisle. The fire was so severe that it totally destroyed the building thus putting over two hundred women out of work for some time until it was re-built. The fire proved to be the largest the police and fire service had had to contend with since the formation of the fire service in 1866. Though one hesitates to consider arson, it is a fact that the factory burnt down once again in 1889, right at the time the cotton industry was going through a severe time ... coincidence?

Also brought into law this year was the Prevention of Crimes Act 1871 which at long last established a register of convicted criminals nationwide and set down regulations for photographing prisoners, as well as establishing penalties for repeat offenders and other areas of prison discipline. The act also allowed for every holder of a licence under the Penal Servitude Act to notify his/her residence plus any change of residence to the police.

For the past few years many police forces had been utilising the services of a recently published newspaper *the Police Gazette* which posted regular items on its most wanted list, plus listing those convicts which had recently absconded. Until now Dunne had not given much thought to its advantages rarely posting items in the newspaper, but at least the new act allowed for county forces to work together for the benefit of all, helped no doubt by the recent introduction of photography and the telex service. With the population of Cumberland (alone) having increased to 220,253, and of which 5.39% of them were or Irish descent, without any recent increase in numbers his small force needed all the help he could get if he was to keep the crime figures acceptable to the Police Committee. Crime was an ever increasing problem. Numbers were indeed up as was indicated by the police reports presented by Dunne at this years Assizes. However not all were murder and manslaughter cases, though it is true there were certainly very many of them throughout his time in office.

However besides the many trials and tribulations that 1871 had brought Dunne, 1872 was to change his life forever. Though he was not to know it at the time it was the actions of his father-in-law, Thomas Barnes that was to later this year bring about these changes. As we have learnt the Barnes family besides owning Bunkers Hill also had a large financial interest in the large estate known as Tring Park in Hertfordshire. Barnes along with the other owners were approached towards the latter end of 1871 to determine whether they would be prepared to sell their interest in the property to the then tenant Baron Lionel Nathan de Rothschild. Having lost his wife just a few months earlier Thomas would no doubt have felt that he had no reason to hang onto to his interest in the mansion, and willingly gave his consent However rather than hold onto the money or invest it back in Cumberland he chose instead to invest again ... this time in the manor of Bunstruex (referred to as Brunstrux in Dod's Peerage) in the village of Berkhamstead, again in Hertfordshire. Like Tring Park this manor also had history. The manor of Bunstreux and Richardyns (as it was correctly named) was originally held of the king as the honour of Berkhampstead. Sir Henry Chauncy, the Hertfordshire historian (writing in Historical Antiques of Hertfordshire) states that this manor was parcel of the revenue of the abbey of Faversham, and was granted by the abbey to Robert Whittingham. In 1462 it was granted to Thomas Montgomery for life as part of the possessions of Sir Robert Whittingham. In 1472 it was settled on Thomas for life, with remainder to Henry Danvers and others. It was settled in 1485 on Catherine, widow of Robert Whittingham and on her death it passed to her daughter Margaret and her husband John Verney. From this point it descended with the manor of Pendley until 1872 when it was bought by Thomas Barnes.

Unfortunately for Thomas he did not live long enough to enjoy his new property, for he died rather suddenly, and certainly rather unexpectedly on the 31st March this same year aged 78. In his will he left Bunkers Hill jointly to his son (and heir) John, and to his four daughters. Bunstreux Manor however, in its entirety was left solely to his daughter Mary, John Dunne's wife – the property was valued at £40,000 (today that equates to around £8 million) John Dunne was now a man of property and very rich in the process.

Though he was of course Chief Constable, and had been so now for fifteen years, there would also have been the nagging thought in the back of his head that he was not quite the person that many thought of him, he knew, though he was probably the only one that did, that he did not come from an influential family. Now all that had changed. He was equal to the many magistrates, justices, and wealthy business people with whom he regularly came into contact on a daily basis. One indication of this was the addition of Esquire (esq.) to his name, normally only used by those holding some academic achievement, or person of property.

One supposes that Dunne was brought down to earth shortly after this stupendous news, when he was asked for his input on plans for a new Licensing Act. This new Act (which was also known as Bruce's Act) was brought into law towards the end of 1872. The paper stated it was one of the most important measures upon the subject passed in modern times. From now on it was an offence to be drunk in charge of a bicycle (or any other vehicle or carriage for that matter) on a highway or in a public place. One month prison sentence and a £200 fine, was the penalties suggested. In addition the new Licensing Act, for the first time actually established licences for public houses and limited the drinking hours, clearly seen as an effort to curb excessive drunkenness. It also created two main kinds of drunkenness offence. Being drunk on any highway other public place, or on any licensed premises. It also provided an offence of being drunk while in charge on a public highway of any carriage which included a bicycle, a horse, cattle (including pigs and sheep) a steam engine or when in charge of a loaded firearm. Clearly there were no immediate results from the new law for in the Chief Constables report to the justices in the October he dwelt somewhat on the then spectacular increase in drunkenness, (especially in the Whitehaven area) over the past few months. And the continuous appearance of certain persistent drunks at the Kendal Magistrates Court would have been a bane not just for his officers but was now turning into a full time job for the magistrates. Sending them to the House of Correction or prison clearly was not sufficient penalty ... Unfortunately this was also the year that the use of the stocks was banned by law, so that method of punishment was now a thing of the past ... Still the opening of the Saint Mary's Home for Fallen Women this year at Coal Fell, Brampton, could just perhaps have helped a little. And the Parks Regulation Act of this year had certain repercussions for Dunne for this new act allowed for 'Park Constables' ... *'with power to take into custody any offender in the park, and also to have such privileges, powers and immunities and liable to all such duties and responsibilities as any police constable has within the police area'. 'Every little helps'* as the expression goes!

Dunne had one additional bit of good news around now. This would have been the retirement of George Bent the then Superintendent of Carlisle City Police – he who insisted on referring to himself as Chief Constable, much to Dunne's chagrin. The man who Dunne appointed was Walter Hemingway who after just three years decided that Carlisle was not for him and transferred to Cardiff Constabulary where he was to stay for the next thirteen years ... happily one supposes. Yet another ending that Dunne would not exactly have been pleased about.

By 1874, there were yet three more of the interminable new Acts which had to be thoroughly 'digested' and acted upon. The Factory Act earlier on in the year at long last established a fifty-six hour working week as well as preventing children from working as chimney sweeps ... though children were still expected to work, by law, ten hour days. (By 1875 the law dictated that all chimney sweeps who employed any assistant or apprentice had to take out a police certificate though whether that law was intended to raise additional income or protect children was never made clear). At first glance this new law would not have affected Dunne greatly, but looking through newspaper reports from the Victorian era, one sees an almost daily contingent of individuals being prosecuted in the courts by the police (though on the orders of factory owners and businesses) who had committed some small offence or other in the workplace usually running away from their contracted work.

Then there was the Houseless Poor Act of this same year. Now individuals whatever their social class could apply for a ticket that entitled them to a nights free food and shelter in the casual ward of a workhouse. Again readers might ask the question *"What has this got to do with the police?"* a lot actually, for amongst their many duties as has already been mentioned was *'assistant relieving officers for relief of tramps and vagrants'*, thus the new law, allowed for ALL who needed succour could get it via the workhouse, increasing the assistant relieving officer's workload substantially, and just to add 'insult to injury' the Licensing Act was amended by Gladstone's government and now allowed for the pubs to stay open longer. Mind you, new government acts were not all bad for the police this year as the Police Expenses Act increased the treasury grant from a quarter (which was the amount set at the time of County Police Act in 1856) it was now to be a half which as far as the ratepayers were concerned would have been excellent news.

For 1875, the most important thing happening to Dunne, and more especially so his wife Mary, was the birth of their third (and last) child. Gerald Fitzgerald Dunne was born in the April, and was a birth that would almost certainly caused some concern for the couple. Mary was now forty-five years of age, considered to be quite old to have a baby even in this day and age with all the accompanying assistance available to mothers, but in 1875 such a birth would have been considered quite unusual. Nevertheless the birth did prove successful, and once again there was yet another child in the Dunne household with connections this time to the 'Darby' Dunne side of the family for the first time, Gerald in recognition of his uncle (his father's brother) whilst Fitzgerald was linked to the Brittas ancestry and a certain Fitzgerald Dunne in particular.

1876 too was to prove something of a memorable year for Dunne, though not for celebrating his twentieth year as Chief Constable of the force (or thirty-five years as a police officer), this time thanks to his attendance at a Carlisle execution ... something which no doubt by now he was thinking of as something which was past history. However that was not to be for on the 19th December he along with the County Sheriff, the new 'Chief Constable' of Carlisle, the newly appointed George McKay, (replacing W. Hemingway) and various other dignitaries attending and witnessing the execution of a certain James Dalgleish committed to death for the wilful murder of Sarah Wright in Penrith in the September.

This was to be the first private execution to take place in Carlisle, and was also the first time that representatives of the Press were neither admitted to view the hanging or to see the body at the inquest.

The crime for which Dalgleish, a Scotsman, was to suffer the extreme penalty was of a very brutal type. His victim was Sarah Wright, a boarding house keeper, and single woman, of forty-nine years of age, with whom he had lodged for some time, and with whom he was apparently on intimate terms. On Sunday the September 24th she was viciously attacked by Dalgleish and was to die from her wounds just a few days after the attack,which it had been determined (and never denied) was by the use of a sledge slasher. The prisoner admitted his guilt right from the start with no attempt being made to prove any motive during the trial. Clearly then he was guilty and the judge was obliged to give Dalgleish nothing less than the sentence of death. Whilst in Carlisle gaol, awaiting the day of execution, he expressed his deep sorrow and contrition for the crime and appeared truly penitent.

With the Scotsman's execution fixed for the 19th December the hangman a certain William Asker of York was sent for as the now ageing Calcraft had been finally and compulsorily retired just two years previously after some forty five years of hanging (and flogging).

There is evidence to prove that this new hangman was no more competent than Calcraft had been on occasions, (on at least two instances the rope had broke and the victim had to be hung a second time) even though he possessed an excellent opinion of his own abilities. The morning of the execution dawned raw and cold. A crowd of some 1800 people gathered outside the gaol as the passing bell began to toll at 7.45am Dalgleish had been busy with his devotions to the very last moment. Now as he finished singing 'Safe in the Arms of Jesus', Asker and his assistants moved quickly to the condemned cell. By all accounts the prisoner was prepared to go quietly which would have been a relief in itself. His arms were swiftly pinioned and he mounted the scaffold resolutely. The hood went over his head and he died without a struggle at 8am.

The *Cumberland Pacquet* in reporting the execution stated:

> *'Outside in the street there was an element of farce. Hushed awe turned to derision as the black flag was thrown loosely over the top of the prison wall, due as later determined by the simple fact that the pulley of the flagpole refused to work. The hardier souls who had perched themselves on nearby roofs where they could see straight down in the gaol were especially disappointed, the execution having gone ahead in complete privacy in a scheduled yard. At 9am the body was cut down and buried in lime, close to the remains of preceding murderers, Thompson, Munroe, Cass and Charlton.'*

CHAPTER SIXTEEN

JOHN DUNNE

1877-1884

Including the trials of: Elizabeth Kirkbride (prolific child murderer).
Sarah Jane Lees, Margaret Messenger, Maynard James Harrison and The Cleator Moor Riots.

There are very few autobiographies of Chief Constables written during the Victorian era, possibly just the one, and this was written by William Chadwick the Chief Constable of Stalybridge, Cheshire. In his book written in the late 1800's and entitled *Reminiscences of a Chief Constable.* it is clear that the one thing that upset him most during his time as a police officer was the crime of murder; not just the need for his attendance at any subsequent hanging, but the abhorrence of the crime itself.

His comments about such a crime is worth noting here if only to try and understand exactly what our own Dunne would have felt about murder, and in particular serial child killers. In the chapter headed *'Murder or Manslaughter'* Chadwick writes:

> *'There is no word in the Queen's English so revolting to a policeman as the word 'Murder'. It conjures up everything that is wicked and cruel about our world, and can have no other meaning than murder means taking the life of another. Whether the method be a knife, gun, poison, or whatever method used it still conjures up images of a horrible act and assumes more shapes on investigation than any other crime. It is generally understood murder is killing with malice aforethought or the committing of a premeditated act, and if there is not strong proof of that, the crime is treated as manslaughter, or what is technically called in law malice prepense, as in a sudden fit of passion, or in a quarrel for example, and as has been proven time and time again over the years juries are only too glad to have a way pointed out to them in trying cases of murder, whether right or wrong, of returning a verdict of manslaughter, on account of the consequences usually attending a verdict for the capital offence, in order to keep their consciences, as they consider, clear of having taken a fellow creature's life under any circumstances'.*
>
> *'In my long experience I have been engaged in many revolting cases, many of which I would rather not have been obliged to take a part, for however zealous*

a police officer may be in hunting up offenders, his pleasure solely consists of doing his duty, and at the same time having no feelings on the matter'.

Thus the following case of baby-killing must have surely tried Dunne, his officers, the jury and the judge to an 'inch degree' at the Court in Appleby in 1877 As has been detailed in the previous chapter, the good people of Penrith had only just got over the recent hanging of James Dalgleish when the newspapers erupted in the January with news of yet another apparent murder ... this time one which was to be far more gruesome than the earlier case.

The Penrith link had started in June 1876 when forty year old widow, Elizabeth Kirkbride, enquired of the landlord of the Griffin Inn if he would store a number of boxes for her until she had finally moved and settled with her son in the Liverpool area. There they were to remain until January 1877, unclaimed and all but forgotten. They could well have remained there considerably longer except for the fact that one of the boxes began to give off a terrible smell. Under the circumstances the landlord felt that he had no option but to open the offending box whereupon to his horror, he discovered the body of a decomposing child wrapped in rags. The child was clearly fully developed though appeared to have been strangled for there was a woman's garter wound round its neck. It was obvious that the child had been dead for a long time. Upon examination of a second box the body of a second child was discovered also in a state of some decay though preserved sufficiently to indicate crude attempts had been made to cut its throat. It was also noticed that their was some serious damage to one of the legs as well as a shoulder blade, the result it was thought of the body being forced into the box. Estimates at the time of discovery were that this body had been hidden for at least two years. With the opening of the boxes the smell was awful with most of those gathered together in the lumber room that day recoiling in disgust whilst at the same time struggling to fight back their nausea.

Such was the scene of a multiple murder which was to prove one of the worst crimes to hit Westmorland, certainly without question the worst that had ever come to Dunne's attention. Regretfully, that was not to be the end of the matter. Since June, of the following year Elizabeth Kirkbride had been living with her eldest son along with his sixteen year old brother in rented accommodation at Tuebrook, Liverpool. It took little time to trace her and she was soon visited by police the Saturday evening following the discovery of the children's bodies at Penrith. She initially denied everything though agreed to return with the police officers to Penrith, simply requesting that she be allowed to leave a note for her sons. A note was left and the group went on its way though rather than go directly to Penrith decided instead to remain in Liverpool for the moment, where it was felt they could start some preliminary enquiries.

It was not until the following Monday morning that the Liverpool landlady a Mrs Orbeti discovered her lodger was missing. As it happened the landlady had a good reason to want to see Mrs Kirkbride, namely suspicion of theft. Mrs Orbeti had missed a coat and in her opinion felt that it could have been Elizabeth that could have taken it, suspecting it could have been pawned. However, it was not just a coat that was missing for she discovered that a blanket and tablecloth had also gone with the suspect nowhere to be found.

The landlady waited until the widow's eldest son arrived home for lunch and immediately confronted him with her suspicions. John Kirkbride felt that he should offer Mrs Orbeti some security and decided to open one of the tin boxes, breaking the lock and prising open the lid. Straightaway he was hit by a ghastly smell which he initially attributed to the dampness of the clothing within the box so did nothing more and returned to work after first telling the landlady to rummage through the box and retain anything she liked by way of further security. Immediately following John's departure Mrs Orbeti had the box carried down into the yard where its contents were removed and sorted through.

Quickly however a discovery was made which made her take the contents to the Liverpool mortuary. Unbelievably the tin box had been found to contain the decomposing bodies of three infants, one of which had a piece of string tied around its neck. All three bodies were at different stages of decomposition. It was clear that all three children had been newly born, with the best preserved having been hidden for possibly five years. Another body had no head and it was thought could have been in the box for as long as eight years, whilst the third lay amongst old clothing at the bottom of the box, close to the missing head of the second child, and which in this case was estimated to have been there for possibly as long as ten years Mrs Kirkbride for her part had now chosen to make a statement which was formally accepted by the authorities. It read as follows: *'I want to tell you who is the father of all the children I am here about. His name is Thomas More and he is a tea and ham and bacon dealer at Askham, near Penrith. He is the only man I have had anything to do with in any way, and I think it is only right that he should be exposed as it is entirely by his own persuasion that I am placed as I am. He has always promised that he would make me his wife, and instead of doing so, when he was in a position to do so, he married another'.*

Thomas More never did come forward to admit or deny his involvement with Elizabeth though there were many who believed him to be involved . Unfortunately the same cannot be said for Elizabeth for she continuously attracted attention. Shortly after her arrest she was brought from Liverpool to

Penrith by train and their were considerable numbers of people assembled at every station en route, no doubt hopeful of catching a glimpse of the mass murderer, or as the press had dubbed her '*The Penrith Horror*'. And not without reason either, for not only was it now known nationally that their had been five dead infant bodies, but only the previous day the body of yet another infant had been discovered this time at the instigation of Elizabeth's younger son, William. He had told the police that he recalled his mother burying something in the garden at Helton some six years previously and upon investigation a grave was discovered under a pear tree containing the body of another child, though it was determined that this one was several years old . Though some bodies had been found at Helton (then in Westmorland) and others near Liverpool, it was nevertheless agreed that the woman should be tried at Westmorland Assizes, located in the town of Appleby. The trial itself was not long in getting under way on 21st February 1877. The outcome of the trial proved something of an anti-climax. Despite the evidence of the garter around one of the children's neck and the obvious attempt to cut the throat of another, as perhaps to be expected, the medical fraternity were not able to swear that any of the children had been born alive.

So it was that Elizabeth Kirkbride was tried and convicted simply on charges of concealment of birth, as had happened before to so many of her contemporaries. The judge ordered to lift her veil and stand up at which point he handed down a sentence of just twenty-seven months imprisonment. He told her: '*It is a matter of grave consideration whether this was not a case in which you should have been tried for murder. I have no doubt that you have been guilty of violence towards these children when they were alive ... in three cases it was clear that violence was resorted to. One of the bodies had been dismembered and beheaded, and two had string marks around their necks. One cannot doubt that you are party to the most inhuman acts of which any human being is capable*'.

The result of this case would not have been the only court case giving Dunne 'grief' at this time ... though on a totally different level. This time it was the late superintendent of Carlisle Police Walter Hemingway (who like his predecessor Bent, preferred the title Chief Constable) who was on the receiving end of the justices, having himself been arrested for '*undue violence in arrest, refusing lawful bail, false imprisonment and slander*' ... and because of his rank it was Dunne who was obliged to arrest him and who prepared the charges. The charge read:

'*For that you, the said Walter Hemingway, on Thursday the third day of August last in a public street, to wit, English Street, in the city of Carlisle, falsely and maliciously spoke and published of the plaintiff the words following: I don't care for your warrant, it is a bad one, you obtained it by false pretences from Mr Nanson, the magistrate. I will repeat it. You obtained that warrant by false pretences. I dare say it and I will. You obtained it under false pretences. And also, for that, upon a charge that the said John Giles Mounsey had committed an assault upon you, you assaulted and beat him and seized him by the neck and with great violence tore his shirt and coat, and then and there dragged him across a pavement into a shop and pinned him down with a violent grip to the counter of the shop, and although he, the said John Giles Mounsey informed you that he would appear to any charge and to any summons for the said alleged assault and requested you not to use such extreme violence, you became more violent and although the said John Giles Mounsey then assured you that if you would only leave go your grip he refused to do so and then with another constable notwithstanding appeals made to you by the said John Giles Mounsey and the bystanders not to use such extreme violence, you became more violent and dragged the said John Giles Mounsey out of the shop through the public streets to a police station and there imprisoned the said John Giles Mounsey. And for that after you arrested him and detain him in prison at the police station and had there charged him with having assaulted you and then and there imprisoned the said John Giles Mounsey there upon the charge aforesaid you then wrongly and maliciously refused to and would not take or receive reasonable and proper bail for the appearance of the said John Giles Mounsey to answer the charge aforesaid although you then acted as such high constable as aforesaid and it was your duty as such constable to liberate the said John Giles Mounsey upon his giving reasonable and proper bail in that behalf and then and there wrongly and maliciously refused to and would not accept any person whatsoever as such bail as aforesaid other than and save and except the brother of the said John Giles Mounsey, whereby the said John Giles Mounsey in order to obtain release from such imprisonment by you, the said Walter Hemingway was forced and obliged to and did send for his said brother and procure him to become such bail and the said John Giles Mounsey was thereby imprisoned upon the charge aforesaid for a much longer time than was necessary or proper in that behalf'.*

Apparently this fracas had all started over the compulsory purchase by Carlisle Corporation of certain properties belonging to the trustees of the late George Gill Mounsey, solicitor and former Mayor of the city. It was John Giles Mounsey who acted on behalf of the trustees and demanded compensation, which to date had been slow in forthcoming. To compensate for this he obtained a distress warrant against the Corporation. By pure coincidence the 3rd August was also the last day of Hemingway's duty as Chief officer of Carlisle Police before taking up his new appointment with Cardiff City Police. At 11am that day a Sheriff's officer, Johnston by name called upon Hemingway in his office and demanded the keys to the safe which contained the Corporation's mace, gold mayoral chain and other civic insignia and items, which the officer demanded be handed over in execution of the warrant. Hemingway refused and even threatened to lock him up if he persisted in his endeavours. That same afternoon Hemingway was accosted by Mr Mounsey who asked him to help him in the execution of the distress warrant. Again Hemingway refused and again he threatened imprisonment to anyone who would dare to attempt to take possession of the Corporations property and going so far as to say to Mounsey *"You have obtained the Magistrate's signature to the warrant under false pretences"*. This statement clearly did not go down too well with Mounsey who thereupon lost his self control, and according to the Carlisle Patriot of the 16th February 1877 *'crashed his umbrella down so hard over the Chief's head that it smashed his new hat and rendered it useless'*. Thereupon Hemingway grabbed hold of Mr Mounsey who according to the same newspaper was *' very very violent, and very much excited'*.

Obviously such a fracas between a well known solicitor and the city Chief police officer attracted a large crowd. Needing help to restrain his prisoner, Hemingway called for help from the watching public even going so far as to offer a 1/- (5p) to anyone who would call a constable ... though without success. Thereupon he dragged Mounsey into a draper's store where shortly afterwards Sergeant Bone of Carlisle City Police put in an appearance. He appeared reluctant to arrest such a well known character, intimated, so Hemingway later reported of the threats of future consequences if he became involved. Still, Hemingway was still his senior officer, so that between them they took Mounsey firmly between them *'each with hold of one side of his collar and marched him up English Street to the police station in West Walls'* amid cheers, it was reported by the Carlisle Journal from the many watching bystanders. In the police court the following morning the Bench found Mounsey guilty as charged thought not without stating that he felt Hemingway had used unnecessary force against him. He was nevertheless fined five pounds, plus an order to pay the costs of the prosecution and costs to replace the policeman's hat. Clearly that was not to be the end of the matter for in the September of this year Mounsey had commenced an action against Hemingway for slander. The case came up for hearing in the Nisi Prius Court in Carlisle on 19th February 1877. The trial lasted for three days, and towards the end the judge stated that Hemingway should have known better than to have used the term 'false pretences' . It was later determined anyway that the warrant of distress had been correctly drawn up and was legally correct. The jury took just under the hour to return a verdict for the plaintiff Mounsey and he was awarded damages of just 20/- (£1.00) This time it was Hemingway himself who was ordered to pay the costs of the action.

It would have been unusual then as now for charges of assault against a member of the public to be brought against a counties or cities Chief officer, but when that happened twice during Dunne's 'watch', and each within a year of one another, that indeed would have been newsworthy. In fact the new Chief officer of Carlisle City Police, namely George McKay, too found himself up before the magistrates by November of '77 when a farmer by the name of Thomas Brown accused McKay of assaulting him in Lowther Street on 11th November, the day of the Martinmas hirings in the city. Apparently the police were in attendance thanks to the large numbers of people attending and with many blocking the shop doorways which was affecting business. Brown stated that not only were the police pushing innocent people around, as indeed he himself was violently pushed by McKay. He apparently remonstrated with McKay telling him not to push him about, and received the response *"I will treat you all alike"*, whereupon McKay took Brown by the shoulders and pushed him into the street *'with a bang'*. McKay later testified that Brown was given two chances to move, but on each occasion refused to do so. Later PC English corroborated McKay's version of events, and the magistrates dismissed the case against the police officer.

Such a charge appears not to have affected his career, for he went on to serve as Carlisle's Chief officer for the next 288 years ... though clearly in 1878 he was having second thoughts about his stay in Carlisle when he applied for the post of Chief Constable of the Midlothian and Linlithglow unsuccessfully as it happened. Other somewhat pleasing news for Dunne this year would no doubt have been hearing that London's Metropolitan Police were inaugurating a Criminal Investigation Department with a plain clothes detective force.

Considering that Dunne himself shortly after taking up his appointment in 1857 had too inaugurated a criminal investigation department, albeit with just one detective, then he must have felt quite proud that he had thought of it first ... and before the long established Metropolitan Police at that! There was a need too for such a department crime figures were increasing annually for in 1877 national crime was up by 88,882, 4.7% up on the previous year, and by 1878 their was a further increase of 93,743, giving an additional 5.47% increase. In fact the magazine Punch (of October 20th 1877) was displaying a cartoon of a lone policeman trying to deal with vagrants, urchins and various members of the public, all of whom are clamouring for his immediate attention.

This cartoon was an illustration of the need to have more policeman on the streets of London and other cities in Britain. Whether such extra policeman as indicated would have been any use to Dunne in respect of both the Weights and Measures Act which was introduced in 1878 (where Parliament had instituted new standards for the weight of a loaf of bread) and later The Adulteration of Food and Drugs Act, is debateable especially as Dunne would have been left in something of a quandary as to how to deal with this Act without putting his own men at risk. He was so confused by this new act that he took it upon himself to write directly to the relevant Government department enquiring as to the powers of magistrates to convict in adulteration cases in which the adulterated article had been purchased by an officer acting on behalf of the local authority.

The somewhat ambiguous and unhelpful reply that he received on the 23rd November from a Walton J Sendall, Assistant Secretary read:

> *Sir. I am directed by the Local Government Board to advert to your letter of the 22nd ultimo in which you request to be furnished with advice as to the course which should be adopted by the officers appointed to carry out the provisions of the Act 38 and 39, Vic.Cap.63, in view of the decision of the Queen's Bench Division of the High Court of Justice in a case to which your attention has been drawn. The Board presume that you intend to refer to certain expressions attributed to the Lord Chief Justice by some of the newspapers in the case of Sandys v Small to the effect that an officer appointed by a local authority to obtain samples could not be considered prejudiced by the purchase of adulterated articles procured under the orders of the local authority. The Board must however point out that the authorised report of that case (Law Reports 3 QRB Div 449) does not contain the words in question, and as a matter of fact, the case itself was decided upon quite a different ground. It should be further stated that in Sandys v Markham reported in the 'Justices of the Peace' 41, page 53, which was the case in which adulterated mustard had been purchased by an inspector for analysis, Mr Justice Lush, in relation to the precise point referred to in your letter, distinctly said that 'if the purchaser did not get pure mustard as he was entitled to, prejudice must be presumed'. The Board may add that several of the police magistrates in the metropolis adopting the opinion of Mr Justice Lush have not hesitated to convict in cases where the purchase has been made not for consumption, but for analysis, and the Board themselves entertain no doubt that this was the correct view.*

Which one assumes left Dunne in something of a quandary – on the one hand the law stated that he was obliged to prosecute offenders under this Act, and in the same breath stated that any officer under his command instructed to obtain samples to assist in the prosecution would also be punished 'Damned if he took action, and damned if he didn't'.

Mind you Dunne's recent additions to his force would perhaps have been better employed in Westmorland this year, and the town of Kendal in particular. Highwaymen were back, though it is doubtful they ever went away, just never got caught. However a certain Thomas Fawcett had no chance of escape this year when a gang of three men and two women robbed him of £15.10 0 (£15.50) at Tarny Banks, Skelsmergh. Eventually the gang was arrested in Manchester, but they were brought back to Kendal where hundreds turned out to watch them be committed at the Town Hall (then Moot Hall) And then, also in Kendal, their was the little matter of James Wallace who was incarcerated for debt but who was sharp enough this year when finding the gatehouse unattended as the warder had 'stepped out on a message into town' stepped into the gatehouse removed the key off the nail by the door, opened the gate and simply set off to walk to his home close to Woolpark Yard. Unfortunately he bumped into the warder as he rounded the corner into Stricklandgate and the two strolled amiably together back to the prison . In reporting this the Westmorland Gazette retorted *'what if he had been a dangerous criminal?'*.

Then like today, there would have been times of the year when extra police would have been warranted especially so in the Windermere and Bowness areas of the Lake District, for thanks to William Wordsworth's book waxing lyrical on the wonders of the 'Lakes', tourism had now to be considered by the constabulary. This year alone the region attracted some 150,000 tourists.

One bit of good news by 1879 was the fact that nationally crime was down by 2.78% (or 91,137)., and another, initially at least, was the introduction of the 1879 Prosecution of Offenders Act which for the first time created the post of Director of Public Prosecutions (DPP) under the direction of the Attorney General to act as the Crown's representative in important cases. However at second glance it was quickly discovered that this new act did little to help Dunne's workload as there was still no body of local prosecutors under the DPP.

As far as the local prosecution was concerned it still remained the police. Police officers would continue to prosecute in the Magistrates Courts and would continue to employ solicitors and barristers to conduct cases in the Crown Courts. In fact many forces established their own prosecuting solicitors departments or had law firms which acted for them regularly. Over the ensuing years various Royal Commissions commented on the unacceptability of having responsibility for investigation and prosecution of crime in the hands of the police. In fact nothing changed until 1885 (NB: Before this Act there was no public prosecutor to take criminal cases to court, people had to find their own lawyers or present the prosecution case themselves.)

Other changes to the criminal law for this year was that English law had begun to distinguish between suicide and homicide, though suicide still resulted in forfeiture of estate though the deceased were not permitted daylight burial until 1882. Branding (solely a punishment for deserters) was finally abandoned this year, (and flogging in the British navy) Oh, and another piece of good news was the interesting fact that Carlisle (or least Carr's Biscuit Company) had played no small part in the Battle of Rorkes Drift this year. That was the battle in which British troops fought (and beat) the Zulus from behind a barricade made of Carr's of Carlisle biscuit tins no less.

There was a lot of excitement in Kendal around the time of the 1880's elections, which took up a lot of time and manpower ... in fact it was the last occasion when their had been such a riot of this nature. The Tory candidates were the Earl of Bective from Underley Hall, Kirkby Lonsdale and (inevitably) the Honorable W.Lowther. For the Liberals there were Sir Henry Tufton, supported by W E Forster, the author of the famous 1870 Education Act. It was when a Liberal procession appeared to be getting out of hand that the Mayor quickly swore in a hundred constables who if anything exacerbated the disturbance and in the resulting police charge four members of the public received scalp wounds from police truncheons. I have yet to find any mention of this incident in any of Dunne's reports for this period, perhaps understandably so.

It could have been that he was far too wound up about the return of an increase in crime, after a gap of just one year. By 1880 national crime was shown as up by an amazing 8.01% (or 98,440) some of which would clearly have rubbed off on Cumberland's crime figures.

Still I'm sure he was pleased to see the appearance on the streets of the first police boxes, which until the introduction of the telephone allowed for a meeting point between sergeants and their constables at regular intervals.

Another standard piece of police equipment from this year was the whistle which replaced the rattle for raising the alarm, In practice the whistle was found to have limited range and a bobby calling for assistance would often beat his truncheon on the pavement to alert nearby colleagues.

Crime and punishment in 1880 was no different as in previous years, and cases involving children were to continually appear for prosecution on Dunne's desk. As we already know Cumberland certainly did have more than its fair share of vulnerable girls and subsequent illegitimate births. There is little doubt today, with the benefit of hindsight that such crimes continued to be compounded by an archaic poor law and the sheer grinding poverty of the times.

The following case of Sarah Jane Lees illustrates this well and which resulted in a verdict which would appear to indicate that the court was especially aware of the circumstances of the time. Sarah Jane Lees appeared at Carlisle Assizes in January 1880 following the death of her child the previous October in a rural area of West Cumberland.The twenty-year-old domestic servant was single, semi-literate and unsupported. In her case however there could be no charge of concealment for Sarah Jane's child was one of those which had clearly lived. In fact for sixteen months she had actually supported it, getting on with her humdrum life,with no apparent hope of any ongoing support from the child's father. In this instance however it was alleged that the mother had deliberately neglected to provide for the child's needs which naturally included the provision of food ... thus the child had subsequently died from malnourishment. For once the prosecution had built up a strong case against her. Fortunately, considering she was being tried for manslaughter there was no fear of her facing execution in the event of a guilty verdict, in fact no woman had ever been hanged in Cumberland that century (though a few had come close to it) and there did appear to be a reluctance on both judge and jury to hang them in any case. She was still in serious trouble however and being of sound mind she couldn't even shelter behind a defence of insanity. On the surface there was nothing especially sinister about Sarah Jane Lees. In court a clear picture emerged however,of not just a deprived child but of an unjust and in-equal society too. The jury clearly had little doubt in their minds too for without specifically blaming anybody and having heard the defending lawyer out, they promptly returned a verdict of not guilty, and the mother left the court never to be heard from again not in the courts at least. The circumstances of the day had ensured that Sarah Jane should not spend time any time at all behind bars, however just eighteen months later thirteen year old Margaret Messenger was to find herself standing in the self same courts in Carlisle, also on a charge of wilful murder though in her case the outcome was not to be the same for the judge donned the black cap and sentenced her to be executed ... the first such sentence on a female in Cumberland for the whole of the nineteenth century and beyond.

Her case was a little different to Sarah Jane's for in the first instance their was little doubt that the charge was indeed premeditated murder, and in the second, two children died, rather than one. There was little doubt that Margaret Messenger was guilty. In the first instance she had deliberately drowned the two year old son of her employers, small time farmers John and Mary Pallister, though initially this was presumed to have been an accident but when just two weeks later their hired help Margaret was telling them that their youngest child six months old Elsie was also dead this time by apparently falling down a well it was clearly too much to be pure coincidence. Clearly this was a case for the police. By the time Superintendent Sempill arrived the parents were convinced that they knew who the killer was. When first questioned Margaret Messenger insisted that "*A big man with a cap on*" had snatched Elsie from her and she had "*found (the baby) in a wet place below the well*". But after persistent interrogation by the parents, she admitted "*I did it all myself and nobody helped me*". It was one of the most horrible crimes recalled by anyone in Cumberland ... the murder of a child by a girl little more than a child herself. At her trial in the November she pleaded not guilty to wilful murder but remained quite composed throughout. The whole sordid story was told yet again to a crowded court though it had received widespread press cover too. It was a comparatively short trial and the prosecution could offer no reason for the killing of the two innocent children. Margaret was tried for murder and subsequently convicted at the Cumberland Assizes in Carlisle on the 2nd November 1881. Immediately after the judge sentenced her to death, having indicated in his summing up that he too had felt her to be guilty all along and there were many among the public who would doubtless have been pleased to see her atone for her ghastly deed, young though she was. Shortly after her conviction and whilst being interviewed by a Dr Orange, the medical superintendent of Broadmoor Criminal Lunatic Asylum along with Dr MacDougal the surgeon of Carlisle Gaol, Margaret confessed to them that she was also responsible for the death of the toddler John Pallister whom she had deliberately drowned after planning the crime a few days beforehand. The hangman was not however to get the pleasure of hanging the thirteen year old Margaret, for shortly after she was imprisoned indefinitely at Woking Prison. She was finally released from Prison to return home and live with her family on license in 1891, after serving a ten year sentence.

1881 besides being a busy year, also proved to be quite good for Dunne financially too. One thinks of 'buying to let' as being a modern idea, but this is far from the truth for back in 1881, and in all probability much earlier the affluent were happily buying properties that would not only increase in value over the years, but also bring in a useful extra income. John Dunne himself was not slow in noticing this possibility and in any case, thanks to his wife's inheritance he had plenty of assets to fall back on, so he purchased Lorne House on Cavendish Terrace in Carlisle. The advertisement for a tenant was shown for the first time in the *Cumberland Patriot* on 23rd April and which declared that this was no ordinary three bed roomed semi detached, rather it offered a dining room, drawing room, breakfast room, library, nine bedrooms, plus lavatory, bath room, stables, coach house, not overlooking separate quarters for the household staff ... clearly indicating that Dunne was looking for someone of 'substance' as a tenant, hopefully long-term.

Dunne and his family continued to live at Moorhouse Hall in Warwick even though his family were growing up fast. Henrietta the first born was now 11, whilst Francis was 10 and the youngest Gerald was now 6. According to the census of this year Mary Dunne apparently managed with just two members of staff, namely Elizabeth Lawson aged 23 and Sarah Brodie, aged 27. Possibly with the children now all at school, less staff were required, compared to the last census return where their were six staff listed.

Once again the law on criminal procedure changed this year with the introduction of the Summary Jurisdiction (Process) Act, which amongst other things meant that a great deal of court documents would now be processed by the police themselves. Just what Dunne needed! One act which came too late as far as Mary Dunne was concerned was the introduction in 1882 of the Married Women's Property Act, which now enabled women to buy, own and sell property and keep their earnings. A wife's legal identity was restored, as the courts were forced to recognize a husband and wife as two separate legal entities in the same manner as if the wife was a femme sole. (single woman). Married womens' legal rights included the right to sue and be sued, as well as being responsible for their debts.

Dunne personal services were once again required in the March of '82 in the investigation relating to the death of 16 year old Lucy Sands who had disappeared on the evening of the 1st December 1881 ... he probably would have been involved sooner but her body was not discovered until some three months after her death, as no one had thought to report her missing. As was later determined she had been with 16 year old Jane Shannon and 15 year old Margaret Cranney on a visit to see Maynard Harrison, who was the son of the manager of the West Cumberland Ironworks at Northside, Workington. 17 year old Harrison had taken the three girls on a tour of the ironworks and then into his parents garden for some fifteen minutes. About 8.45pm Lucy left them, saying she had to meet with a local boy Billy Wilson. Lucy Sands was never seen alive again except for being briefly sighted by local woman Hannah Gibson at 9pm that same evening. The discovery ensured an immediate full-scale enquiry locally whereupon the police focused almost immediately on Maynard James Harrison. Based on evidence received the police soon became convinced that Harrison could well be the killer and on the 9th March he was arrested and charged on suspicion of having wilfully murdered Lucy Sands. The inquest on Lucy Sands was moved from the Bridge Railway Station to the Green Dragon Hotel, Workington, close to the victim's home, on 14th March 1882. Evidence was given by Jane Shannon and Margaret Cranney. Two teenage girls, Alice Atkinson and Liz Smith formerly employed as house servants by Maynard's parents, spoke of the accused arriving home around the time of the supposed killing and endeavouring to get into his bedroom via the wash house roof. Others of this group were even more damning. One of them, Thomas Rosser, stated that Harrison had drunkenly confided, following the discovery of the body, that he had been with Lucy that night. Another, Harry Mainprize, spoke of Maynard saying that he had agreed with Lucy that she should stay on after Shannon and Cranney left. Questions were raised at the inquest as to whether one person alone could have committed the crime. Evidence was given that the body could well have been dragged some distance to its eventual resting place though considerable effort would have been required to pile the stones around it. In any case Maynard had been proved a liar in that medical evidence was given that Lucy hadn't been pregnant, nor was their evidence of sexual violation. And, given the extent of decomposition their was some ambiguity as to what weapon had been used to perpetrate the crime, considering the fact that no weapon had been found. The inquest finally came to a close. The verdict was one of wilful murder against some person or persons unknown. Maynard was elated, but only for a few moments until the police pointed out that they were making further enquiries and there was no question of him being released. Came the trial. Many were anticipating a full trial and a likely conviction of murder, but before that happened Maynard was suddenly discharged by the grand jury at Carlisle on 18th April 1882. There was simply insufficient evidence to proceed further. No one else was ever charged with the offence. The victim's grave in St John's Churchyard, Workington was visited regularly by members of the public who often brought flowers. Today however the grave is untraceable and the stones and tree are of course long gone.

So once again we have a crime where to all intents and purposes the police lost their case – would the outcome have been the same these days with access to fingerprints and DNA one wonders? There is a postscript to this case for there is a report in the Whitehaven Gazette dated April 22nd 1897 that in the will of the late Miss Litt of Richmond Hill, Workington £5,000 was left to a servant James Sands who had lived with her for the last eighteen months. Sands had been a labourer previous to this employment and was a brother to the above Lucy Sands.

So, a number of major trials for 1882 no doubt Dunne would have been quite happy to have seen the end of this year, with so much of his time preparing the police cases for the prosecution, along with time spent actually in court. The only other significant item of information coming to his attention this year would have been the numerous attacks on members of the newly formed

Salvation Army, and not just in Cumberland apparently but all over the country. Salvationists (as they were known) were facing angry mobs who used ammunition in the form of dead rats and cats, tar, rocks, rotten vegetables, and even burning coals and sulphur to show their hatred of the new movement. In this one year alone 669 Salvationists were brutally attacked, with the police in many cases doing very little to help However this did not appear to be the case in Cumberland or Westmorland, for their were many reports in the local press of police intervention though the policy of 'peace at any price' issued by the Home Office generally meant that the police intervened as little as possible. The processions were not illegal they were told, but if the peace of the town was endangered then they should try to prevent disturbances. Many Salvationists found themselves in prison on trumped-up charges made by vindictive police and magistrates.

For the following two years, at least, Dunne found himself more involved in rather more mundane events, rather than murder trials ... mundane things being ensuring the crime rate was kept down and changing his forces emergency devices from rattles to whistles. As it happened the Metropolitan Police, due to increasing numbers of crimes involving firearms told their constables that they could carry firearms if they wished. Dunne chose not to follow that recommendation believing that a truncheon was sufficient defence. Though in truth even if his men had wanted to carry firearms no formal instruction was made available ... Whether Dunne considered the riots in Cleator Moor in the July 'mundane' this year however would be a mute point. In fact they were so serious that not only did a judge in his summing up state *'that it was the first such case of its kind that an English judge had had to deal with'*, but it also necessitated Dunne writing directly to Sir William Harcourt (the then Solicitor-General), it even brought about a number of questions being raised in the House of Commons.

Riots in around Cleator and Cleator Moor were nothing new for Dunne and his men to contend, however the circumstances of the 1884 were something entirely different, both in terms of their savagery and intensity, but importantly also brought about the death of a young lad. To understand more one needs to refer back, and for most of the foregoing I am indebted to Donald MacRaild, and his book *Culture, Conflict and Migration, the Irish in Victorian Cumbria.* There has never been any argument over the statement *'Orangemen and Catholics need little excuse for a fight'*, thus it does not take very long for trifling incidents to escalate out of all proportion. And, of course the most common of these situations commonly arise on or around the *'Glorious Twelfth'* when Catholics congregate wherever there is a large(ish) Irish Catholic community to jostle and jeer the marching Orangemen. Such an instance had previously occurred in July

1876 also in Cleator Moor when around 1500 hostile Catholics met up with Cleator Moor Orangemen as they returned from a regional gathering in Whitehaven. According to the Whitehaven Herald dated July 19th of that year:

> *'The crowd of predominantly women and lads booed and jeered when the local fife and drum band returned after entertaining their brethren in nearby Frizington. As the band progressed into the town playing **'Tommy make room for your uncle'** they were pelted with stones unmercifully by the rabble and had it not been for the prompt action of Inspector Brown and his excellent staff of officers, the consequences might have been somewhat serious'.*

During the following years the pages of the local press were continuously reporting incidents of similar fighting. In the eyes of the newspapers of the time the Catholics were a mere rabble, whilst the Orangemen were perceived as organised and provoked. The events on the 12th July 1884 however totally altered that image. In fact the intensity of the violence on this occasion outstripped even the attack on William Murphy thirteen years earlier.

Such was the extent of the riot that Dunne felt committed to write to the Secretary- General of the extent of the riot immediately afterwards which was probably seen by him as an opportunity for self congratulation over his actions, though based on questions later asked in the House of Commons, he probably wished he hadn't written. In his letter of the 13th July and reported in Hansard (Vol.290 cc 896-7) he wrote:

> *'About fifteen hundred Orangemen had assembled in a field at Wath Brown, near Cleator at 11am yesterday the 12th to hold a meeting by previous arrangement. Speeches were made, and a great deal of excitement existed during the day. The Orange party was armed with pistols, swords, spears etc. They were dressed in Orange costume, with flags, banners and bands of music. Large numbers of the Orangemen were taken to Cleator Moor from Workington and other towns by special train. The Orangemen on their way back to the railway station were hooted by a large crowd of the Roman Catholic party. One of the Orangemen thrust a flag in the faces of some of the crowd, whereupon the crowd, which consisted of about six thousand rushed in upon the Orange party. Several blows were struck on both sides. The Orange party fired several shots, and struck with their swords and spears. One young man Henry Tumelty, aged seventeen years who till recently was a letter carrier at the Cleator Moor Post Office was shot dead on the spot, six others were wounded seriously by pistol shots. Several others were cut by swords and spears. No further deaths have occurred. The Roman Catholic crowd became furious on hearing of the death of one of their party. They made several*

attacks on the Orangemen with sticks and stones, many were cut and wounded, but this was after the firing, and the death of Tumelty. The police succeeded in separating the two parties and by forming lines across the streets the crowd attacking the Orange party were cut off from pursuing them. The Orangemen were at last got to the railway station without further fighting, but while at the station waiting for their train the attack was renewed by large numbers of men and women who had got there by circuitous routes. A body of police were moved on to the railway bridge, from which place the attack was being made. Several shots were fired by the Orange party from the railway station at the attacking party on the bridge, but no persons were wounded there. Two magistrates Mr Jefferson and Mr Ainsworth and forty-five officers and constables of police were on duty to do everything that could be done to preserve the peace, and it was entirely owing to their exertions that a most serious loss of life and destruction of property was prevented. I (Dunne) had previously applied to the Petty Sessions of the district to arrange for a magistrate to be present to read the Riot Act if necessary. The Riot Act was not read, as the peace was restored without resorting to that extreme measure. I was present myself during the latter part of the disturbance, and took command of the police. I kept a large body of men on special duty during the night, as it was feared that the houses of some Orangemen who reside in the district of Cleator would be wrecked, but up to 8 pm this evening all is quiet and orderly. That is all the information I have at present'.

When the letter was read by the Solicitor-General to the House of Commons on the 14th July, one of the MP's present Mr Sexton stated: *"I would say from that report that adequate measures were not taken. It appears that only about fifty police were opposed to a large armed party of Orangemen. I beg to give notice that I shall call attention to the inadequate steps which were taken by the authorities to prevent this collision and loss of life."*

As to be expected a number of the participants were arrested and the Cumberland and Westmorland newspaper report of the 30th July stated that:

'Twenty prisoners were charged with rioting at Cleator Moor. Fifteen witnesses were examined. Cases were dismissed against eleven of the men. Four were committed for trial at the Cumberland Assizes, one of whom John Bawden was the leader of the Orangemen Once again large numbers of the constabulary were in attendance with Dunne taking command throughout'.

At the Cumberland and Westmorland Assizes in the November Mr Justice Day Moore directed the jury to return a verdict of not guilty against Bawden because the evidence was conflicting. All the others pleaded guilty. The judge then stated that he regarded the whole episode as a *'disastrous riot'* and commented that it was the first such case that an English judge had dealt with. In warning the guilty parties and in discharging them, he ordered: *'Be well conducted men and you will hear no more of the offences of which you have pleaded guilty. Go away and take care to keep the peace in future'.* Nevertheless such actions and the judges words did little to pacify the Catholic fraternity further incensed when the verdict of the inquest on Henry Tumelty was announced, namely: *'Death by a shot fired from a pistol or a revolver by a person unknown'.* Notwithstanding the damning words of Mr Sexton MP in the House of Commons on the 13th July, and probably due in part to Dunne's control of the aforementioned riots as well as his earlier control of the cattle disease problems, reminded his peers that they had an excellent Chief Constable in their midst for this was the year that the Cumberland Quarter Sessions presented John Dunne with a gratuity of £300 as some recognition of his services. Their report read: *'His reports upon the system -which should really be called the 'Dunne System' were quoted by the Duke of Richmond and Lord Spencer in support of the measures which the Privy Council afterwards brought before Parliament, and the legislation which has since been introduced for extirpating cattle diseases has been very largely founded upon the suggestions dictated by his experiences. It must be a source of great satisfaction to him to know that besides organising one of the most efficient forces of constabulary in the kingdom he has done so much to promote the interests of the agricultural community among which he has lived and worked during the years. The magistrates appreciated Mr Dunne's services in regard to the cattle diseases. Their recognition of his conduct as head of the county police has been no less complete'.*

Great for Dunne, though no such recognition existed for the lower echelons under his control. In fact they had to wait another fifteen years before their poor pay was given some recognition ... and even then only by they themselves putting pressure on Dunne.

CHAPTER SEVENTEEN

JOHN DUNNE

1885

The murder of Constable Joseph Byrnes, The Netherby Hall Robbery including the capture, trial and execution of Anthony Benjamin Rudge, John Martin, and James Baker

I think it would be safe to say that 1885 witnessed the most notorious murder and robbery in Cumbria's history. No Cumbrian crime before or since has merited such notoriety or interest. (with the possible exception of the Derek Bird massacre in Whitehaven in June 2010).

If Dunne was around today and could choose the one case that affected him the most he would unquestionably reply that it would have been the murder of one of his policemen, Joseph Byrnes, coupled with the jewel robbery at Netherby Hall, near Longtown, the home of Sir Frederick Graham, on the night of 28th October 1885. The crime had it origins on the 27th September when a notorious ladder gang met at the Longtown Coursing Meeting and plotted to burgle Netherby Hall.

The gang members comprised of Anthony Benjamin Rudge, John Martin, James Baker, and (a possible) accomplice William Baker. This group of men proved to be totally ruthless and were not afraid to use brutal force in their life of crime. All the gang had a criminal past. Rudge was wanted for a robbery in Brixton, Martin was wanted for the murder of an Essex police inspector, and William Baker was a suspect in the theft of the Duchess of Montrose Jewels a few years earlier in Newcastle. This was a criminal gang to be reckoned with. The report from the *Cumberland Pacquet* for Thursday November 5th gives us the first full report of the daring robbery.

> *'On Wednesday evening the 28th October the home of Sir Frederick Graham at Netherby was entered by thieves who carried away some diamond jewellery to the value of £300-£400. It appears that between 8 and 9 o'clock when Sir Frederick and a large party of guests staying at the house were at dinner, a housemaid went to Lady Graham's bedroom and to her surprise found the door locked from the inside. She gave the alarm immediately and the door having been broken open, it was discovered that the bedroom had been broken into by thieves who had gained access to the room by means of a ladder, and*

who had stolen from a jewel box; three diamond stars with an opal in the centre of each, two large diamond drop earrings, a gold finger ring, a small blue-enamelled gold watch key in a leather case and a coloured photo of a gentleman in a small oval leather case. The robbers had evidently been disturbed by the housemaid for they had left untouched on the table a gold watch and a large stock of valuable jewellery worth about £30,000, which were in other jewel cases in the room. Information was at once sent to the police at Longtown, by fast horse some two miles distant and thence information was telegraphed to the head office of the county constabulary at Carlisle . Superintendent Sempill took steps immediately to have the roads watched and at 11 o'clock that night Sergeant Roche and PC Johnstone who had been stationed near to Kingstown, about two miles north of Carlisle to keep a look out there, and saw four strangers coming along the road in the direction of Carlisle. They challenged them and announced that they were policemen and intended to search them. One of the four immediately drew a pistol and fired it at Police Constable Johnstone. The bullet entered his right breast below the nipple and traversed along one of his ribs, finally lodging itself in his back. Sergeant Roche immediately attacked the assailants. He got knocked down by blows from a hedge slasher, but got up and while attempting to arrest another, a second shot, apparently from a revolver was fired at him. The bullet entered the fleshy part of his arm. The four men quickly disappeared whilst Johnstone was taken to his home nearby at Kingstown. After leaving Kingstown the fugitives diverged from the main road and crossed into Carlisle by a railway bridge. About 1 o'clock that morning Police Constable Fortune, of the Carlisle City Police, whilst patrolling Shaddongate saw four men walking along the railway line. Having previously been informed of the robbery his suspicions were aroused and he followed them for about a quarter of a mile along the line. At about this time the four men appear to have determined that they were being followed, and turning round they attacked PC Fortune, who received two severe cuts to his forehead as well as other wounds to his head caused by kicks when he fell to the ground. He than lay unconscious for approximately an hour whilst the four men made their escape. As soon as PC Fortune recovered consciousness he went directly to the City Police office and reported what had taken place . The men seemed to have made their way to Plumpton, as about 10 o'clock on Thursday night three men answering their description appeared at Plumpton Station and enquired what time the train left for the south. Finding that no train passed there then, they went to the village of Plumpton where two of them went into the Pack Horse Inn, whilst the third waited outside. The men had a meal of bread and cheese and informed the landlord that they were very hungry after a long drive. In the meantime Mr Thomas Lowthian of Plumpton had observed the men at the station, and informed Police Constable Byrnes who was stationed at Plumpton.

The Constable went towards the Pack Horse Inn, but the men by this time had left the inn and were again making their way towards the railway station. About a hundred yards from the inn they encountered the policeman who challenged them whereupon one of them drew a revolver, pointed it at Byrnes head and fired. The shot entered Byrnes temple and came out at the back of his head. Byrne fell to the ground bleeding profusely .The men apparently then dragged him across the road for part of his beard was later found on the stones and the side of his face was badly grazed, and then threw him over a wall into an adjoining field. The report of firearms alarmed the neighbours and a Mr Stalker of Plumpton along with others ran in the direction of the shot

The men had evidently bolted across the fields towards Penrith, but Mr Stalker and others heard groaning at the back of the wall and on investigating found the injured man who was immediately taken to the Pack Horse Inn. On looking at the place they saw that Byrne had lost a large quantity of blood. Information was at once sent to Penrith of the crime and a cordon of police was set up around the approaches to the town. Dr Matthews, assistant to Dr Montgomery from Penrith quickly arrived to deal with the injured man, though his efforts were to no avail as he died of his injuries at 12.50am on the Friday morning

In the meantime the culprits appear to have made their way to Penrith where they were seen by a guard on the railway entering a wagon on his train near Penrith. The guard had heard of the robbery and suspecting these men had been involved in it instructed the driver not to stop at Shap the next station. As the train passed through Shap the guard threw out a note asking for it to be telegraphed to Tebay. This was done and on arrival at Tebay several railway employees along with the guard surrounded the wagon, but to their surprise found no one inside. It was however soon discovered that in the darkness and as the train was going at full speed the burglars had crept along to another wagon in which they were found hidden under a tarpaulin. One of the burglars drew a revolver from his pocket shouting that he would shoot anyone who tried to arrest them. He was however promptly disabled by the station master of Tebay who hit him on the head with a brake stick, and he was quickly secured with the aid of his colleagues. Two other men scrambled out of the wagon and managed to make their escape, although they were chased for a considerable distance by the railway staff. One of them however was captured at Lancaster whilst attempting to get into the midnight express bound for London. On being brought to Carlisle he was surrounded by a large group of people and the police escort had considerable difficulty in saving him from being lynched'.

The newspaper report went on to state that by this date (5th November) three of the prisoners were now in custody at Carlisle, namely Anthony Benjamin Rudds (Rudge), John Martin (or Morton) and James Baker who were brought before the county magistrates at the county police office at noon on Saturday the 31st October. At the request of John Dunne, two London police officers, Inspector Shore and Sergeant Rolfe visited Carlisle on Monday to view the prisoners in custody. The result of this visit fully realised Dunne's suspicion that a very important capture of notorious criminals had been effected for Inspector Shore identified John Martin as the man wanted by the police for complicity in the murder of Inspector Simmons near Romford. That murder was committed by two men whom the inspector was endeavouring to arrest. One of the criminals was captured and hanged about nine months earlier (James Lee) and Martin has now been identified as the man who escaped and had hitherto eluded the police. Following the visit by the two southern police officers Martin was heard to say to Rudge : I suppose I shall be done for the Romford murder now and for putting a squib up Rolfe's nose. The same newspaper reported that

'the injured policeman Johnstone had been promoted to the office of Sergeant,and Sergeant Roche to that of Inspector for their gallant and courageous conduct in connection with the pursuit of the men now in custody. Inspector Roche is on the road to recovery and Sergeant Johnstone is in an improving condition, though reminded everyone that it was still early days. Police Constable Fortune is also improving well. Great kindness has been shown to all the wounded constables not only by the Chief Constable but by numerous members of the public. Mr Dunne has also received a letter from the Queen in which her Majesty expressed her deep regret at the occurrence and making enquiry as to the condition of the injured policemen. None of the jewellery stolen from Netherby has as yet been recovered and it is supposed that the men had hidden it whilst making their way south across the county'.

The next report about the burglary was not until the 17th December when the *Cumberland Pacquet* wrote:

'After a lapse of more than a month since the robbery of jewellery at Netherby Hall on the 28th October last, the police have now recovered almost the whole

of the missing property. After the murder of Police Constable Byrnes at Plumpton on the night of the 29th October last it will be in the remembrance of the public that the three fugitives now in custody Rudge, Martin and Baker got into a goods train at Penrith and were discovered at Tebay Station when they attempted to escape. Rudge took refuge under an arch of the railway bridge which spans the River Lune at the north end of the station where he was pursued and captured by the railway servants while attempting to draw a revolver from his pocket. A few days afterwards a diamond eardrop which formed part of the missing jewellery was found near that place near the riverside and it was then anticipated that the prisoner had attempted to throw the jewel into the river but it had fallen short of the waterline. Mr Dunne at once placed men on special duty to search the river between Tebay and Lancaster in the expectation that they might be able to discover the remainder of the missing property and after diligent and patient labour their efforts have been crowned with success. On Saturday morning Police Constable Scott discovered on the bank of the River near the railway bridge but on the opposite side of the stream from that on which the prisoner Rudge was apprehended, three diamond stars for head dress, a gold jewel finger ring, and a diamond ear drop, which constituted part of the stolen property. With the exception of a small enamelled gold watch key and a framed photograph which are still missing all the jewellery has been recovered. The police have made a further important discovery in connection with this case. It may be remembered that although only three men have been apprehended and there is no reason to believe that more were concerned in the murder of Police Constable Byrnes at Plumpton, yet four men were seen on the road between Netherby and Carlisle and Police Constable Fortune of the Carlisle City Police Force who was the victim of a murderous assault the same night states positively that four men attacked him. After that point all trace of the fourth man was lost. All the witnesses, however who saw him spoke of him wearing a light overcoat. Such a coat a light Chesterfield overcoat has been found in the River Eden, near Carlisle, the pockets being filled with stones, which had evidently been used to sink it and so conceal it. As nobody was likely to dispose of a good overcoat such as this in this way the police think it may turn out to be the overcoat of the fourth man. With reference to the discovery of the remainder of Lady Graham's stolen jewellery at Tebay, it may be added that the tobacco pouch in which it had been placed was covered with two inches of water and the jewels which had been placed loose in the pouch were, when found, all frozen together in a mass of ice'.

The next, and final report of this case was reported in the *Cumberland Pacquet* on the 21st January 1886 following the trial on the 18th. The judge was to be Mr Justice Day. Initially the newspaper reported on the decision of the Grand Jury, which read as follows:

> *'The Grand Jury at 1.25pm after an absence of two hours returned a true bill (i.e. evidence sufficient to warrant a trial) on all the counts – five in number in the indictment against: Anthony Benjamin Rudge, alias William Walsh, alias William Fennell, John Martin alias John White and James Baker for the Netherby robbery and subsequent outrages and murder. Thus on Monday the 18th January 1886 before Mr Justice Day the three accused. Anthony Benjamin Rudge, alias William Fennell aged forty-five dog trainer, (reads and writes well) John Martin alias John White, aged thirty-six, cigar maker (reads and writes imperfectly) and James Baker, aged twenty-nine, cabinet maker (reads and writes imperfectly) were arraigned upon charges of larceny, attempted murder, and wilful murder. After a trial lasting three days during which time a large number of both police and railway employees gave evidence the jury adjourned to consider their verdict.'*

The final paragraph in the paper of the same date was the somewhat unexpected headline:

> *'Verdict of wilful murder against all the prisoners. Sentence of Death. The jury retired at quarter past seven and after an hour's deliberation returned a verdict of wilful murder against all the prisoners. Rudge then startled the whole court by declaring I confess to the murder myself. He explained that the pistol found on him could not have been used to kill Byrnes, being of a different size and bore to that wounding the constable.* ***"I own it, It was I who did it".*** *he went on.* ***"But you cannot prove it, Martin and Baker are innocent of the crime."*** *He then stated:* ***"if the others were hanged for it, it would be judicial murder".*** *He said this as a dying man who welcomed death. It did no good. The judge placed the black cap upon his head and passed sentence of death on all three prisoners. He declared a specific date for the sentence which as it happened was a date beyond the statutory three weeks allowed after sentencing. The trial complete, the judge took this opportunity to praise the heroic conduct of the police officers, namely Roche, Johnstone and Fortune. He singled out Constable Byrne in particular, who knowing in advance of the armed men still did not hesitate to confront them alone and without any weapon. The judge also highlighted the heroism of the railwaymen who, also being unarmed, had played a vital role in the capture of the three murderers. The judge then ordered that £177 from public*

funds should be shared between the brave public servants and Mrs Byrne'.

Whilst awaiting sentence the condemned men received a number of family visits, and Rudge spent much of his time writing on the conditions in convict prisons, (of which he had had some considerable experience) which he asked to be sent to the Prison Commissioners after his death. The press in the meantime reported that Martin continued to deny any involvement in either the Byrnes or the Romford murder, but in the early hours of the morning of his execution, he confessed that it was he who had shot Constable Byrne, and Rudge and Baker had held Byrne by the arms as he did so.

Later James Berry (the hangman) revealed that as he prepared him for his execution, Martin told him that it was he too who had shot and killed Inspector Simmons. On the morning of the executions, the three men met briefly before entering the shed and were able to say their goodbyes to each other and shake hands. To avoid any chance of the hangings being watched by the public it was decided to use a shed for the erection of the scaffold and the subsequent despatch of the men,. This building had formerly housed the treadmill. All three men were hung simultaneously and promptly at 8am on the 8th February 1886 within the precincts of the old Carlisle jail. They died without incident. Outside a huge crowd waited for the posting of the death notice, for these executions in Carlisle Jail were the first for a decade, notwithstanding the fact that this was triple hanging which was unusual and thus attracted people from all over the country.

In fact before this execution all Carlisle criminals were hung in the prison yard, which now was overlooked by new buildings outside the prison. It is interesting to record that in later months it emerged that James Berry's assistant in the hanging was not Charles Malden, as had been earlier declared but was in fact Sir Claude Champion De Crespigny, a well-known entrepreneur and sportsman. There was a public outcry at the time that an amateur hangman should be allowed to assist at an execution, but Sir Claude argued that at some future date he anticipated being invited to become a County Sheriff, and he would therefore be required to organise and witness executions. It was not, he insisted, in his nature to require anyone to perform any task he was unable or unwilling to perform himself. He had therefore obtained the permission of the High Sheriff of Cumberland to assist at the executions, subject to James Berry's agreement. Somewhat unexpectedly Berry raised no objections after Sir Claude agreed to pay Berry £5 for the privilege of assisting him. Magazines such as Punch,France and Truth had fun with pretend characters such as Lord Fitz-Throttle. It was Sir Claude who reported that two years ago the prisoner Rudge had actually met the hangman Berry whilst at Doncaster Races and had offered to lay him £13 to £2 that Berry *'would never hang him'*. It was not clear whether Berry ever did collect his winnings. In some respects Sir Claude was correct in his assumption that he could be called upon to oversee punishments ordered by the courts in the position of High Sheriff. In fact in capital punishment cases it was the Sheriff's responsibility to organise such executions and appoint the hangman. It was also his responsibility to pay the hangman and his assistants, though he could later claim this expense back through 'sheriffs pleadings' from the Home Office. Indeed the Capital Punishment (Amendment) Act of 1868 required that the High Sheriff or the Under Sheriff be present at any execution.

Of course what was not mentioned was that the appointment of High Sheriff was for one year only, so the likelihood of him actually officiating during such a short term of office was minimal. Though three out of the possible four miscreants had now suffered their due fate it would be true to say that this case was not one of Dunne's better accomplishments throughout his entire career. It would certainly be a case that he would never ever forget, though in truth thanks to considerable mismanagement emanating from his office, he would probably have preferred to forget it. Though these days civilians would never be recruited and placed in such grave danger, things were no different in Dunne's time ... however no instruction had been issued to the police or the public in general by Dunne as to their role if such a situation ever arose.

Policemen were never told NOT to attempt an arrest single-handedly where the odds were strongly not in their favour, and their were many instances over the years where individual policeman had been seriously injured by attempting to handle things on their own. Only the previous year at Hensingham in West Cumbria PC Alexander Forbes had been shot at twice whilst pursuing a certain William Domigan across a field. Domigan later claimed to be drunk and frightened following yet more religious riots in Cleator Moor and had taken to carrying a gun, and when seeing a police uniform felt this was just too much for him. Even the sentence for carrying a gun and indeed firing it with intent to injure or kill was generally paltry for though he was charged with feloniously shooting with intent to kill he spent just three months in prison.

When PC Handley first confronted the men on that moonlight night he at least showed a little common sense by pulling away rather than attempt to arrest the armed men. He could so easily have died if he had done so. Nevertheless the police now had their first indications of the kind of ruthless individuals they were up against, but clearly little was learnt by those directing the ongoing operation. The death of Byrnes itself was clearly an unnecessary tragedy which could have been avoided.

Given the treatment already meted out to Roche, Johnstone, and Fortune along with the lucky escape of Handley, Herington,and Armstrong it must have been evident to those at higher level in the police, and I write of Chief Constable Dunne especially, that the police force had a violent gang of criminals on their hands, all in possession of firearms, and who in all probability wouldn't hesitate to kill if cornered. If the truth was slowly sinking in to those in charge of operations then the warnings (if any) to stay clear of them couldn't have been that emphatic. Indeed there is no evidence of any kind of back-up support such as the military (and Dunne had certainly chosen to use them in the past) or any apparent intention of calling them in to assist. In fact the law allowed for police officers to be armed when deemed appropriate but no such order was ever issued by Dunne's office. Those in command just weren't geared up to staging any kind of tactical search or educating officers (or anyone else for that matter) on the art of protecting themselves. A proper understanding of fundamental human behaviour also left something to be desired, though in fairness to Dunne he never did have sufficient personnel to man such an extensive area. (In 1885 the Secretary of State for the Home Department was warning local councils on the dangers of too few policemen. Indeed, Her Majesty's Inspectors of Constabulary were even threatening to withhold the grant to county forces that did not have a ration of one constable per thousand population, on the grounds of efficiency and Dunne certainly didn't meet that criteria) Byrnes as we know bravely went in armed solely with a truncheon, with tragic consequences, something that should never have happened.

There were many unanswered questions associated with this case, which clearly indicate that the police were weak on all fronts on the apprehension of these criminals. It is clear that they were happy with the arrest of these three men without the apparent need to utilise even more police resources in an attempt to clear up these anomalies. Byrnes funeral took place on Sunday the 1st November when a detachment of police officers marched in front of the hearse on its journey from the Pack Horse Inn to Penrith cemetery., where 3,000 mourners heard Father Meynell conduct the burial service and praise the dead officer for his courage and devotion to duty.

Regretfully this send off didn't extend to a decent burial with headstone for he was buried in a unmarked paupers grave, and it was not until some 121 years later (2006) that funds were raised to erect a proper and permanent memorial gravestone which was unveiled at his last resting place. Again quite why a decent headstone was not erected at the time of his death is not clear especially as he had proved himself more than an able policeman. Clearly a paupers grave was not exactly a fitting tribute to this first class police officer ... unfortunately none of his peers recognised that at the time.

He left a widow and four children, the youngest being just one month old. As earlier stated not one of Dunne's better episodes.

CHAPTER EIGHTEEN

JOHN DUNNE
1886-1895

Including the trial of John William Airey (the killing of PC John Groves)

The year 1886 was not just synonymous with the hanging at Carlisle of the criminals Rudge, Martin and Baker but also with the loss of yet another police officer in the line of duty. This time in the adjoining county of Westmorland and just five months after the untimely death of Joseph Byrnes. Though on this occasion it most certainly did not have the same ending ... far from it!

The officer this time was a certain John Groves, aged 41, who died whilst assisting another officer to apply handcuffs to a man who was violently resisting arrest for being drunk and disorderly at Stramongate, Kendal on the 7th March. He was effectively kicked to death by a drunken lout.

The inquest was heard at Kendal Town Hall but such was the crowd thronging to hear the outcome that the Mayor Mr R Nelson had to order the gallery to be cleared as it was in danger of collapsing. The outrage of his death was so great that it was thought necessary to move the trial to Carlisle. However to everyone's amazement the defendant was found guilty of manslaughter rather than the expected murder charge, and instead of following Martin Rudge and Baker to the gallows, simply served twelve months imprisonment with hard labour.

Once again the deceased man was married and left a large family. This time there had been no large trial, no vast amounts of publicity and no grand funeral yet once again a police officer had laid his life on the line, and for this one there is no indication that Dunne played any part in either the court proceedings or later by attending the officers funeral.

On Wednesday a large crowd turned out for the funeral of John Groves. Sixteen firemen and Sixteen policemen headed by Kendal's Chief Constable,Thomas Cotton, led the cortege to the burial in Kendal cemetery. The grave was marked with a stone inscription: '*In affectionate remembrance of John Groves for twelve years a constable in the Kendal police force, killed in Stramongate whilst in the execution of his duty on Sunday March 7th 1886, aged 41 years. In the midst of life we are in death*'. And at its foot: '*This memorial was erected by the members of the Kendal borough police force as a mark of respect to their late comrade*'.

On Wednesday May 5th, 1886, the case came before Mr Justice Grantham at the Westmorland and Cumberland Assizes in Carlisle. For reasons only known to the Grand Jury they, upon hearing the evidence put before them threw out that indictment for murder and Airey went for trial only on a charge of manslaughter; not surprisingly he pleaded guilty. Nevertheless It was still the prosecution's contention that Airey had kicked Constable Groves deliberately and with intent to cause harm and resist arrest. The defence pleaded that it was a complete accident and that Airey had simply lifted his foot and struck the officer while struggling to get up. The judge told Airey he had been lucky not to have been tried for murder; in his opinion it was not an accident; he thought Airey had intended to kick Groves; and he could not pass a light sentence. But he then passed what could hardly be other than that in the circumstances twelve months with hard labour, adding a comment: *"Take care you make a vow not to take more drink, you evidently cannot stand it".* That seemed more appropriate to a drunk and disorderly charge than one of killing a policeman.

Mr Justice Grantham apparently cared little for the life of PC Groves, and the national press gave his death but a few lines; he was forgotten by all but family and friends. His memorial stone stood for many years but after his wife's name was added in 1919, even that was neglected; eventually falling over, it was soon covered in moss, the inscription lost from sight – no one apparently cared. As it happens that was not entirely the end of the story, for some 96 years later a certain Rev David Searle, the then minister of Lambert Old Church, near Falkirk in central Scotland decided that its 96 year old church pipe organ required overhauling. Concealed inside its working parts, written in ink on a wooden block was the name of the organ builder 'Wm M Skereth, Organ Works, Kendal'.

The block also held a deeper secret ... a message written inside the glued wooden assembly. The minister described its discovery: *"The wooden block was glued to a wooden cap, the two pieces forming an assembly into which the pedal pipe fitted. The two pieces had to be broken open for the overhaul. They had not been opened since the organ was built in 1886. However written on the inside piece of the block, sealed with the wooden cap was the words In memory of PC Groves ... murdered 1886"*. The minister was fascinated. 'Who was 'PC Groves', apparently murdered so long ago? Were the words PC his initials or might he have been a police officer? Was the hidden message a confession to a long unsolved murder and if not what was its meaning?' Intrigued, Mr Searle wrote to the police station in Kendal, to ask for their help in solving the mystery. The name and date were not recognised at first but he was pointed in the direction of the offices of the Westmorland Gazette, who they felt would be able to help, and where he was able to bring to light the background to PC Groves untimely death. Whilst it appeared that no one had cared unduly about the loss of a policemen, clearly William Skereth had cared. PC Groves gravestone still lies just inside the gates of Kendal cemetery, with very few people knowing of the background to his death.

Interestingly for this year one individual who suffered far worse at the hands of a judge proved to be a vicar, rather than hardened criminals or drunken louts. This is in reference to the trial of one Rev. John Henry Latrobe Bateman, the vicar of Haile who was charged with solemnizing a wedding between Robert Little aged eighteen and Mary Jane Cockbain without either a licence or certificate, without due publication of banns, and without the permission of Little's parents, as well as inserting in the register of marriages a false entry relating to the marriage on the 9th May 1886. He was found guilty and sentenced to around eighteen months in prison. Clearly the jury considered his crime far more heinous than that of the death of John Groves.

One wonders if the jury had knowledge of Bateman's previous attendance before the magistrates on March 4th of this year when he was summoned for assaulting one Mary Blanchard his housekeeper. Following a lengthy enquiry Mary withdrew her complaint and the case was closed ... still 'where there's smoke there's fire' There was some attempt by a number of Bateman's friends and relatives to attempt a plea of mitigation but clearly this fell on deaf ears and he remained in Carlisle gaol for the entire sentence. In the meantime his 'living' was awarded to the Rev A.H Cooper in the November.

It might be interesting to learn that it was this year that Dunne was celebrating thirty years as Chief Constable of the Cumberland and Westmorland Constabulary and it appears to have gone completely unnoticed as far as his colleagues are concerned. No record anywhere of such an momentous event, particularly as there were not too many such instances of longevity in the service at this time ... and especially so where the officer concerned was now 62 years of age.

Can't say the same about Queen Victoria for this was the year that the nation was celebrating her Golden Jubilee. Clearly Dunne is showing no indication that it was time for his retirement. Indeed as we shall see Dunne had another fifteen years service in him yet. Mind you he was probably very pleased to see the first telephone line installed into his office this year even if the link so far was solely between Carlisle-Maryport-Whitehaven Possibly it was the Governments' Annual Return of the Judicial Statistics for crime at the latter end of this year that convinced him that he must be doing a good job and was best staying where he was.

The returns for England and Wales published in The Times showed a decrease of 1.4% in the total number of criminal classes at large and known to the police 1886/7 as compared with the numbers in 1885/6. There was also a decrease in the number of houses of bad character equal to 8.1% .The number of indictable offences reported by the police in the same period showed a decrease of 5.6% and in the number of persons sent for trial at assizes and sessions there is a decrease of 682 in number or 4.8%. On the other hand, in the number of persons summarily proceeded against before justices there is an increase of 24,111 or 3.7% while in the total commitments to prison there is a decrease of 6,877 or 3.8%. Perhaps Dunne's war on vagrants and tramps was at long last working.

Cause for celebration did not last long for by 1888 the same department was announcing that national crime for this year was 88,152, namely up 3.26% on 1887... Crime, of course continued unabated in Cumberland too, though as we know such crimes were not always the work of vagrants as Dunne would have us believe. Major crimes continued to be big news and the counties of Cumberland and Westmorland as we have learnt were not slow in producing some monumental crimes throughout the Victorian era. Far more than many other counties though the size of the joint counties and the numbers of population would almost certainly account for that.

A trial this year which would have given Dunne some sleepless nights at this time was that of the four policeman who were put on trial for alleged perjury. The charge was that they had given incorrect information in the trial of burglars Brannigan and Murphy ... a trial which had received widespread publicity at the time, becoming known through the press as the *'Cumberland Burglary'*. As it was not uncommon at this time of first locking up your suspect and then procuring or manufacturing the evidence, it was not too unexpected when the four policemen were acquitted.

In fairness to the police however forensics science,which could so easily have changed the outcome of this trial was still in its infancy at this time. True, science as a whole was advancing as new discoveries were made and the police were only beginning to realise that those advances could help them in their fight against crime. Law enforcement in 1888 was still heavily dependant on the old, tried and true methods of investigation and crime prevention. Even in 1888, before forensic science, the need for preserving the crime scene was there. (as was the case with Dunne and the plaster cast at the Charlton murder case). Many clues could be worked out from the position of the body, along with items found near the body or by studying the condition of the ground around the scene. It was still to be some time before the investigators realised that allowing bystanders to wander around a crime scene, as was still the general practice in those days, vital evidence, such as footwear impressions or blood flow patterns, could be destroyed. Fingerprinting did not become widely accepted as a science until the 1890s and was not considered a positive method for identifying offenders until the New York State Prison at Sing Sing established their fingerprint division in 1903. I suppose one could say that before forensic science the only way to prove someone committed a murder was to catch them in the act, or get the suspect to confess.

Away from serous crimes landing on Dunne's desk this year (1889) it can be assumed that he was pleased to learn that crime, nationally, was for the first time in years, actually down by 86,880 nationally, as it happened or 1.44% on 1888.

As always though new laws and statutes were continually being introduced one of which this year would have been the Prevention of Cruelty to and Protection of Children Act which made at long last the ill-treatment, neglect of or causing suffering to children punishable and additionally prohibited begging by boys under fourteen and girls under sixteen years of age. Considering that a high proportion of Dunne's statistics for vagrants and tramps included young people this should have been good news. The Act was better known as the Children's Charter, and for the first time the police had an Act which enabled them to intervene in relations between parents and children and they could arrest anyone they found ill-treating a child, even entering a home if they thought a child was believed to be in danger. It also gave every child the right to protection from abuse and exploitation and the right to inquiries to safeguard their welfare. Not surprisingly this was also the year that the NSPCC was set up.

An important date for Dunne in 1890 would have been the selection and appointment of Luke Talbot as the new Chief officer of police for Kendal, which happily coincided with the opening of the new police station and courts this year. His was to prove a fairly short-lived appointment though – he stepped down in 1895, though whether this had anything to do with a certain George Graham the newspapers dubbed him *'a Scotchman but an old Kendal slonk'* we shall never know.

Graham was possibly one of the only people to escape (and remain free) from Kendal Prison (originally the House of Correction) in 1890 when he took a bunch of keys from the warder's desk and let himself out of the cell block. Using a rope ladder he had made himself (out of oaken pickings) he then climbed over the wall opposite St Thomas's Vicarage. By doing so he was guilty of another offence – that of stealing prison clothes which were described as of red striped cotton shirt, trousers with a broad arrow almost washed out and dark grey socks with shoes.

The fact that Graham remained free probably didn't help Talbot's career prospects one little bit. Another new appointment this year was of a more temporary nature when in the April Lt. Col Fox Irwin was attached to the Cumberland and Westmorland Constabulary for just one year in the position of honorary Superintendent for the purpose of *'making himself acquainted with the organisation and practical working of the duties of the Police'* when it was stated at the time that he gained considerable experience at Whitehaven, where he spent most of his time. However at the same time as this 'training' was ongoing he was also carrying out a very successful business in Jersey as an army coach, preparing officers for promotion examinations. Precisely what Colonel Irwin's intentions where, we shall never know, for he certainly didn't make a career in the police. Clearly something must have put him off, or someone.

Dunne would no doubt have been pleased to read this year the report by the Royal Statistics Society which declared *'It is conclusive that there has been a continuous and marked decline in crime in England and Wales, and this fact is the more encouraging when a comparison is made in the numbers with the increased population during the same period'.* Now all Dunne had to do was to show that this 'marked decline' also applied to Cumberland and Westmorland. The report coincided with the news that national crime figures were down to 81,773 or 5.88% on previous year. 1890 was also the year that police forces began providing training in first aid. Initially the training was provided by the St John's Ambulance Brigade, though this responsibility was later transferred to doctors employed by the police (called police surgeons). In a retrospect step strangely enough the police in the twentieth century actually reverted to training in first aid by St John's.

Most importantly however 1890 was the year the Police Pensions Act was passed, which meant that all police officers were entitled to a pension equivalent to two thirds of their annual pay after 25 years, rather than it being solely at the discretion of the individual police forces as it had been until now.

Once again, 1891, like the previous year showed that national crime was down, this time to 79,734, which was some 2.49% on previous year. However, this being census year Dunne would probably have been interested to learn that the areas his men were expected to cover now extended to some 1,471,067 acres, making them the fourth largest (joint) county in the country. With the border changes in the twentieth century this of course changed to Cumbria being the second largest county.

The population was up again on 1881 though interestingly the Irish population was reduced by 3.64% due in all probability to railway work coming to an end. It was this same census which brought about the startling news that in the statistics presented by the compilers of the 1891 report which produced inter alia the startling information that Cumberland was one of the most 'overcrowded' counties in England with just over 13% of its people living more than two to a room. Westmorland by contrast had a good record with under 5% of its population in that position, as against an English and Welsh average of 11.23%. Why was this ? The more specific data for urban sanitary districts and municipal boroughs strongly indicated that overcrowding reckoned by a very useful yardstick of tenements with more than two persons per room within them was markedly a feature of the more inbuilt major towns and market centres. These, places like Whitehaven and Carlisle (the two worst cases in the region) but also in Cockermouth, Maryport and Brampton were largely responsible for the very high Cumberland county figure. Next in order of seriousness came the new industrial towns of Workington, Barrow and Cleator Moor which lacked the yard and alley overcrowding of those centres mentioned, but which had their own peculiarities and problems affecting considerable masses of people. Cleator Moor with its large stock of two-up and two-down terrace cottages (some of which still remain to this day) had long been inclined to pack large families into little space.

The year started well for Dunne. Just as he was recovering from a night of partying and the hopes of having a few extra hours off to recover, comes the last piece of news that he wanted to hear that day ... the murder that morning of a woman in Haverigg. This clearly did not bode well for the coming year. The year 1892 was in fact to see the last hanging in the city of Carlisle. (and it was even debatable whether the man should have hung) the criminal this time was to be a Joseph Wilson of Millom, who was hung at Carlisle Gaol on the 22nd March 1892. It would also be the last time that Dunne would be required to be in attendance at such an event, which no doubt was fine by him.

Once again the *Cumberland Pacquet* was quick off the mark in the first reporting of the crime. The article was headed '*Horrible murder at Millom*' and sub-titled '*Woman's brains blown out – Callous behaviour of the murderer*'.

The story went:

'A horrible crime was committed at Haverigg on New Years Day. About 10.30a Mrs Marion Greaves Crossman, a miner's wife, was shot dead by a young man named Joseph Wilson, who lodged with the family. At the time the awful tragedy was committed the husband Richard Crossman was away from home. Everything points to the conclusion that the crime was premeditated. James Crossman a lad about seventeen years of age came home about 5.30am and lay down on a wooden settle in the kitchen and his sleep was undisturbed until Wilson made some noise whilst getting the gun ready to carry out his murderous intention. Young Crossman saw the murderer raise the gun to fire and upon hearing the report and hearing somebody falling he ran out of the house the back way and obtained the assistance of a Mr Jones who resided a door or two away from the Crossmans. A married woman Mrs Williams who lived next door, on hearing the shot came to see what had occurred, but she was forced to leave precipitately as Wilson also threatened to 'do' for her if she interfered. A crowd soon collected and messengers were sent for George Currie the local constable, plus Dr Dunne and Doctor Watson. For some time Wilson stood standing by, seeming to almost gloat over his crime - even telling anyone who would listen that the other barrel of the gun was loaded in case the first shot failed. The gun Wilson used was a double-barrelled one and both barrels were loaded. The weapon was kept upstairs by Mr Crossman to whom it belonged and there were only four cartridges in the house and Wilson had secured three of them, leaving one on the mantelpiece of the back kitchen. When he shot Mrs Crossman he put down the gun in the first instance and when Mr Jones took possession of it he saw that the loaded barrel was half-cocked. The dead woman lay in the position in which she collapsed until the arrival of the police constable. She lay with her face in her hands to protect herself although the bystanders were horrified when they saw that the doors and walls were bespattered with her blood. They could scarcely realise the full effect of the sight until PC Currie moved the body. A moving sight presented itself. The dead woman lay in a pool of blood. The right side of her face between the ear and the nose had been completely destroyed. Part of the left side of the face the ear was also blown away. The shot had gone through the woman's skull and made a cavity through which a closed hand could be put. A portion of the skull was found about fifteen yards away in a field fronting the house. The floor where the woman fell was covered with blood, amongst which were mingled portions of the brain etc. It seemed that at the time Mrs Crossman was shot she was turning round to come into the house after sending one of her lads on an errand. She was probably standing with the door half open and on turning her head round to come in, Wilson

fired. The end of the barrel of the gun would not at the most have been more than six feet from the woman's head when it was fired. Dr Dunne arrived about a quarter to twelve but his professional skill was of course to no avail. At the doctors suggestion a wooden settle was moved from the back kitchen to the front end, and on this the body of the woman was placed. Nothing was however done to remove the effects of the tragedy until PC Currie and Inspector Watson returned, after leaving Wilson in the lock-up. Then with the assistance of a neighbour the blood stains were removed. The murdered woman's children were looked after and removed to some neighbours' houses. The youngest was lying asleep in a cradle, when it was woke up by the shot. Another child, a little boy, who was standing in the front room with the mother, had a narrow escape. Some of the pellets grazed his face and one entered the flesh and had to be extracted by Dr Dunne. The people assembled round the house were burning with indignation at the callous and careless conduct of Wilson, who seemed as if he was delighted that he had accomplished his diabolical purpose. When first taxed with the offence he said "I've done it; I've bloody well shot her". When some individuals tried to bring him to realise his position, he joked about the work the hangman would have to do, and even went so far as to threaten to 'do' for others before the hangman's rope brought his career to a close. "Such a deed is not like shooting a dog" some of the bystanders remarked . "Oh" replied Wilson "it's only a f.....g woman" . The behaviour of the murderer was such that if the police had not speedily taken him away, the bystanders would have torn him to pieces. The only time he betrayed any feeling was when the constable placed the handcuffs on his wrists; he gave a momentary shudder, but directly resumed his ordinary demeanour and on the way to the police station, whilst he was in the hands of Inspector Watson and PC Currie he seemed quite at ease. Meeting an acquaintance Wilson cheerily saluted him, to which the friend replied that he should be ashamed of himself. The husband Mr Crossman had gone away on an early train to Dalton on New Year's morning. He was immediately telegraphed for, and returned by the 3.18pm train. He was informed in the telegram of his wife's death but he attributed it to an entirely different cause, and did not learn the real facts till within a few yards of his own home. Crossman thought his wife's death was due to the fact that she was still near to her recent confinement. A next-door neighbour had promised to remain up all night on New Years Eve with the deceased, but the latter declined and promised to knock for Mrs Williams if she required her'.

Other than a report of the inquest no more mention of this murder was reported until the trial at the beginning of March,under the heading *'The Millom*

Murder' The Cumberland Pacquet reported that following a lengthy trial at which it was clear throughout that Wilson was indeed guilty of the heinous crime ... though the defence lawyers did do their best to prove insanity, both in Wilson as well as family members The jury retired at 4pm to consider their verdict. They returned to the court at 4.25pm.

The jury having answered to their names, the Clerk of Assize said: *"Are you agreed upon your verdict?"*

The foreman of the jury replied: *"Yes, my Lord"*

The Clerk of Assize then asked: *"Do you find Joseph Wilson guilty or not guilty?"*

The foreman replied: *"Guilty, with a recommendation to mercy".*

The Clerk of the Assize then asked: *"You say he is guilty and that is the verdict of you all?"*

The foreman replied: *"Yes".*

The judge then asked of the jury: *"I am afraid I must ask you on what grounds (do you recommend mercy) as I have to communicate with the Home Secretary". The foreman replied "On account of his previous good character".*

The Clerk of the Assize then addressed the prisoner stated *"You stand convicted of wilful murder, have you anything to say why the Court should not give you the judgement of death according to law?"*

The prisoner made no response. The judge after assuming the black cap said: *"Joseph Wilson you have been found guilty, after a most patient trial of the gravest offence which the law of England knows and for that offence the law of England knows but one penalty, and the sentence that I now pronounce is not the sentence of a poor weak mortal but is the sentence of the law, and that sentence is that you must die. You had no mercy. You sent out of this world into the other a person who, as far as appears, had shown nothing to you but affection. But anything I can say must now be addressed, I am afraid to ears that will make little use of it. You will have the advantage of being taught what is your duty by other lips than mine. My duty, and a most painful one it is, is to pronounce upon you the sentence of the law which is that for the crime of wilful murder, of which you are now convicted, you will be taken from the place where you now are to the place from whence you came, and that upon a day to be appointed you will be taken to the place of execution and shall be hanged by the neck till your body be dead, and that your body when dead be buried within the precincts of the prison in which you shall have been last confined. And may Almighty God have mercy on your soul".*

The prisoner who made no comment was at once removed below, and taken to the gaol. Note: Number 4 Moor Moss still exists to this day, though without the name MOOR MOSS imprinted over the door as it did in Wilson's day, and the cottages have since been renamed Marine View with both the original number 4 and 5 made into one property. Only Number 10 Moor Moss still exists as a postal address.

Besides the local newspaper reports of the time, the public learned little more of the history of Joseph Wilson and in all probability weren't especially interested either. To most people he was a nonentity and a nonentity he remained. Even to this day. In fact the writer spoke to a householder who lived for some years at number 6 Moor Moss (now Marine View) who not only knew nothing of Joseph Wilson, but was totally unaware that a murder had been committed just two doors away!

Like many others convicted of murder in the county in Victorian times, he wasn't even a Cumbrian, though he would be in these times given the boundary changes. The crime perpetrated by 23 year old Joseph Wilson in 1892 has little to commend it to posterity. The only notable item about Wilson was the fact that he was the last condemned criminal to be hanged in Carlisle Gaol, as well as being the last in Cumberland. Not because their were no more condemned prisoners, rather the fact that the gaol by now was reaching the end of its life, and prisoners were from this point on transferred to Lancaster once they had been condemned to death.

Not long afterwards, the gaol itself was officially condemned as unsuitable for purpose, and by 1922 it had become cheaper to intern Cumbrian offenders in such prisons as Durham or Lancaster, where murderers could also be hanged as required. By 1933 it had been demolished.

Fortunately for Dunne, this was the only crime of any significance for this year. However having enjoyed reduced crime figures for the past few years, he would have been shocked to learn that murder apart, crime was actually on the increase once again, and greatly so to, for they were up some 6.86% nationally on the previous year ... which in numbers amounted to 85,200. No doubt though the report in The Times of the first conviction worldwide using fingerprints would have given him some encouragement.

Unfortunately this first conviction was in Argentina, when a certain Juan Vucetich made the first criminal fingerprint identification. Apparently he was able to identify Francis Rojas a woman who had murdered her two sons and then cut her own throat in an attempt to place the blame on another. Her bloody print was left on a door post, proving her identity as the murderer. It was to be another nine years before the Fingerprint Branch at Scotland Yard was created in July 1901 and some time after that before the facility became available in the north of the country.

By 1893 their appeared to be a return to a reduction in crime nationally for the Official Judicial Statistics for this year stated *'On the whole there is good ground to think the decrease in crime, though not great as it has often been represented though by no means comparable, for instance, to the decrease in prison population, is nevertheless real and substantial'.* Unfortunately within a month or two they were reporting that national crime was up once again to 86,396 or 1.4% which no doubt left Dunne in a bit of a quandary.

By 1893 Dunne had decided that many of his constables could better patrol their 'beats' with the use of a bicycle, and it was not an uncommon sight to see a police constable racing down the road cape spread out behind him in an attempt to catch other cyclists riding their bikes without either a bell or whistle (a requirement when overtaking) or a lamp for night riding.

In the August Dunne had issued a proclamation that in the event of such 'crimes' the culprit would be fined 40/- (£2) Kendal was also the scene of yet another crime for this year ... not that it had not had a regular supply of them over the years, it's just that some were more serious to report than others.

The Westmorland Gazette was reporting the imprisonment this year of Marcellus Thompson, the cashier of the Kendal Gas Company who in over twenty years in the job had been responsible for the 'defalcation' of £3.600 (around £720,000 in today's money).

The police were in the news nationally this year when their was a discussion (reported in Hansard) of issuing 'silent boots' for the police. The idea being that officers were more likely to catch criminals if they could creep up on them. As nothing further was ever reported on the subject, and we now know that police were never issued with them I think it is safe to say that nothing ever came of the proposal. And continuing with officer's footwear: this was the year that the Police Review and Parade Gossip was first published. One of the first editions reported that police officers were concerned about corns caused by regulation footwear and strict rules that prevented them from loosening their 'stout leather belts' during a heat wave in August 1893.

The paper was set up this year with the help of a philanthropist (John Kempster) who invested his £500 savings because he felt that officers needed somewhere to air their grievances and be given a chance to improve standards of education and training. The paper was to last for many years. It later became better known as The Police Review.

By 1894 Government were again showing interest in at least one of the problems affecting the police, and an item which had been plaguing Dunne throughout his entire working life – habitual criminals. Especially so those of the travelling variety. The Government report of this year declared that there was a real problem with the number of travelling habitual criminals, stating: *'the offences committed by men travelling from county to county or conducting operations in one police district while habitually residing in another and not inconsiderable in number, and are often of a peculiarly serious and dangerous character. If a distinction be made between a professional criminal the man who has deliberately adopted a career of dishonesty or violence as a means of obtaining a livelihood and the man who only lapses into crime occasionally as, as may be said, under stress of circumstance, it is clear that the travelling thief or burglar belongs always to the former rather than the latter category, to the former class also belong as a rule,those criminals who, without being regular travellers, move from districts to where they have become well known to the police to another in which they hope to be rid of their past history and to begin with a clean record a new career of crime'.* It was this same committee that considered that the numbers of travelling criminals were grossly under-estimated by Chief Constables, in their quarterly reports, believing that the main outcome of their inquiry was the recent practice with some forces of taking fingerprints and it appears to them that reliance on such 'fingerprint identification' (which was far from proven) led some forces to abandoning the ideas of separating the criminal population and authorised police supervision of criminals.

Somehow I imagine Dunne didn't go along with those sentiments. Still, he would have been pleased to see that the national crime figures for this year had actually gone down for a change, it was now 86,052, or 0.40%.

1895 saw the arrival of George Hardy the new Chief officer of police for Kendal, following the recent departure of Luke Talbot. His too was to be a short-lived appointment, lasting until 1899. Either Dunne was doing something wrong in his selection process, or more likely, the man had found something better paid. Another arrival, or more correctly a visitor to Cumberland this year was that of the German Kaiser, Wilhelm II to Lowther Castle on the 14th August.

His home during the duration of his visit was on the Raven, a boat belonging to the Ullswater Steamer Company. For his stay the owners made the boat a temporary royal yacht and her decks were painted yellow to mark his visit to the 'Yellow Earl'. Of interest is the fact that the Raven was launched as recently as 1889. One of the shareholders a certain Mr Thomas Cook, whose name today is so closely linked to package holidays, was the reason behind the launch of the company's second vessel. Apparently when the first boat The Lady of the Lake broke down at the height of the season he complained that there was no boat to transport his tourists. John Dunne, as both a friend of the Earl and of course being Chief Constable had the pleasure of meeting Wilhelm at this time, a meeting which would ever remain memorable to him for the Kaiser presented him with an engraved gold watch and chain.

Of course Kendal, like the rest of Westmorland and Cumberland was changing ... this year actually saw the introduction of the first car on the roads. This was a steam powered vehicle designed by W T Carr and built by J Summer of Leyland. Not sure they caught on! Nevertheless at least one police force was ready with their book of speeding tickets to the fore when Hampshire Constabulary handed out the first speeding ticket – fining a man for racing at 6 mph and this at a time when records show their were just 14/15 cars in total on the roads in Britain!

CHAPTER NINETEEN

JOHN DUNNE

1896-1902

Well Earned Recognition

Being a relatively quiet year as far as serious crime was concerned one supposes that the most important item listed in Dunne's diary for August 15th/16th of 1896 would have been the visit to Carlisle of Li Hung Chang, from China, whose official title at the time of his visit would have been Viceroy of Zhili and Minister of Beiyang, another would have been Marquis Suyi of the First Class. It was during his visit to Europe; which was ostensibly to attend the coronation of Emperor Nicolas II of Russia, that he met Queen Victoria who made him a Knight Grand Cross of the Royal Victorian Order.

It was he, just four years later who played a major part in the Boxer Rebellion as well as being the principal negotiator in 1901 when he signed the treaty ending the crisis. It was also this year that Dunne, George Mackay Superintendent of Carlisle City Police, and the Governor of Carlisle Gaol would have had a little 'egg on their face' following the daring escape of a certain William Almond from Carlisle Gaol on the 5th December of this year – more so when it was realised that he had got clean away.

Clearly from newspaper reports for this year there are more cars on the road ... indicated in part by Parliament repealing the 1865 Locomotives on the Highway Act which raised the speed limit for *'light locomotives'* from 4mph to 14, and doing away with that poor individual walking ahead with a red flag. Such changes also reported the news of the first person to be killed in a car accident.

No doubt the streets of Carlisle with now both cars, bicycles, and the introduction of the horse drawn bus (in the January), were a hive of activity, which alone would have posed a whole new set of rules for the able police. Kendal in Westmorland had a bit of a problem which could have caused Dunne's officers a considerable amount of paperwork when what appeared to have started as a child hood tantrum may have been behind a strange and tragic occurrence this year at the home of a certain Charles Butterworth Esq, of Denmark House, Kendal Green, when a maid servant called Isabella Nelson was shot in the head by eleven year old Ronald Kennedy. Fortunately three doctors were quickly on hand and Isabella's skull was trepanned in the house. Unfortunately for Isabella no anaesthetic was used necessitating the patient being held down by Mrs Butterworth and the Misses Butterworth.

Isabella apparently recovered from her ordeal though it is doubtful that Ronald Kennedy was ever allowed anywhere another shotgun. On the good side for this year was the news that national crime was down to 78,614 or 3.33% on previous year. One has to wonder whether Dunne on the 1st January of 1897 and with forty years service with the Cumberland and Westmorland Police under his belt,was aware of the changes that would affect him personally this year ... not least of which was in the February when he was appointed Deputy Lieutenant of Cumberland, in honour of that lengthy service. *The Carlisle Journal* dated Friday February 19th 1897 and headed *'The Honour to Mr Dunne'* described the honour in full detail, and at the same time listing a number of important incidents in his eventful life. The report read:

'The Lord Lieutenant of Cumberland (Lord Muncaster) has conferred upon Mr Dunne, Chief Constable of the Counties of Cumberland and Westmorland, the appointment of Deputy Lieutenant of this county. This act is a grateful recognition of the services of an officer who has been at the head of our county police for a period of over forty years, and who entering upon that office as one of the youngest Chief Constables, now finds himself the eldest. It was in 1856 that Mr Dunne became a candidate for the office of Chief Constable of Cumberland and Westmorland.

The Police Act of that year had made the establishment of police forces in counties obligatory, and he saw that the new order offered him an opportunity for advancement. He sent his name in as a candidate for Cornwall, Somersetshire, Devonshire, Derbyshire, and Cheshire, and also for the combined forces of Cumberland and Westmoreland. He was soon placed upon the 'short leet' of all except Cumberland and Westmorland, but in these counties he was unanimously selected out-of-hand, and eventually elected. Thereupon he withdraw his candidature in the other counties and accepted the office of Chief Constable of Cumberland and Westmorland. He at once set to work to organise the police of these counties upon a basis of economy combined with efficiency and the success which had attended his work in Norwich and Newcastle. From the rules and regulations issued by him for the guidance of his men and from his addresses to them on parade at the annual inspections may be gathered the guiding principles which he inculcated. He laid great stress upon the importance of the police always giving their evidence in courts of justice in a fair and impartial manner without bias or prejudice. If they knew anything that may be favourable to the prisoner or defendant they were to state it candidly, and as readily as they would depose to anything they knew against him. By following those rules, and by the efficient, faithful and fearless discharge of duty the police are in a very different position from that they occupied years earlier. The discipline and efficiency are excellent and Mr Dunne may fairly claim credit for having been a pioneer in the reform of the police system. Fortunately (by 1897) his long service in Cumberland has not been marked by a long list of crimes committed within his jurisdiction, but in dealing with those that have been perpetrated he has displayed great energy, tact and discretion. He was the youngest ever officer ever entrusted with the command of a great force and surviving all his contemporaries to hold the position of Senior Chief Constable in the Kingdom. How well he succeeded in organising the service here or breaking down public prejudice by his just and equitable rule and in gaining general confidence is well known to all who have watched the cause of local affairs. His success is mainly owing to a right conception of the duty of the police force. Since his appointment many important administrative duties have been thrown upon the police, and perhaps nothing more important than that of contagious diseases amongst cattle.

Mr Dunne has on various occasions initiated enquiries which resulted in the passing of useful Acts of Parliament such as the Police Act of 1856, The Licensing Act of 1872, the Poaching Prevention Act, the Police Superannuation Act, The Reformatory and Industrial Schools Act, and other measures of utility. And he was the pioneer in promoting many reforms which have raised the public service to its present state of discipline. Altogether it has been the fortune of few men to donate so long a life to public duty or to be so uniformly successful in its discharge'.

Also this year Dunne was appointed a Senior Justice of the Peace for Carlisle. However as a serving police officer he was unable to take up those duties until he had retired from the force ... still some years hence. Nevertheless both honours were unusual for a policeman to receive and does at least indicate the high regard in which he was held by his fellow peers. On the 29th April 1897 we learn via the *Whitehaven News* that as Cumberland's Chief Constable he was the oldest person holding such rank in the United Kingdom, and as such he was appointed by his fellow peers to preside over a meeting of Britain's Chief Constables, to decide how they, as a body, should celebrate the Queen's longest reign.

Clearly the meeting didn't go without considerable disagreement, for in the May the police Chiefs had issued a warning about the dangers of flags and decorations suspended across the streets, and in fact in the June, Sir Arthur Bigge, the Queen's Private Secretary was even lamenting the fact that a huge fireworks display for London had been ruled out on the grounds that it would put the public at risk.

It was even proposed that plans to illuminate the dome of St Paul's Cathedral be modified to avoid risking a fire and that the Department of Official Works felt the need to ban well-wishers from standing on the top of public buildings for fear they would fall off.

At the time the threat of terrorism was very real and in fact these senior police officers had received a tip-off about a possible 'anarchist outrage' actually brought back many hundred of retired police officers into service to keep the public safe. Rather like today they even discussed the fear of 'binge- drinking'. However they were able to argue satisfactorily that a temporary extension until 2.30 am on Jubilee Day (20th June) would avoid a rush on pubs.

Before that momentous event however their was just one other small matter that Mr John Dunne needed to perform. On the 22nd June following an invitation from St James Palace in London, Dunne was to find himself on one knee before Queen Victoria where he was dubbed 'Sir' John Dunne, in recognition of his outstanding value as a public servant. He was in good company that day as amongst the recipients of awards was Colonel Sir Edward Ridley Colborne Bradford, KCB, KCSI, aide-de-camp to the Queen,and Commissioner of the Metropolitan Police who received a Knight Grand Cross (GCB) AND Honorary Lieutenant-Colonel (retired) Henry Smith CB, Commissioner of the City of London Police who received a KCB. Naturally the local papers amongst which was the Carlisle Patriot were quick to pick up on this award for on the 25th June was the news item: *Royal Honours.* Published in Gazette on Jubilee Day Stated the honours ceremony was a long one, yet great care was taken to prevent it becoming so long as to deprive the honours of distinction. John Dunne was created a Knight along with many others. Following the meeting of the Chief Constables on the 29th April it was unanimously agreed that Sir John Dunne should present the Jubilee address on behalf of the joint police forces of Great Britain, thus on the 21st July Dunne, as the oldest Chief Constable in the country was invited by his fellow officers to present the Jubilee address to His Royal Highness the Prince of Wales (on behalf of Her Majesty the Queen), on behalf of Chief officers and police forces in Great Britain at St James Palace., for his final approval.

Later, Dunne publicly addressed Her Majesty on behalf of the assembled provincial Chief Constables (in total 238), and which was later reported in the London Gazette of the 23rd July 1897. His statement read as follows:

'To Her Most Gracious Majesty the Queen. May it please your Majesty, WE, the under mentioned Chief Officers of the Provincial Police of Great Britain, humbly approach Your Majesty, and beg permission respectfully to submit, on behalf of our Forces, comprising 29,052 Officers and Constables, our loyal and dutiful congratulations on the auspicious occasion of the completion of the 60th Year of Your glorious Reign. The Police Force of Great Britain, as now constituted, was organised in the second year of Your Majesty's Reign, and the most valuable of all Acts benefiting the Police was reached in the 53rd year of Your Majesty's Reign, when an Act of Parliament conferring the inestimable boon of a guaranteed life pension to Police Officers, together with provision for their Widows and Orphans, was passed into law. We humbly submit that, of the many admirable Acts of Parliament passed during Your Majesty's Reign, few, if any, have tended more to the protection and happiness of Your Majesty's subjects than those establishing the present system of Police. We feel it will be gratifying to Your Majesty to learn that the Police have raised, by voluntary subscription, a considerable sum in aid of the Police Orphanage at Redhill, and other charities, as a loyal offering in commemoration of Your Majesty's long and glorious Reign. We earnestly pray, that it may please Almighty God long to spare Your Majesty to the well being of the vast Empire which has so greatly prospered under Your Majesty's most beneficent Rule.

Presented by Sir John Dunne, D.L. 21st July 1897

NB. The orphanage referred to would have been 'The Lodge' at Gatton Point, Redhill, which had first opened its doors in 1895. This was the fore-runner of the Police Orphanages in this country and was originally started by Catherine Gurney, the grand daughter of William B Gurney who played a leading part in the abolition of slavery. The orphanage offered accommodation for 56 boys and 44 girls.

Regardless of the importance of Dunne being in London on the 21st July to make this important address, he still had time the day before to pen the following letter to the Standing Joint Committee, addressed to the Chair Colonel Senhouse:

'Gentlemen. As I am commanded to be at St James Palace on the 21st July to present to his Royal Highness the Prince of Wales on behalf of Her Majesty

the Queen the loyal and dutiful Jubilee address from the Chief officers and Police forces of Great Britain in commemoration of Her Majesty's long and glorious reign, I hope that you will excuse me from attending your meeting tomorrow and personally thanking the Police Committee for their very kind and cordial congratulations and good wishes which are included in their minutes to be submitted to you re the recent honour conferred on me. I therefore write this letter to say how very much obliged I am to the Committee for their kind words of congratulation. I also beg to be allowed to sincerely thank the Standing Joint Committee, the Police Committee, the Quarter Sessions, the County Council, other local authorities for the very fair and impartial consideration and valuable support which I have received from them regarding all matters of public duty during the last 41 years. I think it only right to also mention that when I was unanimously appointed by the Quarter Sessions in 1856 out of one hundred and 23 candidates the Magistrates who took a great interest in the appointment and the subsequent organization of the Police never lost sight of the necessity of having all the duties devolving on the Police carried out in a thoroughly efficient and legal manner in connection with the prevention and detection of crime, the protection of life and property, the maintenance of good order, the extirpation of contagious diseases among cattle, and various other matters affecting the public interest. At the same time they always took a deep interest in the welfare and discipline of the force. The rules and regulations requiring the police to on every occasion give their evidence in courts of justice in all judicial inquiries fairly and impartially without the slightest bias or prejudice on the one side or the other met with their approval and support. These great principles which were initiated in 1856 are the main lines on which all our duties have been based and the present recognition by Her Gracious Majesty the Queen is of the efficiency and discipline of your Police Force is a tribute to the memory of the great magistrates who inaugurated the system and to the existing authorities who have done so much to have it conscientiously fulfilled in every sense in the public interest. I have the honour to be Gentleman John Dunne Chief Constable of Cumberland and Westmorland'.

Possibly to celebrate his promotion, and at the same time add to his growing property portfolio the Carlisle Journal is reporting the sale of Grosvenor House the one-time Police HQ in Warwick Road, Carlisle to a certain Sir John Dunne. At the time the property was no longer a police station having been earlier sold to a certain RJ Baillie in 1895 who after considerable refurbishment opened it as the Grosvenor College.

It is unclear what Dunne did with the property though it is assumed that he rented it out to the original owner to allow it to continue as a college. In later years it was to become a hotel, and a restaurant gaining notoriety of a sort when as The Emperor's Palace Restaurant it was the scene of a 'drug bust' in 2003.

There were also a few changes to the law this year which would have affected Dunne and his officers one was the 'Cleansing of Persons Act 1897', which stated that *'Any local authority shall have the power, when in their discretion they shall see fit, to permit any person who shall apply to the said authority, on the grounds that he/she is infested with vermin, to have the use, free of charge, of the apparatus (if any) which the authority possesses for cleansing the person and his/her clothing from vermin.' (6th August 1897).*

At first glance that may well give the impression that only workhouses and similar establishments had the dubious honour of such work, but of course it was the police too especially the lowly constable (or his wife) in his rural locality who would also be expected to undertake such duties from now on ... which no doubt would give them more reason to consider an increase in their pay.

Another new law for this year would have been the Police (Property) Act 1897 which stated: *'where any property has come into the possession of the police in connection with any criminal charge or under various criminal acts,, a court of summary jurisdiction may, on application, either by an officer of police or by a claimant of the property, make an order for the delivery of the property to the person appearing to the magistrate or court to be the owner thereof, or of the owner cannot be ascertained, make such order with respect to the property as to the magistrate or court may seem fit.'* There is no indication anywhere that proceeds from such property ever ended up in the Police Benevolent Society's funds... but one can assume it was certainly considered.

Not all was so cosy though for this year, national crime was up once again by 0.37% (or 78,905) and in the October their was a report by the same Standing Joint Committees of Cumberland and Westmorland (the one who had spoke so glowingly of Dunne just a few months earlier) which related to claims of inefficiency against Dunne and his force, which after starting on a high was not really the way Dunne would have chosen to end this year.

After such a successful year Dunne must have been completely devastated in the October of 1898 when he lost his wife Mary, the love of his life. *The Cumberland Pacquet* obituary column simply stated:

> *'Lady Mary Dunne, died on the 16th October 1898 at Wetherall, wife of Sir John Dunne D.L. Eldest daughter of Thomas Barnes MD (dec'd) of Bunkers Hill, Cumberland and Tring Park, Herts. Aged 63 years.'*

The newspaper reports of this death also brought to light something about the education of Dunne's three children for the first time. For example his eldest son Francis (better known as Frank) had been educated at Marlborough and Heidleburg, after which he spent time at the Royal Agricultural College, Cirencester. Currently he was an Inspector in the Department of Agriculture.

Gerald, who had been born in 1875, had also been well educated, though in his case it was at Cothill House, Oxford, and thence at Musselburgh, Edinburgh. At the time of his mother's death he was a lieutenant in the 2nd Hussars Regt.

Their only daughter Henrietta, who had been born in 1869 was privately educated at home. In Lady Mary's will she left her farm at Newby consisting of 49 acres ... and a further 24 acres of land in Carlisle to her eldest son Francis.

Eden Mount which at the time of her death was shown to be in her name passed to John.There was also some £15,000 of shares (value £3 million today) in various railway companies which were split evenly between the three children.

She also owned Lime House, Wetherall, which was rented out in 1898 to Gerald and Henrietta, though by the end of October (28th) this was being leased to a Mrs Crosthwaite at a rental of £80 per annum to be run as a school. Interestingly the house had started life as a school for records show that it had been a school back in 1856 for we learn that Elizabeth, Annie and Jane Robinson were advertising the house as a 'Ladies Boarding School', which later became Lime House. The reading of management of Mary's will was not easy however for there is considerable correspondence in Carlisle archives which confirms solicitors were involved sorting out the terms and conditions, especially so her interest in Tring Park as the Barnes family believed they were due a share in it, such reasons dating back to the legalities attached to her original ownership of various properties upon the death of her father Dr Barnes, many years earlier.

It was to be some considerable time before Dunne became part owner of the long owned family estate. Yet again changes to the law ... when would there be a year without them? This time the Act which affected the police force the most was the extension of the Vagrancy Act of 1824 and which stated that any male person living on the earnings of prostitution or soliciting for immoral purposes should be deemed a rogue and vagabond within the meaning of that Act. When the Bill was in the House of Commons it was pointed out that, in view of the provisions of the Act of 1824 regarding incorrigible rogues, this would have the effect of rendering such persons liable to whipping on a second or subsequent conviction of the offence. The Bill was passed in its original form so that persons convicted more than once of these offences were rendered liable to be whipped by order of Quarter Sessions as incorrigible rogues.

Again, though their has not been much mention of prostitution during this era in the pages of this book, all local newspapers reported the appearance of at least one known prostitute appearing before the magistrates – and literally on a weekly basis, so clearly this was a problem, and of course where there are prostitutes there are invariably 'pimps' controlling them. The problem, then as now, was catching them!

Another important change to the law this year was that which allowed for prisoners on trial for felony to give sworn evidence for the first time. Up until now any evidence submitted by a prisoner had not been given on oath, and thus in many cases the jury would not have placed much strength on it ... it would be interesting to learn whether such a change would (or did) make a change to their decisions. This change in the law came within the Criminal Evidence Act 1898 which additionally covered competency of witnesses in criminal cases, evidence of person charged, right of reply, calling of wife or husband in certain cases, provisions as to previous acts.

Today we hear much talk of 'hooligans' and the fact that the situation as regards the youth on our streets causing mayhem, or crowds at football matches, yet the problem was no less severe at the end of the nineteenth century. This year newspapers are warning of the menace of 'hooligans' and of a *'dramatic increase in disorderly behaviour'*. *The Times* was reporting *'organised terrorism in the streets'.* At the same time *The Daily Graphic* of the 15th February of this year stated:

> *'the latest pistol cases have almost all been cases of boys, hardly in their teens, deliberately using pistols as weapons of aggression – these 'gangs' of young ruffians who terrorize certain districts of the metropolis seem, in fact, to be provided with firearms, and to think little more of discharging them than they would throwing stones'.*

It is interesting to record that the word 'hooligan' actually came into the English language this year in the wake of an excessively rowdy August Bank holiday celebration in London when hundreds of people appeared before the courts on charges of assault, drunkenness and assaults on police officers. After the dust had settled, London's 'hooligans' emerged as what we would nowadays call a 'youth culture' having adopted a uniform dress code of peaked caps, neck scarves, bell bottom 'narrow go wide' trousers cut tight at the knee, heavy leather belts with designs worked in metal studs and a hairstyle which was cropped close to the scalp with a 'donkey fringe' hanging over the forehead.

In other cities, similar gangs with the same dress style were known and feared by different names ... the *'Scuttlers'* and *'Ikey lads'* of Manchester and Salford, the

'Peaky blinders' of Birmingham. Fortunately there are no known reports of such individuals in either Cumberland or Westmorland at this time though their was always the usual collection of young tearaways appearing before the magistrates, usually weekly. These lads were possibly the forerunner of the *'Teddy Boys'* that we saw on the streets in the 1950s, when they were the first group in England to differentiate themselves as teenagers.

Still if Dunne didn't have such individuals to contend with at least their was still the knowledge that crime in general, and certainly on a national basis, was up again for yet another year. This time the figure was quite substantial 4.46% or 82,426. However for reasons which, like today, are quite unexplainable this statistic was 'completely turned on its head' for 1899 when the newspapers were reporting that national crime was down 7.7% on 1898 (or 76,025) 1899 was the year that Dunne, along with several other Chief Constables of England and Wales, plus a small smattering of Chief fire officers were part of a Select Committee to enquire into the *'Arrangement for Fire Brigades in England and Wales'*. Surprisingly the general feeling seemed to be against police brigades; in fact the Chief Constable of Bristol remarked that *'personally he would be very glad to be without the fire brigade'*. Police fireman, generally speaking were to be found only in city and borough forces., though the city of Carlisle had for some time had its own fire station and dedicated team of 'fire officers', as indeed had Brampton.

Like the Select Committee on Policing in 1853 at which we know Dunne had a considerable part, this time he had very little to say, though it did, again like the 1853 report, have some quite considerable significance of the running of the fire service in the coming years, and indeed the service as we know it today.

On a more personal front this would have been the year that his eldest son Francis (Frank) embarked for South Africa, to serve as an officer with the Westminster and Cumberland Yeomanry for the duration of the Boer War.

British losses during this campaign were high not just due to enemy action but also the ongoing problems of disease thus Dunne, who of course was now alone, would have been suffering in silence for the next three years. As we later learn however, his eldest son was to return safely home in 1902 – no doubt with others to celebrate his father's retirement.

1899 was also the year that Dunne almost had a riot on his hand from members of his own constabulary. Apparently unlike him, his men had not had a wage increase for some 25 years and they were not happy. First indications of this concern came in the way of a 'round robin' signed by every member of the Cumberland and Westmorland Constabulary.

The *Whitehaven News* of April 27th 1899 reported that:

'A 'round robin' is being signed by the whole of the members of the Cumberland and Westmorland Police, and will be presented before the Standing Joint Committees of the two counties. In this document the police draw attention to the fact that there have been no increases in the rates of pay for the last 25 years, while other neighbouring police forces have had augmentations of pay during the period named. When fully signed the police will forward the 'round robin' to Sir John Dunne, the Chief Constable in order that he may lay it before the proper authorities.'

The letter itself was headed: *'Petition of the Officers and Constables'* and dated 28th March 1899. It read:

'We, the undersigned, being Members of the Cumberland and Westmorland Constabulary, respectfully beg leave through you (Dunne) to memorialise the Standing Joint Committee of these Counties to grant us an increase of pay.

It is 25 years since any increase of pay was granted to the various ranks in this force. During that time a material increase in the scale of pay has been granted to the Police in neighbouring forces. At present their pay is much higher than ours, as can be seen by the annual reports of the Government Inspectors. The social and material well-being of all classes of people in this country have also been greatly improved during the above period. Wages to all classes of workmen have also had an upward tendency during the last two years; and our desire is to progress, keep in pace with the times, and share in the general prosperity of the Country. On these grounds, but principally on the grounds that our pay is lower than that of neighbouring Forces, do we respectfully ask the Police Authorities to grant an increase on the present rates of pay to all ranks. As our duties are not less onerous than those of the members of other Forces, we hope the Standing Joint Committee will see their way to have the scale of pay revised, and made equal to the rates in force in the adjoining Counties and Borough. And your humble and obedient Servants will ever pray. This petition is signed by all the Officers and Constables of the Police of Cumberland and Westmorland.'

This 'round robin' clearly pricked Dunne's conscience along with the '25 years' since their last pay award. His own salary had been regularly increased over the years, starting with the £300.00 per annum in 1857 (plus expenses) to the now £600.00 (plus expenses) i.e. twice as much as his starting pay.

Comparatively speaking newly appointed Police Constables back in 1857 received just £0.19s.0d per week (95p) at the time of their 'round robin' this was now £1.2s 9d per week (£1.12p), thus in other words 'pro rata' their salary has increased by just 21%. (or 1s.9d) over 42 years ... or roughly an increase of 1d per year – and today's police think they are hard done by!

Following discussion with his senior staff, Dunne drew up a lengthy document in which he not only proposed a totally new pay structure for all ranks, but detailed the reasons as to why this should be confirmed by the Standing Joint Committee for eventual approval by the Justices at the next Winter Assizes. It is interesting to report however that Dunne's recommendation were, frankly, a little on the low side compared with other counties, for again using the same example of the newly appointed police constable, the pay he recommended was for an increase to £1.3s 11d, just 1s.2d (6p) per week more (approx 10%) (or £62.3s 8d per annum) Compare that to Lancashire, West Riding, Durham, and Cheshire constabularies which were paying their newly appointed constables £65.7s.11d, per annum then it would be true to say that Dunne was not exactly being over generous.

His detailed report as stated not only listed salaries of lower ranks but also higher ranks too, including himself. He was able to compare his salary with those of other counties, especially so that of Lancashire and West Riding of Yorkshire where their most senior officer received a salary of £1,000 per annum. Thus he was clearly hopeful that his salary too would be considered for an increase.

Following the unanimous approval of the Standing Committee, the application for a salary increase for all ranks was put to the justices at the 1899 Winter Assizes and again approved without question. Dunne himself managed to receive an increase of 15% bringing his annual salary to £700 per annum, compared to the average 10% for all other ranks. Which begs the question, was Dunne thinking more of himself rather than his men when he put forth the under mentioned detailed report for increased pay? Once approved the increase to the local government budget (after deducting the government grant of 50%) was for the two counties just an extra £376.8s.1d. per annum(£376.41p).

His report to the Standing Joint Committees of Cumberland and Westmorland dated 11th September 1899 not only detailed his reasons in full for the proposed salary increase, but is also interesting insomuch as it gives us a clear idea of the work and responsibilities of a Victorian policeman at the end of this era. In producing this printed report as a fictitious question and answer document, it also gave him the opportunity of self-promoting his own worth to the committees – not something Dunne was ever loath to do.

His report was as follows:

'Supplemental Report of Chief Constable re application for Increase of Pay by the Police of Cumberland and Westmorland.

Gentlemen

Several inquiries having been made regarding the petition of the police for increased wages, I think it right to state in addition to my report of the 19th July, last, the following particulars for your information.

1. Question. What number of days in each week are the police required to be on duty; and what are the ordinary duties they are required to discharge?

1. Answer. The officers and constables are on duty seven days in each week, inclusive of Sunday. They are required to see that the public houses are properly conducted, that drunkenness is as far as possible prevented, and to do everything that is necessary to protect life and property on Sundays quite as much as on other days. Each officer and constable is required to do nine hours ordinary duty in every twenty-four hours. This is divided between day and night duty. The night duty is sometimes from 1am to 6am. The hours vary according to the circumstances that may be necessary for the protection of life and property, the prevention of crime, the detection of offenders and the preservation of good order. The average beat of each officer and constable at detached stations is in Westmorland 23 square miles, and in Cumberland 19 square miles. The average miles that each officer and constable at detached stations is required to walk in patrolling and visiting his district in every twenty four hours is 18 miles in Westmorland and 17 in Cumberland. Special duties in connection with inquiries into offences or other matters of complaint often occupies several hours in addition to the ordinary duties. Mechanics, trades people, artisans and labouring men are not required to work on Sundays. Their wages are for six days in each week, and often exceeds what the police receive for seven days. Workmen or men in trade are not required to be on night duty not to be exposed to the risks and responsibilities that police are required to undertake. All classes generally have a day's rest on Sundays. The duties which the police are legally bound to discharge on Sundays makes it quite impossible for them to have the great blessing of that day of rest in conformity with the fourth divine commandment. (remember the Sabbath day and keep it holy)

2. Question. Where the police are not so numerous to population and where crime is not prevalent, the police would surely have less to do than the police of other districts?

2. Answer. In counties were the police are in larger proportion to the population than in Cumberland and Westmorland, their beats are relatively confined to smaller areas. The rule is that all parts of a constable's district has to be patrolled and visited both day and night. The proportion of police to population in these counties has always been materially less than in the counties of the northern district. In Westmorland it was 1 to 1569 previously to the recent addition of two constables at Windermere and Ambleside. It is now 1 to 1,480. To bring the police of Westmorland up to the general average, an increase of 16 constables would be required, at a cost of £1,216.8s.0d per annum (£1216.40p) In Cumberland the proportion is 1 to 1,154. To bring the police up to 1 to 1,000 of the population, an increase of thirty constables would be required at a cost of £2,280.15s.0d per annum(£2280.75p). The duties of the police of the counties are therefore materially more than in the counties where there are larger forces to the population. In this connection it will be seen that the ratepayers have been saved a very large sum of money in having the work done by the smallest possible number of constables. The fact is that in these counties economy consistently with efficiency has never been lost sight of, with the result that the police rates have been materially less than in other districts. Examination of the accounts for the last 43 years will show that by careful supervision many thousands of pounds have been saved to the ratepayers in disallowing exorbitant and unjustifiable claims.

3. Question: Are not the duties of the police in rural districts less onerous and easier than in towns?

3. Answer: The duties of the police in rural districts are far more responsible and irksome than in towns, because in rural districts the police frequently have to act promptly and vigorously upon their own initiative and responsibility in apprehending persons charged with offences or in otherwise dealing with matters of urgency. They are required to discriminate between what is legal and illegal, whereas in towns the police are always near a superior officer, who is able to give necessary instructions as to the apprehension of persons charged with offences, or any other urgent matters of duty. Constables in rural districts are often many miles from a superior officer and are consequently unable to apply for instructions before acting promptly. Patrolling country roads is more laborious and monotonous than police duty in towns and populous places where the assistance of other officers or constables can be at once procured.

4. Question: What classes are the police recruited from; and what are the qualifications required for men to be appointed constables?

4. Answer: Generally from the sons of small statesmen farmers, tradesmen, labourers, mechanics, reservists, yeomanry cavalry, militia and sailors. They must be recommended by trustworthy persons to be men of good character and exemplary conduct, to be able to read and write with a general elementary education, age from 21 to 28, height 5 feet 10 inches, and be medically certified as fit for the service.

5. Question: Does not the Act of 1890 make better and more liberal provisions for the pensioning of officers and constables than the system that previously existed?

5. Answer: The advantage to the police under the Act of 1890 is that an absolute right is given to claim pension of two-thirds pay on the completion of 26 years approved service, whereas under the previous Acts pensions could not be claimed under 60 years of age, and it was even then in the discretion of the local authority to grant the maximum pension of two-thirds pay. Every case had to be considered on its merits and the services of the officers or constables applying to be pensioned. Provision was also made for the pension of officers or constables who were medically certified to be physically or mentally unfit for police duty. The latter is continued under the Act of 1890.

6. Question: Is there any difficulty now in procuring good and efficient men for the service

6. Answer: It has frequently occurred, that the best qualified men go into other districts where they get higher pay. The class of men applying are not so well qualified as they used to be when the wages were substantially similar to the wages of the northern district.

7. Question: Is there any difficulty in retaining the services of men who are qualified for promotion to the higher classes?

7. Answer: Men well qualified do sometimes apply for appointments where they are better paid. The efficiency of the service greatly depends upon the thorough competency and integrity of the head officers. It must be obvious that the safety of a ship, also the successful working of railway trains, or other responsible duties, mainly depends upon the competency and efficiency of the head officers who are responsible for the faithful administration and proper execution of the rules and regulations which they are required to carry out.

8. Question: What is the extra work that the police of these counties have to carry out in addition to their ordinary police duties? What benefit does the county receive from having such extra work done by the police? Can you give any instance to show what the advantages are or have been?

8. Answer: The extra duties are Inspectors of Weights and Measures, Inspectors under the Cattle Diseases Acts, the execution of the acts and orders of the Board of Agriculture, and the regulations of the local authorities, the Explosives Acts, the Food and Drugs Acts, Fire Brigades, and in Westmorland, Fertilisers and Feeding Stuffs Acts. No additional salaries are paid to the police for this extra work. Considerable saving to the ratepayers is effected by the police doing it. The time of the Superintendents and other officers is materially occupied in its execution. The Inspector of Weights and Measures by the police saves at least £1000 a year. The annual reports which are recorded in the County Council minutes fully explain the details. But there is a higher principle than the mere saving of money to be considered. That is, by having the work done by the police the public have the great advantage of having work involved in these various Acts carried out with thorough efficiency and fidelity. It may be mentioned that in 1888, 1889, and 1890 pleuro-pneumonia existed on 52 farms in Cumberland where 325 diseased and 1140 in-contact cattle were slaughtered. Their valuation was £17,479.2s.0d (£17,479.10p). The salvage realised was £9,166.5s.10d (£9,166.29p) The loss to the county was £10,221.7s.5d (£10,221.37p) This loss is inclusive of over £1900 for veterinary expenses, cost of disinfectants etc. I was instrumental in having the salvage of over £9,000 saved to the County. I was compelled to incur considerable expense in the matter. The onerous and responsible work I was obliged to undertake resulted in serious illness. My expenses exceeded £400. I applied for payment by the County Council and also urged that the services of the Superintendents and other officers entitled them to some reasonable remuneration. The minutes of the County Council show that they refused to pay my expenses or to grant anything to the officers. The Westmorland County Council also refused to pay any of the expenses I incurred. It was by the constant efforts of myself and the police in initiating and carrying out an efficient system of slaughter coupled with the thorough isolation and disinfection of diseased premises that this disease was stamped out and the County thereby saved from the serious losses that would have resulted if by apathy and indifference the disease had been allowed to spread through the County. The extirpation of the disease in Cumberland saved Westmorland from its extension into that county from the Penrith district where it existed near the borders of Westmorland. The same system operated with equal advantage to the ratepayers in stamping out and preventing the spread of the Cattle Plague, Foot and Mouth Disease, and Swine Fever. I think I am justified in mentioning this for the purposes of showing the nature of the great advantages the public have derived from having the extra work done by the police.

9. Question: If you approve of the application why have you not submitted any scheme for an increase in the present rate of pay?

9. Answer: I did lay one before the Westmorland Committee, because I was requested to do so. It is less than the average of the Northern district. I did not submit it to the Cumberland Committee because I was not asked to do so. I herewith submit it for consideration and decision.

10. Question: Do you think that the police have reasonable grounds for their application?

10. Answer: Yes. I am quite of the opinion that in consideration of the seven days weekly duty of the police and their public services in the protection of life and property, the prevention and detection of crime, the maintenance of good order, and the material savings resulting from the additional work they discharge without any salary, they are fairly entitled to have their application fully considered on the grounds the wages paid to other forces in the northern district, and in relation to the market value of workmen generally.

11. Question: If the police receive an increase now what guarantee could be given that they would not again apply for a further increase? What are the dates when the present pay in the northern district was granted?

11. Answer: While it would be difficult to hazard anything like prophecy as to what may happen in the future, it may be mentioned that there has not been applications for a general increase in the last 25 years. I think it may therefore be taken as most improbable that a further increase would be asked for in the near future. If the Home Office would make a uniform rate of pay binding in the northern district, I am of the opinion that it would be a great advantage in preventing the men of some counties feeling aggrieved at not being paid wages similar to what is paid in adjoining counties; and that it would prevent men being induced to move from the counties where lower wages are given to those where higher wages are offered. The present pay in the northern district was granted: Lancashire, December 1896, Cheshire, July 1891, and April 1897, Staffordshire, January 1892, West Riding, April 1891, North Riding August 1897, East Riding January and July 1896 and July 1898. Durham, December 1890 and December 1891, Northumberland, August 1890 and July 1891, Carlisle April 1899.

Interestingly in declaring the comparative rates of pay for a total of eight counties in the same document, the listing was headed with the pay of the Chief Constable of Cumberland and Westmorland at £600 per annum for the two counties, pointing out that the average pay for Chief Constables over the eight listed counties was £665.12.s.6d per annum.(£665.62p).

The document then went on to list current rates of pay for all ranks starting with newly appointed constables at £1.2s.9d per week (£1.67) up to superintendents at £3.16s.5d per week (£3.82) followed by a further list of the wages and salaries received by all ranks in the other eight counties mentioned. The document ended with a comparison of the present and proposed scale of pay for all men under his command. This time his request was successful, and though the commission 'hummed' and 'harred' a bit, his request was granted and both Dunne and his constabulary were duly awarded the precise amount requested.

With the arrival of 1900, and the start not only of a new year but also a new century, it surely must have crossed Dunne's mind that the one thing he didn't expect to be doing at the turn of the century was be heading up a police force, especially so at the grand old age of 75. But he was still there, still in charge, and clearly at this point in his life with no intention of retiring. On a more mundane level Dunne would have found himself once again advertising for and finding a replacement for the current Chief Constable of Kendal Constabulary. From a large number interviewed he finally decided upon Charles E Harris who like his predecessor would only remain in the post for just two short years.

For the year once again national crime figures were up once again, 2.51% on the previous year (77,934) 1901 was of course the year that Queen Victoria died, on the 22nd January to be precise at Osborne House, on the Isle of Wight.

She was 81 years of age. She had reigned for a total of 63 years (64 in the June had she lived), which meant that she had reigned longer than other British monarch, and certainly the longest of any female monarch in history. However as we are all well aware our own current Queen, Elizabeth is not so far behind. The chances are that she will out live Queen Victoria's 63 years on the throne and thus by 2016 she will be celebrating 64 years as our Queen at the age of 90.

Sir John, clearly felt he had a small part to play in her demise for his personal records show that he was nothing if not patriotic. Following the Queen's death he sent a telegram of condolence to Balmoral and received the following reply: *'The Private Secretary is desired to thank Sir John Dunne for his kind expression of sympathy with Her Majesty.'* And a further telegram to Osborne House received the following reply: *'The Queen (Alexandra) desires me to convey to you her thanks for your kind message of sympathy'.* Clearly at some point as the most senior Chief Constable for the Kingdom he had been asked to sent a message of condolence on behalf of all the police forces for on the 12th March 1901 he received a parchment letter from the Home Office, Whitehall which read: '*Sir. I am commanded by the King (Edward 7th) to convey to you hereby His Majesty's thanks for the loyal and dutiful message of the Police Forces of Great Britain., expressing sympathy on the occasion of the lamented death of her Late Majesty Queen Victoria and congratulations on His Majesty's accession to the throne*'. Yet another indication, if any were needed, of the position that Dunne held not just in Cumberland and Westmorland, but frankly across the country.

It was in 1901 that the Criminal Registrar noted that Britain has witnessed a marked *'decline in the spirit of lawlessness'.* This (apparently) was due to the *'good work of voluntary organisations from churches to charities'* (rather than the work of the police for the past 40 + years presumably) 'that reform the unruly manners and lax morals of the new mass society. Temperance societies combat the 'curse of drunkenness' philanthropists act as social workers and the godly see it as the Christian duty to help prostitutes change their lifestyles and to aid the 'deserving' poor'.

Clearly they hadn't noted the increase in the national crime rate for this year now 80,962 UP 3.89% on previous year (let alone noted the increase in 1900). Dunne's ratio of population to police officers also got slightly worse this year when we learn from the census returns that the population of Cumberland was now 266,933 (slightly up on 1891) though on the plus side at least the Irish population was down again this time by 2.38%.

Sir John Dunne officially retired on the 31st August 1902 as Chief Constable of Cumberland and Westmorland Constabulary and was succeeded by Charles de Courcy Parry (having transferred from Dunne's old 'stamping ground' of Bath) who was then Chief Constable of the two forces until 1920, after which he went on to become an HM Inspector of Constabulary for Wales, as well as being a leading light of the newly formed Police Athlete Association.

He was awarded a CBE in 1920 at the time of the Civilian War Honours, along with 203 other police officer recipients. Mr Parry who was 32 had considerable police experience. He had been Chief constable of Bath since 1900, deputy Chief Constable of Kent from 1899-1900, superintendent in Monmouthshire 1894-1899, Chief inspector at Bristol 1893-4 and constable and clerk in the Chief Constables office in Derbyshire1887-1893. With such a similar background to John Dunne, particularly the fact that he had been promoted through the ranks, one can only think that panel members selected Parry because of this.

The first notification that the public had of Dunne's imminent retirement was the article in the *Cumberland Pacquet* of April 24th 1902. The article headed *'The Resignation of Sir John Dunne'*, read:

> *'At the meeting of the Cumberland Standing Joint Committee at Carlisle yesterday, Mr Senhouse the Chairman announced that he had received a letter from Sir John Dunne intimating that at the expiration of four months he intended retiring on a pension. A rumour to that effect had been about for a week or two and consequently the announcement of his retirement created little surprise. Sir John has been at the head of the police force of Cumberland and Westmorland for the long period of forty-five years and during all that time he has never ceased in his endeavours to increase the efficiency of the force under his control. The result is that his successor whoever he may be will find his task a comparatively easy one. Apart from the ordinary routine of his official work Sir John has shown on not a few occasions that he was well able cope with great emergencies. Those whose memories can carry them back to the time thirty-five years ago when rinderpest played havoc with the cattle on hundreds of Cumberland farms will remember the extraordinary energy and perseverance displayed by the Chief Constable in dealing with and eventually causing methods to be adopted which resulted in the extermination of the dire disease. There has been more than one occasion when his prescience and the exercise of a wise discretion have prevented the spread of rioting of a serious character. No one will assert of Sir John that he never committed an error of judgement. That indeed can never be truthfully asserted of any human being who has held a difficult position for nearly half a century. But we do say now that he is about to retire from the Chief Constableship that it will be well for the county of Cumberland if his successor is characterized by the same qualities which have made Sir John Dunne one*

of the most efficient officers who have ever held so onerous a position.'

Dunne had been Chief Constable of the two forces for 45 years, though in truth he had been a Chief Constable in total for 52 years, if one includes his time at Bearsted, Newcastle and Norwich. He was at the time 77 years of age.

One wonders if the retirement was entirely voluntary, or was he 'pushed' a little. There is a possible clue in the letter he penned to the Standing Joint Committee the day before he finally retired. Letter from the Chief Constables Office, Carlisle dated 30th August 1902.

> *'Gentlemen. As your meeting on Saturday will be the last at which I shall have the pleasure of acting as your Chief Constable I beg to state that I feel most grateful to you for your kindness, courtesy and valuable support which I have, during the last 45 years and eight months received on all occasions from you and the Quarter Sessions and Mr Bolton the Clerk of the Peace in the execution of my public and various duties and responsibilities. There seems to be some misunderstanding re the reports giving the constitution and distribution of the force. I think it is therefore desirable to explain that I have always laid before you at your monthly meetings a return on Form No.7 showing the station of every officer and constable in the two counties together with the superannuating, reductions, dismissals, appointments, promotions, and removals which took place in each month preceding your meetings. In my quarterly reports I also submitted the returns required by the Police Acts and the Home Office regulations which were duly certified by the Chairman. Colonel Eden, the Government Inspector was engaged with me inspecting the Police of the two counties from the 15th to the 21st July last. He closely examined the officers and constables and fully inquired into every detail connected with their duties. He said that he found everything in a highly satisfactory state of efficiency. I attach my address to the Police on parade during the inspection. There are no vacancies in the force and I have the satisfaction to report that I shall hand over to my successor on the 1st September all official matters and a splendid body of officers and constables whose conduct has been most exemplary and who have discharged their duties in the protection of life and property, the prevention and detection of crime and the maintenance of good order, with exceptional efficiency and fidelity. I have the honour to be Gentlemen Your most faithful and obedient servant (signed) J Dunne Chief Constable of Cumberland and Westmorland.'*

From this letter it is clear that he is certainly a little 'peeved' over comments being made about his force, and possibly his own integrity. For a man with such a background he must have found this letter particularly hard to write ... on two fronts. Amongst other letters written by Dunne at this time was one to his friend William Lowther, who at the time was both a JP and a Deputy Lieutenant for Westmorland and Cumberland, advising of his retirement and received the following reply: Telegram from William J R

'I have received the letter announcing your retirement after 45 years of service. I gladly take the opportunity of thanking you once more for the able manner in which you discharged your duty during my stay at Lowther Castle.'

At the time William Lowther was mostly living at Kensington, London, though he was now spending increasingly more time at his Cumberland home (Lowther Carlisle). As we have learnt Dunne had been an active policeman for more than 50 years in fact it was nearer 62 years in total, starting with his early days in 1839 as a police constable with Manchester City Police until today, a record which has never been equalled by any other officer. In his 45 years as Chief Constable of C & W Dunne had built a highly creditable force of some 240 men, personally wrote over 820 General Orders, 1100 Force Directives, 71,000 official letters and had been instrumental in a number of important changes to the law and national police procedure.

So following such a lengthy career we need to ask ourselves what state had Dunne left his two counties in upon his retirement this year? At first glance it would appear that they were in a rather poor condition for as we know, crime, and especially so major crimes, had been rampant throughout this entire period. Things were reputedly getting better, a recent set of statistics confirmed that, but the national crimes figures at the same time continued to rise. Even three of the most wicked criminals of his time Rudge, Martin and Baker, of course had a place in Madame Tussauds Chamber of Horrors for many years. Others for example Cass and Charlton continue to be relegated to the pages of local publications. It is interesting to learn that the majority of those individuals tried and executed at Carlisle were not even 'Cumbrians' born and bred in the two counties. In fact the majority had been born and brought up many miles away… Pearson, Thompson, Charlton, Dalgleish, Rudge, Martin, Baker,Hunter and Wilson are just some names that immediately come to mind.

Perhaps of more importance, drunkenness and vagrancy had begun to decline nationwide, both, without question had been the cause of more than its fair share of the serious crimes committed in the counties over this period. It was still a problem in 1902 of course though in truth those same statistics were now declaring that there was certainly less drunkenness everywhere than their had been in 1857 when Dunne had taken up his post as Chief Constable though precisely how much we can thank Dunne for is debateable. However what is known is that in the Brampton area, thanks in part to the efforts of the Countess of Carlisle ... Rosalind Howard the well known advocate of both women's suffrage and the temperance movement, (sometimes known as The Radical Countess) the public houses in the region were closed for miles around so at least Dunne had some assistance with this problem, from what he would have originally considered an unlikely area. Coincidentally the Licensing Act 1902. (Protection of Children and Young People) made its appearance this year making it an offence for any person to be found drunk on any highway, public house, licensed premises, public place, building or inn while having charge of a child under seven.

Throughout Dunne's period of office a total of some forty-five years, as we have learnt he was not amiss to self-promotion generally about his police force, but in many instances about himself. Invariably this 'promotion' was linked to his letters in the local newspapers or press releases from his office. But more often than not this could also include long and lengthy letters to the prestigious Times newspaper which would have, naturally, nationwide promotion. Dunne would have had various important duties to undertake this year, one would have been finding a replacement for Charles Harris, the current Chief officer of Kendal Town Police, who had been another officer whose stay had been short-lived – just two years. His replacement, after due consideration was an A.M Berry who had least stayed in position for six years. Another important duty was announced when he received a personal invitation from the King to attend his coronation in Westminster Abbey on the 9th August. Along with other dignitaries attending that day, he too was awarded the King Edward VII Coronation Medal. With just two weeks to go before his retirement one can safely say that such an important invitation was a perfect way to leave office.

Sir John Dunne retired on a pension of £350.00 per annum for Cumberland plus £116.13.4d (£116.62) from Westmorland a total of £466.13.4d (£466. 62) being 2/3rd of his annual pay of £700. In today's money that would be equivalent to £93,400 certainly more than enough for him to live comfortably on.

CHAPTER TWENTY

JOHN DUNNE

1903-1906

Retirement

For Dunne it must have seemed strange to be waking up at Eden Mount, Wetheral on New Years Day 1903, for the first time in 64 years without the need to rush into his office. It is difficult to determine how much he was enjoying his retirement from a very active life, but there is little doubt that he would have found it hard to settle. Possibly settling down with his Daily Mirror and a cup of Typhoo Tipps tea over breakfast may well have helped a little (both were introduced this year).

The letter that he received from the Clerk to the Peace in Carlisle early this year would have been most welcome; this stated: *'I have much pleasure in stating that I have received an intimation that the Lord Chancellor has been pleased to add your name to the Commission of the Peace for the, City of Carlisle and that you qualify for the next Quarter Session'* For the next three years this was to be his life, for records show that he was regularly attending Cumberland Quarter Sessions, with his first attendance at the January Sessions for this year. After that he was a regular attendee, missing just one, in the July of 1904.

There was one distraction at least for him this year when he would have received an invitation to attend the launching of the White Star Line ship SS Ionic. Her sister ships at this time were the SS Athenic and SS Corinthic. (the Titanic wasn't launched for another nine years). Clearly he needed this distraction, for his daughter Henrietta is now the only one living at home, then aged 33 and still unmarried, the eldest son Francis as we know is now 32 years of age and still serving in the Forces. By this time he is a Captain in the Westminster and Cumberland Yeomanry, (Border Regiment) having only recently returned home from a spell serving in the Boer War. Later he was to serve in the First World War with distinction (even though he would be 43 years of age at the outbreak). At this time Francis was living at The Oaks, Dalston, near Carlisle, the one-time home of Susannah Blamire the 18th century poet. The youngest son, Gerald was himself 28 years of age and by this time he too had made a career in the Army, though unlike his older brother he held a commission in a Dragoon Regiment. He had also seen service in the Boer War, and in fact was twice invalided home.

At least 1904 would have given Dunne the satisfaction of attending his son Frank's wedding. Francis Dunne married Laura Constance Helder, the youngest daughter of Sir Augustus Helder MP (1826-1906) at St Nicholas Church, Whitehaven, with the reception at Sir Augustus's home in Corkickle. At this time Sir Augustus was Conservative MP for Whitehaven, though he was also an active solicitor in Whitehaven, a business which traded as Brockbank and Helder (still is, but these days solely under the name of Brockbanks). Helder like Dunne was a regular and busy Justice of the Peace, though their friendship extended way beyond appearances at the Quarter Sessions. In all probability it would have been at one or other's soirées that the young Francis and Laura came to meet such was the occasions at this time.

As to be expected their wedding was a grand affair as reported in the *Cumberland Pacquet* at this time. We even learn from the same newspaper something of their wedding presents; for example, Francis gave his bride a pony and saddle, whilst Laura gave her new husband pearl and enamel buttons and links, plus a writing desk. Sir John gave the newlyweds a cheque, a mahogany wardrobe and a silver tea and coffee service, whilst Francis' brother Gerald gave him a pony and trap, and his sister, Henrietta dining room chairs and an oak chest. Mrs Ismay Barnes, Francis' aunt was generous in the extreme, giving the happy couple a coal scuttle, whilst his cousin (Dr Barnes) generously gave them a silver mustard pot! Possibly indications that the Barnes family were still 'smarting' over the distribution of Mary Dunne's will some years earlier.

Sir John Dunne's long and active life came to an end on the 5th January 1906, and typically for him came about not because of old age or associated illnesses attached to ageing, but simply from running for a train. *The Carlisle Patriot* dated 12th January reported it eloquently:

> *'Death of Sir John Dunne. We deeply regret to announce that Sir John Dunne died at his residence Eden Mount, Wetheral at 7 o'clock on Friday morning the 5th January. Sir John who retired from his position as Chief Constable of Cumberland and Westmorland in April 1902 (sic) was in excellent health until August of last year, when in returning from the Dublin Horse Show he had occasion to run in Crewe Station to catch his train home. The exertion affected his heart and Sir John has since been confined to the house and for three weeks to his bedroom. His spirits were however well maintained, and only two days before his death he arranged to have a bath chair sent to his house so that he might record his vote for Mr Claude Lowther. (As it transpired Lowther was defeated by the Liberal candidate Geoffrey Howard). Sir John*

Dunne was the fourth son of the late Mr W Dunne, a member of the well known Queen's County family, and was born on the 12th February 1824 (sic) .so that at the time of his death he was in his 82nd year. (sic) His whole life was spent in the police service. His abilities were quickly recognised and a few years after he attained his majority he was appointed Chief Constable of Norwich . Mr Dunne was the youngest officer who had ever been entrusted with the command of a police force, but his appointment was splendidly justified, the Norwich force which had previously been corrupt and inefficient, being completely re-organised 'to the great advantage' in the words of the magistrates, 'of the trading, manufacturing and other interests of the city'. Mr Dunne did not remain long in Norwich. His successful administration there gained him a national reputation and in the late forties (sic) he was given the appointment of Chief Constable of Newcastle. Mr Dunne's reign at Newcastle was no less beneficent and when he left the Local Authority officially recorded that 'Mr Dunne under his judicious and able superintendence had brought the police from a state of much disorganisation to one of perfection not to be surpassed by any in the kingdom, and the Judges and Recorder from the Bench as well as the Home Secretary in the House of Commons have adverted to its efficiency under the present management'. Mr Dunne had a narrow escape with his life while at Newcastle. A disastrous fire broke out in a stretch of chemical works and warehouses stored with explosives and an explosion occurring, several persons were killed. Ensign Paynter and Mr Dobson, an architect, were killed by Mr Dunne's side. The Police Act of 1856 directed the establishment of police forces in all counties and Mr Dunne became an applicant for appointment as Chief Constable in several counties. He was on the 'short leet' for Cornwall, Somersetshire, Devonshire, Derbyshire and Cheshire, but withdrew on his unanimous selection from one hundred and twenty candidates as Chief Constable of Cumberland and Westmorland. There were no police in the county before 1856 and the force as we know it today is the creation of Sir John Dunne. The work of organisation was necessarily slow, but the Chief Constable set about it with characteristic energy and in a comparatively short period he gathered around him a body of men, who while loyally administering the law, never forgot the confidence of the public whose servants they are. There is no necessity here to enter into the details of his long and honourable part he played for close on half a century, in the local life of the sister counties, since they are fresh in the public memory. His name will probably be best remembered by reason of the successful war which he raged against the rinderpest, foot and mouth disease, pleuro-pneumonia, and other cattle diseases. He was author of the system-known as the Cumberland and Westmorland system of stamping out disease by slaughtering affected cattle and those in contact with them, and is now universally followed. His reports were freely quoted in the House of Commons in the discussions on cattle disease and there was no higher authority in the country on the methods of dealing with epidemics among stock. Sir John's experience suggested many reforms of the laws and administration which successive Home Secretaries have given effect to. Mr Dunne's eminent services to these counties were conspicuously recognised in 1897 by his appointment as a Deputy-Lieutenant of Cumberland by Lord Muncaster, the Lord Lieutenant, and in the following year, (sic) on the celebration of the Diamond Jubilee of the late Queen, her Majesty was graciously pleased to confer the honour of knighthood on him in recognition of his work in a wider sphere. Sir John retired from the service in April of 1902 (sic) and was immediately afterwards placed on the Commission of the Peace for both the City of Carlisle and the County of Cumberland. On his retirement from office Sir John Dunne was presented by Mr W J Lowther, the Speaker on behalf of the subscribers, who included all the principal residents of the two counties, with an illuminated address and a cheque; and the members of the force gave their old Chief a handsome silver bowl. Sir John after his retirement took an active interest in local affairs, and he was a regular attendee at the magistrates court. Sir John married a daughter of the late Dr Barnes of Bunkers Hill who predeceased him in 1898 and leaves two sons and a daughter. The younger son who held a commission in a Dragoon regiment saw service in the Boer War, being twice invalided home., and the elder son who is married to a daughter of Sir A Helder and lives at The Oaks, Dalston commanded the last detachment of the Volunteer company of the Border Regiment which sailed for South Africa. The funeral itself was on the Monday afternoon when the remains of Sir John Dunne were interred in Wetheral Cemetery. The morning was wet, and although the rain ceased shortly after noon, there was a chilling dampness in the air which probably deterred a number of people from attending the funeral. The cortege which started from the residence of the deceased at Eden Mount, Wetheral shortly after half past two was headed by a posse of police under Superintendent Graham of Carlisle. Then came the hearse, containing the coffin which was of plain oak with brass mountings and bore the following inscription: Sir John Dunne KB DL JP Born 1824 Died 5th January 1906 The coffin was covered with beautiful wreaths. Following the hearse were three coaches, the first of which contained the Chief mourners Mr and Mrs Frank Dunne, Mr Gerald Dunne and Miss Dunne. The second contained Mr Claude Lowther

M.P and other personal friends of the deceased, and the third the nurses and servants. Then followed on foot the remainder of those who had assembled to pay the last mark of respect to one who had for almost half a century had played a prominent part in the life and progress of the sister counties of Cumberland and Westmorland. Amongst those attending the funeral in addition to those already mentioned were: the Mayor of Carlisle (Mr R Crowder) Colonel Irwin, Lynehow, Mr Salkeld, Holm Hill, Mr Crowder, Mr P J C Howard, Corby Castle, Mr C de Courcy Parry, Chief Constable of Cumberland and Westmorland, Mr Sampill, Chief Constable of Stirlingshire, Dr Barnes, Major Webber- Smith, Mr Neil MacInnes, Stanwix, Mr James Watt and Mr J W Watt, Knowefield, Mr F P Dixon and Mr E B Dixon, Blackwell Lodge, Mr H A Dunlop, The Howe, Troutbeck, Mr J J Mitchell, The Knowe Aspatria; Mr G Graham London and Midland Bank, Carlisle, Mr C B Hodgson, Harker Grange, Dr Helm, Mr J.J.Bell, V.S; Mr W C Butler, Carlisle, Mr H S Cartmel, Hayton, Mr Blackburn, Carlisle; Mr Howard Carrick, Scotby, Mr G A Mounsey-Heysham, Silloth, Mr J K Parker, Carlisle, Mr D Main, Harker, Mr W F Bell, Carlisle, Mr W N Ling,, Mr J H Martindale, Wetheral,Mr H W Sewell,Carlisle, Mr Kelsick Wood and Mr Robinson, Carlisle, Mr Wardman, Warwick Bridge, Mr T Clarke, Seascale, Mr Laurie, York, Mr William Coulson, Cumwhinton, Mr J Howe, Cocklakes, Mr T S Strong, Wetheral, Mr W H Kelly, Jnr, Moniative, Dumfrieshire, Mr R M Anderson, Wetheral, Dr Barclay, Wetheral, Mr Burfield, Wetherall Abbey, the Rev W Irving, Wetheral Plains, Mr Thompson, accountant, Carlisle, Mr J Nutsford, Botcherby, Inspector Cooke, N S P C C, Carlisle, Mr J Reay, Wetheral, Mr J R Tiffin, Great Corby, Mr J Gibson, Great Corby, Mr C Platt, Mr J Davis, Carlisle; Mr B Trimble, Wetheral Shields, Mr Dalton Corby, Mr J Thompson, Carlisle, Mr Townson, Wetheral, Mr Fisher, Corby, Mr R Thompson, Wetheral, Mr S Milburn, Wetheral, Mr Robinson, Waterloo, Mr Langhorn, Great Corby, Mr Adams, Wetheral, Mr Green law (Grocer), Wetheral, Mr Roper, Mr Bertioli, Mr Livesay (schoolmaster),Mr R Irving and Mr J Smith, Wetheral, etc. On reaching the cemetery the police lined up on each side of the gates and the funeral cortege was met by the officiating clergy the Rev A G Loftie, Rector of Wetheral and the Rev A Scott, Wetheral. The first portion of the burial service was read by the rector in the Cemetery Chapel and the second at the graveside by the Rev A Scott, the ceremony throughout being of the simplest character. The grave which was at the side of that of Lady Dunne was lined with evergreens, interposed with white chrysanthemums, lilies of the valley etc. Mr Thomas Lawson of Wetheral was the undertaker.'

It is also noticed that the same newspaper submitted the following tribute from Judge Steavenson, which was made on the 6th January the day following John Dunne's demise:

'At Carlisle County Court on Tuesday His Honour Judge Steavenson said that before they proceeded with the usual business of the Court he wished to say a few words about a very notable figure that had passed away. During the whole of his professional career he had known the late Sir John Dunne. As he first remembered him, a handsomer or finer man nobody could wish to see, and not only was he a handsome man but his conduct and his administration of the police forces under him were always based on the highest ideals. He carried out his duties in a manner in which he had never heard any whisper against. Sir John always held the honour of the force high. He held that the duty of the policeman was not to make a case, but always to tell the truth and woe betide the man under him whom he found did not tell the truth. But where he found a man who was actuated by that highest sense of honour, that he himself was actuated by, that man was certain of promotion. He (the judge) as administrator of justice in that Court frequently came into contact with Sir John. A firmer bolder, or more determined man to support those members of the police whom he thought were right they could not wish to find and he honoured him for it. But they all knew that those who did not come up to his ideal did not long remain in the police force. The consequence was that the two places where he (Judge Steavenson) knew him, Newcastle-upon-Tyne and this county-the police force attached a degree of efficiency which, he would undertake to say, had previously been unknown in both forces. Not only did the officers under him become known, but the way in which he administered his office in those forces was initiated in other forces in the Kingdom, and he thought that he was not going too far when he said that Sir John had been a great guide to the better conduct of the police throughout the Kingdom and that he had done a great benefit not only to this district, but also to Newcastle-upon-Tyne and to Norwich. He mourned the loss of a man who had done so much for the administration of justice. He mourned his loss because he was an upright man, because he always set an example of uprightness and because he insisted upon the same honour amongst his force as he showed himself as Chief Constable. He mourned his loss because the county when he retired some years ago lost a man whose position it was almost impossible to fill. Mr T S Strong said he desired on behalf of his fellow solicitors to associate himself with what had fallen from His Honour. With all that had been said they entirely agreed and after the very eloquent tribute paid to Sir John by his Honour, he felt it would be

unbecoming on his part to say any more. There was one thing in the public life and character of Sir John which stood out prominently and to his lasting honour. It was always that he maintained it was the duty of the constable to do justice between man and man and not to seek a prosecution. He desired to associate himself and his brother solicitors with what his Honour had said so eloquently. The end of the road.'

Reports of his death reached far and wide, especially wide. The following is an obituary of John Dunne printed in the *Otago Witness*, Putanga New Zealand … a newspaper particularly popular in the isolated rural areas where poor access prevented newspapers being delivered daily:

'Sir John Dunne, late Chief Constable of Cumberland and Westmorland died at Carlisle on Friday January 5th at the age of 81 years. At an early age he was appointed Chief Constable of Norwich and subsequently he filled a similar position at Newcastle. When only 31 years of age he was appointed Chief Constable of Cumberland and Westmorland and he held that office until he retired in 1902. During his tenure of office Sir John Dunne rather extinguished (sic) himself by drawing up a series of regulations for the extirpation of cattle plague, foot and mouth disease, pleuro-pneumonia and other diseases among animals which have been largely adopted throughout the country. In 1884 the Cumberland Quarter Sessions gave him a gratuity of £300 for his services in connection with cattle disease. At the Diamond Jubilee of Queen Victoria in 1897 Mr Dunne was knighted, as the oldest Chief Constable in the kingdom.'

The *Barrow News* for the 11th January was another newspaper (amongst many) to lament his passing. Their editorial was headed *'An Interesting Career'* and read:

'We regret to announce that Sir John Dunne, late Chief Constable of Cumberland and Westmorland whose health has been failing during the past two or three years and who for some time has been in a condition which gave no hope of his recovery, died at his residence at Wetheral on Friday morning. His death removes an interesting and imposing figure which until three or four years ago was familiar throughout the counties of Cumberland and Westmorland and marks the end of a long career of public usefulness. Sir John who would have attained the age of 81 on the 12th of next month was the son of the late William Dunne, Boley, Queen's County and a descendant of an ancient family of that county. He was educated in Dublin and in France (sic) and practically the whole of his life has been devoted in connection with the police in various parts of the country. Entering the force as a very young man he showed remarkable ability which soon gained promotion, and at an

early age he was appointed Chief Constable of Norwich. He subsequently filled a similar position at Newcastle. On his first acquaintance with the police the force throughout the country was looked upon almost as the enemies of the public but he introduced reforms in the bodies over which he had control which put an end to many corrupt practices, and when he left Newcastle in 1856 it was said that the force had been 'brought to a state of perfection not to be surpassed by any in the Kingdom'. In 1856 when only 31 years of age Mr Dunne was appointed Chief Constable of Cumberland and Westmorland and continued to hold that position of responsibility until midsummer of 1902. He was a strict disciplinarian and his influence was felt throughout the force. In the course of his long experience he was associated with many events which stirred the public mind. In consequence of a tremendous fire at Gateshead he was never in bed for three weeks, and he had a narrow escape from death by an explosion which occurred. He was associated with the suppression of the Orange Riots in Whitehaven and under his direction several crimes of first magnitude were brought home to the perpetrators. The most sensational was the Netherby burglary and subsequent murder which ended in the hanging of three men at Carlisle. During his tenure of office he drew up comprehensive codes of rules and regulations for the police, and the system which he adopted for the purpose of extirpating rinderpest, foot and mouth disease, pleuro- pneumonia and other diseases among animals was found to be so efficacious that it was then, and still is generally adopted and observed throughout the country. During his long career Sir John naturally came into contact with many distinguished individuals and whilst the German Emperor was staying at Lowther, Mr Dunne (as he was then) received a gift from the Kaiser of a gold watch with monogram. In 1897 he was appointed a Deputy Lieutenant of Cumberland and that year the Diamond Jubilee of Queen Victoria he received the honour of knighthood as senior Chief Constable of the Kingdom. Sir John married Mary, daughter of Dr Barnes, Bunkers Hill in 1868 and his wife died thirty years later. He is survived by two sons one of whom is married to a daughter of Sir A Helder M.P.'

The *Cumberland Pacquet* of February 8th for this year further reported on a Motion of the Cumberland County Council as follows: Headed: Cumberland County Council-Quarterly meeting . The late Sir John Dunne.

'The Chairman before the business proceeded with said he thought the Council would like to place on record some acknowledgement of the services which had been rendered by the later Sir John Dunne. He was of course more

> *intimately connected with The Standing Joint Committee but at the same time there were many occasions on which in regard to cattle disease and other questions of that sort, he rendered excellent and valuable service to the county. He therefore moved 'That the County desires to place on record their appreciation of the long services which Sir John Dunne had rendered to the county and also to express their sympathy with Sir John Dunne's family on their recent loss. Mr Johnson seconded the motion, which was carried unanimously and ordered to be sent to Mr Frank Dunne.'*

At the same time *The Barrow News* was reporting on a similar resolution made by the aforementioned Standing Joint Committee . The Chairman, Mr Reginald Marshall, said that before they proceed with the business he thought it would be proper to tell them that a suggestion had been made that some resolution should be sent from this Committee to the family of the late Sir John Dunne whose death had occurred since the last meeting here. They of course were all agreed as to the great value of the services which Sir John rendered for a great many years and through many trying circumstances in connection with the rinderpest and the carrying out of the Contagious Diseases (Animals) Act. He proposed *'That the Standing Joint Committee of the County of Cumberland desires to place on record their sense of the loss which the family of Sir John Dunne DL have sustained by his death; at the same time to express their appreciation of his long and valued services in the office of Chief Constable and Chief Inspector under the Diseases of Animals Act. That the Clerk send a copy of the resolution to the family of the late Sir John Dunne'*. Sir Musgrave Brisco seconded the motion and said he had been acquainted with Sir John Dunne from the time of his appointment to the Chief Constableship of Cumberland and Westmorland. The Chairman said he had read a Letter from Mr W H Watson, The Crofts, Seascale who after expressing his regret at not being able to be present had made a reference to Sir John Dunne which he wished to have read to the Committee. Mr Watson in the letter stated *'I do not doubt but that some suitable resolution of condolence and regret will be recorded on the death of Sir John Dunne, whose able services to the county are vividly impressed on the minds of us all. I had known him personally and intimately for a great number of years and he was connected with me in some important scientific investigations and research I had to undertake more than 25 years ago. The practical knowledge and logical mind he possessed greatly impressed me at that time, while later years when I have had the opportunity of observing closely his ability officially in county and police matters give me the pleasing privilege of expressing a deep feeling of regard for his faithfulness, integrity and uprightness to the county'*. The motion was agreed to.

Shortly after the funeral there was an article in the local newspapers inviting subscriptions for a public testimonial for Sir John. This was sponsored by his friend (and executor) Mr James Watt of Knowefield, Carlisle with the recommendation that the treasurer for Cumberland be himself and that Mr F Punchard of Underley be the Hon treasurer for Westmoreland. Interestingly some 104 years later (7th July 2010) Wetheral Cemetery was the final resting place for that brave young lady Sarah Bryant (no relation to the author) who gave her life whilst serving her country in Afghanistan. Sir John Dunne certainly didn't die poor, clearly showing that over the entire period of his lifetime he had gone from a poor man to one of considerable wealth. His will confirmed that he died on the 5th January 1906 at Eden-Mount, Wetheral, Cumberland. Probate of the will on the 16th February was handled by 'James Watt and James William Watt, seed-merchants and Francis Plunkett Neville Dunne, gentleman'. Effects totalled £44,851 5s.9d., though this was later re-sworn at £43,870.0s.9d or if equated to current values would amount to more than £8 million. For someone whose salary never exceeded £600 per annum this is an extraordinary amount to leave, and clearly shows that marrying Mary certainly did affect his finances.

POSTSCRIPT: Later that year on the 15th August, Dunne's daughter Henrietta, (though she preferred to call herself Julia) married Percy Sheete Lawrie (42 years) of Walstead Grange,Lindfield, Sussex, at Kensington, London ... By referring to the 1911 Census we learn that their main home is 15, Queens Gardens, Hyde Park, London, and by this date they have two children – Percy Andrew Lawrie aged three, and the newly born Rose Mary Lawrie. Clearly from both the London address and Sussex home she too has married well, for we also learn that there are five household staff to care for them. At the time of her marriage her husband Percy is employed as a District Inspector with the Board of Agriculture. At the time of her marriage Julia was thirty-six. Marrying just seven months after the death of her father was in this era quite unusual which pen's the question: Was her forthcoming nuptials known about by the Dunne family prior to his death, or had she continued living with her father to care for him, and his death allowed her then to marry? We shall of course never know.

Dunne's eldest child, Francis (Frank) Plunkett Neville Dunne died at the early age of 60, on the 12th June 1931, in Shropshire. At that time he was living at Loppington Hall, Wem, an early 18th century brick house which at one time had been the home of John Lloyd Dickin. As we know he too had married, Laura Constance Helder, in 1904 the daughter of Sir Augustus Helder MP. Upon his death Frank left £3978.11s.7d, (around £400,000 today) an amount which considering the funds and estates left him both by his mother and father, and that inherited by his wife, also in 1906, meant that he had possibly been living well above his means for some years. In the Supplement to the Edinburgh Gazette dated October 9th 1919 Major Francis Plunkett Neville Dunne is listed as being with the Westminster and Cumberland Yeomanry. He apparently served in the Boer War and also in the First World War, and was later a member of the Royal Board of Agriculture (as of course was his brother-in-law Percy Lawrie). For most of his life he had been a serving army officer living abroad with his wife. There were no children of the marriage. Coincidentally his sister-in-law Caroline, the eldest daughter of Sir Augustus Helder also died this year aged 68, at Callao (Peru) just eight days earlier on the 4th June.

Dunne's youngest son Gerald by 1911 is now aged 39 and living at 'house 2' in Old Town, Naas Urban, Kildare, with his wife Mabel (aged 38) and son Neville Gerald Fitzgerald, who is listed as one year old. Mabel was the widow of Hugo de Burgh, a long and established family who originated in Naas, Kildare though at the time of their marriage were living at Tarnely Lodge, in St Albans Hertfordshire. Hugo was killed in April 1900 during the Siege of Wepener in the Orange Free State. In addition to having a famous heritage this same family produced brave and worthy sons many of whom received awards for their bravery during the first and second world wars, as well as receiving high rank, one of whom was General Sir Eric de Burgh, who was born at Old Town in 1881. Nearly a century later his grandson Chris de Burgh penned a ballad to his memory called 'Old Friend' ... though the same singer /writer was perhaps better known for his rendition of 'Lady in Red'. According to the 1911 census under 'rank, profession or occupation', Gerald has listed himself as 'Retired list of Army'. Both his wife and himself are shown born in England, with the son being born in Co. Kilkenny. From the same census we learn that his house has fourteen rooms, along with seven outhouses., and is listed as 1st Class. The name of the landholder is however shown as Col. Wogan Browne, though in earlier years the same property had been in the ownership of the de Burgh family. Thus it would appear that by this time Gerald Dunne is a gentleman farmer for the same census confirms a number of domestic staff living at the same address. For example their is a Richard Egan who is shown as the butler of the head of the household, plus Rose McEvoy, Nurse, Margaret Call, Ladies Maid, Bridget Keogh, Cook, Agnes Millett, House Maid, Samuel Jones, Coachman, Frederick Whelan, Groom, and Frederick Warner, Chauffeur.... a total of eight staff. The youngest of Dunne's children Gerald had, as stated, married Mabel widow of Captain Hugo de Burgh by the 24th March 1908 and in total they had thirteen children. Based on the aforementioned it is quite clear that Gerald (like his father and brother before him) had married into a wealthy family, which would explain the large house and numerous staff, such things being unavailable to him on a soldier's pay. The eldest of their children was Neville Gerald Fitzgerald Dunne who was born 23rd July 1909, and died March 1985 aged 75., at Honiton, Devon. He is shown in The London Gazette of 31st January 1930 as a Gentleman Cadet from the Royal Military College promoted to 2nd Lt. 30th January 1930, and subsequently appointed to 8th H Cavalry. Their second child William Dunne, chose the priesthood for his career, whilst Margaret Dunne went on to become a Sister of Mercy at Tullamore. County Offaly: Julia Dunne, also chose the church as her chosen career as a Nun of The Good Shepherd, Belgium, (better known as the Sisters of our Lady of Charity of the Good Shepherd). Then their was Nicholas Dunne,Thomas Dunne, James Dunne, Anne Dunne, Catherine Dunne, and Margaret Dunne whom little is known about, Mary Dunne who too chose to be a nun, Honor Dunne of whom all is known is that she married a Mr Griffith, and finally Anne Dunne, who again nothing is known. With such a large and extensive family, (there would probably be in excess of five hundred individuals who by 2014 can claim to be directly related to Sir John Dunne), clearly there has to be many members of the Dunne family living; however researching their family tree is something that family members themselves should undertake, it is certainly not a task for a biographer of Sir John Dunne.

A small collection of John Dunne related photos gathered by the author.

Images courtesy of: The Chief Constables office & the current owners of the 2 houses featured

Sir John Dunne circa 1865

Moorhouse Hall

Sir John's home from 1867

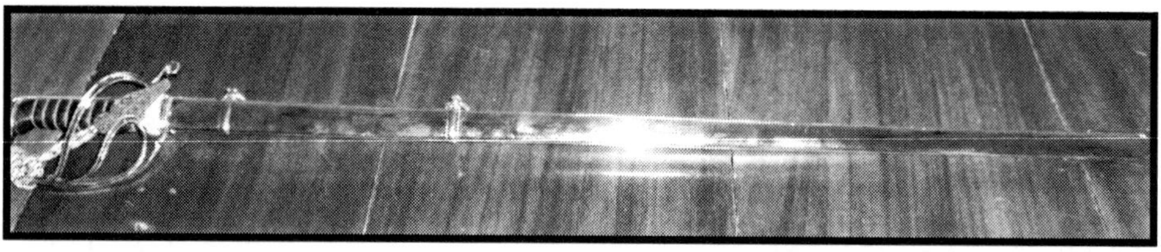

Sword of office

Eden Mount, Wetherall

Sir John's home from 1892

Illuminated scroll and loving cup presented to Sir John on his retirement in 1902

Sir John's last resting place

BIBLIOGRAPHY

Government Publications and Parliamentary Papers

Accessories and Abettors Act 1861
Adulteration of Food and Drugs Act 1878
Anti-Prize Fight Act 1861
Bath Poor Law Union 1836
Burials Act 1857
Capital Punishment (Amendment)Act 1868
Capital Punishment within Prison Act 1868
Cattle Diseases Preventive Act 1865
Cleansing of Persons Act 1897
Commons Select Committee on Policing 1853
Commons Select Committee- Game Law Reforms
Contagious Diseases Act 1864 & 1869
County Police Act 1836
County Police Act 1839
County & Borough Police Act 1856
Criminal Evidence Act 1898
Criminal Law Amendment Act 1867
Criminal Register 1901
Cruelty to Animals Act 1835
Debtors Act 1869
Factory Act 1874 & 1875
Firearms Act 1870
Gangs Act 1869
Garotting Act 1863
General Strike 1842
Habitual Criminals Act 1869
Hansard 11.5.1857
Hansard.Vol 290 cc 896-7
Hansard March 1892
Home Office Statistical Returns 1857
Houseless Poor Act 1875
Industrial Schools Act 1857 & 1861
Larceny Act 1861
Licensing Act 1872 ,1875, 1902
Lighting & Watching Act 1833.
Locomotive Act 1865
Locomotives on the Highway Act 1896
Malicious Damages Act 1861
Married Women's Property Act 1882
Master & Servant Act 1867
Metropolitan Police Act 1829
Municipal Corporations Act 1835
Night Poaching Prevention Act 1862
Obscene Publications Act 1857
Offences against the Person Act 1861
Parish Constables Act 1842
Parks Regulation Act 1872
Parliamentary Committee in the Health of Towns 1840
Peoples Charter May 1838
Poaching Prevention Act 1863
Police Expenses Act 1875
Police Pensions Act 1890
Police (Property) Act 1897
Police Superannuation Act 1875
Police Town Clauses Act 1867
Poor Law Amendment Act 1834
Prevention of Crimes Act 1871
Prevention of Cruelty to Children Act 1889
Prisons Act 1865
Prosecution of Offenders Act 1879
Protection of Children Act 1889
Reformatory & Industrial Schools Act 1866
Sanitary Act 1866
Select Committee On Policing 1853 (Dunne's evidence pages 115-124)
Summary Jurisdiction (Process) Act 1881
Superintending Constables Act 1850
The Town Police Clauses Act 1847
Vaccination Act 1867
Vagrancy Act 1864& 1898
Weights & Measures Act 1878
Women's Property Act 1870 & 1872
Youthful Offenders Act 1854

Newspapers

Barrow News 11th January 1906
Barrow News 18th January 1906
Carlisle Journal 26th July 1861
" 18th November1869
" 16th February 1877
" 19th February 1897
" 8th August 1897
Carlisle Patriot 25th June 1897
" 12th January 1906
Cumberland Pacquet 11th January 1814
" 3rd March 1857
" 15th September 1857
" 22nd September 1857
" 14th January 1858

" 26th January 1858
" 9th February 1858
" 16th February 1858
" 8th June 1858
" 15th June 1858
" 19th October 1858
" 26th October 1858
" 4th January 1859
" 13th December 1859
" 16th April 1859
" 9th July 1861
" 1st December 1863
" 17th February 1863
" 15th April 1863
" 12th May 1864
" 4th February 1867
" 13th October 1868
" 9th March 1869
" 5th January 1870
" 19th December 1875
" 23rd April 1881
" 5th November 1885
" 17th December 1885
" 21st January 1886
" 3rd January 1892
" 12th March 1892
" 23rd October 1898
" 24th April 1902
" 18th October 1904
" 8th February 1906

Cumberland Patriot 9th January 1858
" 16th February 1877
Daily Graphic 15th February 1898
Edinburgh Gazette 9th October 1919
France. 14th January 1886
Kendal Mercury 12th October 1969
Liverpool Mercury. 7th January 1857
London Gazette 24th June 1897
" 31st January 1930
Morning Chronicle 18th May 1839
Newcastle Courant 12th March 1854
Otago Witness 24th January 1906
Police Gazette- Various
Police Review May 1893
Punch 20th October 1877
" 19th February 1886
The Times. 6th October 1854
" 19th February 1857
" 8th March 1866
" 4th September 1858
" 17th May 1898
Truth January 1886
Westmorland Gazette 14th March 1878
Whitehaven Gazette 22nd April 1897
Whitehaven Herald 19th July 1876
Whitehaven News 29th April 1897
" 27th April 1899

Books, Essays, and Theses

A Force Remembered. The Illustrated History of the Norwich City Police 1836-1967: Maurice Morson.
A History of Britain: Simon Schama
A History of Cumberland & Westmorland: William Rollinson
A History of Police in England and Wales: 900-1966: T A Critchley
A History of Policing in Manchester: E.J.Hewitt.
A History of the Queen's County : Michael Corey
Annals of the Four Masters
A Plaque of Blue Locusts: Robert Storch
Blind Eye of History: Charles Reith
Crime & Society in England: Clive Emsley
Culture,Conflict & Migration.The Irish in Victorian Cumbria : Donald MacRaild
Dod's Peerage 1900.
Essex Constabulary. Orders and Instructions framed and issued for the Superintendents and Constables of the Essex Constabulary: Captain McHardy
Essex Survivals with Special attention to Essex Smugglers. 1929: Roe
General Sir Charles James Napier: Prof A J Pointon
Griffiths Valuation
Guide to the Lakes: William Wordsworth
Historical Antiques of Hertfordshire.
History of the British Navy: Sir William Laird Clowes
Hop Pickers of Kent & Sussex.2008 :Hilary Hefferman
Juvenile Delinquency in Manchester , Its causes and history and some suggestions concerning its cure : W B Neale
Landed Estates

Nineteenth Century criminal statistics and their interpretation: V.A.C.Gatrell
Order, Rules ,Regulations and Instructions framed and issued for the Government and guidance of the Cumberland & Westmorland Police: J Dunne. July 1857.
Policing and its Context: C. Emsley
Policing Northamptonshire: R Cowley
Policing Provincial England 1829-1856: Phillips.D and R. D. Storch.
Policing Shropshire 1836-1967: D J Elliott
Policing the Victorian Community: Carolyn Steedman
Poor Law & Constabulary :Edwin Chadwick
Rationing Crime- the political economy of criminal statistics since the 1850's: Howard Taylor
Recruiting the English Policeman: C Emsley and M Clapson
Reform of the Borough Police 1835-1856: Jennifer Hart
Reminiscences of a Chief Constable: William Chadwick
Report on the State of the Irish Poor in Great Britain 1836: Father Daniel Hearne.
Standing Rules and Regulations for the Constabulary Force or Ireland : Anon.
The British Police: J.Hart.
The Chartist Movement :Mark Hovel
The Chief Constables of England and Wales: The Socio-legal history of a criminal justice elite: David Wall
The Condition of the Working Class in England: Friedrich Engels.
The Constable's Oath and Instructions to Constables and Other Peace Officers: Kendal. 1840
The Dagenham Murder. The Brutal Killing of PC George Clark: .Linda Rhodes, Lee
Shelden, Kathryn Abnett .2005
The Decline of Theft and Violence in Victorian and Edwardian England: V.A.C.Gatrell
The English Police .A Political and Social History: C Emsley
The Essex Police: J Woodgate
The History of the Workhouse: Peter Higginbotham
The Making of a Chief Constable: Maureen Scollan
The Making of the English Working Class : E.P.Thompson
The Moral and Physical Conditions of the Working Classes: John Kay
The new police in nineteenth century England, Crime Conflict and Control: D.Taylor.
The Plague of the Blue Locusts. .Police Reform and popular resistance in northern England 1840-1857: R D Storch
The Policeman as domestic missionary; urban discipline and popular culture in Northern England 1850-1880: R.D.Storch.
The Sanitary Conditions of the Labouring Population 1842: Edwin Chadwick
Thump of wood on a Swede turnip: Clive Emsley
Vagrancy and the New Poor Law in late Victorian & Edwardian England: Rachel Vorspan

Internet

Dublin & Liverpool Steam Packet Co- Wikepedia.
Manchester Police
Surrey Constabulary
History of Essex Constabulary

THE AUTHOR

Alan Bryant was born in London in 1936 and after attending Sloane Grammar School, Chelsea served as 2nd Lieutenant in the Royal Army Pay Corps. Following a stint as a Police Constable in Hampshire and Isle of Wight in the early 1960s he took work, amongst other things, as an international estate agent, a buyer for Saudi department stores, a resort director and freelance journalist.

A prolific writer since 1989 with almost 20 books under his belt, he continues to occupy his time doing voluntary work in the local community and studying for his many academic achievements including B.A (Hons) (at age 68) an M.A (at age 72) and M. Humanities (at age 75). This book will be included as part of his on-going academic PhD thesis.

OTHER BOOKS BY ALAN BRYANT

Towns and Villages of Britain series including:

Towns & Villages of the Lake District and Cumbria

Towns and villages of Lancashire

Towns & Villages of the Peak District and Derbyshire

Towns and Villages of Cheshire.

Towns & Villages of Yorkshire

Western Lakes

Northern Lakes

Southern Lakes

Kendal Town Guide

Murder most 'Orrid

What's on

The Festival of Britain

Birds of Britain

Cumbrian Poems by Cumbrian Poets

History of Barrow Police - Second World War

Artful Dodger

Romanies

Herdwicke Sheep

Lightning Source UK Ltd.
Milton Keynes UK
UKOW05f1328270115

245213UK00010B/502/P

9 780992 751470